The "Other" Students

Filipino Americans, Education, and Power

The "Other" Students

Filipino Americans, Education, and Power

edited by

Dina C. Maramba

State University of New York at Binghamton

Rick Bonus

University of Washington

INFORMATION AGE PUBLISHING, INC.
Charlotte, NC • www.infoagepub.com

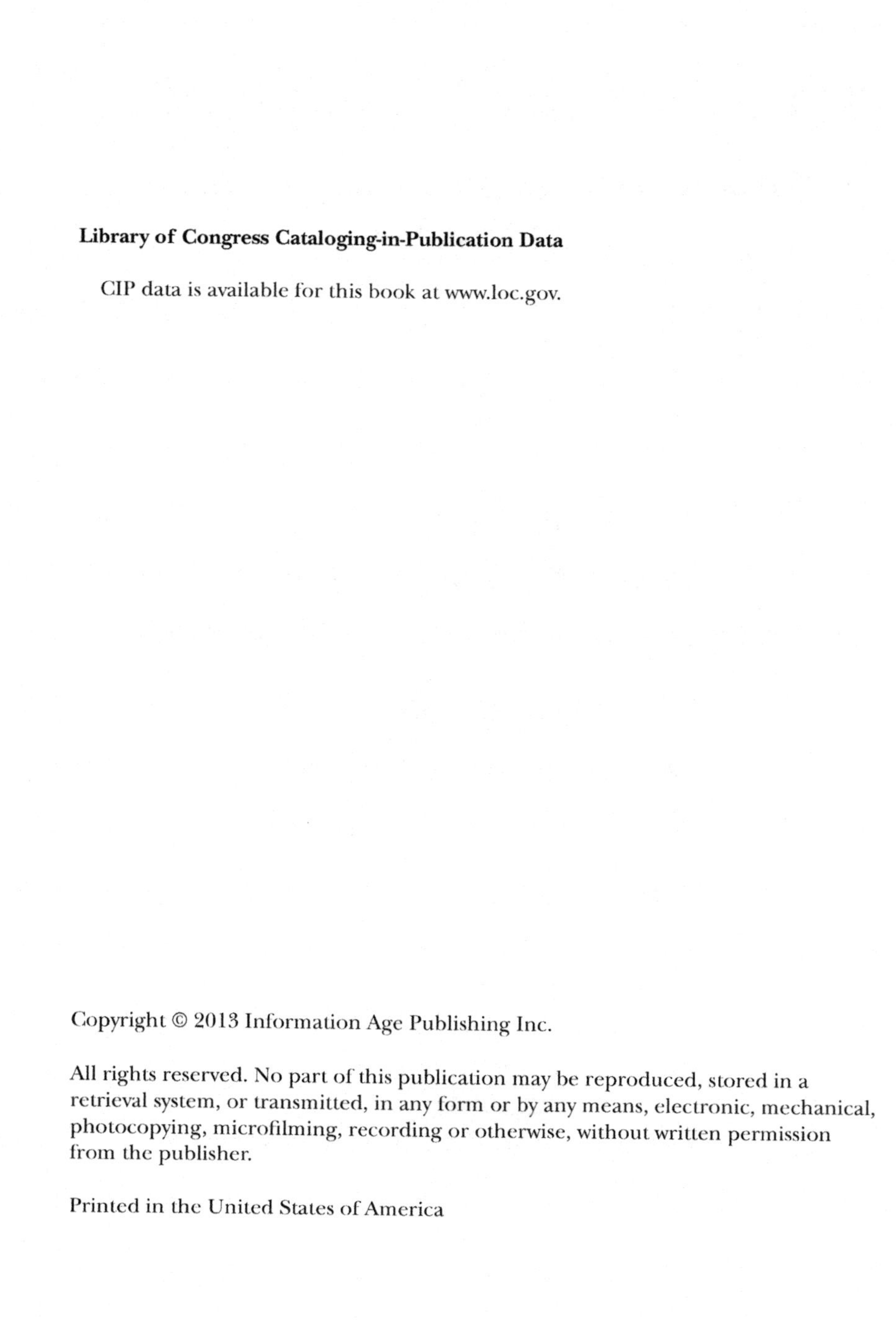

Library of Congress Cataloging-in-Publication Data

CIP data is available for this book at www.loc.gov.

Printed in the United States of America

CONTENTS

PART II

EDUCATION AND THE MAKING OF IDENTITIES

PART III

FILIPINO AMERICAN STUDIES AND PEDAGOGIES

PART IV

FILIPINO AMERICANS AND POLICIES IN EDUCATION

ACKNOWLEDGMENTS

This book started out as an idea between the two of us when we organized a panel on Filipino Americans and education for the annual conference of the Association for Asian American Studies in Atlanta way back in 2006. What we imagined as a small group of academics and community activists whose work focused on U.S.-based Filipinas and Filipinos and their relationships to issues of education, and whose academic projects we wanted to cohere into one book, turned out to be a most remarkably vibrant set of authors whose contributions have enabled us to transform the ways in which we conceive, critique, and change education in the lives of Filipino Americans historically and in contemporary times. Add to this list Shirley Hune, whose feedback in the early stages of this work was extremely helpful; Tyrone Nagai, whose suggestions and copyediting were invaluable; Jon Okamura, whose wisdom and support always motivated us; Jane C. Maramba, who generously agreed to design our cover; and Anthony Barretto Ogilvie, who agreed to write our book's Foreword. To all of them, we offer our profound gratitude. We also thank them for patiently waiting for an inordinate amount of time for us to convince a publisher to believe in our collective project. After numerous attempts to persuade more than a handful of presses about the merit and necessity of our book, it was George F. Johnson and his staff at Information Age Publishing who swiftly communicated their faith in us. We thank them for the confidence with which they have regarded our collective work.

Dina C. Maramba: I wish to thank my family: Mom, Dad, Wendy, Jane, grandparents, aunties, uncles, cousins, relatives, and family friends, whose uncon-

The "Other" Students, pages ix–x

ditional love and support keep me grounded and inspired. To my mentors, your consistent encouragement and "reality checks" continue to play an integral role in my academic career: Antonia Darder, Daryl G. Smith, Alberto Ochoa, Ruben Espinosa, Rick Bonus, Patrick Velasquez, Robert Teranishi, Marybeth Gasman, Mitchell Chang, Frankie Laanan, Leo Wilton, Gladys Jimenez-Muñoz, Reynaldo I. Monzon, Lubna Chaudhry, and Lisa Yun. To my sisters and brothers in academia: Robert T. Palmer, Kimberly A. Griffin, Kevin L. Nadal, Rachelle Winkle-Wagner, V. Thandi Sule, Nana Osei-Kofi, contributors to this book, and so many other important allies, your immeasurable support has made our academic terrain easier and more enjoyable to navigate together. I am grateful to my former and current students, who motivate me to do the work I love. I am also appreciative of the faculty and staff at the State University of New York, Binghamton. *Maraming salamat sa inyong lahat.* I am deeply thankful to all of you.

Rick Bonus: I want to thank the members of my "juju" writing group—Kiko Benitez, Chandan Reddy, Ileana Rodriguez-Silva, and Stephanie Smallwood—for all the productive energies you have generously shared with me. To my colleagues and students, especially Dina C. Maramba, Martin Manalansan, David Palaita, Michael Tuncap, Nestor Enguerra Jr., Brukab Sisay, Deborah Tugaga, Staliedaniel Uele, Michael Peralta, Reuben Deleon, Micah Bateman-Iino, Brady Angeles, Taylor Ahana, Arthur Sepulveda, Sarah Ledbetter, Daniel Tugaga, Linda Vo, Mary Yu Danico, Lauro Flores, James E. Banks, and George Lipsitz—including countless others who nurture and inspire me—I am most grateful. The administration, faculty, and staff of the Department of American Ethnic Studies, the Diversity Minor Program, the Southeast Asia Center, the Office of Minority Affairs and Diversity, and the dean's office in the College of Arts and Sciences at the University of Washington have been most supportive of my work, and the officers and members of the Filipino American Educators of Washington have always given me a community to turn to. And of course, my beloved siblings Nanette, Maritel, Bobby, Vida, and Emma, including all the rest of my family members in Washington, California, Nevada, Michigan, and especially those in the Philippines, have unwaveringly blessed me with immense love and care. To all of you, I am so profoundly thankful.

PREFACE

Although the Filipino American population has increased numerically in many areas of the United States, especially since the influx of professional immigrants in the wake of the 1965 Immigration Act, their impact on schools and related educational institutions has rarely been documented and examined. *The Other Students: Filipino Americans, Education, and Power* is the first book of its kind to focus specifically on Filipino Americans in education. Through a collection of historical and contemporary perspectives, we fill a profound gap in the scholarship as we analyze the emerging presence of Filipino Americans both as subjects and objects of study in education research and practice. We highlight the argument that one cannot adequately and appropriately understand the complex histories, cultures, and contemporary conditions faced by Filipino Americans in education unless one grapples with the specificities of their colonial pasts and presents, their unique migration and immigration patterns, their differing racialization and processes of identity formations, the connections between diaspora and community belonging, and the various perspectives offered by ethnic group-centered analysis to multicultural projects. The historical, methodological, and theoretical approaches in this anthology will be of interest to scholars, researchers, and students in disciplines that include education, ethnic studies, Asian American and Pacific Islander studies, anthropology, sociology, political science, urban studies, public policy, and public health.

The "Other" Students, page xi

FOREWORD

As the editors of *The "Other" Students: Filipino Americans, Education, and Power* note, the examination of the relationship between the U.S. school system and Filipino American students must include the history between the two nations that started some 200 years ago. During this bicentennial period, we see the unequivocal transformation of two different countries that became entwined in a dominant power-colonial relationship that has had powerful and continuing impact on the shaping of the identity and psychology of Filipinos in both the Philippines and the United States. Symptomatic of this relationship has been the persistent and perplexing issue of Filipino American student academic performance at all levels and Filipino American parent and community involvement with the U.S. school system at the local level.

From the perspective that schools are apparatuses that prepare future citizens to be productive and competitive in a global economy, it is incumbent upon the United States to have a highly skilled and educated workforce. We are not doing well in this regard, as the media are replete with warnings by educational scholars, politicians, and business leaders alike about the dire academic performance of Native Americans, African Americans, Latinos, and many immigrant K–12 public school students. When combined with their few numbers entering and completing certificates and degree programs in postsecondary educational institutions, especially at the university level in degree programs requiring high level math and science, the situation becomes more alarming; they forebode a herculean effort to ensure that many of our students of color are prepared to meet our national economic imperatives while engaged in self-satisfying vocations and high-wage incomes.

In some of our largest urban areas, Filipino American students are demonstrably among those in the highly profiled, underachieving groups. This was

The "Other" Students, pages xiii–xiv

noted by a group of Filipino American research and community scholars, who in 2007, were convened by the National Federation of Filipino American Associations (NaFFAA) to examine how Filipino American public school students were doing academically. Their task was made difficult by the lack of specific data on Filipino American students in all 10 urban areas that were examined; in fact, only five cities and areas provided such data. Nonetheless, information gathered from interviews of community-based organizations and agencies, along with limited information on Filipino American students at the university level, when combined with the limited disaggregated statistics on Filipino American students, portrayed a community that should act with concern and speed before low academic performance by Filipino American students becomes endemic nationwide and beyond the tipping point.

It is noteworthy that there was recognition for the need for more detailed analyses of Filipino American students and the relationship between the school system and the Filipino American communities within their service areas. One of the first tasks at hand was to seek the disaggregation of Filipino American student data at all levels so that the picture of Filipino American student performance could be more clearly and more widely identified and studied. Moreover, given the mix between Philippine-born, American-born, and mixed-race Filipinos, there was the further need to look at the issue of the quest for identity by Filipino American youth and the impact of colonialism on the Filipino American students' perception of self and place in the U.S. school system. All of these elements play a critical role in Filipino American students feeling well and doing well in school, regardless of grade and college level.

This work by Maramba and Bonus, along with other authors who have studied these topics and issues, more definitively responds to the questions that have been begging to be answered with regard to Filipino American student academic performance and educational strategies that demand engagement. The literature on Filipino American students has been conspicuously lacking, so with this work, we now have a major starting point for the U.S. school system to learn how to more appropriately respond to the needs of these students and their families. If this is done, all schools will become, as the editors state, "avenues of collective opportunity for all... [as] sites of possibility [and] hope" rather than institutions pushing uniformity and compliance while failing to consider the needs of groups of equal or greater need.

Anthony Barretto Ogilvie, EdD
Executive Dean, Professional and Continuing Education
Seattle Central Community College
and
Coordinator, National Study group on Filipino American
K–12 Public School Students: A Study of Ten Urban
Communities Across the United States

INTRODUCTION

Filipino Americans as "Others"

Rick Bonus and Dina C. Maramba

What does it mean to talk about Filipino[1] Americans as the "others" in the field of education and within the context of relationships of power in contemporary society? Frequently, many research projects that focus on minorities in education start with the growing number of diverse students, faculty, and administrators in schools as the reason and basis for scholarly inquiry, referencing the ostensible if not palpable impact of such population groups on the state of education in American society and on the very ways in which scholarly inquiry is conducted (Chan, 2005; Gándara & Contreras, 2009; Hune, 1998). Hence, many studies on the changing demographics within American schools and universities have sought to clarify the necessity and importance of considering otherwise missed or invisibly treated populations with a view toward either accounting for the differences that their presence would have made in relationship to grand theories and trends, or for the specificities that they present in comparison to larger, more dominant, and well-studied groups (Hirabayashi, 1998). For us, this is an important reason why we emphasize the labeling of Filipino Americans as "other," for they usually fall out of numerical significance in data collection, they are lumped in categories with other groups, or they are deemed

The "Other" Students, pages xv–xxxvii

to be different from the majority.[2] It is within and across these vectors that we place our anthology.

But in more important ways, we would like to imagine our collection of essays as principally located in a scholarly terrain that grapples with "minorities in education," not merely to correct previous exclusion, although that is indeed significant work even by itself, but to offer alternative ways of configuring the connections between education and power, including the politics of and challenges to differential inclusion, using the historical and contemporary experiences of Filipino Americans. We would like to situate the essays in our anthology as interventions, both in their political and academic sense, into the ways we can begin questions and pursue answers regarding underrepresentation, invisibility, and power in education, without resorting to additive solutions or reinforcing exploitative situations. As such, our collective intent is not so much to merely fill in the missing gaps in our knowledge and practices about the American educational system in order to be assimilated into it, but to make legible the histories and experiences of Filipino Americans as they interrogate, reimagine, and propose other ways of configuring such knowledge and practices. In these cases, Filipino Americans as "others" signal for us a different way of understanding difference, one that enables not only a comprehension of exclusion and its consequences, but a generation of practices of understanding, equity, inclusion, and transformation.

In the first instance then, we present in this anthology a collection of perspectives on the emerging presence of Filipino Americans both as subjects and objects of study in the field of education. Even though the Filipino American population has increased numerically, at 2.5 million (U.S. Census, 2010) in total, it is scattered in many metropolitan areas of the United States, especially since the influx of professional immigrants in the wake of the 1965 Immigration Act. Notwithstanding their presence in American society now for more than 200 years (Cordova, 1983; Espina, 1988; Fujita-Rony, 2003), their impact on schools, social service institutions, and local and larger political communities has rarely been documented and examined. Filipino American groups have usually (if ever) been studied—especially in the social sciences and education—by placing them within, and only as they are a constitutive part of, larger racial group assignments such as minorities, Asian Americans, Hispanics/Latinos, and Pacific Islanders (Chan, 1991; Parrillo, 2011; Schaefer, 2010). While we do not intend to discredit the usefulness and coalitional import of such studies, we seek to problematize the assumed homogeneity of these traditional aggregations as they are used in the field, by offering instead the research approaches and claims more aptly suited to the study of Filipino Americans as a heterogeneous group (see Vea, this volume). Beyond this, we also want to offer the specificities of this group as indices of comparison with and possible application to larger claims about other interrelated groups (Isaac, 2006; Nakanishi & Nishida, 1995).

We want to highlight the argument in this book that one cannot adequately and appropriately understand the particular histories and contemporary conditions faced by Filipino Americans in education unless one reckons with the specificities of their colonial pasts and presents, their unique migration and immigration patterns, their differing racialization and processes of identity and community formations, their unequal placement in local/global capitalist arrangements, and their multilevel relationships to each other and with dominant as well as other minority groups. Specifically, the Philippines, an archipelago of more than 7,100 islands in Southeast Asia in the western Pacific Ocean, was colonized by Spain from 1521 to 1898, by the United States from 1898 to 1946, and occupied by Japan from 1942 to 1945. Its history of deploying workers overseas is extensive and continuing, from the recorded exploits of "Manila men," who jumped ship via the Manila-Acapulco galleon trade during the period of Spanish colonization, all the way to the recruitment of farm and fishery laborers to Hawai'i, the Pacific coast states of the United States, and Alaska in the first quarter of the 20th century and continuing with the massive immigration of professional-degree workers into the United States commencing in 1965. By the beginning of the 21st century, Filipino workers, mostly in the domestic service sector, have gone "global" and transnational. Racialized as non-White, they have mostly occupied low-rung work positions, while others have struggled as middle-class income workers or enjoyed professional elite statuses. Given the diversity of their migration and immigration histories, income and settlement patterns, as well as age and educational experiences, they exist in isolation from each other or, for those who can and are willing, they find the time and resources to create and sustain networks of support and alliance. These communities face a wide and deep range of social and political issues, from media invisibility and political disenfranchisement to mental anguish, job discrimination, and isolation caused by stereotyping, misrecognition, and devaluing of one's own culture. The consequences of colonization and labor migration—in structural, physical, and psychic terms—continue to linger (Bonus, 2000; David, 2011; Pido, 1992; San Juan, 2000).

Considering also that Filipino Americans by themselves have multiple, diverse, and complex histories, cultures, and communities, the essays we have gathered here explore in different ways a variety of questions and issues regarding, for example, the fraught relationships between U.S. imperialism and identity formation, the uneven connections between diaspora and community belonging, and the different perspectives offered by ethnic group-centered analysis to multicultural valances—all contextualized within and animated by the field of education. What does it mean to have a national or ethnic identity as Filipinos and Americans in the face of a vexed and lingering history of colonization and immigration? How does a group reckon with labor migration displacement, multiple forms of racism, and continuing exploitation? How can teachers and students engage with the specific histories and contemporary experiences of Filipinos that make them different from others, yet teach others how to understand difference? In this sense, we can imagine these essays as references available for application into curricula, pedagogy, and educational policy from the purviews of both ethnic-specific and multicultural emphases.

In the second instance, and perhaps more critically, we collectively argue that one cannot fully appreciate the importance of a minority group's experience in American schools unless one has an ample appreciation and understanding of schools as sites and purveyors of systemic and institutional inequalities as much as they are locations of possibilities and potentials for transformation (Freire, 2000; Leistyna, Woodrum, & Serblom, 1995; Pizarro, 2005). American schools have been imagined historically both as repositories and privileged locations for the production and dissemination of knowledge. They are regarded as enduring symbols of hope and intrinsically sutured into the mythology of the American dream, providing the supposed means for social mobility and advancement, including the possible enhancement of one's stature and position of power (Thelin, 2004). In reality, however, as many studies have shown, schools have historically obtained benefits only for a few at best and have effectively maintained, if not reinforced, social, political, and economic inequalities at worst (Apple, 1995, 2004; Darder, 1991; Hochschild & Scovronick, 2003). It is then unjustifiable to us to offer the specificities of Filipino American experiences as "learning points" that American schooling can benefit from to the degree that such schools will harness more effectively its capacities to reproduce inequality. Rather, we provide in this collection a set of scholarly considerations specific to Filipino American schooling experiences that expressly challenge, among others, the cores of American educational values that disallow or impede the provision of opportunities for others, those practices of schooling that follow or privilege only universal or dominant understandings of the ideal student, and the ethnocentric views of education that statically and conservatively normalize singular and limited sets of curricula, pedagogical stresses and strategies, assessment variables, and extracurricular programming.

Similar to many previous groundbreaking projects that have articulated the "problems" of school as fundamentally resting not on the students' shortcomings but on the failures of the "system" that produces them, we want to take advantage of the possibilities of educational transformation by probing deeply into what can be changed beyond its surface, and we offer these essays as tools and avenues for those possibilities that have been realized, and those that have yet to be (Delpit, 2006; Giroux, 1983; Valenzuela, 1999). In this vein, we consciously connect our energies with, as much as we draw inspiration from, the legacies of antiracist and other civil rights struggles, including anti-imperialist movements, mounted in the spaces of academia and productive of such transformative changes in our schools, from increasing access to underserved students to institutionalizing marginalized multidisciplinary departments such as ethnic studies; women studies; and gay, lesbian, and sexuality studies. We are members then of a generation of teachers and scholars who have been privileged to obtain the benefits and challenges of these enduring struggles, and we wish to share and act upon this privilege.

On the whole, we attend to these two instantiations of scholarly emphases as if they are fundamentally dialogic and not distinct from each other. The pursuit of disaggregated inclusion in data gathering projects, of access to classroom and faculty spots, and of integration into curricular offerings are remarkably important agendas for anyone committed to Filipino American representation and voice, particularly in determining educational policy. At the same time, we also believe that inclusion alone can never be enough and that fixing the system that produces inequality without transforming the core logics and power structures of that system can only result in empty, temporary, or unsatisfactory results. We intend to intervene in these regressive uses of race and other forms of difference in scholarly work in the field of education. That is, the essays we put together in this volume track the Filipino American "other" student both as identity and community formations whose histories, nuances, and complexities beyond their mere appearance in our classrooms we have yet to adequately reckon and connect with other groups. Within these political formations, whose uneasy relationship to education in specific ways forms the very basis for the critique of underrepresentation and the reproduction of inequality and exploitation in schools, we ultimately present the twin directionality of Filipino American histories and cultures impacting on education as well as American education's varied, uneven, and productive forces exerting their consequences upon Filipino Americans.

All of the essays in this volume assume the historical and continuing significance of race in American society to the degree that it endures both as a reality of quotidian existence structurally and relationally with other categories of difference and as a flashpoint for educational policy that determines career training, access, resource allocation, curricular material, and indices of academic performance and success. In a straightforward way, we can limn at least two opposing points of contention here: policy that seeks to overcome the so-called baggage of race by disregarding its import (or more boldly, by eliminating its named appearance) as it simultaneously invokes the language of civil rights for all through "equal" treatment and policy that affirm the significance of race in excluding or overprivileging groups by circumscribing or mitigating its effects through token, nominal, and safe means (Buenavista, Jayakumar, & Misa-Escalante, 2009; McCarthy, Crichlow, Dimitriadis, & Dolby, 2005; Taylor, Gillborn, & Ladson-Billings, 2009). Such has been mistakenly referenced as multicultural or diverse education, subfields in education and the social sciences in which we are in particular conversations with, while mindful of the ways in which their transformative orientations are oftentimes misperceived or reappropriated as assimilative (Banks & Banks, 1993; Gay, 2000).[3] Both avenues of policy, whether labeled as color-blind or color-conscious, merely end up alleviating conditions of racial inequality temporarily as they exacerbate the grip of White supremacy on positions and practices of power in schools by not paying attention to it (Howard, 1999). Our authors, therefore, explicitly and implicitly grapple with these tensions and otherwise broken promises of educational policy by harnessing the powers and potentials of scholarly writing that take into consideration the institutional forces of racism as they are experienced differentially and differently by groups, as they are constitutively embedded in practices of privilege distribution and as they interact with other categories of difference to produce various hierarchical permutations and their criticisms.

Our project proposes Filipino American "others" as an alternative site of resistance for traversing the histories and contemporary realities of race and power in American education. Even though the category "other" may signal a position of exclusion, an inability to name, or a condition of shame, we do not intend to merely mark minority status and argue against its ability to disempower. This is not satisfactory for us. Instead, we aim to understand "others" as a site of difference, and by that, we seek to harness the generative powers and potentials of alternative voices, perspectives, experiences, and visions that can be brought to any and all discussions and practices regarding education. These are what variance and dissimilarity can offer. But to a good extent, we do not propose this site of otherness to actualize a potential return neither for an investment in narrow demands for an exclusive group nor for a more benevolent distribution of scarce resources for insular gain once Filipino American "culture" is putatively determined. We do not seek to "celebrate" Filipino Americaness in the name of compensatory and decorative diversity, nor do we intend to make visible something that was once unrecognized simply to eke out a privileged spot in a smorgasbord of cultural curricular considerations.

Most of all, we do not aim to provide our readers with a definitive, absolute, and homogeneous set of origins and attributes of authentic and pure Filipino American histories and cultures that could be appropriated as benchmarks for inclusive representation in civil society. Instead, we invoke the category Filipino American "others" to locate the shared vectors of differential treatment and unequal power that bind an otherwise heterogeneous racial/ethnic group with their dominant and nondominant counterparts while simultaneously submitting navigational instruments and examples for treading critiques and dialogues with those who care about minorities in education (Giroux, 1992). Even though we look to the category Filipino American as a distinct and specific group, we hold its distinctiveness and specificity only insofar as it is interdependently contextualized and constitutively related with other groups and categories. We therefore invite our readers to imagine with us a strong sense of community and collaboration in, first, defining a set of shared contours and possibilities that may be specific to Filipino American "others" but are in actuality conjunctured with other groups, both dominant and nondominant, and second, in delineating an engagement with mostly unquestioned and assumed knowledge and practices of education and race in American society using the purviews of Filipino American otherness as a provisional and open-ended location.

We highlight four particular themes, precisely tracing the organizational flow of this collection. First, in Part One: Historical Coordinates, we want to mark the historical parameters and delineations of the Filipino American experience. We want to frame the histories of colonization, imperialism, and racialization as indices for proposing an understanding of the contexts within which matters concerning Filipino Americans and schooling are understood. But we submit here that instead of locating the progeny of Filipino Americaness in that moment in which people from the Philippines set foot on primary United States territory, or its corollary, that we begin from the so-called distant shores in the Pacific where Filipinos originally boarded ships on their way to America, we consider as an alternative the interstitial coast-to-coast historical entanglements of domination, control, and resistance between the United States and the Philippines (Cordova, 1983; Tiongson, Gutierrez, & Gutierrez, 2006). In doing so, we wish to clarify that the Filipino American historical experience, unlike most immigrant narratives, does not begin with immigration to the United States, but rather prior to departure from the Philippines in which centuries of Spanish colonization (1521–1898); American imperial occupation and colonization (1898–1946), including the recruitment of White teachers to inculcate a foreign educational system in the islands; and lingering but exacerbated postcolonial conditions of exploitation and injustice have, in fact, constituted who gets access to America (and beyond) and on what terms and consequences (Bonus, 2000; Fujita-Rony, 2003; San Juan, 1993).

This proposition bears directly on how we can begin to reimagine Filipino American students, for example, not as subjects whose present or potential incorporation into the American state has already been predetermined, but as bodies who always already bear the traces of these colonized histories, with all their supposed advantages ("They speak good English, like their parents"), erasures ("They do not have a culture of their own"), and appropriations ("Are they Hispanic? Asian? Black?")—all of which render as problematic societal incorporation itself. As Zeus Leonardo and Cheryl E. Matias emphatically assert in our inaugural chapter, "Betwixt and Between Colonial and Postcolonial Mentality: The Critical Education of Filipino Americans," these colonized histories loom largely in their makeup, and any education worthy of the term "critical" must take this fact into account. They thread their periodization of Filipino colonial and postcolonial experiences, all productive of displacement, trauma, and homelessness (especially for those who are in the diaspora), to a provocative exposition of the continuities across these experiences that have also generated restlessness, anxieties, and multiple possibilities that we have to, at the very least but with much care, consider as affirming and buoyant.

We then approach connected matters of American-style tutelage in the colonial Philippines to further underscore the fact of American intrusion into the Philippines prior to Filipino immigration (again, a matter that confuses those who incorrectly assume that all kinds of immigration start with "coming into" the host country), to cast some illumination on the progenies of images and imaginations about the Philippines, Filipinos, and their cultures, for an American audience also prior to and then extending into initial contacts between Americans and Filipinos on the mainland and the colony, and to gauge the circumstances of such encounters through such modalities as infantilization, debasement, and discipline. In Benito M. Vergara Jr.'s "'The Real Filipino People': Filipino Nationhood and Encounters With the Native Other," we are provided with an opportunity to understand how, in the 1904 World Exposition held in St. Louis, Missouri, indigenous schooled and nonschooled Filipinos, approached as comparisons, were used as exemplary representations of American benevolence and might, and as spectacular testimonies for the ascendancy of U.S. global imperial power at that time. In Vergara's account were the voices of the *pensionados* during this remarkable moment when such U.S. government–sponsored students from the islands contested the depictions of indigenous Filipinos as savage, inferior, and "other." It will be illuminating to see how these struggles over the terms by which Filipinos can be monolithically defined despite the heterogeneity of their archipelagic origins resonate with contemporary practices of population lumping. In "Colonial Lessons: Racial Politics of Comparison and the Development of American Education Policy in the Philippines," Funie Hsu explicates the constitutive processes of establishing and coordinating colonial schooling overseas as mediated by, among others, U.S. domestic educational policies, with specific reference to Native Americans and African Americans. Her chapter prods us to draw distinctions regarding the colonial legacies of schooling for Filipinos and possibly their deep linkages with schooling issues, especially for Filipinos in the United States.

In these chapters, Filipino collective experiences in American colonial education are refracted in at least three interrogative ways. First, since American public education as it was introduced in the colonial Philippines constituted Filipinos as unenlightened savages whose civilized salvation depended on its very subjugation, what degrees of such a constitution endure today, even with other groups, as we persist in regarding schooling as a disciplinary apparatus? Second, in learning how such colonial education projects also stimulated uneasy and unexpected discussions about the proper integration into and thus consequent impact of the native on the American nation, how are these histories of Philippine colonization also histories of uneven American national formation, fraught with inconsistencies and contradictions? And third, in considering the oft-hidden processes of constructing a national culture, especially of a nation that has experienced centuries of foreign intervention and of a people who have travelled away from their original land, how may "culture" as it is depicted in texts, exhibitions, and curricular materials also be imagined as contested, dynamic, and open-ended processes, whose horizon of articulation may not be limited only to the nation form? We ask these questions as alternative gestures to practices in education that produce disavowals, aversions, and exclusions in the teachings of U.S. imperial and transnational histories, state-sanctioned nation forms vis-à-vis America's racial others, and colonial/postcolonial, even transnational, popular culture.

In these historical essays, we submit the deep necessity of foregrounding both the physical and psychic artifacts of Filipino American colonial histories within any educational project that seeks to make sense of both the trauma and resiliency of those whose postcolonial presences find their way into American schools. And from a larger context, we put forward the proposition that any analysis of the American schooling system, from its ideological groundings all the way to the range of practices it deploys, must place in its center a thorough consideration of the legacies of U.S. imperialism, so that race, which is its constitutive and material form, is understood as a determining force of students' lives.

In Part Two: Education and the Making of Identities, we highlight the relationships between knowledge and identity construction as well as their implications in schools and school environments, including the promulgation of educational values. In this section, we venture to reveal at the outset the difficult questions and mixed outcomes of positioning identity as the focal point in which to argue about recognition, value, and affirmation of otherness in the schooling environment. Admittedly, this is a complex and sometimes dangerous move to tackle. On the one hand, we strongly attend to the desire and commitment to insist on the materiality and concomitant distinctiveness of the box that will specify to us who we think we are and how we want to be seen and treated by schools and society. Hence, we offer the emphatic call for a "culturally responsive teaching framework" with particular road maps for plotting self-determined Filipino American heritage into expanded, integrative, and empowering curricula, the pertinent literature of which Third Andresen's chapter surveys and historicizes. In "Knowledge Construction, Transformative Academic Knowledge, and Filipino American Identity and Experience," he lays out the tight connections between group validation for students and empowerment on their way to becoming social-political actors. These connections are keys to addressing the ravages wrought by marginalization and subjugation, the experiences of which Filipinos hold in common with Native Americans and African Americans, among others. Similarly, but focusing more on analyzing empirical ethnic identity survey instruments and findings, Belinda Butler Vea's chapter, "Disaggregating the College Experiences of Filipino Americans from the Aggregate Asian American/Pacific Islander Experience," tracks the contours of large-group categorization in educational settings to reveal both the capacity of aggregated identity markers to make visible commonalities across heterogeneous groups bound by panethnic solidarities, as in the case of "Asian American and Pacific Islander" or AAPI population groups, and its otherwise detrimental incapacity to render the remarkable peculiarities of certain internal groups, as in the case of Filipino Americans. She argues therefore for the separate treatment of Filipino Americans on the basis of their ethnic identity assertions and valuations, apart from such a larger group as AAPI.

On the other hand, while we subscribe to the noteworthy force that such an advocacy for ethnic identity specificity can bring into the struggle for individual group recognition, we are at the same time open about its durability and efficacy in many other struggles, which necessitates inclusionary modalities in the pursuit of justice and coalitional alliances across group differences, so that building democracy or combating social violence can be more efficacious. Groups that are too exclusivist and narrowly inclusionary run the risk of being perceived as isolated, segregationist, and limited in their impact. Indeed, we believe that there is no guarantee of meaningful liberation from injustice worth holding on to for those involved in exclusionary politics.

Moreover, we seek not to be eventually embroiled in the trap of the very thing that we critique—an authentic, unchanging, and pure identity in a totality identified as Filipino American. So we place our trust instead in putting out our calls for a provisional consideration of the specifics of Filipino American sets of identities only to the degree to which we hold such social and political constructions to be context-specific, dynamic, and contingent both in the sense that they are impermanent as much as they are dependent on historical social relations. The chapter by Kevin L. Nadal exemplifies this stance. In "Counseling Filipino American College Students: Promoting Identity Development, Optimal Mental Health, and Academic Success," Nadal proffers that mental health treatment for Filipino American college students must take into account the uniqueness of Filipino American identities as an index of difference that is produced through formal recognition, varying sets of cultural values (mostly connected with socioeconomic status) and once again, colonial experience. Such unique attributes are quite context specific. In California state surveys and data-gathering activities since the 1990s, for example, Filipino Americans have been counted as "Filipinos," not "Asians" or "Hispanics," making group identification activities for Filipinos there more ethnic specific. Nadal provides a discussion of counseling techniques that may help engage these specificities, underscoring the importance of history, context, and culture in the lives of Filipino American college students.

In Part Three: Filipino American Studies and Pedagogies, we draw a tighter rein on the connections among history, identity consciousness and politics, scholarly-community formations, and curricular design as sites that attempt to draw out particular approaches to research, teaching, and mentorship. In order to come within reach of a proper appreciation of these connections by way of contouring our objects of study, we have chosen as an entry optic Allyson Tintiangco-Cubales' chapter, "Struggling to Survive: Poverty, Violence, and Invisibility in the Lives of Urban Filipina/o American Youth." This chapter pries open a window into what are usually disregarded or undetected segments of the Filipino American population. On the surface, the numbers of Filipinos attending the schooling system in the United States closely approximate the cumulative school attendance percentages of the U.S. general population. These are true for the numbers of enrollees in preschool or nursery (5.8% for Filipino Americans; 6.2% for U.S.) kindergarten (4.9% for Filipino Americans; 5.1% for U.S.), elementary school (38.2% for Filipino Americans; 40.8% for U.S.), and high school (20.5% for Filipino Americans; 22.1% for U.S.). Filipino American college enrollment is even higher than the national number (30.6% for Filipinos Americans; 25.8% for U.S.), and the numbers of those in the Filipino American population that have bachelor's degrees are twice as high as the national percentage (37.2% for Filipino Americans; 17.1% for U.S.) (U.S. Census, 2006; for additional information, see National Commission on Asian American and Pacific Islander Research in Education, 2010, 2011; National Federation of Filipino American Associations, 2008).

But upon closer examination of such census statistics, some of these bachelor's degrees may have not necessarily been obtained in the United States, and in the case of Filipino Americans, this education does not easily translate into commensurate U.S. employment (see Buenavista, this volume). Filipinos' lower per capita income ($24,405 for Filipinos; $25,267 for U.S.) and higher labor participation rate (70.2% for Filipinos; 65% for U.S.) show a different, slightly complicated picture, which Tintiangco-Cubales nuances by way of an ethnographic peek into the lives of low-income urban Filipino American youth (U.S. Census, 2006; National Federation of Filipino Associations, 2008). The members of this subpopulation group usually elude the notice of those who still faithfully subscribe to the Model Minority Myth ascribed to many Asian Americans so much so that many teachers and counselors pathologize these youths' nonsuccess in the school system as merely individual malaise or internal group aberrations, or exceptions attributable to a so-called "culture of poverty" (Lewis, 1966). Tintiangco-Cubales boldly offers some critical insights in view of and against this attitude, through the voices of the youth in her study, including their experiences with her in a mentorship-empowerment program that she herself cofounded—the Pin@y Educational Partnerships (PEP) project. We learn here a remarkable example of how an organically based, situation-specific, and culturally conscious mentorship program can actually enable productive linkages between histories of colonization and contemporary culture, between structures of poverty and their impact on the lives of urban youth, between community service as an instantiation of advocacy and the teaching profession as an ethical-political calling, and between theory and practice in academic work.

Indeed, in *Teaching to Transgress*, bell hooks (1994) reminds us that "When our lived experience of theorizing is fundamentally linked to processes of self-recovery, of collective liberation, no gap exists between theory and practice" (p. 61). This is the spirit behind Tintiangco-Cubales' chapter, as it is correspondingly the will that propels Patricia Espiritu Halagao's "Theorizing from Pain, Passion, and Hope: The Making of Filipino American Curricula and Pedagogy." This essay delves into the profound implications of growing up as a Filipina in White America from a very personal point of view and in conditions that made her devalue her own culture in favor of the dominant one, which precisely produced the impulses that motivated her to help start a multicultural curriculum project when she was still a graduate student. Called Pinoy Teach, this program also took shape organically, as its development into a full-fledged curriculum personally and collectively traced an uncharted set of maps through what many would call a group "decolonization" process, but with an added component of having its participants locate Filipino-specific histories side by side with other racial/ethnic grids. Halagao theorizes this process more formally as a postevent rumination, and even though this multicultural process is not unconventional, its uniqueness springs from the rarely acknowledged perspectives that Filipino American history and identities comparatively illuminate. Teaching and mentorship here become prime locations of possibility and empowerment, as the Pinoy Teach model encourages its participants not only to become teachers but also to give back to their communities through service-learning partnerships. Halagao's project has inspired the creation of at least two other curriculum/pedagogy projects that are detailed in her chapter. They are wonderful evidences of the longevity and applicability of such meaningful work.

Both PEP and Pinoy Teach are truly exciting and innovative projects that do not conform to simplistic additive methods, and their rich and ever-expanding curricula are accessible to all kinds of educators, whether new or advanced in their professions. These projects are critically important mainly because in fact, whether one is new or advanced in the teaching professions, especially for those involved in secondary education, there is unfortunately a lack of documented information to rely on except for the rare ones exemplified above. This is proven empirically in Roland Sintos Coloma's chapter, "Invisible Subjects: Filipina/os in Secondary History Textbooks." Here, the tiring argument about pervasive Filipino "invisibility" gets differently cast not as a woeful injunction to complain for not being included but as a warning against irresponsible knowledge production about American history and its diverse populations. Coloma's research on the quantitative and the *qualitative* non- or rare appearance of Filipino and Filipino American histories in U.S. and world history textbooks used in American high schools opens up a number of intriguing permutations. One is the connection between many teachers' desire to expand the imposed curricula they use beyond what top-down-determined textbooks can accommodate and the universalizing demands of regulations like No Child Left Behind to standardize testing in narrow terms, which effectively places absolute limits on curriculum expansion. It is also reminiscent of the hidden curriculum in schools, which works to reinforce dominant ideologies and obliterate experiences of particular groups (Giroux & McLaren, 1996), thus affecting ways in which a critical agenda for curriculum and pedagogical reformation becomes less likely. A second is the significance of public education in the Philippines, whose history as a crucial element of U.S. colonial rule (it being introduced right after military pacification and the setting up of the colonial administration) can also be viewed precisely as a history of the significance of education in American society, governance, and immigration, if only it were not elided in many books.

This history of American educational presence in the Philippines is the same one that brought the very first Filipinos to mainland United States: the U.S. government-sponsored students who came mostly from the elite sectors of Philippine society to study in American universities so that they could return home after schooling to become the administrators, teachers, and professionals of the new country. Textbooks could have used the history of these so-called *pensionados* (see Vergara, this volume) to again highlight the centrality of colonial tutelage in American history here and abroad. At the very least, this history could have been used to mark one of the waves of modern migration of Filipinos into the United States, which Coloma precisely suggests for inclusion in textbooks. This third set of points—the visibility of Filipinos in the Philippines whenever it is mentioned in the texts, compared to the peculiar absence of Filipinos in the United States in *all* of the texts—emphasizes how students in many of our high schools unfortunately learn about Filipinos only as they are distantly and unreachably located spatially and temporally, but never as actual members of American society with their own immigration and settlement histories. Consequently, this has led to detrimental experiences of identity development and sense of belonging for students at the postsecondary level (Maramba, 2008a, 2008b; Maramba & Museus, in press; Maramba & Velasquez, in press; Museus & Maramba, 2011; Nadal, 2004; Nadal, Pituc, Johnston, Esparrago, 2010).

Coloma attempts to make critical connections between invisibility in knowledge production and erasure as its consequence, which in turn reproduces marginalization, substandard education, and low group esteem for those students who are not able to see reflections of themselves (and those like them) in the texts that discuss society and the world in which they assume to be a participant. But even though textbooks, as Coloma claims, are incredibly vital in arbitrating and proclaiming what counts as knowledge and what does not (by means of erasure), one need not be limited to or completely dependent upon them insofar as the pursuit of alternative knowledge can be activated. In "*Kuwento* and Karaoke: Literacy Perspectives on Culture and Education," Korina Jocson provides us with an analytic glance at what appears to be merely a simple teaching strategy of storytelling that goes beyond what mainstream textbooks can provide. Utilized by a high school teacher in California for a class called Filipino Heritage Studies, Jocson's chapter about it captures both the power and potential of active/dynamic classroom discourse in teaching Filipino and Filipino American histories in view, and against the grain, of how regular books limit, erase, or skew such histories.

Heretofore, what indeed appears as a simple pedagogical tool of making *kuwento*, the Tagalog term for storytelling, is actually a set of rich and stimulating dialogues facilitated by the teacher who is able to make history come alive, not by enumerating Filipino and Filipino American achievements (e.g., doing "famous firsts") in the contributionist style of conservative ethnic studies and practicing noncritical traditional pedagogical techniques, but through conversations that animate, for example, the links between war and empire. In these cases, students are able to appreciate the importance of the Philippines in relation to Puerto Rico and Cuba, and as all three intersect with Spanish and U.S. imperialisms and the relevance of the Vietnam War to contemporary critiques of U.S. intrusion into the Third World. Through this active incorporation, students are able to grasp the value of interspersing once-discretely written histories and themes with each other while simultaneously gaining a more illuminating consciousness and therefore a more substantive valuation of Filipino as well as American histories. And more than learning history and, constitutively, identity, *kuwento,* as it is complementarily understood with karaoke or "singing along," opens up a wide and deep array of possibilities for tapping into other kinds of literacies, ways of building community, and co-constructing knowledge, culture, and identity.

We end this section with a chapter written by Antonio T. Tiongson, Jr., entitled "Reflections on the Contours of and Trajectory for a Critical Filipino Studies," to highlight yet another set of curricular, pedagogical, and intellectual paths that crisscross ongoing and constantly changing questions about identity, history, and social formations in a way that underscores the *in process* approach we advocate for studying Filipinos and Filipino Americans. Tiongson explicates new and uncommon, but thought-provoking, insights and inquiries into our collective studies of Filipinos by mapping the significance of empire in a post-9/11 context, the convergences (and disjunctures) of colonial and postcolonial histories that collectively implicate Filipinos with Chicanos, Puertorriqueños, and Pacific Islanders, and what he calls the "interconnections between Black and Brown formations"—all articulated through the works of emerging and seasoned scholars of Filipino and Filipino American studies. On many levels, these scholars offer stimulating and provocative opportunities to think about Filipinos "outside of the box," so to speak, and in conversation with many other communities that they may not be traditionally associated with, but otherwise linked through intersecting threads of history and politics.

Finally, in Part Four: Filipino Americans and Policies in Education, we look into school environments as sites for negotiating relationships of power between Filipino American communities and the larger society. Although not all of the chapters in this section directly and formally impact educational policy, all of them explore various ways of influencing the nature, emphasis, and direction of policy in several domains: access to public higher education; campus climate in connection with student self-esteem; the determination of meanings, practices, and contexts of college education for a minoritized student population; sexual health education; and faculty recruitment and development. We start this section with college access.

Policies and programs that regulate and oftentimes inhibit student access to colleges and universities are the objects of study in "Filipino American Access to Public Higher Education in California and Hawai'i," written by Jonathan Y. Okamura. Primarily examining the impact of and response to the elimination of race-based affirmative action admissions programs in the University of California system, compared to the consequences of a regime of steady state cutbacks in public university support in the University of Hawai'i system, Okamura offers a frank assessment of both gains and disadvantages for Filipino American students. He also provides relevant comparisons with other groups—African Americans, Latinos, and Native Hawaiians—for a richer account of the kinds of cross-racial divergences and conjunctions that have fueled or can inspire future proactive and coalitionally driven politics in this area. Such politics may hopefully counter persistent attacks on the recruitment, representation, and retention of minority students in higher education. These advocacies, especially those situated in California that Okamura writes about, have flourished chiefly through the inspired leadership and unrelenting involvement of students; but in places such as Hawai'i, in which groups with low socioeconomic status get to be the stakeholders with the least advantage in the politics of school access, college access issues are the most demanding with which to contend. These are how the reasons for tracking the links between access to school and access to power become ever so acute.

Policies that help determine the most conducive climates in which to foster student retention and graduation are the indirect targets (and beneficiaries) of Reynaldo I. Monzon's meticulous attention to survey schemes, variables, and validities as they are conducted in schools. In "Collective Self-Esteem and Perceptions of Family and Campus Environments Among Filipino American College Students," he carefully evaluates the accuracy and appropriateness of correlating specific manifestations of psychological well-being with academic performance, comparing, for example, the applicability and relevance of values that denote personal self-esteem versus those that refer to collective self-esteem for Filipino American students. Monzon demonstrates how a survey scale that identifies Filipino American collective self-esteem, compared to other surveys that identify "universal" personal values, may be a more useful and responsible way of examining the academic performance, retention, and persistence of Filipino American college students. To some degree, and illustrative of a catch-22 situation, Monzon's study pokes at the difficulty of obtaining and tracking "statistical significance" for an underrepresented group when that group is precisely numerically low. In addition, he challenges and brings to light the often-misinterpreted statistical data that arise when Filipino Americans are again aggregated with other larger groups in obtaining quantitative data. His study demonstrates that when quantitative methodologies are carefully administered and their data analyzed, the outcomes become critical interpretations that are relevant to Filipino Americans.

Our collective injunction to make Filipino colonial, imperial, and postcolonial histories the shadows that both trace the genealogical and contemporary routes as well as the very same ones that generate affirming possibilities for Filipino Americans continues with Tracy Lachica Buenavista's "Pilipinos in the Middle: Higher Education and a Sociohistorical Context of Contradiction." Hers is an ethnography-based study that reveals the lingering ghosts of Philippine colonial education that find their way into U.S.-based conditions of underemployment, circumscribed social mobility, unfamiliarity with the dynamics of college application and attendance, and conflicting prioritization of demands brought in by family, work, and school that are jointly experienced by Filipino American college students and their parents. Buenavista and her subjects argue that such spectral presences, which are productive of contradiction and persistence, lead us to name and activate a "middle" location in education, which we hope policymakers engaged in student counseling, assessment, and instruction will pay attention to. Resonating with Tintiangco-Cubales' subjects, these are Filipino American students who find themselves anxiously situated between the struggles of their college-educated but proletarianized parents and their aspirations to do well in college while simultaneously dealing with obligations to help their families financially.

Students undergo many life challenges, conflicts, and contradictions that can be misunderstood, go unnoticed, or become silenced. Nadal's coverage of mental health issues, Monzon's critical assessment of self-esteem measurements, and Buenavista's attention to socioeconomic status and college unpreparedness for Filipino American youth are evidence and stark reminders of how much work there is to be done for us to recognize the multivalent and intersecting dimensions of identity, history, structural context, and culture in the lives of our youth. For Charlene Bumanglag Tomas, whose chapter is on "Sexual Health and Responsibility: The Role of Public Schools in Filipina American Teenage Mothers' Lives," such challenging life issues become even more pressing and precarious given the high rates of HIV/AIDS, teenage pregnancy, and sexually transmitted diseases among young adults. We join Tomas in approaching the subject of sexual health with a good measure of trepidation, which is understandable for those of us who are aware of and live through the taboos and shame associated with sex and sexuality among many Filipino communities. But Tomas seriously tackles the issues head-on in her chapter by providing a straightforward but sensitive and multi-analytic set of accounts of Filipina teenage mothers' experiences during their pregnancy and beyond—accounts that usually fall by the wayside in determining policy and institutionalizing classroom priorities regarding sex education. These voices of the young Filipina mothers themselves eventually become the bases for a collection of recommendations that Tomas highlights and discusses in order to address both schoolwide and culture-specific situations and initiatives regarding sexual health practices and instruction or counseling. What we proffer here is the sustenance of a social environment of sex-related practices that are responsibly healthy, well meaning, mature, and meaningful.

This section on policy matters related to education concludes with Dina C. Maramba and Kevin L. Nadal's essay entitled, "Exploring the Filipino American Faculty Pipeline: Implications for Higher Education and Filipino American College Students." Their study presents a virtually unexamined area in higher education that challenges the continuing concern of the dismal numbers of Filipino American tenured and tenure track faculty. As an initial and exploratory study, their attention is focused particularly on those faculty members in the social sciences. Their findings signify the potential gravity and deep ramifications of a lack of Filipino American faculty in general. In particular, Filipino American faculty, although already low in numbers, are mainly located in ethnic and American studies, with only a spattering in other academic fields such as education and psychology. The implications of this study bring to the surface the negative impacts that such invisibility or low faculty visibility can have on potential students who are entering such fields and even further pursuing the professorship altogether. This culminating chapter signals optimistic thinking and a supplication on our part to imagine a more expansive educational policy environment that would include minority faculty recruitment and retention as one of its top priorities, considering the often-unmentioned, understudied, but grave and glaring situation of severe underrepresentation of Filipino American faculty on so many campuses.

* * *

In the beginning of this introductory essay, we asked, what does it mean to talk about Filipino Americans as the "others" in the field of education and within the context of relationships of power in contemporary society? We underscored the necessity of answering this question satisfactorily by engaging with the possible gains as well as the potential limitations of responding to "otherness" by mere representation and through shallow non-disruptive recognition, or by instead offering "otherness" as viable nodes that can make possible strategic interventions against inequality and injustice in education in general and through specific practices of schooling. Giroux (1992) asserts that those designated as "other" must find ways to "reclaim their own histories, voices, and visions as part of a wider struggle to change material and social relations" that have appeared to be "forgotten" or erased (p. 33). We offered a set of thematic arguments and critiques, articulated individually by our authors and gathered in summary form and as parts of a collective in this anthology, to remark upon both the heterogeneous sources and collaborative energies that can be produced out of such an otherness. Now we end this introduction by briefly ruminating on the relationship of identity to education as an attempt to reconnect our bearings with those who we believe should pay special attention to our project.

We agree, most certainly, that schools are apparatuses, among many, for disciplining and regulating diverse subjects, for nurturing and promoting social behavior, usually in the interest of dominant groups, and for managing and training populations in the service of local and global economies. Schooling then produces uniformity as it emphasizes commonality. It also manufactures consent, pushes for compliance, and primarily rewards individual attainment. But what if we imagine schools in other ways as well; that instead of schools being only mere instruments for the enrichment of a few, that they are also avenues of collective opportunity for many? In this case, if identity in its nonsingularity is a site for finding one's meaning in the world, we venture to pay attention to schooling as a significant location for creating, nurturing, challenging, and transforming one's identity personally, socially, and politically. Therefore, we critically imagine education as a constitutive producer as much as it is a product itself, of processes of identity formation and sustenance that then gives meaning to an individual in relationship to others. And in so imagining, we name schooling as sites of possibility, hope, and as a critical part of that process, which enables its participants to coproduce knowledge, tools, and practices that fundamentally engage and connect such partakers with their social worlds (Apple, 2002; Darder, 1991; Freire, 2000). This process is of course complex and conflict ridden, for its stakeholders are varied, differently interested, and unequally invested, and its relationship to the social, political, and economic spheres, both local and transnational in range and scope, within which it is embedded, is multiply determined.

For these reasons, we advocate for greater inclusivity into those spaces of power that determine and put into practice the visions and missions of our schools, and we pursue this advocacy both in the name of those groups, like Filipino Americans, which have been traditionally cast out of recognition and voice, and in the spirit of a desire, willingness, and capacity to reconfigure the terms and relationships of power that undergird the management of differences in our educational system. We cannot stress enough the importance of demarcating the crucial difference between such an advocacy, which entrusts political participation to a reductive politics of identity that stops at numerical presence versus a political engagement that hears and respects dissent, builds coalitions across groups, and pursues transformation while remaining considerate of how different groups have been differentially incorporated in schools.

As Filipino American scholars and educators, we know too well how our attempts at alleviating the costs of our exclusion in schooling will not produce transformative change if we simply and inadequately base our demands on the mere "presence" of our racialized bodies in schools. For such an attempt to be significant and change-worthy, we call for an activist-oriented critical mass of broadbased alliances, which will qualitatively value the work of justice and power in schools while simultaneously weighing the historical vectors of colonialism, racism, and resistance that Filipino American presences hold in specific and share with other similarly situated groups. In doing this, we cast multiple angles of attention as a collective in conversation with other collectives to works and practices that trace our colonial/postcolonial genealogies; consider our ongoing histories with U.S. imperialism; acknowledge and understand our multidimensional, heterogeneous identities and socioeconomic statuses; recognize our multigenerational and transnational communities; and reckon with our multilevel struggles with schooling access and knowledge production. Finally, we ask that such a more critical attentiveness to our otherness be organized in ways that value our situational diversity as disaggregated from larger groups, along with the positive uses of our multidisciplinary range. We call on educators, social scientists, humanists, policymakers, and community activists to be sensitive to these perspectives as we collectively strategize within and outside of our schools to combat invisibility and exclusion and to find productive ways of problematizing education. To us, all of these constitute what it means to speak of Filipino Americans as the "others" in the field of education and within the context of relationships of power in contemporary society.

NOTES

1. We refer to the category "Filipino American" in this anthology as one that is inclusive of those who identify with it ethnically, racially, and culturally. While the "o" in "Filipino" may technically include only those who are male, we use the term provisionally to include male, female, and other kinds of social identities linked with this category.
2. In 1986, Filipinos were eliminated from affirmative action recruitment and admissions programs in California. In this example, though, they technically fall out of the "other" category, suffering the brunt of being mistakenly included in the majority. (Lew, 1995; see Okamura, this volume).
3. The most influential and prolific production of scholarly materials regarding multicultural education comes from the Center for Multicultural Education, based at the University of Washington and pioneered by James A. Banks.

REFERENCES

Apple, M. (1995). *Education and Power* (2nd ed.). New York, NY: Routledge.

Apple, M. (2002). *Power, meaning, and identity: Essays in critical educational studies.* New York, NY: Peter Lang.

Apple, M. (2004). *Ideology and curriculum* (25th anniv. 3rd ed.). New York, NY: Routledge.

Banks, J. A., & Banks, C. A. M. (1993). *Multicultural education: Issues and perspectives.* Boston, MA: Allyn and Bacon.

Bonus, R. (2000). *Locating Filipino Americans: Ethnicity and the cultural politics of space.* Philadelphia, PA: Temple University Press.

Buenavista, T. L., Jayakumar, U. M., & Misa-Escalante, K. (2009). Contextualizing Asian American education through critical race theory: An example of U.S. Pilipino college student experiences. In S. D. Museus (Ed.), *Conducting research on Asian Americans in higher education* (pp. 69–81). New Directions for Institutional Research, 142. San Francisco, CA: Jossey-Bass.

Chan, S. (1991). *Asian Americans: An interpretive history.* Boston, MA: Twayne.

Chan, S. (2005). *In defense of Asian American studies: The politics of teaching and program building.* Urbana: University of Illinois Press.

Cordova, F. (1983). *Filipinos: Forgotten Asian Americans.* Dubuque, IA: Kendall Hunt.

Darder, A. (1991). *Culture and power in the classroom.* Westport, CT: Bergin and Garvey.

David, E. J. R. (2011). *Filipino/American postcolonial psychology: Oppression, colonial mentality, and decolonization.* Indianapolis, IN: AuthorHouse.

Delpit, L. D. (2006). *Other people's children: Cultural conflict in the classroom.* New York, NY: New Press.

Espina, M. (1988). *Filipinos in Louisiana.* New Orleans, LA: Laborde.

Freire, P. (2000). *Pedagogy of the oppressed.* New York, NY: Continuum International.

Fujita-Rony, D. B. (2003). *American workers, colonial power: Philippine Seattle and the transpacific west, 1919–1941.* Berkeley: University of California Press.

Gándara, P., & Contreras, F. (2009). The Latino education crisis: The consequences of failed social policies. Cambridge, MA: Harvard University Press.

Gay, G. (2000). *Culturally responsive teaching: Theory, research, and practice.* New York, NY: Teachers College Press.

Giroux, H. A. (1983). *Theory and resistance in education: A pedagogy for the opposition.* South Hadley, MA: Bergin & Garvey.

Giroux, H. A. (1992). *Border crossings: Cultural workers and the politics of education.* New York, NY: Routledge.

Giroux, H. A., & McLaren, P. (1996). Teach education and the politics of engagement: The case for democratic schooling. In P. Leistyna, A. Wodrum, & S. A. Sherblom (Eds.), *Breaking free: The transformative power of critical pedagogy.* Cambridge, MA: Harvard Educational Review.

Hirabayashi, L. R. (1998). *Teaching Asian America: Diversity and the problem of community.* Lanham, MD: Rowman & Littlefield.

Hochschild, J. L., & Scovronick, N. B. (2003). *The American dream and the public schools.* New York, NY: Oxford University Press.

hooks, b. (1994). *Teaching to transgress: Education as the practice of freedom.* New York, NY: Routledge.

Howard, G. R. (1999). *We can't teach what we don't know: White teachers, multiracial schools.* New York, NY: Teachers College Press.

Hune, S. (1998). *Asian Pacific American women in higher education: Claiming visibility & voice.* Washington, DC: Association of American Colleges and Universities, Program on the Status and Education of Women.

Isaac, A. P. (2006). *American tropics: Articulating Filipino America.* Minneapolis: University of Minnesota Press.

Leistyna, P., Woodrum, A., & Serblom, S. A. (1995). *Breaking free: The transformative power of critical pedagogy.* Cambridge, MA: Harvard Educational Review.

Lew, G. A. (Ed.). (1995). *Common ground: Perspectives on affirmative action and its impact on Asian Pacific Americans.* Darby, PA: Diane.

Lewis, O. (1966). *La vida: A Puerto Rican family in the culture of poverty—San Juan and New York.* New York, NY: Random House.

Maramba, D. C. (2008a). Immigrant families and the college experience: Perspectives of Filipina Americans. *Journal of College Student Development, 49*(4), 336–350.

Maramba, D. C. (2008b). Understanding campus climate through voices of Filipino/a American college students. *College Student Journal, 42*(4), 1045–1060.

Maramba, D. C., & Museus, S. D. (in press). Examining the effects of campus climate, ethnic group cohesion and cross-cultural interaction on Filipino American students' sense of belonging in college. *Journal of College Student Retention, 15*(1).

Maramba, D. C., & Velasquez, P. (2012). Influences of the campus experience on the ethnic identity development of students of color. *Education and Urban Society, 44*(3), 294–317. doi:10.1177/0013124510393239.

McCarthy, C., Crichlow, W., Dimitriadis, G., & Dolby, N. (Eds.). (2005). *Race, identity, and representation in education* (2nd ed.). New York, NY: Routledge.

Museus, S. D., & Maramba, D. C. (2011). The impact of culture on Filipino American students' sense of belonging. *Review of Higher Education, 34*(2), 231–258.

Nadal, K. L. (2004). Pilipino American identity model. *Journal of Multicultural Counseling and Development, 32*(1), 44–61.

Nadal, K. L., Pituc, S. T., Johnston, M. P., & Esparrago, T. (2010). Overcoming the model minority myth; Experiences of Filipino American graduate students. *Journal of College Student Development, 51*(6), 694–706.

Nakanishi, D. T., & Nishida, T. Y. (1995). *The Asian American educational experience: A source book for teachers and students.* New York, NY: Routledge.

National Commission on Asian American and Pacific Islander Research in Education. (2010). *Federal higher education policy priorities and the Asian American and Pacific Islander community.* New York, NY: USA Funds.

National Commission on Asian American and Pacific Islander Research in Education. (2011). *The relevance of Asian Americans & Pacific Islanders in the college completion agenda.* New York, NY: USA Funds.

National Federation of Filipino American Associations. (2008). *Filipino American K–12 public school students: A study of ten urban communities across the United States.* Washington, DC.

Parrillo, V. N. (2011). *Strangers to these shores* (10th ed.). Boston, MA: Allyn and Bacon.

Pido, A. J. A. (1992). *The Pilipinos in America: Macro/micro dimensions of immigration and integration.* New York, NY: Center for Migration Studies.

Pizarro, M. (2005). *Chicanas and Chicanos in school: Racial profiling, identity battles, and empowerment.* Austin: University of Texas Press.

San Juan, E. (1993, July 8). Filipino writing in the United States: Reclaiming whose America? *Philippine Studies, 41,* 141.

San Juan, E. (2000). *After postcolonialism.* Lanham, MD: Rowman & Littlefield.

Schaefer, R. T. (2010). *Racial and ethnic groups* (12th ed.). Upper Saddle River, NJ: Prentice Hall.

Taylor, E., Gillborn, D., & Ladson-Billings, G. (2009). *Foundations of critical race theory in education.* New York, NY: Routledge.

Thelin, J. R. (2004). *A history of American higher education.* Baltimore, MD: Johns Hopkins University Press.

Tiongson, A. T., Gutierrez, E. V., & Gutierrez, R. V. (2006). *Positively no Filipinos allowed: Building communities and discourse.* Philadelphia, PA: Temple University Press.

U.S. Census Bureau. (2006). *American community survey.* Retrieved from http://www.factfinder.census.gov/faces/tableservices/jsf/pages/productview.xhtml?pid=ACS06ESTS1501&prodType=table

U.S. Census Bureau. (2010). *Race reporting for the Asian population by selected categories: 2010.* Retrieved from http://factfinder2.census.gov/faces/tableservices/jsf/pages/productview.xhtml?pid=DEC_10_SF1_QTP8&prodType=table

Valenzuela, A. (1999). *Subtractive schooling: U.S.-Mexican youth and the politics of caring.* Albany: State University of New York Press.

PART I

HISTORICAL COORDINATES

CHAPTER 1

BETWIXT AND BETWEEN COLONIAL AND POSTCOLONIAL MENTALITY

The Critical Education of Filipino Americans

Zeus Leonardo
University of California, Berkeley

Cheryl E. Matias
University of Colorado, Denver

Recorded in the history of human suffering is a cancer so malignant that the least tough irritates it and awakens such agonizing pains. Thus every time in the midst of modern civilization I have wanted to invoke you, either to accompany me with your memories or to compare you with other countries, each time, your beloved image appeared to me with a social cancer.

Desiring your health which is ours, and searching for the best treatment, I will do for you what the ancients did for their sick: they exposed them on the steps of the temple so that each person who came to invoke the Supreme Being might propose to them a remedy.

The "Other" Students, pages 3–18

> And to this end, I will try to reproduce faithfully your condition without any indulgence, I will lift part of the veil that conceals the evil, sacrificing all to the truth, even my own pride, for as your son, I also suffer from your defects and weaknesses. (Rizal, 2006)

In the dedication page of his book, *Noli Me Tangere* (1886), Jose Rizal speaks to the people of what would be later known as the Philippines. He relates the Spanish colonialism of the Philippines to a cancer that makes the Philippines sick. He continues by stating that the only way to ameliorate this social cancer is to painfully expose it, despite its taboo status. What Rizal did in his controversial book is to clear the lens of reality for both the Spanish and Filipino people. His book parallels the emotional and social outcry of Harriet Beecher Stowe's (1852) *Uncle Tom's Cabin* with respect to American slavery. Rizal anticipated the social pain that would be caused by writing his book. However, he did not anticipate that the social cancer to which he refers would continue to grow for over a century and become ubiquitous among the following generations of Filipinos and Filipino Americans. Filipinos and Filipino Americans are no longer formally colonized subjects by the Spaniards or the Americans, but generations have inherited a certain cancer of the mind that subjugates their true sense of culture, identity, and history. Following Rizal's invocation, this cancer is called colonial mentality and wreaks havoc on Filipino American educational development.

There is a general agreement that Filipino Americans have entered a social condition that is markedly different from previous eras because of colonialism. In the postcolonial condition, they have entered a domain of social hybridity and diasporic movement that challenges the assumptions of colonialism as a reliable discourse to explain the experiences of Filipino Americans. In this chapter, we promote the continuity, rather than the radical break, between the colonial and postcolonial conditions. Existing within a social life that has not been sufficiently theorized, Filipino Americans experience education as a combination of colonial and postcolonial tendencies. In other words, the oft-invoked trope of "colonial mentality" exists within the uneasy space of a postcolonial hybridity in which the legacy of colonialism functions less as a metanarrative and more as a condition of possibility for the education of Filipino Americans under postcolonialism. As such, Filipino American education has not stepped fully out of colonial mentality to assume a postcolonial mentality but rather is located in the continuity between them. However, before we examine the potentiality of a postcolonial hybridity, it is essential that we explicate the formation of colonial mentality as produced by a colonial education system of both its Spanish and U.S. colonizers. In the next section, we outline the beginnings of Filipino education as part of a racialized colonial project.

EMERGENCE OF COLONIAL MENTALITY

Remnants of colonialism, such as the valorization of light skin, the straightening of hair, sharpening of one's nose, the all-for-America attitude, and the linguistic dominance of English, stand as a few obvious markers of Spanish colonization and the more recent U.S. colonial domination. However, one of the less obvious markers of Filipino colonization is the lack of historical self-understanding by the Filipino people. Likewise, Filipino history that is free from colonial tutelage and its distortions remains elusive. Similar to how Albert Memmi (1965) argues that the French colonized native Algerians for so long that Algerians were forced to see themselves through the eyes of the colonizer, Filipinos and Filipino Americans have suffered a similar fate. They have been forced to identify themselves through the lens of their Spanish and American colonizers. That is, their "orientalized" image and identity were molded through the eyes of their colonizer and not themselves (Said, 1979). After years of being told who and what they are, the indigenous and natively constructed Filipino identity and history have become lost, which has real consequences for the development of an entire people. This diasporic identity and history was a key strategy for European and U.S. colonizers to exercise influence over its conquest (Spring, 2001). In her book, *Methodology of the Oppressed*, Chela Sandoval (2000) uses Roland Barthes to describe this loss of history as a "robbery by colonization." This robbery of history is described as the "most serious blow suffered by the colonized" because it strips them of any notion of freedom and the right to "actively participate in history" (Memmi, 1965, pp. 91–92). Similarly, colonized people become nothing more than an object of a superimposed history similar to the characters in George Orwell's (1949) novel, *1984*.

This lack of historical self-understanding leads to more problems. What choice do the colonized have if they have no history to offer themselves? Memmi (1965) addresses this condition when he states the "colonized is forced to accept being colonized" (p. 89). For if the colonized were to go beyond the confines of the colonial system, it becomes an uncertain journey into an unknown realm. This is precisely because the colonizer has forced the colonized to assume their role as a subjugated people. In turn, this makes it difficult for the colonized to see beyond their subjugation. Metacognitively speaking, insofar as the colonized have no history, they can only accept the history that is offered, even if it derogates their self-image. In this condition, what other choice do they have?

Colonization encompasses a history of disadvantages, racial discrimination, social injustice, and biased education. Typically, colonization is defined as the "act of colonizing, or the state of being colonized." Our questions then become, "Who is the colonizer and who is the colonized?" and "How do the dynamics between the two influence the education, identities, and cultural traditions of people?" (cf. Memmi, 1965). As a result of Spain's paternalism and the United States' imperialistic tutelage of the Philippines, Filipinoness is subject to a long history of colonization. In the following sections, we first explore how the Philippines' colonial history affects its educational practices and how such practices set the basis for a colonized view of Filipino and Filipino American cultural identity. This enables a better understanding of how colonial mentality was spread. Later, we describe the postcolonial moment to explicate the subjectivities that colonization produced but did not determine. In other words, the project of colonization was incomplete and produced Filipino self-understandings that escape the ultimate control of empire. Within the postcolonial condition, the Filipino diaspora has lived with the resulting ambiguity and ambivalence with respect to notions of homeland, national identity, and cultural essence. In short, Filipinos around the world have been educated as *exiles*, and this exilic condition is productive and not merely repressive (see Matias, forthcoming).

THE DIALECTICS OF THE FILIPINO

The term *Filipino* itself recognizes the 400-year colonial rule of the archipelago, which started in the early 1500s. Because the term *Filipino* derives from the nation of the Philippines and because the Philippines was named after King Felipe (Philip) II of Spain, identifying oneself as *Filipino* recalls the colonial subjection of the archipelago's people. Thus, the very term that Filipinos use to identify themselves is part of colonialism. It contains the history of colonization because it interpellates every Filipino as a subject of a colonizing power, hails him by that name, and recognizes him as a member of the colonized. Calling oneself "Filipino" negates the identification and existence of native inhabitants who lived on the archipelago before Spanish colonial rule and whom Europeans conveniently labeled as *Indios* or *Negritos*. Despite this understanding, many Filipinos and Filipino Americans still label themselves as such because there is no viable alternative, other than using regional labels, such as Batangeño, whose accent also bears the marks of colonialism. The idea of being Filipino is so deeply ingrained in the associated cultural identity that to deny it would be like taking the connotations of "Black" away from African Americans. In short, the birth of the Filipino is coterminous with the birth of a particular colonized subject.

Phonetically, the use of the /f/ sound in the word Filipino already assumes the sounds imposed by the English and Spanish languages. Because indigenous languages, such as Tagalog, do not contain the /f/ sound, the pronunciation of *F*ilipino would actually be Pilipino with a /p/. Some may argue the /f/ pronunciation in itself adheres to the linguistic dominance of English or Spanish, and the predominance of the label Filipino is so commonplace that to change it would be to alter the meaning of Filipino identity (Leonardo, 2000). However, others argue that the Filipino/Pilipino people have "taken back" that label and have strategically reclaimed it for themselves in order to own their identity. In many respects, the label of Filipino is dialectical in that it functions as a form of self-recognition as well as a sign of imposition by a colonial power. Hence, to understand the dialectical nature of "Filipino" and what it means, we must first understand the sociopolitical, historical, and colonial timeline of what is now called the Philippines. It is not our intent to decipher what is right or wrong in the use of terminologies. It is certainly a complex issue, and tracing an identity prior to "Filipino" is riddled with problems, such as the search for a sense of belonging that is perpetually deferred to previous namings or a politics that becomes meaningless at the level of practice. Rather, we assert the need to be critically aware of the dialectical context of words that bind Filipino identity.

COLONIAL CATHOLICISM AND INFERIORIZATION OF THE FILIPINO

In addition to the Spanish Galleon trades between Acapulco, Mexico, and Manila, Philippines, which heightened the Spanish economic control over the islands and the reorganization of lands from *datu*-ruled villages to the serf-like *encomiendo* system, the commitment to evangelical Catholicism as a form of education contributed to the subjugation of Filipinos. From the outset, we want to assert Filipino ambivalence toward education. With the fervent sentiments of Christian expansionism, the church became a key political player in the Spanish domination of the Philippines and the reeducation of the indigenous inhabitants, thus sanctioning the friars as the Filipinos' first teachers. Under the *patronato real*, missionaries not only brought the gospel but also stood as a symbol of Spanish colonial power (Nepomuceno, 1981). Their roles extended well beyond passing "the word of Christ" and included infiltrating the political-educational domain. This means that the Filipinos' first form of colonial education was religious in content. Because of the Filipinos' constant uprisings against Spanish colonial rule, the friars were expected to pacify the natives, to "restore them [Filipinos] to the state of subjection" (Nepomuceno, 1981, p. 68). The friars' message contained important contradictions. On the one hand, they reminded Filipinos that in order to be saved, they must fully convert to Christianity. On the other hand, to obtain full Christian status meant that Filipinos must have "ipso facto subjection to colonial power" (Nepomuceno, 1981, p. 79). Hence, Filipinos were manipulated into believing that in order to be "saved" they must learn subservience and accept their culture as inferior to Spanish culture.

The colonizer recognized the natives' forced internalization of inferiority, which reaffirmed the assumed passivity of the Filipinos in the minds of the Spanish. In later times, this was described as indolence by U.S. colonizers (Rafael, 1995). As a result, Filipinos have been described as "docile" and "ambient." Admiral George Dewey himself used these exact words to describe the Filipinos in a January 1902 Senate Hearing (Graff, 1969). The idea that Filipinos are "childlike, indolent, intellectually inferior, and morally retarded" stemmed from the "orientalist" (Said, 1979) literature about Filipinos written by European imperialists (Sullivan, 1991, p. 54). The Spaniards' denigration of the Filipino native culture created a superiority complex among the Spaniards (Sullivan, 1991; cf. Fanon, 1967). This coercive and manipulative ploy to construct Filipinos as passive and in need of Christian redemption also paved the way for future foreign powers, such as the United States, to justify their colonial tutelage of the Philippines. By absolving the church of its colonial role in the character defamation of Filipinos, the colonizers were able to pacify the colonized and continue to prostitute its culture and pillage its land. Conversely, by accepting inferiorization, Filipinos inadvertently participated in the creation of their own colonial mentality. This process confirms Foucault's (1980) observation that we are all complicit in the reproduction of power.

The dual role of the missionaries or friars is of grave importance here. First, they were ordered to pacify the indigenous people. Second, by maintaining the significance of Christianity, they downplayed the significance of the natives' existing cultural norms. The Spaniards unabashedly spread the idea that Spanish humanity was exceedingly superior to the natives' sense of humanity (Nepomuceno, 1981). Thus, in the eyes of the Spanish, the natives must be saved from themselves, like children who do not know what is good for them.

This deduction of mythic proportions became the rationale and justification for Spanish colonization. Far more important to note here, the subjects of power become the objects of its precedence (Foucault, 1980). In other words, the native inhabitants internalized this forced arrangement, and a sense of inferiority pervaded the minds of the Filipinos. Memmi (1965) described this internalized colonialism best as when the colonizers justify their position by insinuating that the colonized is too indolent and lazy for self-governance (see also Alatas, 1977). After years of being told that the colonized is inferior to the colonizer, the colonized develop a complex and contradictory sentiment of fear and admiration for the "superior" colonizer (Freire, 1993). The colonized subject begins to question his status by muttering, "Is he partially right? Are we not all a little guilty after all? Lazy, because we have so many idlers? Timid because we let ourselves be oppressed?" (Memmi, 1965, p. 86). Hence, colonized people experience a split subjectivity in terms of whether or not they are inferior and whether or not the colonizer has a right to govern. As a result, a formidable neurosis sets in for the colonized (Fanon, 1967).

This colonial education transformed into what Gloria Ladson-Billings (1998) terms "psycho-cultural assaults" against the native cultural traditions. Eventually, colonial education blurs the lines between "the new, enforced ideas of the colonizers and the formally accepted native practices" (www.emory.edu/ ENGLISH/Bahri/Education. html). The colonized begin to accept cultural hegemony and internalize the colonizer's standards (Freire, 1993). They assume wrongly that once assimilated, they will become a superior person. Fanon (1967) warns of this impossibility when he claims that the Black man is trapped in his Blackness, a body that betrays him in the end. If the Spanish set the stage for education through colonial subjugation, then this first injury taught other nations how to regard the Philippines and Filipinos. Thus, at the beginning of the 20th century, another foreign power awaited the Filipinos: the United States.

THE HIDDEN CURRICULUM OF COLONIAL EDUCATION AND AMERICAN BENEVOLENCE

Education always has a purpose (Spring, 1997), and it is always directed and never neutral (Freire, 1993). Whether it consolidates a sense of national unity or pacifies a colonized people, education in a colonial situation served and still serves as a masked "benevolent pathologizer" of its students (Ladson-Billings, 1998). Education is neither apolitical, beyond the influence of social structure, nor is it passive (Meyer, Ramirez, & Soysal, 1992, p. 129). Rather, education is an active process that reinforces, and sometimes challenges, institutionalized racism, sexism, class exploitation, and other existing relations of power (Leonardo, 2003). It often becomes a reflection of society's accepted norms and is used to perpetuate the existing status quo and social stratification. According to functionalist theory, schooling maintains the "dominance of the elites (through co-option)" (Meyer et al., 1992, p. 129). When you put the term *colonial* in front of the word *education*, the connotations are strong and obviously oppressive. For the term *colonial* inherently implies a construction whereby the colonizers are the subjects of power and the colonized are the objects of power (Memmi, 1965).

The intention and aspiration for using colonial education was to model the paradigms and social norms of the colonizer. It was expected that the colonized in a colonial education system would forcibly conform to the normative, hegemonic practices of the colonizer. In this manner education in the Philippines played an assimilating role whereby indigenous people were expected to strip their native learning structures to adopt one that was both foreign to them and rationalized as superior by their colonizers. Again, colonial education had its purpose: "to equip a colonized society with the skills needed to administer the colonial enterprise" (Arnove & Torres, 2003, p. 54). Therefore, colonial education became the medium that upheld the oppressive state of a capitalistic enterprise, racist relations, and cultural imperialism. Nowhere is this more apparent than the United States and Spain's colonial relationship with the Philippines.

After the Spanish-American War at the end of the 19th century, the United States assumed control of the Philippines. Because of Filipino resistance, America realized it needed to fight the Philippine "insurgence" (also known as the Philippine-American War) on two battlefronts: military and civilian. It is a textbook case of what Gramsci (1971) calls hegemony or the struggle over ideology and common sense through cultural, rather than purely coercive, means. In order to culturally pacify the Filipino insurgency, Americans instituted colonial education. They wanted to teach the Filipinos about the "benevolent" intention of American control. Flanked by the repressive military on one side, U.S. colonialism used the educational apparatus on the other (see Althusser, 1971). President McKinley himself affirmed the idea of a "benevolent assimilation" when he spoke to the American public on December 21, 1898.

The introduction of the Thomasites and the Pensionado Program were two methods designed to instill colonial education among the Filipino people. In 1901, the Philippine Commission (run by American military officers and diplomats) initiated Act No. 74, which required the transport of 600 teachers from the United States to the Philippines. These teachers were called the Thomasites after the Minnewaska cattle cruiser they arrived in—later named the U.S. Thomas (www.thomasites100.org/thomas_hist.html). These were White men and women who came to the Philippines in hopes of educating the "savages" about the superiority of American democracy. Hence, Philippine colonial education continued its racial project with a new master: the United States.

The Pensionado Act of 1903 gave birth to a Pensionado Program, designed to institute a "formal" U.S. education in the Philippines at the expense of the colonial government, much like the Illustrados, a program that sent wealthy Filipinos to Spain for formal education during Spanish colonial rule. The Pensionado Program's intent was to generate a pool of highly trained, U.S.-educated Filipinos who embodied American ideals. It is important to note that by this time, Filipinos already internalized (through years of Thomasite teaching) the idea that American education was superior to any teachings indigenous to the Filipinos. Although initially designed for the wealthy classes, eventually Filipinos who were "not necessarily wealthy" also participated in the program, and upon return to the

Philippines they had access to better opportunities in the colonial bureaucracy (http://opmanong.ssc.hawaii.edu/ filipino/filmig.html). Furthermore, the Pensionado Program developed the "counter consciousness" that Renato Constantino (1970) described in his book *Dissent and Counter Consciousness.* If colonial education is described as both an overt and covert assimilation process of colonized minds, then any extensions of it are implicated, such as the Pensionado Program. It simultaneously preached American ideals and forced Filipinos to mentally juggle the duality of their cultural existence. On the one hand, Americanism and all its glory represented the ultimate utopia, which was promised through assimilation. On the other hand, Filipinos were colonial subjects inserted into the existing racial hierarchy of America. It did not matter how many showers they took and how hard they scrubbed, the brown did not wash off.

If there is one thing to be learned about the Pensionados' sojourn in U.S. society, it is that race matters. Filipinos were exposed to the cruel reality that, despite all the teachings about the American Dream, meritocracy, and Horatio Alger stories of picking one up by one's bootstraps to succeed in a capitalist society, there still existed one barrier: the fact of being Filipino. Carlos Bulosan's (1973) *America is in the Heart* is the poignant story chronicling this contradiction as Bulosan moved from city to city, job to job, and met with racism at the beginning of the day and exploitation by the end. Constantino (1970) describes this struggle best when he writes,

> The Filipino is estranged from his society, isolated from his fellow men, and alienated from himself. His estrangement is manifested in the daily confusion of our national life and is the cause of our general pessimism and frustration. We have so degraded our concept of human community that it has become a caricature of itself and human life has been reduced to mere existence. The violence that surrounds our lives, the meaningless activities we frantically engage in, our limited social and individual goals—all of these have distorted the human bond and are indications of our failure to appreciate fully the limitless potentialities of the human being. We have measured our relations and our worth in terms of cold cash. Our goals, our happiness, our possibilities have thus been reduced to crude economic terms. (p. 31)

Here, Constantino describes a Filipino pyrrhic victory when it comes to U.S.-sponsored Filipino education. Filipinos succeeded in adopting and mastering the "superior" Western education, yet, by accepting this tutelage, they also had to realize that such an education taught them the inferiority of their own native culture. Hence, the Pensionado Program gave Filipinos a chance to experience a Westernized, White man's world, but upon receiving their graduate degrees, they became subjects of a U.S. regime based on racism. Consequently, recipients of such a program not only returned to a colonized land after experiencing a colonizer's educational system, but they also brought with them a colonized mind.

Colonial education is a fact of Filipino history. It succeeded in assimilating Filipinos into accepting the American ideals of government, education, and language as well as producing conditions for dissent against its imposition. It also rendered the native Filipino culture antiquated and obsolete, similar to Said's (1979) observation of the Occident's treatment of the Orient. Yet, paradoxically, by reducing their identities and cultures, colonialism also allowed a transformationally resistant spirit to develop, a new conceptualization of who Filipinos are as defined by themselves (see Matias, forthcoming). Therefore, colonial education is both the point of subjugation and the potential point of resistance and self-definition.

In the end, colonial education in the Philippines helped establish the Filipino diaspora, which since has spawned subjectivities even the colonizer could neither have predicted nor controlled. The rudimentary elements of Filipinoness were undermined, because for too long the Filipino self-conceptualization was defined by a superior other. This internalization of Western standards and colonialism make the discovery of authentic Filipino identity confusing, because Filipinos find themselves struggling for a sense of belonging that must acknowledge they were uprooted (Leonardo, 2003). However, this irony is not just repressive but productive in Foucault's (1980) sense that power creates and produces new subjects. Whether classified as *indios*, *negritos*, *savages*, *Pilipino*, or *Filipino*, the inhabitants and the descendents of what is now called the Philippines live in an utter state of ambivalence, reconceptualization, and activism regarding true identity. They seldom realize that there exists no box to check, because the box was originally placed there *for* them and not designed *by* them. Yet in realizing this, they also now have the opportunity to redefine their identity (see Matias, forthcoming).

REFERENCING FILIPINO AMERICAN HISTORY AND THE DIALECTICS OF EXILE: CONTINUITIES IN THE CRITICAL EDUCATION OF THE FILIPINO

The history of Filipino American migration involves a complex relationship with American colonial rule. That is, it is impossible to understand Filipino American migration without putting its history in the context of American colonization. Almost every Philippine historical event that occurred for the past century occurred mainly in relation to the United States. Therefore, it is important to understand that the United States shaped the plight of Filipino Americans. By acknowledging the Philippines' colonial history, one can then understand how the current social structure, plight, stereotypes, identities, and development of colonial mentality among Filipino Americans are extensions of that history.

Ultimately, colonial mentality is a cancer that continues to spread its disease in the hearts and spirits of the Filipino people. The most destructive and murderous aspect of this cancer is that it has become so prevalent in Filipino American society that it is seen as unremarkable and invisible. For the Filipino diaspora, habituating to this cancer becomes a form of social death because it will distort people's minds, self-understanding, history, and identity.

Despite this dire outlook, all is not lost. Filipinos and Filipino Americans can and must emerge from their colonized state of being. Education has the potential to decolonize and "cut through illusions" (Memmi, 1965, p. 146). Filipinos must understand "one prize of victory is that the winners get to write the history books" (Francisco, 1976, p. 2). History is thus slanted toward the colonizer's perspective, which subjugates the voices, attitudes, and beliefs of the colonized. Accepting Filipino history without questioning its distortions will deny the concrete existence of an oppressed people. Colonialism will not be remembered as merely a legacy, but an event bound up with the fact of being Filipino.

Filipinos now live in a postcolonial age marked by the fall of official colonialism. The Philippines is no longer a colony of either Spain or the United States, but this does not suggest that the lingering effects of colonialism are not formidable. On the contrary, Filipinos must, as Gramsci (1971) would suggest, take an inventory of their coloniality in order to learn what it has made of them. In order to re-form Filipino education, we must come to terms with the forces that have formed the Filipino in the first place, specifically the colonial interaction. In our attempts to understand the process of colonialism, there is perhaps no better group whose experience showcases survival and resilience from multiple colonizers: first Spain, then a failed attempt by Japan, and finally the United States. So, whereas colonialism has ended, *coloniality* continues (see Quijano, 2000) and necessitates re-forming the Filipino through discourses that accept but do not grieve the condition of the colonized. In other words, colonialism may have wreaked havoc on the Filipino's sense of self and group development, but colonialism was an incomplete project of domination that produced subjectivities that neither the colonizer nor colonized could have predicted or controlled.

To the extent that colonial power was repressive, it also produced knowledge, ambivalence, and new associations that currently make up the *Filipino as exile.* For as Said (2000) remarks,

> Exile can produce rancor and regret, as well as a sharpened vision. What has been left behind may either be mourned, or it can be used to provide a differ-

> ent set of lenses... using the exile's situation to practice criticism... [and] to show that no return to the past is without irony. (p. xxxv)

Appropriate and critical education for the Filipino must acknowledge that colonialism may have developed the Filipino identity (i.e., the Philippine nation-state did not exist before Spanish colonization), but it did not end there. In the postcolonial moment, Filipino subjectivity results from the multiple recombinations made possible by colonialism and exile. We gain a set of discourses through exile that puts into focus a set of concrete, historical experiences that are not just disabling and relegating the colonized to an impossible corner in order that he may sulk, but one out of which the exile creates a life (see Matias, forthcoming). As Jacques Ranciere, in a recent colloquium at UC-Berkeley, says of the Left in France, there has been a loss, or the realization that there remains a gap between their goals during the cultural revolution and current French reality. This loss goes by the name of "melancholy." But Ranciere goes further and suggests that there are "idiots" who do not recognize that there has been a loss and those who do. He advises that those who do may as well enjoy it. Likewise, Filipinos have experienced a loss through colonial violence that some may not recognize. The exile accepts the loss and may as well enjoy this life.

Filipino education is about picking up the pieces left from the ashes of colonialism. With the rise of the Filipino diaspora, the dispersion of identity challenges the notion of a stable, unproblematic, and singular identification. This allows for Filipino agency insofar as the exile not only reproduces the determinisms of colonial mentality but produces the ambiguities of postcolonial mentality as well. This is the nexus of Filipino education. The Filipino has experienced a historical break, a juncture that disrupts any essentialist association with "home," because his ethnicity and nationality are bound up with the fact of colonialism. When he attempts to find a resting spot for an authentic identity, the history of colonialism reminds him that he is doubled (Bhabha, 1990) rather than split. In the specific context of the United States, it is difficult for the Filipino exile to claim either the Philippines or the United States as his home, for he knows very well that he has been changed by his interaction with U.S. life. He is both/and as well as neither/nor a Filipino and American. To the extent that he has rightful claims to the history of the Philippines through continuity and belongs to the United States because he contributes to it, he is both. Yet the Filipino American is neither because the claim to a "homeland" so integral to the exile's schizophrenic self-understanding is denied through geographical and cultural distance from the Philippines at the same time that the land he does occupy denies him full access to its privileges as a perpetual foreigner (Bulosan, 1973; Wu, 2002). He is a stranger in both lands and a member of their national narratives, all at the same time. He is more than one thing but not completely anything. If Chinese immigrants are frequently called sojourners on U.S. soil, then Filipinos are its perpetual example.

Having once been owned through colonialism, the Filipino knows that ownership does not characterize his historical attitude to his condition in which "the world is not what I think, but what I live through . . . I am in communication with it, but I do not possess it" (Merleau-Ponty, as cited in Said, 2000, p. 5). The postcolonial Filipino understands, like Du Bois' (1989) "twoness," a peculiarity to his existence. He wants to belong but resists its confirmation. He knows that belonging means to own and be owned, so he envies yet resents those who feel a sense of belonging. After all, belonging is not just a personal search but a historical condition for the colonized who were once possessions of the colonizer. The Philippines literally came with a price tag of $250 million when Spain relinquished her colony to the United States as a result of the Spanish-American War. The Filipino knows better than to prize belonging. Yet he seeks after his people. As every Filipino American knows, "spotting" a compatriot in public is quite an event, and the "I too" statement inevitably gets invoked: "You're Filipino? I'm Filipino too!" Or, to mimic Fanon (1967), "Look, a Filipino!" This utterance recalls the coloniality of being (Maldonado-Torres, 2007), and the exilic circumstance is not negated by these moments of recognition but confirmed by them, which are simultaneously forms of misrecognition. The fact that Filipinos are so exuberant to find their mirror image in the other completes their alienation within a nation that makes it a crime to be Filipino (Bulosan, 1973). If the Filipino belonged to U.S. life in general, then there should be little reason to seek his brother or sister, as is common for many White Americans who see themselves reflected in public life and rarely feel starved to seek out their image. So the Filipino's moment of recognition through his mirroring is an irony, because it misrecognizes the other for the self. It is a representation of Filipinoness twice removed because it detours through the other and is not a direct confrontation with the self. Furthermore, it does not represent the Filipino's otherwise "human" self, but a colonized self, a (mis)representation of his elusive authenticity. It is a momentary comfort as he makes his way back to solitude. Colonialism continues to educate him.

The opposite of nationalism, which as Said (2000) reminds us, is about the politics of groups. The exile recognizes his radical solitude. His discontinuous state of being, which resulted from colonialism, then the displacement that followed and the out-migration that became a logical consequence, cut him off from a feeling of rootedness, not unlike Deleuze and Guattari's (1983) postmodern trope of the rhizome that has no original source. If he is nationalistic, the Filipino belongs to the provisional nation of exiles. This nation is predicated on antinationalist nationalism in which members do not band together but are nonetheless tied with one another through an anonymous history. The Filipino's literal nation of the Philippines resulted from the injury of colonialism, so any thought of homeland lacks security. He may even speak of returning to the Philippines either for a visit or upon retirement, but he is afraid of the disappointment that awaits him because he knows too well that the Philippines has moved on without him, and the country does not cry for him in his absence. His very identity was created through colonialism, which as far as he is concerned "has no outside." He cannot think beyond the confines of this history, although he attempts to escape it daily. He would like to break out of it, even crush it like a mosquito, but he knows it would signal his death. His whole being has been built around the struggle to reconcile his colonized twoness, and he is afraid that there is nothing on the other side, a life without tension. This is the postcolonial's dance; it is awkward and beautiful at the same time. The Filipino's schooling is truly the education of the exile made possible by the lessons of colonialism (see Matias, forthcoming).

To be an educated Filipino means to learn about one's coloniality in order to forget it. But the act of forgetting is not just an act of denial. Rather, it is the condition of possibility that makes further learning possible for the postcolonial. The Filipino's search for the self is precisely to abolish it, to become something different from what he knows of himself: the colonized.

If this discussion so far sounds a bit theatrical, essentialist, and stereotypically Filipino, Said (2000) reminds us that the exile is prone to willfulness, exaggeration, and overstatement. He is restless because there is no rest for the colonized. He is anxious because something has been lost, and to regain it means a decision to lose even more, to risk oneself, to disappear. He is Filipino and he owes this fact to colonialism. So even the common, cultural perception of the Filipino as overdramatic may be a vestige of colonialism and the revenge of the exile. The performance of his coloniality produces new subjectivities as he tries to make sense of life after the death of colonialism. No one told him it was going to be like this.

REFERENCES

Alatas, S. (1977). *The myth of the lazy native.* New York, NY: Routledge.

Althusser, L. (1971). *Lenin and philosophy.* New York, NY: Monthly Review Press.

Arnove, R., & Torres, C. (2003). *Comparative education: The dialectic of the global and the local* (2nd ed.). Lanham, MD: Rowman & Littlefield.

Bhabha, H. (1990). Interrogating identity: The postcolonial prerogative. In D. T. Goldberg (Ed.), *Anatomy of racism* (pp. 183–209). Minneapolis: University of Minnesota Press.

Bulosan, C. (1973). *America is in the heart.* Seattle: University of Washington Press. (Original work published 1943)

Constantino, R. (1970). *Dissent and counter-consciousness.* Quezon City, Philippines: Malaya.

Deleuze, G., & Guattari, F. (1983). *Anti-Oedipus: Capitalism and schizophrenia.* Minneapolis: University of Minnesota Press.

Du Bois, W. E. B. (1989). *The souls of Black folk.* New York, NY: Penguin. (Original work published 1904)

Fanon, F. (1967). *Black skin White masks.* New York, NY: Grove.

Foucault, M. (1980). *Power/knowledge.* New York, NY: Vintage.

Francisco, L. (1976). The Philippine-American war. In J. Quinsaat (Ed.), *Letters in exile.* Los Angeles, CA: UCLA Asian American Studies Center.

Freire, P. (1993). *Pedagogy of the oppressed.* New York, NY: Continuum.

Graff, H. (1969). *American imperialism and the Philippine Insurrection.* Boston, MA: Little, Brown.

Gramsci, A. (1971). *Selections from prison notebooks.* New York, NY: International.

Ladson-Billings, G. (1998). From Soweto to the South Bronx: African Americans and colonial education in the United States. In C. Torres & T. Mitchell (Eds.), *Sociology of education: Emerging perspectives* (pp. 247–264). Albany: State University of New York Press.

Leonardo, Z. (2000). Betwixt and between: Introduction to the politics of identity. In C. Tejeda, C. Martinez, & Z. Leonardo (Eds.), *Charting new terrains of Chicana(o)/Latina(o) education* (pp. 107–129). Cresskill, NJ: Hampton.

Leonardo, Z. (2003). *Ideology, discourse, and school reform.* Westpoint, CT: Praeger.

Maldonado-Torres, N. (2007). On the coloniality of being: Contributions to the development of a concept. *Cultural Studies, 21*(20/23), 240–270.

Matias, C. (forthcoming). Who you callin' White?: My counterstory of colouring White identity. *Race, Ethnicity, and Education.*

Memmi, A. (1965). *The colonizer and the colonized.* Boston, MA: Beacon.

Meyer, J., Ramirez, F., & Soysal, Y. (1992). World expansion of mass education, 1870–1980. *Sociology of Education, 64*(2), 128–149.

Nepomuceno, J. (1981). *A theory of the development of the Filipino colonized consciousness* (Unpublished doctoral dissertation). University of Michigan, Ann Arbor.

Orwell, G. (1949). *1984.* New York, NY: New American Library.

Quijano, A. (2000). Coloniality of power, Eurocentrism, and Latin America. *Nepantla, 1*(3), 533–580.

Rafael, V. (1995). *Discrepant histories: Translocal essays on Filipino cultures.* Philadelphia, PA: Temple University Press.

Rizal, J. (2006). *Noli Me Tangere* (English Translation: Touch Me Not). New York, NY: Penguin Books.

Said, E. (1979). *Orientalism.* New York, NY: Vintages.

Said, E. (2000). *Reflections on exile.* Cambridge, MA: Harvard University Press.

Spring, J. (2001, 1997, 1994). *The American school 1642–2000.* New York, NY: McGraw Hill.

Sandoval, C. (2000). *Methodology of the oppressed.* Minneapolis: University of Minnesota Press.

Stowe, H. (1852). *Uncle Tom's cabin.* New York, NY: Bantam Dell Classic Books.

Sullivan, R. (1991). *Exemplar of Americanism: The Philippine career of Dean C. Worcester.* Ann Arbor: Center for South and Southeast Asian Studies, The University of Michigan.

Wu, F. (2002). *Yellow.* New York, NY: Basic.

CHAPTER 2

"THE REAL FILIPINO PEOPLE"

Filipino Nationhood and Encounters with the Native Other

Benito M. Vergara, Jr.
Independent Scholar, Oakland, California

The Louisiana Purchase Exposition, held in St. Louis in 1904, was one of America's most definitive acts of self-representation, serving as a display of American colonialism at its height. This commemoration of America's mid-century expansion, together with the recent colonization of the Philippines, was both a literal and symbolic embodiment of the narrative of Manifest Destiny. Money and scale was no object: the centerpiece of the Exposition, the Philippine Reservation, cost over a million dollars, with almost 100 buildings spread over 47 acres. Aside from displaying the obsessions of the colonial mind, the Exposition also provides an instructive illustration of the constitution of Philippine nationhood and the politics of representation (and misrepresentation).

The catalog of the Philippine exhibits at the 1904 Louisiana Purchase Exposition serves as compelling testimony to the archival and acquisitive impulses of the colony's metropole. The Philippine collection, almost sur-

The "Other" Students, pages 19–38

real in its variety and specificity, was composed of, among thousands of other items, 21 Juan Luna paintings, kegs of San Miguel Beer, guitars from Negros Occidental, crocodile eggs from Sorsogon, paperweights from Bilibid Prison, coffins from Bacolor, whips from Abra, and white worms from Antique. Also included in the array of colonial spoils were "18 Tinguians, 30 Bagobos, 70 Bontoc Igorots, 20 Suyoc Igorots, 38 Negritos and Mangyans, 79 Visayans, 80 Moros, 413 Philippine Scouts, and its 40-piece band" (Official Catalogue, 1904, p. 263).

Not included in the list, however, were 98 students, called *pensionados*, who were sent to be educated in the United States, and who later formed the backbone of the Philippine independence movement and the succeeding Commonwealth government. How the *pensionados* arrived at the fair, what they thought of their fellow Filipinos (and how, as "real Filipinos," they sought to distance themselves from the so-called "savages") is the subject of this chapter.

AT THE FAIR

With almost "75,000 catalogued exhibits and 1,100 representatives of the different peoples of the archipelago," the Philippine Reservation at the 1904 World's Fair was not only a demonstration of colonial order, but of an evolutionary progression as well. The exhibition presented "the principal lines of tribal demarcation" in a hierarchy of stages of civilization, from "the Negrito aboriginal [*sic*]" and "the fierce Moro" to "the civilized Visayan" (The Philippine Exposition, 1904). At the other end of the civilization continuum were the Philippine Scouts[1] and the model school, where schoolchildren, ably representing the Philippines under colonial tutelage, recited their ABCs in front of spectators.

One brochure contrasted "one hundred bare-limbed Igorot" sacrificing a dog and "four hundred well-trained" Philippine Scouts standing at attention: "The Igorot represent the wildest race of savages, the scouts stand for the results of American rule—extremes of the social order in the Islands." Emphasizing the evolutionary schema by which the Filipinos were seen, William McGee, head of the Fair's anthropology department, wrote:

> The primary motive of the ethnologic exhibits is to show the world a little known side of human life; yet it is the aim to do this in such manner that all who come may learn something of that upward course of human development beginning with the Dark Ages of tooth and claw and stone and tools, and culminating in the modern enlightenment. (McGee, 1904, p. xi)

The American colonial project in the Philippines was one built on maintaining contradictions and walking a fine line between them. Filipino "primitiveness" was emphasized, but due to the demands of the "White man's burden," Filipinos' potential for civilization—as exemplified by the Philippine Scouts, the *pensionados*, the schoolchildren, and the *ilustrado* members of the Honorary Commission, set up by the Philippine Exposition Board—also had to be demonstrated. It was this constant, tense, vacillation between nature and nurture, culture and savagery, childhood and maturity—a discourse circulated in newspapers and in the halls of Congress, and reflected in colonial administrative policies—that would make intellectuals like Maximo Kalaw, head of the Philippine Press Bureau in Washington, DC, write,

> The policy of indefiniteness, of drifting without knowing where, could be maintained only by convincing the American people that the enterprise in the Philippines was bringing unprecedented results in the way of uplifting a people, but that at the same time the end of that mission was yet a long, long way off. (Kalaw, 1916, p. 151)

Such a policy was physically embodied a decade earlier in the scientifically authorized arrangement of Filipinos at the fair. This was in keeping not only with ethnological principles, but also with the colonial ideology that guided the exposition. As Marshall Everett (1904) wrote, regarding the role of anthropology:

> It was necessary for the visitor to understand the meaning of Anthropology... in order to see the unity of the exposition. Otherwise he would... say that the great Filipino Reservation, the medley of many strange peoples... and other exhibits of savage and semi-savage life, were... unmeaning shows, without educational value or unity of purpose. When he understood that these strange exhibitions... were all presented to furnish a living illustration of the various degrees of man's development on this earth, he became a thoughtful spectator. (p. 278)

Such an arrangement provided the organizing and clarifying lens through which to view and understand the exposition. The (American) spectator was, of course, at the apex of this anthropological hierarchy of development, and the Reservation was an indelible reminder of this fact—such was the "educational value" of the exhibits.

Pensionados, representing the pinnacle of Filipino potential, could cling in vain to an idea of acceptance by Americans as civilized equals, but such hope was dimmed by the popularity of "the savage." Scientific value aside, it was the more exotic elements—half-naked "natives," 20 dogs slaughtered daily—that drew the biggest crowds. The so-called Igorot village was the Reservation's biggest moneymaker (and the exhibit remembered most vividly by visitors in later years), featuring people at work daily, with hourly dancing; "at intervals spear throwing and native ceremonies were to be seen" (Francis, 1913, p. 572). Everett wrote that "stray canines in the vicinity of their camp were always in danger of sudden death" (Everett, 1904, p. 302). In this respect, the Reservation was a contradictory combination of anthropological precision and carnivalesque sensationalism.

In the midst of this sideshow atmosphere were the *pensionados.* Participants of an ambitious program to send Filipino students in the United States for education, the *pensionados* were both apart from the exhibition and part of it as well. Prior to the beginning of the fall semester, the students were brought to St. Louis to work three hours a day for a month as guides, waiters, and secretaries at the Reservation. But they were also considered part of the exhibition, since "one of the purposes of the participation of the Philippine Government... is that the people of the Philippines should become acquainted with those of the United States, as well as the United States itself," as Colonel Clarence Edwards of the Bureau of Indian Affairs put it (Lawcock, 1975, p. 99). We shall see later, however, that the *pensionados* felt quite out of place.

A *Federalista* who supported annexation and U.S. citizenship, Felipe Buencamino initiated the *pensionado* program, grandly referred to by their superintendent, William A. Sutherland, as "the Pensionado Movement." Buencamino was the first to push for a provision in the civil government bill that created "an allowance of $100,000 per annum... for the education of young Filipinos in America." Act No. 854 was finally drafted and approved in 1902, providing for 100 students "of good moral character, sound physical condition" and between the ages of 16 and 25 to be selected for education in the United States. A total of 75 of those would be chosen by examination, and 25 would be selected by then-Governor General William Howard Taft. The latter was especially supportive of the program, as he wrote,

> In no way can young Filipinos, whose ancestors have been physically and intellectually removed from contact with modern life, acquire a thorough knowledge of Western civilization.... it may be well to hold out the privilege of some years of residence in an American institution of learning as a reward for extraordinary achievements. (Philippine Commission, 1904, p. 272)

He further recommended that students be brought to the exposition to show "the intelligent Filipinos what our country is and what our institutions mean" (Philippine Commission, 1904, p. 520).

"Of the one hundred, twelve were to receive instruction in agriculture and the useful mechanical arts and twelve to receive 'special courses of instruction'"[2] (Lawcock, 1975, p. 85, 89). The only thing required from the students (apart from good grades and behavior) was that they take the civil service exam when they returned and that they accept an appointment in the Philippine Civil Service (p. 90).

The selection of the students was, however, a more calculated process, and one not completely dependent on their exams. Sutherland, picked by Taft to be the *pensionados*' superintendent in the United States, had sent Taft selection guidelines, which included the following: "Each student must be of unquestionable moral and physical qualifications, no weight being given to social status." Taft crossed out the word "no" before "weight," insuring that weight *would* be given to social status. As Sutherland (1953) recounts it, "The Governor, more realistic than I, scratched out the word 'no' before the word 'weight.' He saw the importance of this, particularly with those first boys going over" (p. 28). The *pensionados* were, in effect, the cream of the Philippine elite; Sutherland's ostensibly democratic project of social equality had come to naught.[3]

In all, 98 students (28 from Manila) were finally selected. The Philippine government would sponsor almost 100 more students in the next three years, and another 100 when the program was revived in 1919. But it was that first batch of students who set sail for America in October 1903, and their presence at the Exposition is what threw into sharp relief what it meant to be Filipino to the members of the Philippine elite at that point in history.

THE FILIPINO

Larry Arden Lawcock, in his exhaustive and wide-ranging 1975 dissertation, explored the connection between the *pensionados* and the independence movement in the Philippines. He argued that their "political agitation," begun in the United States, was continued upon their return to the Philippines, and it later evolved into the crusade for independence from America. This was accomplished by a propaganda campaign with a dual focus: "(i) to correct misinformation and (ii) to charm the colonizers into granting the political objective sought" (p. 13). It is the nature of this "misinformation" and how it ran counter to the *pensionados'* concept of "the real Filipino," which primarily concerns me in this chapter.

The main mouthpiece of the Filipino students in the United States was the popular *Filipino Students' Magazine* (later called the *Philippine Review*), started by University of California at Berkeley students. Partially subsidized by the Boston-based Anti-Imperialist League, the magazine completed a popular run from 1905 to 1907 (Lawcock, 1975, pp. 106–107).

Its East Coast counterpart was the more conservative journal, *The Filipino*, which was edited out of Washington, DC, by Jose Maria Cuenco and Asterio Favis. Lawcock dismisses *The Filipino* as "an inept, ill-considered, semi-official attempt to counteract the independence stand of the senior and relatively successful" *Filipino Students' Magazine.* Partly supervised by Sutherland, the journal had a relatively limp run from January to November 1906, because of its "unpopular political policy" (Sutherland, 1906, pp. 117, 120–121).

But it was *The Filipino* that typified the contradictions among the sons (and the few daughters) of the elite. Although Lawcock stresses the continuities between the *pensionados'* propaganda campaign and the independence movement back home, *The Filipino*'s view of "the Filipino" may have been a more accurate reflection of the attitudes at the beginning of the century. And what outraged the *pensionados* most was the exhibition of Filipinos, although not for the obvious reasons that immediately come to mind.

The first issue of *The Filipino* carried the following unsigned editorial, entitled "Igorots and Americans":

> It seems as though the Filipino people have before them a long lifework in attempting to counteract the impressions spread broadcast throughout America by those who so thoughtlessly exhibit savages belonging to our wild, uncivilized tribes in the islands... we do not relish the dubious looks we receive when we explain that we are as yet ignorant of that delicacy which we may politely denominate "fricasseed canine," ... one of our companions was disgusted to see exhibited in a sideshow at a country fair in a little town in Vermont a miserable, deformed semblance of humanity, advertised as "Laduca, the Wild Filipino Woman." There are "Filipinos" at Coney Island, "Filipinos" at Portland, "Filipinos" at Los Angeles, "Filipinos" everywhere, all on exhibition for visitors at 10 cents apiece. We are thinking of catching up a few of those large, fat, long-necked, waddling birds, whose voice is a melodious squawk, and taking them to the Philippines on exhibition as "True Specimens of "Americanos!" (Igorots and Americans, 1906)

Such a distancing is not altogether surprising, considering the writers' class and educational background. Their protests of stereotyping—that not every Filipino eats dogs—are clear. But the telltale quotation marks surrounding "Filipinos" also make it evident that the *pensionados* did not consider their "wild" counterparts as "true specimens" of Filipinos; they were merely "savages belonging to our wild, uncivilized tribes," and indeed analogous to animals such as turkeys. By this, the *pensionado* writer draws the boundaries of Filipinoness to exclude the "native."

Sutherland himself elaborates in an article:

> Much of the good impression that should have remained with the thousands of visitors to the Philippine exhibition was lost or at least prejudiced by an unfortunate arrangement of the native Filipinos who were a part of the Philippine reservation. Of all the natives of the Philippines who were within the various inclosures... only a relatively small number, the Visayans, belonged

> to the civilized or Christianized races of the Islands. The Visayan concession itself was unattractively presented... Visitors flocked to those concessions that were well advertised... and which made much of the uncouth habits of certain of the tribes. As a consequence, to many the word "Filipino" became synonymous with "Igorot, Moro, Negrito, Tinguian, Bagobo," and the like.... We shall constantly try to represent the Filipino and the Philippines only in a true light. (Sutherland, 1975, p. 1906)

Although Sutherland blames the publicity that surrounded the so-called uncivilized tribes, it is clear that the problem is once again of representation. The word "Filipino" is exemplified by these tribes, and not the "civilized or Christianized races." Such a misrepresentation, Sutherland concludes, can be corrected by exhibitions that represent Filipinos "in a true light."

Such pious talk on Sutherland's behalf apparently did not constitute a conflict of interest when he agreed to arrange a similar Philippine exhibit at the Jamestown Tercentennial Exposition in 1907. An unsigned editorial entitled "The Filipinos Do Not Want the 'Wild Tribes' Exhibited," in the Filipino newspaper *El Renacimiento* voiced people's complaints:

> We are most decidedly opposed to Mr. Sutherland's again taking over a group of the Igorrotes. We shall always protest against a recurrence of that exhibition. We cannot understand his insane mania for it. What object have the promoters in view for this exhibition... It certainly is not merely to assemble everything good and bad from the country... but to exhibit that which is best in a nation and marks its highest degree of progress.... This surely is the fundamental idea underlying any exhibition. No nation and no race now considered civilized would think of sending to such exhibitions examples of backwardness, ignorance or savagery which might exist within its borders.... Why, then, this intention and desire to exhibit the Igorrotes at such a critical period when it is so desirable that the United States and the world in general may form a correct opinion of the Philippine nation? We protest against the sending of Igorrotes again because they do not represent any of the manifestations of real progress and advance of our people. (The Filipinos Do Not Want, 1907)

In contrast, the reaction of Filipino students in Spain a full two decades earlier is instructive, because they were, on the whole, remarkably compassionate in tone. Long enshrined in popular Filipino history as the architects of Filipino nationalism, if not the first to articulate a Filipino consciousness, the students aspired (and later, agitated) for full recognition (and later, independence) from Spain.[4] Jose Rizal—nationalist, novelist, doctor, poet, and inarguably the most important Filipino historical figure—was a student in Spain at the time, and along with his fellow students, similarly encountered fellow "Filipinos" at the Philippine Exposition in Madrid in May of 1887.

Even before the *Exposicion de las Islas Filipinas*, members of the Filipino community were already complaining bitterly about yet "another iniquity among those that formed the uninterrupted chain of domination." "[We] are all agreed," Evaristo Aguirre wrote Rizal, "that the show will be ridiculous, that... [it] will be a moral and material misfortune for the Philippines... and what is more painful, the children of that country... [i.e., the Philippines] will come to be the object of the mocking, stupid, and rude curiosity of this truly savage people [i.e., the Spaniards]" (as cited in Rizal, 1930, p. 76). In this same letter, Maximo Kalaw's translation renders Aguirre's "*indigena filipino*" into "native Filipinos"—here, with a small "f," but it is also revealingly inclusive of the *indigenas*.

Tragedy befell the Exposition when Basalia, described in the annotations to Rizal's letters as a Muslim woman, the wife of a respected Jolo leader, died from pneumonia, making her one of four exhibited people who would eventually die in Madrid. An outraged Rizal wrote to his friend, the Austrian ethnologist and historian Ferdinand Blumentritt, that he had done all he could do in order to prevent the degradation of his poor compatriots from being exhibited like animals and plants, but to no avail. "I wish that all of them would die like the poor Basalia so that they will not suffer anymore," Rizal wrote. "Let the Philippines forget that her sons have been treated like this—to be exhibited and ridiculed!" (Rizal, 1938, pp. 153–156).

Historian John Schumacher argues that the Exposition galvanized the Filipino community:

> The humiliating treatment of the Filipinos... seemed to have touched the core of nationalism... In the Philippines the pagan Igorots and Muslim Moros were considered and treated by Christian Filipinos as outside the civilized Filipino community. Now a new feeling of solidarity with the Igorots and Moros at the exposition was displayed by the educated, middle or upper-class Filipinos in Madrid.... The efforts of Spaniards in Manila to use these poor people to portray the Filipinos as still without civilization and culture stung many of the educated Filipinos into identifying themselves with these their "brothers" and "countrymen." (1997, pp. 72–75)

Schumacher argues that the educated Filipinos' identification with the "non-Christian tribes" was a reaction against being characterized as without "civilization and culture"—a reminder perhaps of their marked "inferiority" vis-à-vis the peninsular Spaniards. This may not have been completely the case. Rizal had earlier dismissed the exposition in a letter to Blumentritt: "Don't bother yourself about the Exposition of the Philippines in Madrid. From what I understand... it's no Exposition of the Philippines but only of the Igorots, who will play music, do their cooking, and sing and dance" (Scott, 1975, p. 13).

That this empathy may lead to glimmers of nationalism can perhaps be seen in the embrace of the "ethnic minorities" into a more inclusive "*filipino.*" But one can argue that the dialectic could have gone either way: either resulting in identification, that is, recognition of a particular commonality or, striking a defensive mode, in disavowal, much like the *pensionados* did.

THE "NATIVE OTHER"

The distinctions made by *pensionados* between the "savage" and the "real" Filipinos were made more comprehensible to a supposedly ignorant American audience by employing a readily available idiom. In much the same way that the Louisiana Purchase Exposition officials utilized anthropology as an explanatory lens, the figure of the Native American was employed in *pensionado* discourse as the analogous American other. This was, in effect, a replication of the discursive categories in which American colonial officials understood the Filipinos.

As early as July 1904, Vicente Nepomuceno, a member of the Philippine honorary commission, was comparing Native Americans with "uncivilized" Filipinos, "who, like all backward and non-progressive races, are rapidly dying out." In an interview with the *St. Louis Post-Dispatch,* Nepomuceno said: "The Moros, Negritos and Igorrotes no more represent the people of the Philippines than the dying Indian represents the American people" (Filipinos Are Preposterously Misrepresented, 1904, p. 1).

The *pensionados* would draw the distinctions even further. In an editorial for *The Filipino,* called "The Hunt-Igorot Incident," Favis recounted a case in which Truman K. Hunt, governor of the subprovince of Bontoc and director of the Reservation's Igorot Village, was jailed in Memphis for embezzling the villagers' wages (Rydell, 1984, p. 19). But although he decried the treatment of the Igorots, Favis ultimately lamented the misrepresentation—indeed, the symbolic violence—committed:

> Those who saw these people and who had no right idea and did not possess true knowledge of the real Filipino people . . . were more than ever convinced of the incapacity of the Filipino branded by his enemies. Americans who know the Filipino people—and when we speak of the Filipino people we mean the seven million Christians who represent the Philippines politically, intellectually, socially, and religiously, and not the Negritos, Igorots, and Moros who are to us what the most savage Indians are to the civilized Americans—may smile at this statement and regard it as absurd. (Favis, 1906, p. 27)

Here, Favis clearly delineates the boundaries between who is Filipino and who is not. For him, the "native" is the false Filipino, and authenticity is located within intellectuals like him. His reasons are understandable on the surface, that is, the *pensionados* were afraid that it would make the Philippines look unfit for independence. But Favis' vision is by no means that of a plural nation; it is one that is specifically Christian. One can perhaps argue that the Philippines' insistence upon its identity as "the only Christian nation in Asia" finds its roots upon such national imaginings as early as the turn of the century.

By 1919, similar arguments were still being made by the Washington, DC-based Philippine mission, which was led by Kalaw, Conrado Benitez, and Arsenio Luz (Churchill, 1982). Writer Jose P. Melencio (1919) stated in one of their pamphlets,

> We protest against the insidious tactics of some American writers who, in the haste to cripple the Filipino plea for independence, invariably decorate their magazine and newspaper articles with pictures of the backward, scantily dressed, peoples of the Philippines. We call that foul play. For those people are by no means representative of the bulk of Filipinos. They constitute the decided minority... *It is not fair to predicate Filipino capacity for self-government on the looks, attire and backwardness of those mountain people. They are to the Philippines what the Indians are to America—no more, no less.* (p. 27; emphasis in original)

It should be emphasized that these Filipinos, as Lawcock (1975) reminds us, were engaged in a propaganda campaign. Writing for an unconvinced (and more likely, indifferent) American public, the *pensionado* writers took it upon themselves to explain and clarify the situation in easily comprehensible terms. The Native American is used here as the "American primitive"—American indeed, but an inferior and unrepresentative one—and therefore analogous to "the backward, scantily dressed, peoples of the Philippines."

The figure of the Native American was similarly used to make Filipinos more intelligible or, to extend the metaphor further, more "assimilable." The connections were, in any case, fairly explicit: the Filipinos were, after all, housed in the Philippine *Reservation.* McGee, as head of the Anthropology section, also reconstructed the Indian School at the World's Fair, and he made the link clearer in a report:

> The [Indian] school is designed not merely as a consummation, but as a prophecy; for now that other primitive peoples are passing under the beneficent influence and protection of the Stars and Stripes, it is needful to take stock of past progress as a guide to the future. Over against the Indian on the grounds, just beyond Arrowhead Lake, will stand the Filipino, even as over against the Red Man on the continent, just beyond the Pacific, stands the brown man of the nearer Orient; and it is the aim of the Model Indian School to extend influence across both intervening waters to the benefit of both races. (McGee, 1904, p. 7)

Everett makes the unambiguous connection between both groups: "It has been said that the Igorrotes are cannibals and head-hunters, and that they are to the Philippines today what the wild Kiowas of Kansas and Nebraska were to the United States sixty years ago—a warlike, savage people preying upon whomsoever happened their way" (McGee, 1904, p. 297). Even the army generals sent to fight the Filipino "*insurrectos*" came fresh from the "Indian wars," like the infamous General Jacob "Howlin' Jake" Smith, a Wounded Knee veteran. In contrast, Christian Filipinos were ostensibly culturally closer to the civilized White Americans.

These same comparisons were also legitimized within the colonial bureaucracy itself: the use of particular colonial administrative categories in censuses like "Christian or Civilized Tribes" and "Non-Christian or Wild Tribes" stressed continuities with previous American experience in dealing with Native Americans. The word "tribe" functioned as both denotative and connotative index; Dean Worcester, the infamous zoologist and member of the Philippine Commission, would authoritatively (though erroneously) write of "more than 200 native tribes, each with its peculiar language, laws and customs" (Worcester & Bournes, 1897, p. 6).

The numbers of "tribes," which, as Rodney Sullivan points out, were Worcester's inaccurate classifications of what were "essentially homogeneous peoples" (Sullivan, 1991, p. 154), were then cited by both travel writers and colonial administrators as proof of the Philippines' nonstatus as a nation, too culturally diverse and unable to govern itself. "There never was a Philippine nation," one book declared, "only a collection of many tribes, speaking different languages" (Greater America, 1900, p. 98). This, more importantly, also presented the colonial government with further rationale for implementing the "civilizing process." Later on in the decade, the image of the Philippines as a mere collection of tribes was entrenched enough for a writer for *El Renacimiento* to complain,

> Mr. Sutherland may promise that [the "Igorrotes"] shall be well treated and kept apart from the Tagals and Visayans. This is not the question. The question involved is the unfavorable impression which their representation will create... in making this division the impression would be created that we were still living divided into tribes, which is untrue... Sutherland is perfectly aware of the difference between the Igorrotes and civilized Filipinos, but it is not so with the rank and file of his countrymen, who, seeing nothing but specimens of the wild tribes... might readily confound them with the Filipinos in general, as has in fact already proved to have been the case. (The Filipinos Do Not Want, 1907)

Such insistence on clarity—the public must not confuse the "Igorrotes" with "civilized Filipinos," for they are like Indians, after all—takes a slightly different turn with the *ilustrado* students in Europe in the 1880s. The story has been retold in different versions: Rizal and his companions are at the *Exposition Universelle* in Paris in 1889, where Buffalo Bill's Wild West Show will be performing to huge crowds for 7 months. Rizal attends the show, listens to the applause for the Indians' horseback skills, and, as Gregorio Zaide dramatically relates, Rizal turns to his companions and says,

> Why should we resent being called Indios by the Spaniards? Look at those Indios from North America—they are not ashamed of their name. Let us be like them. Let us be proud of the name Indio and make our Spanish enemies revise their conception of the term. We shall be Indios Bravos! (Zaide, 1970, p. 172)

Thereafter, Rizal starts signing his letters "Gran Indio Bravo" (or "grand brave/wild Indian"), and forms a semi-Masonic organization "which has its only purpose the propagation of all useful skills, be they scientific, artistic, literary, etc., in the Philippines" called naturally, *Los Indios Bravos* (as cited in Schumacher, 1997, p. 237). Rizal would later enjoin the rest of the *Indios Bravos* in his many epistles "to create a [Filipino] Colony [in Madrid] which is serious, hard-working and studious." "It is the only way," he continued, "to make the tyrants respect us and to get foreigners to make common cause with us" (p. 238).

While the organization dissolved soon after (to be remade, however, as the "*Solidaridad*" Masonic lodge in 1890 and the more influential *La Liga Filipina* in Manila in 1892), the reappropriation of a derogatory term and its transformation into *Los Indios Bravos* is enlightening. "*Indio*" is transmuted into a badge of pride; the next step, as Schumacher put it, was "to make Spaniards revise their idea of the indio" (Schumacher, 1997, p. 237). Here, the Native American functions as a source of identification, not just in terms of solidarity, but also of validation. "Filipino," "*indio*," and "Indian" were semantically distinct categories that were nevertheless overlapping in particular ways for the *ilustrados* on its way to a budding Filipino nationalism, categories that the *pensionados*, two decades later, would be taking great pains to separate.

MISREPRESENTATION AND THE NATION

The *pensionados* were not alone in their anxieties over the exhibits; the visualization of the civilizing process ran into complications for the exposition organizers, where the representation of Filipinos at the fair itself became an issue. Although they failed to gain an audience in the United States, the *pensionados*' protests were not politically insignificant either; as I will argue in this section, their concerns regarding Filipinoness, tribes, and nationhood would later inform the discourse of the Philippine independence movement.

In *All the World's a Fair*, Robert Rydell (1984) described how the Filipinos' nudity worried the American government. Taft was afraid the press would think that the Philippine government was "seeking to make prominent the savageness . . . to depreciate the popular estimate of the general civilization of the islands" (p. 172). While the Democratic Party was at least nominally anti-imperialist, it employed racist arguments to support its platform, and public perceptions about the supposed savagery of Filipinos might lead to the defeat of the Republican incumbent Theodore Roosevelt in the coming elections. "Short trunks would be enough for the men, but . . . for the Negrito women there ought to be shirts of some sort," Taft suggested. W. P. Wilson, the chair of the Philippine Exposition Board, "preferred that the Igorrotes remain in their loincloths even though temperatures warranted warmer clothing. He felt that people would not pay to see them clad in western clothing" (as cited in Vostral, 1993, pp. 23–24).

Following the president's orders, D. K. Hunt then issued the order to have the men wear pants, and, as the *St. Louis Post-Dispatch* reported, this "boosted visitation, since all wanted to see the islanders before their clothes arrived" (as cited in Vostral, 1993, pp. 23–24). Newspaper writers and anthropologists censured the government's efforts, with editorial cartoons portraying Taft, checkered pants in one hand, chasing Sambo-like natives around the village. The plans to make them wear "bright-colored silk trousers" were soon abandoned.

The incident reveals the government's awareness of how crucial the issue of representation was at the Exposition. It gave fuller embodiment to the formation of knowledge about the Philippines, with its human exhibits functioning as representative, living artifacts. In this sense, one might say that, in hindsight, the *pensionados* understood why representation was so crucial; they knew exactly what was at stake at the heart of their debate on exhibiting Filipinos.

The controversy caused major repercussions back in the Philippines. By January of 1908, the Philippine Legislature would pass a law stating "no tribal people should be exhibited except those who were customarily fully clothed." As Secretary of the Interior, Worcester, who would later embark on speaking tours (complete with lantern slides and films) campaigning against Philippine independence, was blamed for the exhibitions, but he in fact endorsed a 1906 petition banning the display. His reason for preventing such exhibition, though, was that "experience shows that men and women thus taken away from their natural surroundings are apt to be pretty thoroughly spoiled and to be trouble makers after their return" (Worcester, 1930, pp. 32–35).

As argued by Lawcock (1975), one of the *pensionados*' objectives in their propaganda campaign in the United States was the correction of mistakes. "Letters to editors correcting misinformation in the press with regard to the Philippines would fill a scrapbook," Lawcock wrote (p. 123). Tomas Confesor and Mariano V. Osmena, along with other students from Chicago, produced a pamphlet addressing those same issues. Entitled "The Truth About the Philippines," the brochure included "well-chosen pictures representing the real Philippines" with "fully attired students, lawyers, officials and 'typical Filipina ladies'" (as cited in Lawcock, p. 138).

By 1919, the Philippine Press Bureau, based in Washington, DC, would regularly publish the Philippine Commission of Independence Press Bulletin as part of a more organized, government-sanctioned propaganda campaign, designed, as Maximo Kalaw put it in a report to the Commission of Independence in Manila, to counter media distortion.

> Editorials appearing in even the largest city newspapers reveal an almost unbelievable ignorance on the Philippine question. Ex-officials of the Philippines have long carried on a campaign of misrepresentation, picturing the Filipino people as a mere coterie of savage or semi-civilized tribes devoid of any sense of nationality and separate from one another by warring jealousies and hatred. (as cited in Churchill, 1982, p. 18)

Kalaw was as prolific a writer as he was outspoken a proponent of independence. Among his works was the 1916 book, *The Case for the Filipinos*, an impassioned but sober argument for the necessity of granting independence to the Philippines. All throughout the long essay, as befitting his role as an updated *propagandista*, are angry passages decrying the misrepresentation of Filipinos:

> Many... publicity agents have gone to the extreme of deliberately misrepresenting conditions in the Philippines... They sent Igorrotes to the St. Louis Exposition who created in the minds of hundreds of thousands of Americans the indelible impression that the Filipinos have not yet emerged from savagery. There was hardly a magazine in the Union which did not embellish its pages with photographs of "head-hunters" conveying to the lay mind that they were typical Filipinos. (Kalaw, 1916, pp. 159–160)

By the 1930s, when Congressional hearings on Philippine independence were being held, testimonies from Filipinos were still haunted by mention of tribes. This time, however, the rhetoric was somewhat different:

> In many quarters in the United States we find a considerable misconception concerning the Filipino people.... those who are not well acquainted with the true conditions there speak of the Filipinos as a conglomerate of tribes, greatly different from one another. The fact is that after more than 400 years

> of national life with the same religion, the same aspirations, the same economic and social interests, the Filipinos are to-day a nation at least as much as any people inhabiting any of the independent countries in the world can claim to be. (Independence for the Philippine Islands, 1932, p. 10)

The above passage comes from Speaker of the House Manuel Roxas, who would later become President of the Philippines from 1946 to 1948. During the 1932 Congressional hearings on the Hare-Hawes-Cutting Act, Roxas addressed the usual themes: correction of misconceptions and repudiation of the plurality of tribes. But what is clear here is that he was appealing to a more popular, more temporally sweeping model than his predecessors had: a nation already united in its diversity, a nation oddly birthed at the moment of Spanish colonialism. After the trappings and symbols of Filipino national culture are assembled and circulated by way of American colonial education, there is no question, certainly, as to what "the Filipino people" means here. It is a model that is generously inclusive, but Roxas's plea—the Philippines' recognition as a sovereign nation[5]—here is still entirely dependent on the absence (both in his present and historically) of the "non-Christian tribes."

Writer James Blount echoed *pensionado* sentiment when he wrote in his book, *The American Occupation of the Philippines*, that "no deeper wound was ever inflicted upon the pride of the real Filipino people than that caused by [the Louisiana Purchase Exposition]" (as cited in Worcester, 1930, p. 643). Worcester defended himself in the pages of his book, *The Philippines Past and Present*, by attributing the attacks against him "to certain Filipino politicians who [attempt] to conceal the fact of [the non-Christian tribes'] existence, and to the efforts of certain misguided Americans to minimize the importance of the problems which their existence presents (Worcester, 1930, p. 643). "The Moros are as 'real' as the Tagalogs," he continued.

> In his heart of hearts he resents his Malay blood, and he particularly objects to anything which reminds him of the truth as to the stage of civilization which had been attained by his Malay ancestors a few centuries ago. (Worcester, 1930, p. 644)

Whether or not one agrees with his generally odious politics, Worcester may have come close to the heart of the anxiety over the "uncivilized tribes." That is, they function as a kind of secret, one that is acknowledged as existing but not one to be circulated outside among strangers. The *pensionados*' protestations that the ethnic minorities are, indeed, in the minority confirm this status; they are to be whisked away, out of sight, as quickly as possible. One may argue that this form of embarrassment may be what anthropologist Michael Herzfeld (1997) refers to as "cultural intimacy," as he defines it, "the recognition of those aspects of a cultural identity that are considered a source of external embarrassment but that nevertheless provide insiders with their assurance of common sociality" (p. 3). But it is difficult to argue this in the case of the Philippines. So-called tribal minorities (or *lumad*) in the Philippines are neither seen to embody ethnic essence nor are they romanticized as "noble savages" in Philippine popular culture. At best, they make their appearance as signs of domesticated otherness in such instances of reified Filipino culture as music festivals and dances. Otherwise, they are made to linger at the periphery of Filipino "civilization," as unassimilable beings in the Filipino body politic.

AMERICAN BOYS

As a postscript, it is relevant to note that the *pensionados*, who considered themselves to be Filipino exemplars, were branded as "American boys" upon their return, probably the first people to be called as such. Celia Bocobo Olivar, herself the daughter of *pensionado* and former University of the Philippines president Jorge Bocobo, wrote in her 1950 thesis, *The First Pensionados—An Appraisal of Their Contributions to the National Welfare*:

> The biggest problem faced by the returned *pensionados* was prejudice—both on the part of their own countrymen and that of the Americans. The Filipino *Pensionados*... had to readjust themselves to the lower standard of living in the home country. All of the new things they did appeared queer and artificial. They were looked upon with distrust, even to the extent of ridicule. They were mockingly referred to as... "American Boys..." They did not find in the Philippines the freedom and democracy which they had enjoyed in America... The result was that instead of being pro-Americans... these *pensionados* became more nationalistic. (as cited in Sutherland, 1953, p. 36)

Both Sutherland (1953) and Lawcock (1975) cite Olivar's conclusion that such a reception later evolved into nationalism. Lawcock in particular very explicitly sees the independence movement as a specific outgrowth of their propaganda campaigns in the United States. But it is revealing to read *The Filipino* as manifesting a more exclusive (or exclusionary) nationalism—by no means similar to "the elimination almost to the vanishing point of racial prejudice and discrimination" in the country, which Sutherland (1906, p. 38) attributes to the *pensionado* program. We cannot, of course, generalize concerning the *pensionados*, but one can posit shared subject positions among them, depending on their class identification.

It is ironic (or perhaps illustrative of the many contradictions of colonialism) that the "American boys" were sent to the United States to ostensibly "Filipinize" the commonwealth-to-be. The *pensionados* were themselves caught up in competing definitions of what it meant to be Filipino: according to the logic of colonial tutelage, the students had to go to America to become better Filipinos. In a way, the meaning of the word "Filipino" was as much in flux in the early 1900s as it was before the turn of the century. But by the early 1900s, however, "Filipino" had already hardened into an ethnoracial category—a radical and more exclusive change from the Creole "*filipino*" of the 1880s as well as Rizal's more inclusive and transcendent term years later—but one whose parameters were nonetheless still constricted by class, religious, technological, cultural, or, more likely, semiracialized barriers.[6]

The problem was that the Philippines was eager to prove its worth as it entered the world of nations. The Philippines was moving from its benighted colonial state to an age of even greater modernity. But caught at the same time in the throes of nation-building, the national elite found itself hard-pressed to include the so-called non-Christian tribes in their myopic national vision. The constitution of the Filipino nation, then and now, did not include its uncivilized embarrassments.

NOTES

1. By 1903, the recruitment of Filipino troops was permitted, allowing American soldiers stationed in the Philippines to return home. The Philippine Scouts therefore served as cheaper replacements and through their drill exhibitions at the Exposition, proved "that the Filipinos were capable of providing military service for the American empire in the Philippines" (Laurie, 1995, p. 54). See also Paul Kramer's section, in his excellent article (1999), on the Philippine Scouts, which marked the earliest of many anti-Filipino riots that revolved around Filipino men in the company of White women.
2. Forty-five Puerto Rican students were sent to the famous Carlisle Indian School, a clear precedent to the *pensionado* program. The stress on "useful mechanical arts" is echoed in later education policy implemented by the Americans in the Philippines, itself directly taken from education programs for African Americans. See Glenn May's *Social Engineering in the Philippines* (1984) for an in-depth examination of industrial education.
3. Among the more prominent *pensionados* were Delfin Jaramilla and Mariano de Joya (former Chief Justices of the Supreme Court), Ambrocio Magsaysay (future President Ramon Magsaysay's uncle), Camilo Osias, Ernesto Quirino (future President Elpidio Quirino's brother), Jose Maria Cuenco (Archbishop of Cebu), Francisco Benitez (University of the Philippines College of Education dean), Conrado Benitez (University of the Philippines College of Business Administration dean), and dozens of political functionaries and landowners. In the field of education alone, Sutherland writes, "The *Pensionados* have furnished their country with three university presidents, four university deans, twenty university professors, eight professional lecturers, and some thirty or forty other teachers" (1953, p. 99).

4. Careful attention must be paid here to the (semantic) differences between the *propagandistas*: these students were initially composed of creoles (or *insulares*), i.e., Spaniards born in the Philippines, who were considered politically and culturally subordinate to the *peninsulares*, or Spaniards born in Spain; this was therefore the root of their dissatisfaction with the colonial administration. Students like Rizal, on the other hand, were *mestizos*, of "mixed blood"; some were members of the native elite (the derogatory term *indios*, meaning "Indians"). The word "*filipino*," with a small "f," referred almost exclusively to the creole, although, as Benedict Anderson writes, "It was also, almost imperceptibly, starting to be claimed by upwardly mobile Spanish and Chinese mestizos" (1998, pp. 246–247). It is only after the turn of the century that "Filipino," with a capital "F," was used in the same ethnic/national sense that it is today.
5. Kalaw writes in *The Case for the Filipinos* (and it is as vivid an argument for the modularity of an ethno-nationalism as there ever was): "One fact must be conceded in studying the Philippine question: the Filipinos are *a people*, like the Cubans or the Irish or the French—a distinct political entity, with a consciousness of kind and with national feelings and aspirations" (1916, p. xiii; emphasis in original).
6. I argue that the same can be said concerning general middle-class outrage over domestic helpers and mail-order brides—that it is more a matter of anxiety over misrepresentation than genuine compassion over their situation. The disparaging, semiracialized manner in which the two groups are often discursively characterized—not to mention by class and language—hints at something closer to *pensionado* embarrassment.

   To bring more balance to this project, a crucial avenue of exploration would be to consider what Muslims and people of the Cordillera thought at this time. Works by Peter Gordon Gowing and P. N. Abinales, for instance, make it clear that Muslims actively resisted their forced incorporation into the "Filipino" nation. In the 1920s, for instance, Muslims constantly petitioned the United States government for retention of the Sulu archipelago as "permanent American territory" as protection against a Christian Filipino government (Gowing, 1983, pp.168–169). Abinales argues that the colonial government's paternalistic attitudes, the datus' orientation in a Southeast Asian (and not Filipino) context, and Mindanao's (and the Cordillera's) practically autonomous administration under military rule, were all contributing factors to the continuing management of Muslim Mindanao with policies predicated on an "essential" difference (1998, 2000).

REFERENCES

Abinales, P. N. (1998). An American colonial state: Authority and structure in southern Mindanao. In P. N. Abinales (Ed.), *Images of state power: Essays on Philippine politics from the margins* (pp. 1–62). Quezon City: University of the Philippines Press.

Abinales, P. N. (2000). *Making Mindanao: Cotabato and Davao in the formation of the Philippine nation-state.* Quezon City, Philippines: Ateneo de Manila University Press.

Anderson, B. (1998). *The spectre of comparisons: Nationalism, Southeast Asia and the world.* London, UK: Verso.

Churchill, B. R. (1982). *The Philippine independence missions to the United States, 1919–1934.* Manila, Philippines: National Historical Institute.

Everett, M. (1904). *The book of the fair.* Philadelphia, PA: P.W. Ziegler.

Favis, A. (1906, November). Hunt-Igorot incident. *The Filipino,* 26–28.

Filipinos are preposterously misrepresented. (1904, July 19). *St. Louis Post-Dispatch.*

Francis, D. R. (1913). *The universal exposition of 1904.* St. Louis, MO: The Louisiana Purchase Exposition Co.

Gowing, P. G. (1983). *Mandate in Moroland: The American government of Muslim Filipinos, 1899–1920.* Quezon City, Philippines: New Day.

Greater America: Selections from The Youth's Companion. (1900). Boston, MA: The Perry Mason Co.

Herzfeld, M. (1997). *Cultural intimacy: Social poetics in the nation-state.* New York, NY: Routledge.

Igorots and Americans. (1906, March). *The Filipino, 4.*

Independence for the Philippine Islands. (1930). Committee on Territories and Insular Affairs. Washington, DC: Government Printing Office.

Kalaw, M. M. (1916). *The case for the Filipinos.* New York, NY: The Century Co.

Kramer, P. (1999). Making concessions: Race and empire revisited at the Philippine Exposition, St. Louis, 1901–1905. *Radical History Review, 73,* 74–114.

Laurie, C. D. (1995). An oddity of empire: The Philippine scouts and the 1904 world's fair. *Gateway Heritage, 15*(3), 44–55.

Lawcock, L. A. (1975). *Filipino students in the United States and the Philippine independence movement: 1900–1935* (Unpublished dissertation). University of California, Berkeley.

May, G. A. (1984). *Social engineering in the Philippines: The aims, execution, and impact of American colonial policy, 1900–1913.* Quezon City, Philippines: New Day.

McGee, W. J. (1904). Anthropology. *World's Fair Bulletin, 5*(4), 4–9.

Melencio, J. P. (1919). *Arguments against Philippine independence and their answers.* Washington, DC: Philippine Press Bureau.

Official Catalogue, Philippine Exhibits, Universal Exposition, St.Louis, USA, 1904 (1904). St. Louis: The Official Catalogue Co., Inc.

Philippine Commission to the President. (1904). *Report.* Washington, DC: Philippine Commission.

The Philippine Exposition (1904). St. Louis. Print.

Rizal, J. (1930). *Epistolario Rizalino, 1877–1887.* Manila, Philippines: Bureau of Printing.

Rizal, J. (1938). *Epistolario Rizalino: Cartas de Rizal a Blumentritt en Aleman, 1886–1888.* Manila, Philippines: Bureau of Printing.

Rydell, R. W. (1984). *All the world's a fair: Visions of empire at American international expositions, 1876–1916.* Chicago, IL: University of Chicago Press.

Schumacher, J. N. (1997). *The Propaganda movement, 1880–1995: The creation of a Filipino consciousness, the making of the revolution.* Quezon City, Philippines: Ateneo de Manila University Press.

Scott, W. H. (1975). The Igorots who went to Madrid. In W. H. Scott (Ed.), *History on the Cordillera: Collected writings on mountain province history* (pp. 12–13). Baguio City, Philippines: Baguio.

Sullivan, R. J. (1991). *Exemplar of Americanism: The Philippine career of Dean C. Worcester.* Michigan Papers on South and Southeast Asia, no. 36. Ann Arbor: University of Michigan Center for South and Southeast Asian Studies.

Sutherland, W. A. (1906, July–September). The Philippine exposition at the Jamestown tercentennial exposition in 1907. *The Filipino.*

Sutherland, W. A. (1953). *Not by might: The epic story of the Philippines.* Las Cruces, NM: Southwest.

The Filipinos do not want the "wild tribes" exhibited. (1907). El Renacimiento. In *The Public 9*(418), 1169–1170. Retrieved September 5, 2012, from http://books.google.com/books?id=RDIfAQAAMAAJ&lpg=PA1153&ots=LRW5UOYL6C&dq=The%20Filipinos%20do%20not%20want%20the%20%E2%80%9Cwild%20tribes%E2%80%9D%20exhibited.&pg=PA1169#v=onepage&q=The%20Filipinos%20do%20not%20want%20the%20%E2%80%9Cwild%20tribes%E2%80%9D%20exhibited.&f=false

Vostral, S. L. (1993). Imperialism on display: The Philippine exhibition at the 1904 World's Fair. *Gateway Heritage,* 18–31.

Worcester, D. C. (1930). *The Philippines past and present.* New York, NY: Macmillan.

Worcester, D. C., & Bourns, F. S. (1897). Spanish rule in the Philippines. *The Cosmopolitan, 23*(6), 587–600.

Zaide, G. F. (1970). *Rizal: Asia's first apostle of nationalism.* Manila, Philippines: Red Star Book Store.

CHAPTER 3

COLONIAL LESSONS

Racial Politics of Comparison and the Development of American Education Policy in the Philippines

Funie Hsu
University of California, Berkeley

co·lo·nial les·son *noun* \kə-lō-nē-əl, -nyəl\ \le-sən\
1: *something learned from colonial comparison or experience*
2: *a course of instruction*
3: *a teachable moment of critical interrogation*

In 1902, David P. Barrows, Chief of the Bureau of Non-Christian Tribes, sailed from the Philippines back to the United States on a fact-finding mission. Upon his arrival in California, he contacted the Commissioner of Indian Affairs, W.A. Jones, in Washington, DC:

> Dear Sir:
>
> I should be pleased to receive a copy of your last annual Report of the Bureau of Indian Affairs. I have arrived in this country under directions from the U.S. Philippine Commission to make certain investigations both of the scientific and admisistrative [*sic*] work for the American Indians, that may assist us in organizing similar measures in the Philippines. (Barrows, 1902b, p. 1)

The "Other" Students, pages 39–62

Barrows carefully reviewed a variety of U.S. policies enforced upon Native Americans, paying particular attention to those regarding the organization of schools. Just months before his departure, he fulfilled the duties of Superintendent of Manila, overseeing the newly established American public schools in the capital. His research on U.S. Indian education policy would serve him well when the Philippine Commission appointed him General Superintendent of Education in 1903. As was the case for the American officials before and after him, Barrows' comparison of U.S. colonial and racial schooling models shaped the development of American education policy in the Philippines.

Although official U.S. rule of the archipelago ended in 1946, such colonial legacies continue to haunt the organization of contemporary U.S. experiences (Maldonaldo-Torres, 2007; Quijano, 2000), fundamentally influencing the development of American educational practices (Kliewer & Fitzgerald, 2001; Leonardo & Porter, 2010; Macedo, 2000). For this reason, educational research requires an analysis of colonialism. Renato Constantino (1966) is one of many scholars (Alidio, 2001; Coloma, 2004; Encarnacion, 1932; Martin, 1999; Racelis & Ick, 2001; Tupas, 2008) who have examined the role of American colonialism in the development of education in the Philippines. In doing so, he details the crucial, complementary function of American education in implementing colonialism. Constantino wrote, "The education of the Filipino under American sovereignty was an instrument of colonial policy. The Filipino had to be educated as a good colonial" (p. 4). U.S. colonial education, Constantino explained, was therefore miseducation, serving to construct Filipinos as a racial and colonial other. The Filipinos, though, were not the only ones to have experienced U.S. colonial conquest nor were they the lone students of American colonial miseducation. Educational policies directed at Native Americans, argues Historian Anne Paulet (2007), served as a blueprint in building the structure of colonial education in the Philippines. In other words, Native Americans were also miseducated and constructed as a racial other as part of an earlier U.S. conquest.

Paulet (2007) focuses on the relationship between U.S. colonial education policies domestically and in the Philippines, but her work also signifies the need to examine connections across other colonial contexts. For example, she references Glenn Anthony May's (1980) work on the influence of industrial training schools in the American South, which aimed to produce working-class African Americans in the service of an expanding nation, on the development of American education in the Philippines. It is a significant fact, however, that in addition to being informed by Native American policy and industrial schooling institutions of the Reconstruction South, the formation of U.S. education policy in the Philippines was influenced by, and contributed to, policies at colonial education institutions in Hawai'i,

Cuba, and Puerto Rico. This chapter examines all of these colonial connections, illuminating new dimensions of the relationships among American racism, colonialism, and education.

These relationships were made possible by what historian Ann L. Stoler (2006) terms a "politics of comparison" (p. 23), which suggests that increased attention be paid to the role comparison served in articulating and deploying a colonial project. Nowhere was this more apparent than in the colonization and establishment of American education in the Philippines, and it serves as a prime example of the "practices of colonial comparison by colonial governments themselves" (p. 23). Highlighting the formation of American education policy in the Philippines as a racial politics of comparison that relied on other cases of U.S. expansion and colonial education, I demonstrate how colonial education administrators in the Philippines, such as David P. Barrows, looked to other American models of racial and colonial schools to develop the public education system in the islands across the Pacific. To formulate a trivalent understanding of the racial politics of comparison in the development of American education policy in the Philippines, I conceptualize "colonial lessons" as an organizational and analytical tool.

In the following sections, I begin with an overview of the colonial fact of American education in the Philippines after the Spanish American War. I then present the first interpretation of the colonial lesson—*something learned from colonial comparison or experience*—to highlight moments of comparison among colonial education administrators in the Philippines and in other colonial and racial schooling projects across the U.S. territories. In this first part, I argue that colonial administrators were themselves students of colonialism by participating in a racial politics of colonial schooling comparison, gathering data from earlier U.S. colonial schools and studying previous experiences in American conquest as lessons in implementing colonialism. I explore the establishment of education policies in the colonization of the Philippines as part of a larger network of U.S. colonial education and thus examine how the racial politics of comparison resulted in colonial lessons on American conquest. The second interpretation of colonial lessons—*a course of instruction*—illuminates the manner in which the racial politics of colonial comparison produced the daily lessons and activities that were taught to generations of Filipino students. Through the comparison of colonial education models, educational administrators designed a curriculum of racial othering in the Philippines that borrowed from previous pedagogies of othering, through implementation of English instruction and industrial education. In this way, the colonial lessons learned from cases of U.S. expansion formed the basis of the colonial lessons of instruction carried out in the American schools. The chapter concludes with the third and final interpretation of colonial lessons—*a teachable moment of criti-*

cal interrogation—which presents the critical knowledge that can be gained from unearthing the hauntings of colonialism.

co·lo·nial les·son ***noun*** \kə-lō-nē-əl, -nyəl\ \le-sən\
1: *something learned from colonial study or experience*
2: *a course of instruction*
3: *a teachable moment of critical interrogation*

COLONIAL CONTEXT OF AMERICAN EDUCATION IN THE PHILIPPINES

The terms of peace outlined in the Treaty of Paris officially drew the Spanish-American War to an end on December 10, 1898. Articles I, II, and III of the treaty detailed the conditions that would result in official U.S. overseas expansion, ceding "Porto [*sic*] Rico and other islands now under Spanish sovereignty in the West Indies," Cuba, Guam, and the Philippine Archipelago to the United States (Philippines Commission, 1903, p. 1049). However, having already established the Philippine Republic in June of 1898, six months prior to the signing of the Treaty of Paris, Filipino nationalists had asserted their autonomy. An American military regime was quickly established in the Philippines to quell Filipino resistance to American rule and to establish colonial governance. By the following year, the United States had instigated another war, the Philippine-American War, in an attempt to subdue Filipino nationalists who demanded full independence from foreign rule.

The U.S. military government in the Philippines turned toward education as part of the strategy for pacifying the insurgency, and schooling was used as an element in the broader directive of organizing the new colonial order (Constantino, 1966; Marquardt, 2001). In an attempt to distinguish American rule from Spanish imperialism, U.S. colonials rationalized that, although the Spanish occupied the Philippines from 1565 to 1898, a systematic public education structure for Filipinos was not emphasized during Spanish colonial rule (Barrows, 1905).[1] Similarly, they ignored the Philippine Republic's provisions for free public schools as declared in the Malolos Constitution of 1899. The American colonial administration prided itself on the construction of what it deemed a cohesive, systemic public schooling structure for the Filipinos. Organizationally, the American education system provided a model for schools in the Philippines following the increasingly popular principles of progressive education that shaped educational management in the United States (Coloma, 2004). Yet strategically, public education in the Philippines was explicitly tied to the goal of conquest. Education was seen as a vital element in the military's pacification campaign. In the 1901 Annual Report of the War Department, Military Governor of the Philippines Arthur MacArthur asserted,

> I know of nothing in the department of administration that can contribute more in behalf of pacification than the immediate institution of a comprehensive system of education. The matter is so closely allied to the exercise of military force in these islands that in my annual report I treated the matter as a military subject and suggested rapid extension of educational facilities as an exclusively military measure. (War Department, 1901, p. 258)

Indeed, in MacArthur's eyes, the appropriation of funds to build schools needed to be viewed "in the same light as the appropriation for military roads for which the War Department recently authorized an allotment of $1,000,000" (p. 258). Education was, as Constantino (1966) wrote, "a weapon" (p. 3) in the colonial conquest of the Philippines.

As the American military occupied the physical terrain of the islands, they simultaneously engaged in ideological warfare, building the first public schools on Corregidor Island. In addition, U.S. military personnel served as the first teachers in the Philippines (Constantino, 1966). Although American colonial education in the Philippines fulfilled the purpose of pacification, it was not presented to the public in this light. Instead, education was touted as "the kindergarten of liberty" (Depew, 1900, p. 21) and a foundational element of Filipino nation building that was provided under the auspices of the United States. (Kramer, 2006).

As a republic that was founded on the premise of independence from foreign rule, engagement by the United States in the overseas conquest of the Philippine Islands posed an ideological dilemma. The invasion of the Philippines produced widespread charges that the United States was behaving no differently from other imperial powers. Given this problem, U.S. colonials took heed from precious experiences of imperialism and made great effort to present American colonialism as different. "The Spanish failure has its lesson," warned David P. Barrows, "and that lesson must be seen by other colonial nations or the failure will be repeated elsewhere" (Barrows, 1910, p. 158). Drawing from this colonial lesson, U.S officials packaged public education as a symbol of America's commitment to Filipino national development. Such a rhetorical maneuver served to position the United States as a patron of liberty rather than a usurper of independence. Education in the Philippines was therefore essential in maintaining the political welfare of the continental United States as the possession of overseas territories posed a threat to American democratic ideals.

co·lo·nial les·son *noun* \kə-lō-nē-əl, -nyəl\ \le-sən\
1: ***something learned from colonial comparison or experience***
2: a course of instruction
3: a teachable moment of critical interrogation

RACIAL POLITICS OF COMPARISON

Acquiring the Filipino "Problem"

Education was also viewed as the mechanism to relieve what poet Rudyard Kipling claimed to be the "burden" that the so-called dependent peoples of the new colony posed upon the White man (Kipling, 1899). The acquisition of new U.S. territories had historically resulted in the governance of additional peoples, a fact well documented by colonial officials debating the Philippine issue (Depew, 1900). Such "acquisition" of people as part of conquest was predicated upon a colonial ideology deeply rooted in notions of race, difference, and inferiority. Within this rationality, Filipinos were constructed, or racialized, as non-White "others" and therefore deemed uncivilized (Go, 2004; Kramer, 2006). A July 1, 1900, newspaper article in the *New Haven Union* announced the acquisition of "Our New Ape Men" and declared the Negrito people of the Philippines as "the curious black dwarves of our newly-acquired archipelago" and "probably the most monkey-like people in the world" (Our new ape men, 1900, p. 12). It was a scholarly perspective supported by leading colonial figures, such as Dr. Dean C. Worcester, anthropologist and one of five members of the Philippine Commission (Our new ape men, 1900). Filipinos, then, embodied a colonial dilemma as they represented a population of semihumans that needed to be managed.

Discourse in the United States went so far as problematizing the very existence of Filipinos. New York State Commissioner of Education Dr. Andrew S. Draper proclaimed, "The Philippine problem has come to be the problem of pressing concern to us" (Draper, 1907, p. 648). In Draper's speech, titled "The Philippine Problem," which was published in the 1907 issue of *The Southern Workmen,* he describes Filipinos as savages incapable of assimilation and self-government:

> There are more people in the Philippine Islands than in the State of New York—perhaps twenty times more than the Indian population ever was. The conditions are hard and the outlook uncertain. It is a hard matter to have such a mass of unlettered, semi-savage, or wholly savage people under our flag, without the possibility of assimilating them as we do the millions who come to us from other lands, and with some inevitable doubts about their ever being able to govern themselves. We are coming to the serious stage of the undertaking and the problem looms even larger than at first. (p. 648)

The argument that the "savage" Filipinos were ill-equipped for self-rule, as echoed by Draper, justified ongoing American rule in the Philippines but also presented a colonial conundrum. In addressing the question "Should republics have colonies?" General Thomas McArthur Anderson (1906) noted, "The government of an inferior race is a difficult problem . . . We have learned this within our own borders in our dealings with the Indian and the Negro" (p. 1225). McArthur's statement points to both the racial lessons learned from previous episodes of American expansion and the fact that U.S. colonial and educational figures looked to these lessons in developing policies for the Philippines. Comparison within a racial framework proved to be an essential method for implementing American colonialism in the archipelago.

Racial Politics

Insofar as Filipinos were made into a racial, political, and moral "problem," they joined Native Americans, African Americans, and other "dependents" in U.S. territories as colonially racialized people that needed to be removed, improved, or dealt with in some way to advance U.S. development. It was no mere coincidence that Draper referenced the "Indian population" in "The Philippine Problem." He first gave this address at the 1907 Lake Mohonk Conference of the Friends of the Indian (later known as the Lake Mohonk Friends of the Indian and other Dependent Peoples), a society established specifically to deal with the "Indian Problem" that surfaced as a result of continental expansion. *The Southern Workmen,* "a magazine devoted to the interests of undeveloped races" (The Southern Workmen, 1907), was a publication of Hampton Normal and Agricultural Institute, a school that aimed to turn the "Negro Problem" in the Reconstruction South into a productive, accommodating labor force.

Opened in 1868 by the American Missionary Association, Hampton was the industrial training ground for Booker T. Washington, an African American educational leader who championed industrial education as a solution to the "Negro Problem." Washington would later serve a foundational role in advising U.S. colonial officials in the development of education in the Philippines (May, 1980).

Washington's most vocal critic, W.E.B. Du Bois,[2] accurately observed that such an educational model bode well with many White Americans. In 1903, Du Bois wrote, "The prevailing public opinion of the land has been but too willing to deliver the solution of a wearisome problem into his hands and say, 'If that is all you and your race ask, take it,'" (p. 33). In other words, Du Bois criticized Washington for allowing Whites to persist in imagining the "problem" as contained within non-White groups. Du Bois, however, viewed that the problem was not with particular racialized peoples but rather with the political economic system of race and colonialism itself: "The problem of the twentieth century is the problem of the color-line—the relation of the darker to the lighter races of men in Asia and Africa, in America and the islands of the sea" (p. 10). It was precisely the U.S. colonization of the "islands of the sea" that prompted David P. Barrows to reiterate Du Bois' declaration. In his article, "What May Be Expected From Philippine Education?" published in the 1910 issue of the *Journal of Race Development*, Barrows professed,

> The most pressing problems of the twentieth century are those occasioned by racial contact and collision. Over a large part of the earth, the white man is master of the political fortunes of the backward and dependent peoples of other races, but it is doubtful if he can longer generally maintain his superior position except by generous concessions. The future is full of trouble and will tax the capacities of the white race as perhaps they have never been taxed before. (p. 157)

In this interpretation of the "problem," Barrows reveals that the undercurrent of anxiety coursing through White racial power in fact motivates the system of race, the very system that produced the "color-line." Thus, colonialism in the Philippines was infused with a racial politics that served to manage White dominance by racializing Filipinos as problematic others. Racial comparison along the color line of "problem" groups served as a foundational strategy for implementing colonial institutions, and specifically education, in the Pacific Islands.

The Kindergarten of Liberty

In the comparison of colonial cases, education emerged as the primary process by which to solve the Filipino "problem." Schooling was employed as both a metaphor for tutelage under American rule (Kramer, 2006) as well as a foundational social structure by which the United States enforced the colonial and racial othering of Filipinos. In a February 27, 1900, speech to the U.S. Senate, Hon. Chauncey M. Depew compared American rule in the Philippines to that established in Cuba, thereby presenting a colonial lesson for his fellow senators on how best to proceed with the Pacific colony. Passionately invoking education, he expressed,

> The kindergarten of liberty, under competent instructors, rapidly develops its pupils for larger responsibilities for citizenship, respect for law, for judicial duties and for a constantly increasing share in their local and general assemblies. One year of rule by the United States in Cuba is a convincing

> object lesson. Brigands have become farmers, and revolutionists conservative citizens. Order has taken the place of anarchy, and law of license. The Cubans are developing their industries and rapidly developing habits of self-government. So the uplifting of the people of the Philippines to the comprehension and practice of orderly industry, respect for individual rights, confidence and then participation in government will add enormously to their happiness and reciprocally to the strength, prosperity and power of our country [Applause in the galleries]. (p. 21)

Depew's suggestion that the Philippines be instructed into U.S. "liberty" in the same manner as Cuba was an idea well received by his fellow Americans. Indeed, in the mindset of many American officials, it made sense that the same colonial policies would rule overseas territories of the United States, including a similar racialized system of education. U.S. colonial occupation would serve as the "kindergarten of liberty," providing lessons in democratic principles and practices. Through a system of public education, American officials would disseminate skills to the population of racialized others. The 1899 political cartoon, "School Begins" (Figure 3.1), depicts the Philippines, Hawai'i, Porto [*sic*] Rico, and Cuba as little brown schoolboys forced into the same classroom, a condition of the colonial lessons learned and imposed by American foreign rule. Racialized as burdens of

Figure 3.1 "School Begins" by Louis Dalrymple (*Puck*, January 25, 1898). Caption: Uncle Sam (to his new class on civilization)—"Now, children, you've got to learn these lessons whether you want to or not! But just take a look at the class ahead of you, and remember that in a little while, you will be as glad to be here as they are!"

conquest, they were all rendered dependent children in need of tutelage within the U.S. colonial schoolhouse.

Published in *Puck*, a Democratic-leaning humor magazine with high circulation, "School Begins" illustrates that Americans were politically and socially engaged in a practice of racial comparison between U.S. colonial projects. Although the immediate "problem" races were those associated with the overseas colonies acquired after the Spanish-American war, they were always contextualized within domestic racial politics in relation to the homegrown "problems" of the African and Native American.

The satirical cartoon depicts Uncle Sam sternly admonishing the "Brown problem" kids, representing the territories in the Pacific, squirming in the front row. In the background, two male figures—a Native American and an African American student—provide both the racial framework of American continental conquest and the resulting educational policies in which the new colonial students are inscribed. The Native American student sits alone just beyond the class, forlornly holding a book in English upside down in front of him. Across the room, the African American student assumes an ambiguous role in the classroom. Busy wiping the schoolhouse window and looking at the rest of the students in the classroom, it is unclear whether he is actually a student in the class or a laborer assigned the duties of maintaining the infrastructure of Uncle Sam. These two older colonial students remain isolated from the rest of the class, a foreshadowing of the social and educational trajectory that may befall the newly enrolled classmates if they do not master the skills of civilization provided in the colonial lessons. Thus, "School Begins" depicts U.S. colonialism as an educational practice, illuminating such schooling as a pancolonial project. Outside the open door, a little Chinese boy peers into the classroom with a book tucked under his arm, ready to begin his first day of school. A direct reference to the Open Door Policy issued that same year, which provided for U.S. economic expansion into China, the cartoon implies that the American school of democracy is preparing to admit yet another student into its classroom. "Now, children," reads the caption, "you've got to learn these lessons whether you want to or not! But just take a look at the class ahead of you, and remember that in a little while, you will be as glad to be here as they are!" The new school children of the colonies have, in fact, two model classes ahead of them. One class is represented by the obedient students sitting directly behind them, and their books depict the names of the more recently annexed states to the Union (i.e., Alaska, Arizona, New Mexico, Texas, and California). The second class is represented by the African and Native American students who are relegated to the corners of the classroom as "others." The anti-imperialist bent of the cartoon, demonstrated in part through a racial comparison of these other dark-skinned male students and their alienation in the classroom, suggests that these new students will follow in the footsteps of the second class and thus become second-class peoples.

Indeed, when designing the system of education in the Philippines, colonial officials looked to models of schooling that were geared toward the other "problem" races instead of examining the educational systems popularly used in the recently incorporated U.S. states, revealing that the intended goal of education in the Philippines was not to train Filipinos for participation in democracy but rather to produce them as racialized "others." Presenting a critique of U.S. imperialism as effective schooling in democracy, "School Begins" ultimately highlights the fact that the practice of racial comparison of colonial cases also contains the potential for critical perspectives.

Students of Colonialism

With the initial expansion of U.S. education in the Philippines—from the expedient teachings of American soldiers to a more comprehensive system of public schooling—the question of organization arose. Although President McKinley established the first Philippine Commission, also known as the Schurman Commission, in 1899 to aid in organizing colonial institutions in the Philippines, it wasn't until the second Philippine (Taft) Commission in 1900 that a plan for an official system of education was detailed. Adapting the approach of colonialism as democratic schooling (Kramer, 2006), it was clear to colonial education administrators in the Philippines that they would instruct Filipinos with American ideals of civilization, but the specific method of carrying out these lessons remained an issue for consideration.

When Bernard Moses was appointed to the U.S. Philippine Commission to tackle this problem, he brought with him the legitimacy of an academic and the ideology of White racial domination. A March 10, 1900, newspaper report identified Moses as a "professor of history and political economy in the University of California" (Berkeley University Prof., 1900). The article further explained that "The special subject of Prof. Moses' historical researches has been the colonization and development of North and South America." In a speech entitled "Colonial Enterprise," Moses (1905) shared the following conclusions on the study of colonialism:

> In all these undertakings, [the] student discovers his chief interests not in the events of the conquest, not in the formation and establishment of a government, not in the efforts to eliminate the unruly and to preserve order, but in questions concerning the relations the white man holds and is to hold in the future to the numbers of the less developed races. (p. 291)

Matters of race, therefore, were at the center of the project of conquest. More accurately, according to Professor Moses, matters of White racial domination served a foundational purpose of colonialism (Brechin, 2006). Moses saw his work in the Philippines as a reflection of his expertise on conquest, a project that went hand in hand with what he identified as concerns of maintaining the "color line" and racial positioning. In specific regard to developing appropriate educational policy in the Philippines, Moses (n.d.) expressed the following:

> The American policy provides for educating the members of another and an alien race. This work is to solve a practical problem of education in the broader sense, a problem which comprehends all the influences that make for enlightenment, and which embraces many factors that do not come into consideration in the administration of the ordinary educational affairs in the United States. It is the problem of educating the stranger, and its solution must be based on a proper comprehension of the relation of the people of the Orient to the people of the Occident. Therefore, at the foundation of our educational administration in the Philippines lie the facts of race distinction and the question or the relation of one race to another. (p. 235)

Since Filipinos were constructed as "members of another and an alien race," their education posed a "problem," as it did with the other races birthed out of U.S. continental expansion. Also, Moses advocated for the teaching of "race distinction," which echoes the type of racial segregation practiced in the Jim Crow South.

Upon being appointed the first Superintendent of General Education in the Philippines on April 17, 1900, Fred Atkinson contacted the director of Tuskegee Institute, Booker T. Washington, to seek advice on industrial training. One month later, before arriving at his post in the archipelago, the Harvard-educated high school teacher from Massachusetts journeyed to the American South. As a guest of Washington, Atkinson visited both Tuskegee and Hampton Institutes, where he made firsthand observations of the manual training program implemented at the schools. Atkinson had identified the method of industrial training designed to rectify the "Negro Problem" as a fitting model for the schooling of the newly acquired "little brown brothers" (Go, 2004) in the Philippines (May, 1980). "Education in the Philippines must be along industrial lines," he communicated to Washington, "and any and all suggestions for you and your work will be invaluable" (as cited in May, 1980, p. 89). The basis of his comparison between the two groups rested on the process of racial othering or "problem" making, which was reinforced by American national development. "Thirty-nine years have now passed since the close of the Civil War and the negro problem is still unresolved," Atkinson (1905) wrote in *The Philippine Islands*, "at the end of a like period of time we shall be struggling with the Philippine question" (p. 14).

Like Atkinson, other colonial and domestic U.S. officials found Tuskegee's method of manual education to be a comparative example of the type of schooling that could be established in the Philippines. Immediately following the Spanish-American War, President McKinley toured the United States to capitalize on the good sentiments fostered by the American victory. One of the stops in the southern portion of his tour included the Tuskegee Institute. The President was so impressed with the industrial work at Tuskegee, that *The Post* (1898) reported, he "told members of the Alabama Legislature, who were in the audience to-day, that the assistance from the state ought to be materially increased" (Uplifting the negro, 1898). Secretary of the Navy John D. Long, also present at the event, found the Tuskegee model of industrial training to be "the solution of the negro problem" (Uplifting the negro, 1898). Washington's curriculum of manual labor was lauded as an effective method of turning African Americans into productive, accommodating members of society. Secretary of Agriculture James Wilson found in Washington's Tuskegee Institute a model for the educational task facing the United States in the Philippine Islands. "Here is the lesson that teaches us," he said, "that we can face the great problem of our new possessions with equanimity" (President at Tuskegee, 1898).

Tuskegee, in turn, was developed from several comparative lessons derived over the course of American expansion and schooling. Most directly, it was influenced by the mode of industrial training that sprang out of Hampton Institute. Established by Samuel Chapman Armstrong and the American Missionary Association in 1868, Hampton served as the preeminent manual education school for African Americans in the Reconstruction South, with Booker T. Washington as its most celebrated alumnus. However, inspiration for the industrial program at Hampton had been garnered years before, as lessons learned from Armstrong's previous colonial education experience as the son of Reverend Richard Armstrong, an influential missionary and educational figure in the formation of Hawai'i's public school system (Benham & Heck, 1998). From these lessons, Samuel Armstrong rationalized that, "there was worked out in the Hawaiian Islands the problem of emancipation, and civilization of the dark skinned Polynesian people in many respects like the Negro race" (Benham & Heck, 1998, p. 90). Thus, both the Hampton Institute and Tuskegee Institute instructed racialized pedagogies mastered from colonial lessons derived by Armstrong senior in Hawai'i generations earlier. The education of African Americans in these institutes was therefore intimately entangled with the history of racial oppression and economic exploitation in the Hawaiian Islands. Philippine educational administrator Fred Atkinson took these colonial lessons to heart. As superintendent, he attempted to establish a similar training regimen in the Philippines to train Filipinos for work in the practical industries that would benefit American economic interests in the islands.

Following Atkinson's resignation, and that of his short-termed successor, Elmer Bryan, in 1903, David P. Barrows was assigned General Superintendent of Education in the Philippines. This was a promotion from his initial colonial appointment in 1900 as Superintendent of Manila Schools. Before his service in the Philippines, David P. Barrows had conducted doctoral research on the Coahuilla Indians of Southern California. It was research that served him well in 1902 in his second colonial position as Chief of the Bureau of Non-Christian Tribes for the Philippine Islands. As Chief of the Bureau, Barrows was committed to staying abreast of U.S. Indian policy, with the intention of developing policies for those "natives" of the Philippines. He returned to the United States for the explicit purpose of studying colonial comparisons in the management of indigenous peoples:

> My business in the United States is first to get all the light I can from the results of Indian policy inaugurated under Morgan: lands in severalty, Indian police, courts for the trial of Indian offences, schools, agriculture, etc. (Barrows, 1902a, p. 1)

Barrows had been actively engaged in a racial politics of comparison to gather data that would inform his decision making in the Philippines. In 1903, Barrows was reassigned to the work of colonial education and promoted to General Superintendent of Public Schools in the islands. In this position, he continued his study of the colonial policies geared toward Native Americans, but with a particular focus on schooling. Under his direction, education in the Philippines shifted its focus from industrial education to English instruction.

However, Barrows had also engaged in personal study of industrial education models in the United States, making arrangements to visit Carlisle boarding school and Native American reservation schools for the purposes of comparison. Established by Captain Richard Pratt in 1879, with the intention to "kill the Indian" in Native Americans and to, "save the man" (Pratt, 1973, p. 1), Carlisle Indian Industrial School shared close ties with General Samuel Chapman Armstrong and his Hampton Normal and Agricultural Institute in Virginia. Pratt had begun his Native American educational project by directing a group of Indian prisoners to Hampton for manual training (Fey & McNickle, 1959). Although Pratt left Hampton when funding was secured for the construction of Carlisle in Pennsylvania, Hampton continued to enroll Native Americans into their industrial training curriculum, a program viewed as effective in instilling the middle-class norms of the White settlers. Thus, colonial lessons on racialized educational practices were exchanged between models applied toward solving the "Hawaiian,"

"Indian," "Negro," and "Filipino" problems that arose as a condition of U.S. continental expansion. Former Military Governor Colonel George LeRoy Brown provided an explicit example of colonial officials in the Philippines engaging in a racial politics of comparison in his 1902 "Observations on School Work in the Province of Paragua." Directly referencing his study of Hampton and Carlisle, he wrote,

> Early in the seventies, in connection with the development of school work among the Indians in the Western territory, the idea of varying routine schoolwork with a training of eye and hand, indoors and outdoors, was conceived and carried info effect successfully. Later, this idea was further developed into industrial training at Carlisle Indian Training School, Pennsylvania, and also at Hampton, Virginia, to both of which institutions I was detailed at different times. (Brown, 1902, p. 2)

Colonel Brown went on to encourage the model of "varying routine schoolwork with a training of eye and hand" for the students in Paragua schools. In anticipation of a colonial field trip to Carlisle in 1902 in order to partake in similar comparisons, Barrows informed Commissioner of Indian Affairs, W. A. Jones of his plans "to stop off at Carlisle for a day, although I notice that your last report is unfavorable to the boarding school for Indian pupils" (Barrows, 1902, p. 1). Like Jones, Barrows found the Carlisle boarding model of schooling impractical and unsuitable for emulation in the Philippines. He saw boarding schools as being exceedingly expensive and ineffective, preferring on-site schools instead (Paulet, 2007). Manual training, however, persisted in the schools of the islands, although too a lesser degree than Atkinson had originally desired.

The colonial lesson learned from the comparison of educational models imposed upon Hawaiians, Native Americans, and African Americans in the United States served as the foundation upon which colonial education administrators in the Philippines built the system of public schools. This makes clear that the Philippines functioned as part of a larger colonial project. In "The Philippine Problem," Draper wrote, "We do not overlook little Porto [*sic*] Rico or our good friends in the Hawaiian Islands . . . both of these peoples will quickly get the benefit of any insular policies which the overwhelming situation in the Philippines may induce" (1907, p. 651). The institution of colonial education that developed in the Philippines as a result of the racial politics of comparison would serve as another lesson in the handbook of U.S. pancolonial education.

co·lo·nial les·son *noun* \kə-lō-nē-əl, -nyəl\ \le-sən\
1: *something learned from colonial comparison or experience*
2: ***a course of instruction***
3: *a teachable moment of critical interrogation*

COLONIAL CURRICULUM IN THE PHILIPPINES

The colonial lesson in the "School Begins" cartoon can also be interpreted as the literal content material or curriculum that comprised the educational system in the territories in general and the Philippines in particular. In the cartoon, a book sits on Uncle Sam's desk. Titled "U.S. First Lessons in Self Government," it spells out in clear English that the lessons of self-government were to be conducted in the language of the colonizers. The African American window washer represents the pedagogy of productive industry, such as that endorsed at Tuskegee and Hampton and studied by Atkinson, Barrows, and Brown. Indeed, these two modes of instruction served as the pillars of the educational system in the Philippine Islands. "As to the subject of instruction, the English language should be the subject most insisted upon," proclaimed Fred Atkinson, the first Superintendent of Public Instruction in the Philippines, "There should be industrial and commercial courses as well as general courses" (Atkinson, 1901, p. 2). Atkinson was thoroughly invested in pursuing educational ventures like Tuskegee as exemplars of industrial education in the archipelago. English instruction, though, became the bedrock of education in the Philippines, especially under Barrows' direction.

English Instruction

As the Philippine Commissioner overseeing education, Bernard Moses established English as the medium of instruction as one of his first orders in constructing a comprehensive educational structure in the Islands. In fact, it was an educational policy mandated by Philippine Public Law Act 74 in 1901 (Philippine Commission, 1903, p. 103). English was seen as the only suitable language for imparting the moral and civic values of American democracy (Kramer, 2006; Martin, 1999; Tupas, 2008). It was also an essential element in positioning the U.S. administration in contrast to that of the previous Spanish imperial rule. By granting access to the language of the dominant power through public education, Americans claimed beneficent assistance in their occupation. In regard to teaching English to the Filipino, Moses declared,

> To teach them the English language and open them to the views of the world that may be gained through the use of that tongue is not to subject them to any intellectual loss, but, on the other hand, to furnish them a most powerful stimulus to intellectual progress. (Use of the English, n.d., p. 10)

An education in sciences and letters was thus given through English as the mandated medium of instruction.

The policy of English instruction itself was a colonial thread that ran through public schools in Hawai'i, Native American boarding schools, the industrial education institutions of the American South, and the newly developing educational systems in Cuba and Puerto Rico. In detailing the accounts of former boarding school students and their experience with English instruction, Brenda J. Child (1998) referred to the "strict policy that forbade Indian students from speaking tribal languages, the languages of their mothers and fathers" (p. 28). She documented that many students at boarding schools caught speaking a language other than English were punished with brute force: "Beatings, swats from rulers, having one's mouth washed with soap or lye, or being locked in the school jail were not uncommon punishments" (p. 28). The physical enforcement of English as a foundational colonial lesson reveals the violent, racialized ideals of Anglo superiority integral to English instruction policies. In Hawai'i, the 1902 Report of the Superintendent of Public Instruction noted that it was necessary to employ English as a common language to teach the racially and linguistically mixed student body: "The whole mass is taught in the English language, and that we should have the success which has attended our efforts argues well for the system which has been instituted and carried on for the last fifteen years" (p. 8).

The need for English instruction, it was argued, in Hawai'i (Benham & Heck, 1998) and in the Philippines (Tupas, 2008; Kramer, 2006; Bernardo, 2004; Martin, 1999) was dire, as it allowed for the unification of diverse peoples, languages, and cultures.

The mandate of English instruction in the Philippines was thus interconnected with other U.S. colonial education enterprises. It is no surprise then, that the *U.S.S. Thomas* made a stop in Honolulu, "for three days rest and recreation" on its educational journey to the Philippines (Gleason, 1901, p. 26). In fact, a handful of the teachers aboard the transport *Thomas* had previously served as instructors in the Hawai'i public schools. One, Henry S. Townsend, would climb the colonial education ladder in the Philippines to become a noted principal and regional educational administrative figure. Not surprisingly, several of the American teachers who departed for the Philippines and Puerto Rico had also taught at Indian schools (Walsh, 1991, p. 9). These colonial ties continued to be woven throughout the course of American public education in the Philippines, with some teachers leaving the Philippines for educational opportunities in other U.S. territories.

English also facilitated the use of American teachers, deemed uniquely suited to the colonial civilizing project. "As soon as practicable," relayed the Schools of the Western Islands report, "American teachers and equipment should be provided all schools" (Brown, 1901, p. 2). Although American soldiers fulfilled the initial teaching positions, they were transferred out of duty in the classroom and replaced with trained educators imported from the continental United States. "Over 200 hundred teachers have been appointed," Atkinson reported in 1901, "and are now awaiting transportation in the United States" (General Superintendent of Public Instruction, 1901, p. 61). In 1901, just over 500 White American teachers departed from San Francisco's Pier 12 aboard the cattle carrier *U.S.S. Thomas.* The Thomasites, as they were known, set sail for the new American colony of the Philippines with the intended goal of implementing the colonial policy of English instruction.

The employment of American teachers from the United States for the purpose of English instruction mirrored educational developments in Puerto Rico. There too, English was established as the medium of instruction, although Harris had cautioned the speed at which it should be introduced for fear of riling suspicions about the intent to replace Spanish. The use of Spanish in the schools was allowed during the initial 10 years of American colonial rule, but it was to be replaced by English thereafter (Walsh, 1991, p. 11). In the meantime, American teachers were needed to impart English in the Puerto Rican schools. Paralleling the Philippines, educators from the continental United States were shipped to Puerto Rico in 1901, replacing the soldiers who initially served as teachers.

Industrial Education

Industrial education comprised a second focus in the Philippine schools, "An integral and essential feature of the public school organization is the system of industrial education," (White, 1913a, p. 265) wrote Frank R. White, Director of Education. Along with English instruction, manual labor and training in domestic skills were part of the daily curriculum. Harking back to the values of hard work and productivity espoused at institutions such as Carlisle, Hampton, and Tuskegee, industrial education in the Philippines was seen as an important strategy for developing the territory for the economic needs of colonial government. The stated aim of the policy of industrial education was to "prepare the Filipino to serve his own country as an intelligent, industrious, and useful citizen" (White, 1913, p. 266). To develop "useful citizens," industrial education was tendered at a young age, beginning with the first grade of primary instruction. A typical day of instruction for a young student of this grade level followed the regimen below, as outlined by the Department of Public Instruction:

> Primary Course *First year-* Reading, 20 minutes daily; language, 20 minutes; numbers, 20 minutes; writing, 20 minutes; recreation exercise, 60 minutes including (a) singing, (b) physical training, (c) busy work: stick laying, col-

> oring, paper cutting, paper tearing, paper folding, braiding, bead and seed stringing, knot tying, outline drawing with pencil; industrial work, 30 minutes. (White, 1913b, pp. 378–379)

Evident in these activities, are the "varying of routine work with that of eye and hand" as recommended earlier by Colonel Brown's comparative observational experience at Hampton and Carlisle. In the Philippine schools, instructional time devoted to industrial training increased to 60 through 100 minutes by the fourth year. Manual work remained an integral part of the training for public school students throughout the duration of their academic careers.

As it did in other colonial education institutions, the practice of industrial instruction in the Philippines took on a gendered dimension. Industrial training for girls in the Philippines involved an education in sewing, weaving, lacemaking, and other such domestic work. Some girls received training in the School of Household Industries located in Manila, an institute designated to produce new domestic workers to staff the homes of colonial families. Such gendered instructions were seen as fundamental in developing useful women for the new nation. Boys, in turn, were schooled in such tasks as rattan making, gardening, and hat making. They were also trained in construction so they could learn how to build the homes, buildings, and infrastructure that would supposedly pave the way toward national growth. The practice of gendered industrial education emulated that which had already been established in the United States. Included in Colonel Brown's observational notes on industrial training at Hampton and Carlisle were references to gendered curriculum: "Calisthenics, gymnasium work, outdoor sports, and military training were found to be useful factors in the development of the boys. All kinds of house-work; cooking, sewing, embroidery, for girls" (Brown, 1902, p. 2). These lessons were later mimicked in the Philippine provinces as classes were established in "sewing for the girls and an effort made to start a cooking class, for girls" (Brown, 1902, p. 2).

The colonial structure of the gendered industrial education enterprise bore striking resemblances to educational practices applied in Native American boarding schools and the industrial institutions of the South. Indian girls in boarding schools across the United States were prepared in the fields of baking, housekeeping, laundry, and nursing. Many were sent on so- called educational outings to hone their craft in the homes of White middle-class families (Child, 1998). At Hampton,

> The girls were taught to cook and sew, to set a proper table, to acquire all the graces that would make a good housewife—or housekeeper. Habits of neatness and cleanliness, never required of many slaves, were insisted upon for both sexes. (as cited in Wexler, 2000 p. 108)

These colonial education portraits demonstrate that the vocational instruction of those in colonized territories served to benefit the personal and economic gains of those at the helm of American conquest. Although touted as intellectual and democratic tutelage, the colonial lessons of industrial education produced a racialized and gendered labor force for the maintenance of U.S. expansion.

co·lo·nial les·son *noun* \kə-lō-nē-əl, -nyəl\ \le-sən\
1: *something learned from colonial study or experience*
2: *a course of instruction*
3: ***a teachable moment of critical interrogation***

DEVELOPING CRITICAL ANALYSES OF COLONIALISM

The development of the Philippine education system under U.S. rule relied upon racial politics established through the history of American nation building and schooling. In creating the colonial institution of education in the Philippines, American officials had a network of colonial and racial models to compare from. Industrial training schools in the domestic United States, such as Hampton, Tuskegee, and Carlisle, served as important racial points of comparison. U.S. colonials also looked to educational models in other overseas territories, such as Hawai'i, Puerto Rico, and Cuba, in determining a suitable system for the Philippines. That U.S. officials in the Philippines compared these specific schooling projects was not natural. Instead, it reveals a troubling pattern of structured racial difference. On the one hand, it seems that making educational comparisons was a logical strategy, but on the other hand, these colonial administrators did not look, for example, to elite White women's boarding schools. They looked in particular "problematic" racial places and for particular racial educational practices. Many of these colonial officials drew from their personal experiences as participants in, or scholars of, U.S. conquest. Through these firsthand comparisons, they gathered many colonial lesson plans from which to build the American government in the Philippines.

The educational policies that emerged in this shared colonial context directly affected the academic content and curriculum of the Philippine public schools. The racial and gendered ideals that upheld American conquest were infused in the daily colonial lessons of the schoolhouse. English instruction and industrial education, the pillars of colonial education policy, structured the educational opportunities of Filipino youth around time-tested colonial strategies of racial othering. Although American education in the colony claimed to impart democratic knowledge and the values of advanced civilization, it actually functioned to disseminate notions of White racial superiority and to maintain, in Philippine Commissioner Bernard Moses words, "the facts of race distinction" (n.d., p. 235).

However, Filipinos did not always internalize the colonial ideology propagated by colonial educators. In fact, within these very colonial lessons existed an opportunity for alternative interpretations of American democracy. Indeed, in 1898, a committee of Filipino nationalists took it upon themselves to become scholars of U.S. colonialism and engage in their own racial politics of comparison (Banganiban et al., 1899). In a letter addressed to the Schurman Commission, these scholars decried the rule of a hypocritical American government, denouncing

> the violent and destructive character of American people in their dealings with the colored race, quoting as example the extermination of the Indians in the different states of North America, whose population has been disappearing from those extensive plains, and adding an American maxim which says that "A good Indian is a dead Indian." (p. 5)

Through a comparative study of previous American conquest, Filipino nationalists exposed the contradictory nature of the colonial lesson of U.S. rule being imposed on them by the American military regime. Therefore, although colonial education has been used as a weapon of oppression, as Constantino (1966) states, it can also be employed critically. Colonial lessons, then, can serve as the material from which we develop our most intelligent critiques of historic educational inequality and unveil the problematic logic of the persisting color line.

NOTES

1. There remains a scholarly debate as to the scale and effectiveness of the system of public education under Spanish rule. Here, I am highlighting the U.S. colonial official's portrayal of Philippine education during Spanish colonial rule as insufficient and underdeveloped.
2. Du Bois was the first African American to receive a doctorate from Harvard University. He was also the leader of the National Association for the Advancement of Colored People (NAACP) and a professor at Atlanta University (now Clark Atlanta University).

REFERENCES

Alidio, K. A. (2001). Between civilizing mission and ethnic assimilation: Racial discourse, U.S. colonial education, and Filipino ethnicity, 1901–1946 (Doctoral dissertation). The University of Michigan, Ann Arbor, MI.

Anderson, T. M. (1906). *Should republics have colonies?* Boston, MA: A. T. Bliss.

Atkinson, F. (1901). *Report of General Superintendent of Public Instruction.* [Report]. Bancroft Library (Bernard Moses Papers, C-B 944, Carton 2).

Atkinson, F. (1905) *The Philippine Islands.* New York, NY: Ginn.

Banganiban, P. et al. (1899). *Untitled.* National Archives, Records of the Bureau of Insular Affairs, RG 350.U.S. Commission to the Philippine Islands.

Barrows, D. P. (1902a, January 15). [Letter to Charles Lummis]. Bancroft Library (David Prescott Barrows Papers, C-B 1005, Box 1).

Barrows, D. P. (1902b, January 20). [Letter to W. A. Jones]. Bancroft Library (David Prescott Barrows Papers, C-B 1005, Box 1).

Barrows, D. P. (1905) *History of the Philippines.* Indianapolis, IN: Bobbs-Merrill.

Barrows, D. P. (1910). What may be expected from Philippine education? *The Journal of Race Development, 1,* 156–168.

Benham, M. K., & Heck, R. (1998). *Culture and educational policy in Hawai'i: The silencing of native voices.* Mahwah, NJ: Lawrence Erlbaum.

Berkeley University Prof. Moses to go to Manila. (1900, March 10) *The San Diego Union.* Bancroft Library (Bernard Moses Papers, C-B 944, Carton 2).

Bernardo, A. B. I. (2004) McKinley's questionable bequest: Over 100 years of English in Philippine education. *World Englishes, 23*(1) 17–31.

Brechin, G. (2006). *Imperial San Francisco: Urban power, earthly ruin.* Berkeley & Los Angeles and London, UK: University of California Press.

Brown, G. (1901). *Schools in the Western Islands.* Bancroft Library (Bernard Moses papers, C-B 944, Carton 2).

Brown, G. (1902). *Observations on school work in the province of Paragua.* Bancroft Library (Bernard Moses Scrapbook, Banc Mss 71/229 C, Vol. 7)

Child, B. (1998). *Boarding school seasons: American Indian families, 1900–1940.* Lincoln: University of Nebraska Press.

Coloma, R. S. (2004). *Empire and education: Filipino schooling under U.S. rule, 1900–1910* (Doctoral dissertation). The Ohio State University, Columbus, OH.

Constantino, R. (1966).*The mis-education of the Filipino.* Manila, Philippines: Erehwon.

Dalrymple, L. (1898, January 25). School begins [Political cartoon]. *Puck.* New York, NY: Keppler & Schwarzmann.

Depew, C. M. (1900). The government of the Philippine Islands. Washington, DC: U.S. Senate.

Draper, A. S. (1907). The Philippine problem. The Southern Workmen, 648–652.

Du Bois, W. E. B. (1903). The souls of Black folk. New York, NY: Bantam.

Encarnacion, A. (1932). *A history of education in the Philippines, 1565–1930.* Manila: University of the Philippines Press.

Fey, H. E., & McNickle, D. (1959). *Indians and other Americans: Two ways of life meet.* New York, NY: Harper & Brothers.

General Superintendent of Public Instruction. (1901). [Report]. Bancroft Library (Bernard Moses Papers, C-B 944, Carton 2).

Gleason, R. (Ed.). (1901) *The log of the Thomas: July 23–August 21, 1901.* American Historical Collection, Manila, Philippines: Ateneo de Manila University.

Go, J. (2004). "Racism" and colonialism: Meanings of difference and ruling practices in America's Pacific empire. *Qualitative Sociology, 27*(1), 35–58.

Kipling, R. (1899). The White man's burden. *McClure's, 12.*

Kliewer, C., & Fitzgerald, L. M. (2001). Disability, schooling and the artifacts of colonialism. *Teachers College Record, 103*(3), 450–470.

Kramer, P. A. (2006). *The blood of government: Race, empire, the United States, and the Philippines.* Manila, Philippines: Ateneo de Manila Press.

Leonardo, Z., & Porter, R. K. (2010). Pedagogy of fear: Toward a Fanonian theory of "safety" in race dialogue. *Race Ethnicity and Education, 13*(2), 139–157.

Macedo, D. (2000). The colonialism of the English-only movement. *Educational Researcher, 29*(3), 15–24.

Maldonado-Torres, N. (2007). On the coloniality of being: Contributions to the development of a concept. *Cultural Studies, 21*(2/3), 240–270.

Marquardt, F. S. (2001). Life with the early American teachers. In M. Racelis & J. C. Ick (Eds.), Bearers of benevolence: The Thomasites and public education in the Philippines (pp. 23–27). Pasig City, Philippines: Anvil.

Martin, I. P. (1999). Language and institutions: Roots of bilingualism in the Philippines. In L. S. Bautista & G.O. Tan (Eds.), The Filipino bilingual: A multidisciplinary perspective (pp. 132–136). Manila: Linguistic Society of the Philippines.

May, G. A. (1980). Social engineering in the Philippines: The aims, execution, and impact of American colonial policy, 1900–1913. Westport, CT and London, UK: Greenwood.

Moses, B. (n.d.). "The work." Bancroft Library (Bernard Moses Scrapbook, Banc Mss 71/229 C, Vol. 6).

Moses, B. (1905). *Colonial enterprise* [Speech]. Bancroft Library (Bernard Moses Papers, C-B 944, Carton 1).

Our new ape men. (1900, July 1). [Clipping from *The New Haven Union* newspaper]. Bernard Moses Scrapbook, Bancroft Library, University of California, Berkeley. Banc MSS 71/229 C, Vol. 6. (Bernard Moses Papers, C-B 944, Carton 2).

Paulet, A. (2007). To change the world: The use of American Indian education in the Philippines. *History of Education Quarterly, 47*(2), 173–202.

Philippines Commission. (1903). *Public laws passed during the period from September 1, 1900, to August 31, 1902: Acts Nos. 1 to 449, Inclusive.* Manila, Philippines: Bureau of Public Printing.

Pratt, R. (1973). *Official report of the Nineteenth Annual Conference of Charities and Correction* (1892). Reprinted in Richard H. Pratt, "The advantages of mingling Indians with Whites," Americanizing the American Indians: Writings by the "Friends of the Indian," 1880–1900 (pp. 260–271). Cambridge, MA: Harvard University Press.

Quijano, A. (2000). Coloniality of power, Eurocentrism, and Latin America. Nepantla, 1(3), 533–580.

Racelis, M., & Ick, J. C. (2001) Bearers of benevolence: The Thomasites and public education in the Philippines. Pasig City, Philippines: Anvil.

Stoler, A. L. (2006). Tense and tender ties: The politics of comparison in North American history and (post)colonial studies. In A. L. Stoler (Ed.), *Haunted by empire* (pp. 23–67). Durham, NC and London, UK: Duke University Press.

Superintendent of Public Instruction. (1902). *Report to the Governor General of Hawaii.* Honolulu, HI: Bulletin.

The Southern Workmen. (1907). Hampton Normal and Agricultural Institute.

Tupas, T. R. F. (2008). Bourdieu, historical forgetting, and the problem of English in the Philippines. *Philippine Studies, 56*(1), 47–67.

Uplifting the negro. (1898, December 16). [Clipping from *The Post*]. Library of Congress (William McKinley Papers, Series 13, Box 1).

Use of the English language in schools and official business. (n.d.). Bancroft Library, (Bernard Moses Papers, C-B 944, Carton 1).

Walsh, C. E. (1991) *Pedagogy and the struggle for voice: Issues of language, power, and schooling for Puerto Ricans.* New York, NY: Bergin and Garvey.

War Department. (1901). *Annual report for the fiscal year ending June 30, 1901* (Vol. 1–4) Washington, DC: Government Printing Office.

Wexler, L. (2000). *Tender violence: Domestic visions in an age of U.S. imperialism.* Chapel Hill: University of North Carolina Press.

White, F. (1913a). *Industrial education in the Philippines Islands.* National Archives (Records of the Bureau of Insular Affairs, RG 350, 23406-16).

White, F. (1913b). *Industrial education in the Philippines Islands, Part II.* National Archives (Records of the Bureau of Insular Affairs, RG 350, 23406-16).

PART II

EDUCATION AND THE MAKING OF IDENTITIES

CHAPTER 4

KNOWLEDGE CONSTRUCTION, TRANSFORMATIVE ACADEMIC KNOWLEDGE, AND FILIPINO AMERICAN IDENTITY AND EXPERIENCE

Third Andresen
University of Washington

The purpose of this conceptual chapter is threefold. First, I will discuss Banks' (2003) stages of identity framework and utilize them to help the readers understand how the Philippine colonial history is portrayed in high school textbooks and how it influences Filipino American experiences. Second, I will discuss approaches that clarify perceptions about self and outline a brief history of Philippine colonization and its effects on student attitudes toward self. I will examine how various factors such as the legacies of colonization and limited curricula contribute to the creation of Filipino and Filipino American identity. Finally, I will discuss researchers' findings and their curriculum recommendations, including facilitating teachers to

The "Other" Students, pages 65–85

understand deficit thinking in order to deconstruct stereotypes and allow positive identity development to unfold as it relates of Filipino Americans.

The invisibility of Filipinos in U.S. history books is one of many issues surrounding Filipino identity, and it has been discussed by scholars and Filipino American community members as a substantial factor in the experiences of contemporary Filipino Americans. Cordova (1973) presents an argument that Americans have slight or no knowledge about Filipinos, and "Filipinos do not know themselves" (p. 136). Scholars such as Flores (1998), Lott (1980), San Juan (1991), and Santos (1982) also explain how the curriculum that Filipino students receive in U.S. educational institutions functions to transmit their invisibility. These scholars note that invisibility is one of the factors that made the formation of a positive Filipino American ethnic identity difficult to attain, and it has led to what Santos (1982) and Flores (1998) call ethnic confusion and inherited colonial mentality. Banks (1994) suggests that "schools should help students to clarify their ethnic, national, and global identifications for an individual can attain a healthy and reflective national identification only when he or she has acquired a healthy and reflective ethnic identification" (p. 98).

Moreover, Filipino American scholars and community members have identified internalized colonialism as a significant factor in the experiences of Filipino American students (Lott, 1980; San Juan, 1991). Internalized colonialism parallels Banks' (2003) notion of cultural psychological captivity. He defines cultural psychological captivity as a person's "negative ideologies and beliefs about his or her ethnic group that are institutionalized within society" (p. 63). It is analogous to Phinney's (1989) "diffuse" identity wherein people of color are formally educated to embrace Eurocentric cultural and historical perspectives. Karnow (1989) argues that American educational policies, which center on Western cultural-historical perspectives, affected the way Filipinos are perceived and identified in the United States. He states that Filipinos "readily accepted American styles and institutions, learned to behave, dress and eat like Americans, sing American songs, speak Americanized English and absorbed American democratic procedures, displaying unique skills in American parliamentary practices" (p. 198). In doing so, Filipinos effectively "reeducated" themselves and cultivated an identity that stemmed from what Cordova (1973) described as invisibility in society and what Flores (1998), Lott (1980), San Juan (1991), and Santos (1982) attributed to the curriculum taught to Filipino students.

Even though Filipinos established communities in the continental United States as early as 1763 in the bayous of Louisiana, "little is known about Filipinos in the United States and even less information is available in libraries, resource centers, or institutions of higher education" (Cordova, 1973 p. 4). Cordova further states that despite their involvement in preserving the United States during the War of 1812 and their contributions in the agricultural and fishing industries, Filipinos remain invisible in our society. Various scholars in the field, such as Flores (1998), Lott (1980), San Juan (1991), and Santos (1982) cite that invisibility does not only occur in larger societal views of Filipino Americans, but it is also in the curriculum they receive in educational institutions. Although I acknowledge that Filipino American families and communities play a major influence in shaping students' attitude toward self, schools have been significant instruments as well in influencing students' attitudes toward self-perception and their role in society. Foster (2005) argues that schools have become more than just a place where students come to learn. Following a progressive model, schools have become a place where students learn to think, and it is the site where students are taught to be socialized into becoming Americans (Foster, 2005).

IDENTITY FRAMEWORK

The development of a stable sense of identity is one of the central processes of childhood and adolescence. Maintaining the wholesomeness of one's identity is one of many ongoing struggles people undergo throughout adulthood. Identity dictates how individuals view themselves both as a person and in relation to ideas, nature, and others. Identity also refers to the "capacity for self-reflection and the awareness of self" (Leary & Tangney, 2003, p. 3). According to Harris (1995), it also refers to an individual's sense of uniqueness or knowing who one is. A student of color's "identity is intimately tied to how an individual responds to the socializing agents" (Spencer, 1987, p. 111). These socializing agents could be the media, literature, school, and society.

Furthermore, identity formation begins at an early age through the knowledge-construction process. Banks (2004) defines knowledge construction as the "procedure by which social, behavioral and natural science create knowledge and the manner in which the implicit cultural assumptions, frames of references, perspective and biases within discipline influence the way knowledge is constructed" (p. 4). Examining the knowledge-construction process provides insight into the students' identity issues and academic achievement. As we become adults in a culture that historically marginalizes communities of color, "we continue to experience forces, which tend to make us question who we are and which push to embrace attitudes and ideas that are alien to us" (Harris, 1995, p. 1). Phinney's (1989) "diffuse" identity, wherein people of color are formally educated to embrace Eurocentric cultural and historical perspectives, illustrates this tendency. Such internalization may lead to feelings of inferiority about self and one's ethnic or cultural group as well as feelings of shame, embarrassment, or resentment about being a person of his/her ethnicity or culture. According to Gay and Baber (1987), the terms "Oreo," "Toms," "Aunt Jemimas," and "Afro-Saxons" developed into labels of African American individuals in this stage. The terms "Banana," "Coconut," American Born Chinese (ABC), and "Popcorn," on the other hand, became labels describing assimilated Asian Pacific Islander Americans. The label symbolizes that although the appearance of an individual may be of Asian Pacific Islander heritage, their psychological and cultural attributes are based on White standards.

Banks (2003) develops a typology to describe some of the distinctions that exist between individual members and cultural groups. For example, he developed the stages of cultural identity typology, which may be useful in understanding the development of Filipino American identities. This typology presupposes that individual members of ethnic and cultural groups are at various stages of development and that these stages can be identified and described. The specific stage I am going to discuss here is *cultural psychological captivity*, which is defined by Banks as "negative ideologies and beliefs about his or her ethnic cultural group that are institutionalized within society (p. 63). This stage is when the individual has low self-esteem, feels isolated, and internalizes negative images and ideologies of his or her ethnic group. I will discuss how with this specific stage, Filipino American identity has developed a sense of self-rejection as described in cultural psychological captivity. I will also provide data that would substantiate this claim through previous and current related research.

Another relevant theory that relates to Filipino and Filipino American identity is Cross' (1991) model of "Nigrescence." Cross describes a preencounter stage that puts low or no priority on being Black. Individuals at this stage denigrate their race and place value on other aspects of their lives, like work, religion, civic involvement, or social status. The stage parallels Phinney's (1989) idea of a "diffuse" identity. Individuals in the preencounter stage are formally being educated to embrace a Western cultural-historical perspective. Preencounter Filipino Americans cannot help but experience varying degrees of miseducation when it comes to learning about the experiences of people of color (Cross, 1991).

David and Okazaki's (2006) Colonial Mentality Scale (CMS) for Filipino Americans conceptualized psychological captivity among Filipino Americans as a form of internalized oppression, which is characterized by a perception of ethnic and cultural inferiority that is believed to be a specific consequence of centuries of colonization under Spain and the United States. It involves unquestioning refutation of anything Filipino and a preference for anything American. Colonial mentality is conceptualized as an individual difference variable on which Filipino Americans likely vary in the levels of their endorsement. Five major cultural and psychological captivity themes corresponded with the Colonial Mentality Scale (CMS) for Filipino Americans. These themes include the following: (a) colonial debt or tolerating historical and contemporary oppression; (b) deficit perceptions of being Filipino; (c) deficit perceptions of other Filipinos; (d) deficit perceptions of culture; and (e) deficit perceptions of physical characteristics.

According to David and Okazaki (2006), the first theme of the CMS scale, colonial debt, is defined as tolerating historical and contemporary oppression of Filipinos and Filipino Americans. It assumes that this type of "oppression is accepted as the appropriate cost of western civilization and advancement" (p. 242). An example of this factor could be the notion that Filipinos and Filipino Americans might believe that they should feel thankful and fortunate that "Spain and United States had contact with them" (p. 245).

The second theme, deficit perceptions of being Filipino, involves feelings of inferiority, shame, embarrassment, resentment, or self-hate about being a person of Filipino heritage. An example of internal inferiority is the notion that people in situations feel ashamed of their ethnic or cultural background or that being members of their particular ethnic or cultural groups is not as good as being White.

David and Okazaki (2006) describe the third theme, deficit perception of other Filipinos or within group discrimination, as "discriminating against less-Americanized Filipinos to distance oneself from the inferior characteristics attached to being Filipino and become as American as possible" (p. 242). Similarly, Banks (2003) describes these characteristics as "avoiding situations that lead to contact with other cultural groups or striving aggressively to become highly culturally assimilated" (p. 63). An example of this would be a Filipino American making fun of, tormenting, and mocking Filipinos who are not very Americanized in their behaviors.

Deficit perception of physical characteristics is the fourth theme of colonial mentality. It is defined as believing "anything Filipino is inferior to anything White, European, or American" (David & Okazaki, 2006, p. 242). Examples of this include body image, skin tone, and material products.

David and Okazaki (2006) describe the last theme of colonial mentality as deficit perception of Filipino culture. It is the belief that all Filipino cultural things are inferior to White, European, or American cultures. Examples of this notion would be the preference for anything made in the United States, a person feeling ashamed of Filipino culture and traditions, or a person believing that there are very few prideful things about the Filipino culture.

In order to understand the influence and role of colonial mentality in schooling, Banks' (1996) concepts of mainstream and transformative academic knowledge will be discussed. Banks defines mainstream academic knowledge as "the concepts, paradigms, theories, and explanations that constitute traditional Western centric knowledge in history and the behavioral and social science" (p. 8). As a result of the mainstream academic knowledge received in school, students of color often experience cultural psychological captivity. Since identity is an important issue in communities of color, learning through a mainstream academic paradigm is a major factor in people of color's internalization of their psychological and cultural captivity. With regard to Filipino Americans' contributions and experiences in the United States, the repercussion of this captivity is invisibility or limited visibility, particularly in terms of merely acknowledging the contributions of groups of color in the classroom. To counter this invisibility, transformative academic knowledge is suggested. Banks defines transformative knowledge as "the concepts, paradigm, and explanations that challenge mainstream academic knowledge and expand the historical and literary canon" (p. 17).

This invisibility in the curriculum influences how Filipino and Filipino American students construct knowledge. As a collective, Filipinos view the long-lasting effects of 400 years of Spanish and American colonization as a "crisis of dislocation, fragmentation, uprooting, loss of tradition, and alienation" (San Juan, 1994, p. 207). Colonization forces many people of color to undergo an immeasurable spiritual and physical affliction (San Juan, 1994). The Filipino experience represents one of the outcomes of domination wherein "populations are expediently shuffled around for the sake of capital expansion" (San Juan, 1994, p. 207). On occasion, many educators are often unaware, if not uninformed, of the diversity and complexity within the Asian Pacific American student population. San Juan (1994) further explains this experience as "something most cannot even begin to fathom, let alone acknowledge distinguishing Filipinos from the Chinese, Japanese, Koreans, and others from the Asian continent" (p. 206). These factors influence Filipino American students' self-concepts and attitudes toward learning about their ethnic history and culture. Many Filipino American students subsequently face the challenge of deconstructing an immense history of subjugation to find a self-concept that positively removes them from the loss of tradition, capitalism, and the spiritual and physical ordeals of colonization.

A BRIEF HISTORY OF PHILIPPINE COLONIZATION AND EFFECTS ON THE SELF

When the United States challenged the Philippines' claim to independence and "purchased the islands from Spain for $20 million under the terms of the Treaty of Paris that ended Spanish-American War, Filipinos found themselves in another fight for their independence" (Banks, 2003, p. 431). This time they "fought for independence from the United States in the Filipino-American War" (Banks, 2003, p. 41). In U.S. high school history courses, this war was labeled the "Filipino Insurrection" and was defined as a less organized rebellion against an established authority (Espiritu, 2001). The insurrection as described by American textbooks portrays the events from an entirely U.S. perspective. According to Agoncilio (1990), the Filipinos were organized and on the brink of victory over the Spanish forces when Spain and the United States undermined the Filipino efforts by staging a mock battle wherein the United States would prevail against Spain. Recognizing a U.S. deception, General Emilio Aguinaldo, one of the Filipino upper-class revolutionary generals and first president of the Philippine Republic, declared war on the United States (Agoncilio, 1990) thus leading the Philippines into the Filipino-American War or Filipino Insurrection, as it is called in U.S. history texts.

This change in wording from *war* to *insurrection* influences Filipino American students' knowledge-construction process. In the minds of the majority of American students, it suggests the belief that Filipinos were incapable of attaining their freedom from Western dominance. In Banks' (2004) dimensions of multicultural education, the knowledge-construction process "relates to the extent to which teachers help students understand, investigate, and determine how the implicit cultural assumptions, frames of reference perspectives, and biases within a discipline influence the ways in which knowledge is constructed within it" (p. 5). By calling the Filipino-American War an *insurrection*, it implicitly suggests the idea that the Filipinos had no role in the victory over Spain, the declaration of Philippine independence was not recognized by the United States, and that the United States liberated the Philippines from Spain. This perspective affects the Filipino American identity and psyche by implying that Filipinos are an incapable group of uncivilized heathens who benefited from the "White Man's Burden" (Karnow, 1989).

Kipling, a British poet remembered for his celebration of British Imperialism, wrote the poem "White Man's Burden: The United States and the Philippine Islands" (1899) to deliberately justify the need for American occupation and consequently described Filipinos as an inferior race. This view played a major role in shaping a part of Filipino identity by instilling an eternal gratitude to the United States for helping them to establish democracy and civilization. The poem was an example of how social positionality placed a presumably inferior Filipino race squarely in an "assumption of rightness." Howard (2006), founder of the REACH center for multicultural education, defines the assumption of rightness as one of the elements of the notion of White Supremacy, whereby Whites are inclined to claim truth, fairness, and balance as their private domain. Howard further states that as Whites, "we usually don't think of ourselves as having culture: we're simply right... dominant groups don't hold 'perspectives' they hold 'truth'" (p. 54).

As mentioned earlier, David and Okazaki's (2006) definition of this indebtedness or colonial debt is "tolerating historical and contemporary oppression of Filipinos and Filipino Americans because such oppression is accepted as the appropriate cost of western civilization and advancement" (p. 242). This suggests that some Filipinos may believe that maltreatment from European American leaders in the United States is well intentioned and meant to promote the perception by the dominant group of viewing Filipinos in a positive, albeit patronizing, way (e.g., United States' "little Brown brothers").

Filipino Americanization through President McKinley's Benevolent Assimilation policies drew on this social positionality and described a distinction "not only in terms of in-group and out-group but also in terms of dominance and subordination" (Howard, 2006, p. 29). The assumption of rightness was created through the Filipino social positionality and the ensuing "truth" about their position in society. Filipinos became the "little Brown brothers" that McKinley described, and it was not long afterwards that other stereotypes of Filipinos and their roles in the U.S. economy would create an image of what and who Filipinos should become.

With this perception, scholars such as Constantino (2002) present American colonial educational policies in the Philippines as evidence to support the argument that Filipinos and Filipino Americans have developed a negative attitude toward self. After President Emilio Aguinaldo's defeat in 1901, the United States began to remold the Philippines in its own image. The most effective method of remolding and subjugating a group of people is to encapsulate their minds (Constantino, 2002). He also argues that education was also utilized as a weapon in wars of colonial conquest in order to reconstruct people's knowledge about themselves. The 1903 census reported that the primary reason for the rapid introduction of an American-style public school system in the Philippines was the "conviction of the Military leaders that no measure would so quickly promote the pacification of the islands" (U.S. Census, 1903). With this notion, the implementation of an American education policy in the Philippines was intimately connected with a larger military campaign. Karnow (1989) stated that implementing the American educational system "would Americanize the Filipinos and cement their loyalty to the United States" (p. 196). This creates the groundwork for assimilating Filipinos into a system in which Whites benefit the most. The Filipino American identity evolved from this mode of colonization. American education was instrumental in laying the groundwork for a new public school system in the Philippines that was "shaped in the American way" (Bonus, 2000, p.33). Before United States occupation, "schooling was not mandatory, was available to only a few, and was conducted in local languages" (Bonus, 2000, p.33). The United States introduced a free public education system, which opened schools to many who were formerly denied access.

Paulet (2007) argues that the model to construct this uniquely American form of endeavor was similar to the Native American educational system implemented in the United States. According to Paulet, "the goal of Americanization was accomplished by constructing schooling in the archipelago along the lines of Indian education" (p. 194). She cites that there were numerous studies of both Indian and Filipino educational polices, but none of them connect the two policies. Specifically, she mentions the investigations conducted by the Bureau of Insular Affairs in the U.S. War Department of Native American reservations to see if they could serve as a possible guide for actions in the Philippines. In addition, she and other scholars claim that the implementation of the English language curriculum was another form of Americanization. The Americanization program mandated English as the primary language of instruction in subjects "that focused on United States history and culture" (Bonus, 2000, p. 33). One of the Commission's reports from the General Superintendent for Public Instruction stated that all schools under government control "be conducted in the English language" (Philippine Commission Report, 1903). This mandate was the beginning of the Filipinos' "miseducation, for they learned no longer as Filipinos but as colonials" (Constantino, 2002, p. 181).

According to the 1901 Philippine Commission Report, English was implemented as a tool to unify the Islands and teach the American way of life. The 1900 Report of the Commissioner of Education prescribed textbooks to be used in Philippine schools that have American representations in English such as the image of George Washington, apples, children playing in the snow, and the American flag. Racelis and Ick (2001) reveal a list of suggested American and other western literature such as *Beauty and the Beast, Gulliver's Travels, Jungle Book,* and *Ragged Dick* from libraries for Philippine public schools. This indicates that the curriculum that the American educational policy used to pacify and "Americanize" the natives was in fact put into practice in Philippine schools. This cultivated in the minds of the Filipino students an idealized picture of America and what it meant to be a good American. They began to perceive the United States as "a desirable place to be and Americans in general a desirable people to emulate" (Bonus, 2000, p. 33). Many Filipinos "readily accepted American styles and institutions, learned to behave, dress and eat like Americans, sing American songs, speak Americanized English and absorbed American democratic procedures, displaying unique skills in American parliamentary practices" (Karnow, 1989, p. 198). A lot of Filipinos had effectively been "reeducated" by the U.S. education policies in the ways of the Americans and created an identity modeled by and centered on American ideology. In the process, this knowledge construction creates a Filipino American identity that rendered their Filipinoness invisible and no different from the other Asian Pacific Americans in American society.

The Philippines has been discussed in U.S. history texts as fortunate for being "blessed with American citizenship," and Filipinos were made to believe that all things American were positive (Rodriguez, Reyes-Cruz, & Olmedo, 2004, p. 291). The pattern in the Philippines demonstrates the effect of stereotypes and education created under colonial rule. Although the United States provided the Philippines free access to education, the "little Brown brothers" were seen by policymakers as inferior and often paralleled to "American Blacks" (Karnow, 1989, p. 198). Filipinos' role in American society had become fixed due to American economic and strategic interests. The policymakers believed that like African Americans, Filipinos did not have the capability to succeed academically and therefore should focus on developing their vocational skills. Anderson (1988) cites that White planters of the South believed that Blacks should be "politically disenfranchised and fitted for physical drudgery of unskilled farm and domestic labor" (p. 41). The Philippines' first governor, William Howard Taft, received reports from different advisers that "like Negroes, Filipinos were unfit for academic studies and ought to acquire practical skills as pig breeding, carpentry, handicrafts suited for a deficient race" (Karnow, 1989, p. 206). Stereotypes like these continued to shape Filipino identities as residents of the islands who gradually internalized the stereotypes that were created by their "liberators." Wealthy Filipinos, who regarded manual labor as demeaning, saw formal education "as an opportunity for their children to climb the social ladder" (Karnow, 1989, p. 206). The education system and curricula created and implemented in the Philippines by Americans were now the defining measurements of Filipino identity. As stereotypes, government reports, and historical texts relating to Filipino and Filipino American identity evolved, Filipinos assumed the identity that American colonization created and instilled through education.

Despite the structures set up by the United States to indoctrinate Filipinos into accepting and believing their own inferiority and the superiority of Americans, Filipinos "resisted attempts to be completely assimilated or to be recreated as marginal laborers 'in the White man's image'" and expressed their dissatisfaction with U.S. policies like the English-only policy by "continuing to speak their language" (Rodriguez et al., 2004, p. 290). This resistance and perspective is often overlooked, absent, or minimized in historical textbooks.

THE RESISTANCE OF COLONIZATION

Theodore De Laguna was an American philosopher who taught at Bryn Mawr College, and went to teach in the Philippines in 1901. In his description of the condition of the American educational policy, he stated that on their arrival, the teachers assigned to the Philippines were told that Filipinos were eager to learn English (De Laguna, 1903). He came to a realization through his teaching experience that the inadequacy of supplies and compulsory English immersion was attributed to the Filipinos' dismay toward the American education policy.

In 1903, recent college graduate Carter G. Woodson, an African American, also decided to leave the United States and teach in the Philippines. On the boat ride from Hong Kong to Manila, a missionary tried to persuade Woodson not to "Americanize" the Filipinos and to immerse himself in their language, culture, and history (Goggin, 1997). Woodson did not heed this advice. He was attracted to the $100 per month salary (which is equivalent to nearly $2,400 per month in today's terms) that was promised to American teachers who volunteered to work in the Philippines (Goggin, 1997). Woodson started teaching at a school in San Isidro (Nueva Ecija Province) outside of Manila. A year later, he was promoted to supervisor of schools and placed in charge of teacher training in Pangasinan (Goggin, 1997). Woodson's letters to his brother and sister inspired them to also want to teach in the Philippines, and he twice renewed his annual contract. What makes Woodson such an interesting case study is that he participated in the American colonization effort in the Philippines in the early 1900s, yet three decades later, he wrote one of the most critical and influential books on American education: *The Mis-Education of the Negro* (1933). Thus, even though Woodson did not look back at his experience in the Philippines critically, many of the ideas he later espoused could have been easily written about Filipinos as well as African Americans. For example, one of his most famous quotes from the book is the following:

> When you control a man's thinking you do not have to worry about his actions. You do not have to tell him not to stand here or go yonder. He will find his "proper place" and will stay in it. You do not need to send him to the back door. He will go without being told. In fact, if there is no back door, he will cut one for his special benefit. His education makes it necessary. (p. 6)

In many ways, Woodson's ideas in the *The Mis-Education of the Negro* echo the challenges faced by Filipinos subjected to the same American educational system that "mis-educated" African Americans and Native Americans.

George Counts was a member of the Philippine Educational Survey Commission, which was engaged in the investigation of the school system of the Philippines in 1925. He wrote the popular article "Dare a School Build a New Social Order?" and his article "Education in the Philippines" provided De Laguna's account and recommendations for an adequate justification of school reform. His main claim was that since the beginning of the 20th century, one of the most daring experiments in "human enlightenment ever attempted had been in progress in the Philippines" (Counts, 1925, p. 94). He made a connection between the Spanish influence, the language problem, the curriculum, and teaching staff as being the factors of ineffective educational policy. Counts also claimed that the accomplishments of the school system were not to be measured altogether by the "multiplication of school buildings and the growth of enrollment" (1925, p. 98). This indicated that although the schools in the Islands had grown in numbers, the quality of education was yet to be determined.

The experiences of Counts, Woodson, and De Laguna reveal that some Americans began to question the purpose and quality of colonial schooling. De Laguna witnessed Filipino resistance to the colonial educational policies instituted by the United States and documented the inadequate supplies provided to Filipino students by their American educators. Woodson encountered a missionary who cautioned against "Americanizing" Filipinos. Likewise, Counts found the American colonial educational policies to be ineffective. The observations made by these early American educators in the Philippines remain relevant to understanding the educational challenges of Filipino Americans today.

MISEDUCATION AND FILIPINO AMERICANS

When the concept of miseducation is applied to Filipino Americans, it reveals both the legacies of colonial education in the Philippines as well as the impact of those legacies on today's youth. According to Cross (1995), the "most damning aspect of miseducation is not necessarily poor mental health, but the development of a worldview and cultural-historical perspective which can block one's knowledge about, and thus one's capacity to advocate, embrace, the cultural, political, economic and historical interest" (p. 56). Although miseducation does not automatically lead to self-hatred, it most certainly distorts how people discuss cultural and historical issues (Cross, 1995). Being liberated from a Spanish education system only to be reeducated in an American system after the Spanish-American War contributed to the miseducation of Filipinos who were "socialized to favor a Eurocentric cultural perspective . . . a perspective in which notions of beauty and art derived from a White and decidedly Western aesthetic, as reflected in the content in numerous cultural and academic preferences" (Cross, 1995, p. 56).

Furthermore, when Filipino culture is invisible in the curriculum, it is difficult for Filipino youth to "carve a positive sense of self and ethnic identity because of the Philippine-U.S. colonial relationship" (Flores, 1998, p. 28). Freire (1970), a Brazilian educator and activist, further contended that because of the inferior connotations attached to their cultural and ethnic characteristics, the colonized individual might develop an intense desire to distance himself or herself from such mythical, stereotypical, and inferior identities and try to become as much like the colonizer as possible.

Lott (1980) argued that one of the greatest issues facing the Filipino American community is its "colonial mentality." This mentality "impoverishes [the colonized] tearing himself from his true self and reinforces the belief that they are psychologically and intellectually subordinate and inferior people" (p. 28). Colonization positioned the Filipino American identity in the first stage of Banks' (2003) Stages of Cultural Identity, which is cultural psychological captivity. Colonization also positions Filipino Americans in Cross' (1991) preencounter stage. Banks (2003) stated that consequently,

> The Stage 1 person [or group] exemplifies cultural group and identity during this stage and may respond in a number of ways, including avoiding situations that lead to contact with other cultural groups or striving aggressively to become highly culturally assimilated. (p. 63)

In a random sample of 1,788 high schools students in the San Diego Unified School District who completed a survey about coping with assimilation, Filipino American females had seriously considered attempting suicide within the past 12 months of the survey more than any other group (Pang, 1998). In the study, "45.6% of Filipino American women who filled out the survey had considered suicide; this compared with 33.4% among Hispanic females, 26.2% among Caucasians, and 25.3% among Black female... in addition 39.2% of Filipino females had made plans about how they would attempt suicide and 23.3% had attempted suicide" (Pang, Pak, & Kiang, 2004, p. 554). "Filipino American counselors have indicated that the findings of the survey reinforced their beliefs that Filipino American adolescents are uncertain about how to cope with cultural conflicts and social pressures to assimilate" (Pang et al., 2004, p. 554). Although colonial mentality and assimilation do not share the same definition, they are connected. These cultural conflicts such as deficit perception of ethnic self or colonial mentality are among the factors that add more pressure on the students to culturally assimilate—to give up one's cultural identity.

Lee (2005) states that cultural assimilation was understood to be a prerequisite for social economic assimilation, social mobility, and the successful achievement of the American dream. While the importance of assimilation is central to the "melting pot" metaphor, cultural assimilation to communities of color meant being subjected to Anglo conformity. Lee cites that "while immigrants may imagine an idealized America that is open and free, what they find is a society where race and White supremacy structure identities, experiences, and opportunities" (p. 3). Failure to assimilate into the dominant culture was understood to be "problematic for the immigrant, the colonized, and the larger society" (p. 8).

Espiritu (2001) conducted a study that showed the influence of this cultural identity stage when she found that Filipino American students who experienced a multicultural curriculum felt uncomfortable and resisted their own history and culture more so than their African American and Caucasian peers. Her findings described how the Filipino American students inherited "colonial attitudes" from their parents. In interpreting Philippine history, "they revered the colonizer's perspective and degraded the colonized which they viewed Spanish and American as good" (Espiritu, 2001, p. 121). Many of the Filipino American students internalized the belief that anything related to their ethnic identity was negative and that the education they received from their colonizers was assumed to be true and without fault.

Colonization creates an image of Filipinos that stems from their identification with the environment and the lessons learned in an educational system implemented by Whites. These images place Filipinos in stereotype threat of invisibility and inferiority. Steele (2003) explained that

> Stereotype threat is specially frustrating because, at each level of schooling, it affects the vanguard of these groups, those with the skills and self-confidence to have identified with the domain... ironically their susceptibility to this threat derives not from internal doubts about their ability (e.g., their internalization of the stereotype), but from their identification with the domain and the resulting concern that they have about being stereotyped in it. (p. 682)

Stereotype threat is a response that arises when intelligent students do not want to reaffirm stereotypical notions of their perceived intellectual inferiority, which can result in "disidentification and a reconceptualization of one's self and values so as to remove the domain as a self identity, as a basis of self evaluation" (Steele, 2004, p. 683). Many Filipino and Filipino American students find themselves in an identity crisis as they try to neutralize the threat of these domains and stereotypes. "Disidentification offers the retreat of not caring about the domain in relation to the self" (Steele, 2004, p. 683). With this notion, offering an opportunity to enlighten the self about Filipino and Filipino American contributions to society can have positive results.

RECOMMENDATIONS FROM SCHOLARS

The following is a discussion of researchers' findings and recommendations with regard to curriculum, including ways to facilitate effective teaching as it relates to Filipino Americans. Banks (1996) suggests that transformative academic knowledge and scholarship could be useful to reeducate Filipino American students and diminish disidentification. This type of knowledge and scholarship "has provided significant new perspectives on the experiences of ethnic groups in the United States and has helped us to transform our conceptions about the experiences of American Ethnic groups" (Banks, 1996, p. 18). With transformative academic knowledge, a reduction in the deficit thinking of Filipino American students can be achieved. Educators should also find time to understand this knowledge to decrease their own deficit thinking and invisibility by first becoming aware of the diversity and complexity of students, particularly Asian Americans. San Juan (1994) proposes that Filipino Americans should not be subsumed under the rubric of Asian Americans given their vast historical, political, and cultural differences from other Asian ethnic groups. This will allow students to construct their own thoughts and definitions of their identity (Collins, 2000).

In order for transformative knowledge and scholarship to transpire, various teaching strategies and dimensions in multicultural education must be considered. Miramontes, Nadeau, and Commins (1997) point out that knowledge is best acquired when learners "actively participate in meaningful activities that are constructive in nature and appropriate to their level of development" (p. 148). The academic achievement of students who have been historically oppressed hides the less visible but more important reason for their performance: the asymmetrical power relations of society that are reproduced in schools and the deficit view of minority students that school personnel uncritically, and often unknowingly, hold. The asymmetrical power relations between students and teachers have been a contributing factor to low academic performance and backlash. Bartolome (1994) asserts that asymmetrical power relations relegate certain groups to a subordinate status and continue to affect the way students create identities that devalue their own experiences.

When students are valued and when they are reflected in their education, the relevance and importance of academic achievement will increase. Utilizing the students' cultural datasets or cultural displays of knowledge that are inherent in their everyday experiences and scaffolding students' learning can facilitate the development of critical consciousness in youth of color. Within multicultural education, Gay (2010) provides Multicultural Education Principles and Culturally Responsive Teaching characteristics that are important in educating such ethnic groups of color as Filipino American students. Culturally responsive teaching could be utilized in deconstructing the Filipino American colonial mentality and stereotype threat. Culturally responsive teaching uses students' cultural referents, "such as their cultural knowledge, prior experiences, and performance styles to make their learning encounters more relevant and effective" (Gay, 2010, p. 136).

Some studies about the "student-of-color experience of a curriculum about self" show that history courses involving their group's history has positive effects on the students (Gay, 2010, p. 136). In other words, by including the experiences of people of color, students' cultural background, and contributions within the curricula, the self-concepts of students are improved. In addition, a curriculum involving Filipino experiences should then help to make them visible and less dependent on cultural psychological captivity or colonial mentality. Furthermore, learning about their cultural heritages aids in the elimination of the self-denigrating beliefs about their culture and helps students create a positive self-concept (Gay, 2010). Culturally responsive teaching "validates the teaching of cultural heritages of different ethnic groups in mainstream curriculum" so that students can create an ethnic identity from a non-Eurocentric perspective (Gay, 2010).

Phinney (1989, 1990) characterized ethnic identity as the part of a person's social identity and self-concept that comes from knowledge, values, attitudes, affiliations, and the emotional significance of membership within a specific ethnic group. Ladson-Billings (1992) explained that culturally responsive teachers develop intellectual, social, emotional, and political learning by "using cultural referents to impart knowledge, skills, and attitudes" (p. 382). Learning about the significant contributions of Filipinos and Filipino Americans and using their cultural datasets allows students to "perceive good prospects in the domain, that is, that one has the interest, skills, resources, and opportunities to prosper there as well as that one belongs there, in the sense of being accepted and valued in the domain" (Steele, 2004, p. 683). According to Steele, (2004), theory of domain identification is used to describe achievement barriers that are still faced by marginalized groups in schools. The theory assumes that "sustained school success requires identification with schools and its subdomains that societal pressures on these groups (e.g., economic disadvantage, gender roles)" (p. 682).

The teachers, textbooks, and schools' role in clarifying and validating student identity will help students "clarify personal attitudes and cultural identity, reduce intrapsychic conflict, and develop positive attitudes towards his or her cultural group" (Banks, 2003, p. 64). Multicultural education includes more non-Eurocentric representations of cultural diversity in curriculum content and not only involves students' experiences but validates them as well. Within such an educational system, Filipino Americans and other students would be less susceptible to stereotypes and colonial mentality while making themselves visible and viable parts of American curricula. Gay cites that "the results are improved achievements of many kinds. Among them are more clear and insightful thinking; more caring, concerned, and humane interpersonal skills" (Gay, 2010, p. 35).

Espiritu's (2001) study on *Pinoy Teach,* Filipino American students' experience in curriculum, reveals that empowerment from learning Filipino American history was the result of teaching youth about one's ethnic history and culture. *Pinoy Teach* is a 10-week multicultural curriculum that focuses on Filipino American history taught by University of Washington undergraduate students in Seattle and Bellevue public schools. The program supports the claim that culturally based curriculums increased an individual's sense of ethnic identity, which is an aspect of self-esteem (Godina, 1996). The participants in the study gained an even greater sense of empowerment by having the knowledge to refute erroneous information about the Philippines and combat prejudicial comments people made about Filipinos (Espiritu, 2001). "In addition to confidence, they became more certain of their knowledge when they were able to share it with youth" (Espiritu, 2001, p. 129).

Daus-Magbual's (2010) research on Pin@y Educational Partnership (PEP), a teaching pipeline, high school retention program, and a space for the development of critical Filipino American curriculum, teaching, and research in San Francisco, reveals that PEP teachers mentioned a loss of identity and history during their childhood and adolescent years. Daus-Magbual reports that when the participants learned about the colonial influences that shaped the identity of the Filipinos and the mass exodus from the Philippines, "PEP teachers felt angry, disappointed, and confused" (p. 122). The research participants shared that their involvement in PEP provided a "sense of agency as educators to re-remember, re-discover, and to engage others in learning Filipino and Filipino American studies" (p. 122). PEP participants' reading of Filipino and Filipino American historical narratives provided an opportunity to perceive themselves in history as agents dedicated to constructing new frames of references of being Filipino American.

Including Filipino and Filipino American history and contributions from a non-Eurocentric perspective would allow many Filipino Americans to free themselves from cultural psychological captivity and form a healthy ethnic identity. The first principle of ethnic identity formation is "participation in ethnic social networks, and therefore in activities controlled by ethnic groups" (Heller, 1987, p. 181). Students are capable of reaching Banks' fifth stage of cultural identity: the multiculturalism and reflective nationalism stage, which is the "idealized goal for citizenship identity within a culturally diverse nation" (Banks, 2003, p. 65). In this stage an individual performs at "least at minimal levels, within several cultural communities and to understand, value, and share the ideals, symbols, and institutions of several cultures" (Banks, 2003, p. 65). In learning about their ethnic contributions and other minority group contributions, Filipinos and Filipino Americans would not only have respect for their cultural heritage but for other minority heritages as well. This outcome would decrease the stereotype threat and help students identify with their academics despite the "limits on educational access... segregating school practices and restrictive cultural orientations, limits of both historical and ongoing effect" (Steele, 2004, p. 682). They would then be less susceptible to stereotypes and colonial mentality while making themselves visible and viable parts of American curricula.

The process of deconstructing the colonial internalization could be achieved through one of Banks' (2004) dimensions of multicultural education and knowledge construction. In order for knowledge construction to transpire, content integration should first take place because the "knowledge construction process cannot be included in the curriculum without content integration" (Banks, 2004, p. 4). Content integration "deals with the extent to which teachers use examples and content from a variety of cultures and groups to illustrate key concepts, principles, generalizations, and theories in their subject area or discipline" (Banks, 2004, p. 5). Espiritu (2001) recommended that when teaching a multicultural curriculum that emphasizes the history and culture of the students, teachers should consider: (1) "discussing students' ethnic backgrounds, prior knowledge, and experiences, (2) moving from safe to controversial topics, (3) learning through concepts, (4) linking learning about their ethnic history and culture to social action; and (5) acknowledging the teacher's ethnic and cultural background as an influencing factor on curriculum" (p. 130).

If these recommendations are incorporated in the curriculum, the degree of consistency among the "student's behavior, perception, and values and that of his or her group will materially affect the child's identity development" (Rotheram & Phinney, 1987, p. 216). The student learns that the colonial subjugation through education can no longer render her or him invisible because the knowledge of cultural heritage deconstructs the stereotypes and allows the student to positively and effectively develop their ethnic identity with the strength of the knowledge gained in his/her reeducation and knowledge deconstruction. Their self-concept is no longer rooted in Eurocentric ideologies but now involves "the different ethnic groups in mainstream curricula" (Gay, 2010, p. 136). Invisibility, ethnic confusion, colonial mentality, and stereotypes that shaped the Filipino and Filipino American identity would decrease. The identity created through multicultural education would incorporate content integration and cross-ethnic awareness, a "relationship between groups" that will encourage citizens to acquire the sense of intelligence, identity, and skills needed to become a reflective member of our pluralistic society (Rotheram & Phinney, 1987, p. 218).

The curriculum in schools must be transformed in order to help students develop the skills needed to participate in knowledge-construction processes (Banks, 1994). Transformative academic knowledge and the dimensions of multicultural education will help students develop higher-level thinking skills and empathy for the people who have been mistreated by the expansion and growth of the United States (Banks, 1994). Furthermore, teaching transformative academic knowledge as a construction process will develop the skills to critically analyze Filipino and Filipino American history and (a) give Filipino American youth a vehicle to develop cultural awareness, (b) mobilize the community and raise parental involvement in schools, (c) raise the self-esteem of Filipino American students, and (d) expose mainstream communities to Filipino American culture, thus reducing invisibility (Flores, 1998). If Filipino Americans and educators are given the opportunity take up these tasks, they will constitute a force not only in transforming education but improving our society as well, for education is an integral part of the struggle for a truly democratic and transformative curriculum (Constantino, 2002).

REFERENCES

Agoncilio, T. (1990). *History of the Filipino people.* Quezon City, Philippines: Garotech.

Anderson, J. D. (1988). *The education of Blacks in the south.* Chapel Hill: University of North Carolina Press.

Banks, J. A. (1994). *Multiethnic education: Theory and practice* (3rd ed.). Boston, MA: Allyn and Bacon.

Banks, J. A. (1996). *Multicultural education, transformative knowledge, and action.* New York, NY: Teachers College Press.

Banks, J. A. (2003). *Teaching strategies for ethnic studies* (7th ed.). Boston, MA: Allyn and Bacon.

Banks, J. A. (2004). Multicultural education: Historical development, dimensions, and practice. In J. Banks & C. A. M. Banks (Eds.), *Handbook of research on multicultural education* (2nd ed., pp. 3–29). San Francisco, CA: Jossey-Bass.

Bartolome, L. (1994). Beyond the methods fetish: Toward a humanizing pedagogy. *Harvard Educational Review,* 64 (2), 173–194.

Bonus, R. (2000). *Locating Filipino Americans: Ethnicity and the cultural politics of space.* Philadelphia, PA: Temple University Press.

Collins, P. H. (2000). *Black feminist thought: Knowledge, consciousness, and the politics of empowerment.* New York, NY: Routledge.

Constantino, R. (2002). Miseducation of Filipinos. In A. V. Shaw & L. H Francia (Eds.), *Vestiges of war* (pp. 177–192). New York: New York Press.

Cordova, F. (1973). The Filipino American: There's always an identity crisis. In S. Sue & N. Wagner (Eds.), *Psychological perspectives* (Vol. 1, pp. 136–139). Science and Behavior.

Cross, W. (1991). *Shades of Black: Diversity in African-American identity.* Philadelphia, PA: Temple University Press.

Cross, W. (1995). In search of Blackness and Afrocentricity: The psychology of Black identity change. In H. Blue, H. Harris, & E. E. H. Griffiths (Eds.), *Racial and ethnic identity: Psychological development and creative expression* (pp. 53–72). New York, NY: Routledge.

Counts, G. S. (1925). Education in the Philippines. *The Elementary School Journal, 26*(2), 94–106.

Daus-Magbual, R. (2010). *Political, emotional, and powerful: The transformative influence of Pin@y Educational Partnership (PEP).* (Unpublished doctoral dissertation). University of San Francisco.

David, E. J. R., & Okazaki, S. (2006). *Colonial mentality: A review and recommendation for Filipino American psychology. Cultural Diversity and Ethnic Minority Psychology, 12*(1), 1–16.

De Laguna, T. (1903). Education in the Philippines. *Gunton's Magazine,* 494.

Espiritu, P. (2001). *Collisions, conjunctions, and community: How Filipino American students experience a curriculum about self.* (Unpublished doctoral dissertation). University of Washington, Seattle.

Flores, P. (1998). Filipino American students: Actively carving a sense of identity. In V. O. Pang & L.-R. L. Cheng (Eds.), *Struggling to be heard: The unmet needs of Asian Pacific American children* (p. 351). New York: SUNY Press.

Foster, S. J. (2005). "Pinko teachers and commie educators": The National Education Association confronts the "red scare." In B. Field & L. M. Sherry (Eds.), *Explorations in curriculum history research* (pp. 387–405). Greenwich, CT: Information Age.

Freire, P. (1970). *Pedagogy of the oppressed.* New York, NY: Continuum.

Gay, G. (2010). *Culturally responsive teaching: Theory, research, and practice.* New York, NY: Teachers College Press.

Gay, G., & Baber, W. (1987). *Expressively Black. The cultural basis of ethnic identity.* Westport, CT: Praeger.

Godina, H. (1996). The canonical debate—Implementing multicultural literature and perspectives. *Journal of Adolescent & Adult Literacy, 39*(7), 544–549.

Goggin, J. (1997). *Carter G. Woodson: A life in Black history.* Baton Rouge: Louisiana State University Press.

Harris, S. (1995). Psychosocial development and Black male masculinity: Implications for counseling economically disadvantaged African American male adolescents. *Journal of Counseling & Development, 73*(3), 279–287.

Heller, M. (1987). The role of language in the formation of ethnic identity. In J. Phinney & M. Rotheram (Eds.), *Children's ethnic socialization* (pp. 180–200). Newbury Park, CA: Sage.

Howard, G. (2006). *We can't teach what we don't know.* New York, NY: Teachers College Press.

Karnow, S. (1989). *In our image.* New York, NY: Ballantine.

Kipling, R. (1899, February 12). The White man's burden. *McLure's Magazine, 12*(4), 290–291.

Ladson-Billings, G. (1992). Culturally relevant teaching. In C. A. Grant (Ed.), *Research and multicultural education* (pp. 106–121). Washington DC: Falmer.

Leary, M. R., & Tangney, J. P. (2003). *Handbook of self and identity.* New York, NY: Guilford.

Lee, S. J. (2005). *Up against Whiteness: Race, school, and immigrant youth.* New York, NY: Teachers College Press.

Lott, J. T. (1980). Migration of a mentality: The Pilipino community. In R. Endo (Ed.), *Asian Americans: Social and psychological perspectives* (Vol. 2, pp. 132–140). Palo Alto, CA: Science and Behavior Books.

Miramontes, M. B., Nadeau, A., & Commins, N. L. (1997). *Restructuring schools for linguistic diversity: Linking decision making to effective program.* New York, NY: Teachers College Columbia University.

Pang, V. O. (1998). Educating the whole child: Implications for teachers. In V. Pang & L. L. Cheng (Eds.), *Struggling to be heard: The unmet needs of Asian Pacific American children* (pp. 265–304). Albany: State University of New York Press.

Pang, V., Pak, Y., & Kiang, P. (2004). Asian Pacific American students: Challenging a biased educational system. In J. Banks & C. Banks (Eds.), *Handbook of research on multicultural education* (2nd ed., pp. 542–563). San Francisco, CA: Jossey-Bass.

Paulet, A. (2007). To change the world: The use of American Indian education in the Philippines. *History of Educational Quarterly, 47*(2), 173–202.

Phinney, J. S. (1989). Stages of ethnic identity development in minority group adolescents. *Journal of Early Adolescence, 9*(1/2), 34–39.

Phinney, J. S. (1990). Ethnic identity in adolescents and adults: Review of research. *Psychological Bulletin, 108*(3), 499–514.

Racelis, M., & Ick, J. C. (2001). *Bearers of benevolence: The Thomasites and public education in the Philippines.* Manila, Philippines: Anvil.

Rodriguez, C., Reyes-Cruz, M., & Olmedo, I. (2004). Deconstructing and contextualizing the historical and social science literature on Puerto Ricans. In J. Banks & C. Banks (Eds.), *Handbook of research on multicultural education* (2nd ed., pp. 288–313). San Francisco, CA: Jossey Bass.

Rotheram, M. J., & Phinney, J. (1987). Ethnic behavior patterns as an ethnic identity. In J. Phinney & M. Rotheram (Eds.), *Children's ethnic socialization* (pp. 201–218). Newbury Park, CA: Sage.

San Juan, E. (1991). Mapping the boundaries: Filipino writers in the USA. *The Journal of Ethnic Studies, 19*(1), 117–131.

San Juan, E. (1994). The predicament of Filipinos in the United States. In K. Aguilar (Ed.), *State of Asian America: Activism and resistance* (pp. 205–218). Boston, MA: South End.

Santos, R. (1982). The social and emotional development of Filipino American children. In G. Powell (Ed.), *The psychological development of minority group children* (pp. 131–146). New York, NY: Brunner/Mazel.

Spencer, M. (1987). Black children's ethnic formation: Risk and resilience of castelike minorities. In J. Phinney & M. Rotheram (Eds.), *Children's ethnic socialization* (pp. 103–116). Newbury Park, CA: Sage.

Steele, C. (2003). A threat in the air: How stereotypes shape intellectual identity and performance. In J. Banks & C. Banks (Eds.), *Handbook of research on multicultural education* (2nd ed., pp. 682–698). San Francisco, CA: Jossey-Bass.

U.S. Bureau of the Census. Philippine Commission. Census of the Philippine Islands. (1903). *Education under the Americans.* Washington, DC: Government Printing Office.

Woodson, C. G. (1933). *Miseducation of the Negro.* Washington, DC: Associated.

CHAPTER 5

DISAGGREGATING THE COLLEGE EXPERIENCES OF FILIPINO AMERICANS

From the Aggregate Asian American/ Pacific Islander Experience

Belinda Butler Vea
University of California

Research literature in higher education has underscored the importance of diversity to college communities. While the literature has stressed the value of examining student populations based on race/ethnicity, many studies continue to examine diverse student communities in the aggregate, particularly the Asian American and Pacific Islander (AAPI) student population. A review of the literature reveals a virtual void in the empirical study of the AAPI subpopulations (David & Okazaki, 2006a, 2006b; GAO, 2007; Maramba, 2008a, 2008b; Monzon, 2003; Nadal, 2004). Over the last few decades, research on particular AAPI subgroups in higher education has remained almost negligible, with the misperceptions that AAPIs are aca-

The "Other" Students, pages 87–102

demically successful, overrepresented, persisting, and graduating at higher rates than Whites (Hune & Chan, 1997; Yeh, 2002). A growing body of literature suggests, however, that the various AAPI cohorts are not homogeneous, based on factors such as economics, geographic location, immigration patterns, and educational attainment (Teranishi, Ceja, Antonio, Allen, & McDonough, 2004). However, still missing from the literature is empirical evidence on the impact of college and college experiences (including academic achievement and performance) of specific AAPI subgroups in postsecondary education.

Assumptions made about AAPI college students as the model minority are based on aggregated data, or at the very least, data on three prominent subgroups. According to Yeh (2002), most research tends to focus on Chinese, Japanese, and Korean Americans. This is due in part to their large representation within the United States and within higher education. These three "main" groups overshadow other subgroups, resulting in the misperception that all AAPIs are similar and can be studied as an aggregate group. When data are disaggregated, there are 43 various AAPI subgroups (GAO, 2007), whose students experience college on different levels based on various factors such as socioeconomics, cultural affinities, immigrant status, and parents' educational background. For example, in a 1997 Educational Testing Service study, AAPIs as a group appeared to be excelling in secondary education; however, when disaggregated, the data revealed high dropout rates for Filipino/as (46%), Southeast Asians (50%), and Samoans (60%) (Yeh, 2002).

Although the 2000 U.S. Census lists Filipina/os as the second-largest immigrant population, they and Southeast Asian groups continue to be a distinct minority in higher education research and literature (U.S. Census, 2000; Yeh, 2002). Therefore, for the purposes of this chapter, I discuss Filipino/a students as separate from the AAPI population. In addition, current research and literature in the fields of higher education and educational psychology on Filipina/o students and other AAPI subgroups is predominantly based on qualitative inquiry. Through interviews and focus groups, the scholarship on Filipina/o students details the impact that culture and ethnicity, familial backgrounds, and family support (Espiritu, 1994; Maramba, 2008a) have on their college experiences and overall emotional and psychological well-being. While this form of methodology gives a much-needed voice to Filipina/o students who typically are omitted from the higher education discussion (e.g., Espiritu, 1995; Maramba, 2008a, 2008b; Strobel, 2001), there remains the need to have quantitative evidence that can provide substance to those voices. Indeed, there exist a few useful quantitative studies that examine the influence of social and cultural integration of Filipina/o college students (e.g., Maramba & Museus, in press; Monzon, 2003; Museus & Maramba, 2011). However, these studies specific to Filipina/o students in higher education do not focus on their academic performance. The current study attempts to address Filipina/o student and their academic achievement.

The existing scholarship, along with institutional factors, point to the need for more empirical research on Filipina/os in higher education. For example, there is a need to address stereotypes associated with these students, their lack of representation through the educational pipeline, and their level of academic achievement. Through an analysis of quantitative data, this study seeks to add yet another dimension in understanding the impact of college on AAPIs, more specifically, the Filipina/o population.

According to Pascarella (2006), research in higher education is geared toward traditional students rather than the growing population of nontraditional college students from various ethnicities, cultures, and socioeconomic levels. A review of the literature reveals a failure to recognize the relationship between student inputs (student demographics such as ethnic designation, nativity, generational status, and parents' background as well as college experiences including work and academic responsibilities, selected major, and peer interaction) and student outcomes (academic development, classroom engagement, and institutional satisfaction) of widely divergent student populations. This relationship includes what students bring with them upon entering higher education (social, cultural, and educational capital) and how this capital matches with the process of transitioning into college and the expectations of the institution. Although some outcomes appear the same (major selection, institution selection), these students do not always share the same experiences nor will the "magnitude or even the direction of [college] impact be the same for students with different characteristics and traits" (Pascarella, 2006).

To help address concerns in the literature, the purpose of this chapter is to emphasize the need for empirical evidence on the proposition that Filipina/os students are underrepresented, face institutional barriers, and confront cultural obstacles that tend to hinder their academic achievement (Agbayani-Siewert, 2004; Agbayani-Siewert & Revilla, 1995; Alvarez, 2002; Espiritu, 1994, 1995; Okamura, 1998; Posadas, 1999a, 1999b; Strobel, 2001; Wolf, 1997). For purposes of this study, I examined 2006 data on AAPI students enrolled at the University of Western California (UWC; a pseudonym). UWC is a highly selective public university in California, with a highly diverse AAPI student population. Comparison is made between the general AAPI population to Filipina/o students as a means of illustrating how aggregated data—by race/ethnicity or within ethnic groups—can mask the realities of academic achievement and performance by individual AAPI groups (see Table 5.1).

Table 5.1 illustrates the total student population at UWC, aggregated. Table 5.2 illustrates the diversity of AAPI students enrolled at UWC, disag-

TABLE 5.1 Total UWC Student Population

Race/Ethnicity	Total UWC Enrollment	% Race/Ethnicity Subgroup by Total UWC Enrollment
American Indian/Alaskan Native	840	0.5
Black/African American	4,565	3.0
Chicano/Mexican-American	16,121	10.5
Latino/Other Spanish-American	5,477	3.6
White/Caucasian	54,122	35.3
AAPI	61,692	40.2
Other	3,128	2.0
Decline to State	7,543	4.9
University Total	**153,488**	**100.0**

TABLE 5.2 Disaggregated UWC AAPI Student Population

AAPI Subgroups	Enrollment by UWC AAPI	% AAPI Subgroup by Total UWC AAPI Enrollment
Chinese/Chinese-American	23,868	38
East Indian/Pakistani	4,553	7
Japanese/Japanese-American	5,357	9
Korean	8,444	14
Pacific Islander	698	1
Thai/Other Asian	3,963	6
Vietnamese	7,498	12
Pilipino/Filipino	7,311	12
Total	**61,692**	**100**

gregated. Table 5.1 indicates AAPIs represented slightly over 40% of the UWC student population in 2006.

Table 5.2 presents the data for the total 2006 AAPI enrollment at UWC. The data illustrate the discrepancy in size within the AAPI category. This is particularly true given the size of UWC's Chinese/Chinese American students (N = 23,868) compared to the next largest group, Koreans (N = 8,444). As such, the use of aggregated data on AAPIs in higher education does indeed mask the academic realities of smaller AAPI groups.

The study underlying this chapter examined significant factors and college experiences that influence postsecondary academic achievement, student engagement, and student satisfaction of Filipina/o students. The primary questions that guided the study were the following: Do Filipina/o students differ from AAPIs in key background characteristics, college experiences, and college outcomes? and Are the key factors that predict college experience similar or different for Filipina/o and AAPI students? Findings for this study are presented first by comparing demographic similarities between the general Filipina/o students to AAPI students, including immigrant status and parents' educational background, both of which can contribute to student academic success. And, second, the study discusses the predictors affecting Filipina/o students' academic outcomes.

CONCEPTUAL FRAMEWORK

Older research models, theoretical frameworks, or paradigms that previously excluded minority student groups are problematic when applied to underrepresented minority (URM) groups. For example, the use of traditional research methods, without revision, to study previously excluded URM groups including AAPIs and Filipina/os do not take into consideration the significant factors and experiences (such as race/ethnicity and culture) that influence student outcomes. To help address this concern, the AAPI Undergraduate Socialization Model (Vea, 2008) was developed to study the AAPI college student experience. The conceptual framework for the new model was derived from two older models for understanding college impact: Astin's Inputs-Environment-Outputs (I-E-O) Model and Theory of Involvement (1965) and Weidman's Model of Undergraduate Socialization (1989). According to Astin (1970), the relationship between student inputs and the college environment is critical in determining the predictors of student outcomes. Weidman (1989) emphasized the socializing influences experienced by undergraduates from a variety of sources, including aspects located within and outside of postsecondary institutions. The new model adapts and advances concepts from Astin and Weidman to examine Filipina/o and AAPI student inputs such as ethnicity, student characteristics, parents' demographics and education, and student experiences.

DATA SOURCE AND METHOD

In 2006, the overall AAPI population at UWC was 61,692 students or almost 42% of the total enrollment in the system. The number of AAPI respondents was 23,428 or 42% of the total UWC survey respondents (N = 58,160). Table 5.3 illustrates the distribution of the total AAPI respondents.

To measure college outcomes, the study utilized quantitative statistical analyses and included descriptive analyses and regression analyses. College outcomes were defined as (a) academic achievement, operationalized by academic development, classroom engagement, and UWC GPA satisfaction;

TABLE 5.3 2006 AAPI Enrollment and Respondents

AAPI Subgroup	Enrollment by UWC AAPI	% UWC AAPI Subgroup by Total UWC AAPI Enrollment	UWC Survey AAPI Responses	% Responses by Total UWC Survey AAPI
Chinese/Chinese-American	23,868	38	10,156	43
East Indian/Pakistani	4,553	7	1,722	7
Japanese/Japanese-American	5,357	9	1,374	6
Korean	8,444	14	2,751	12
Pacific Islander	698	1	260	1
Thai/Other Asian	3,963	6	1,564	7
Vietnamese	7,498	12	2,871	12
Pilipino/Filipino	7,311	12	2,730	12
Total	**61,692**	**100**	**23,428**	**100**

(b) student satisfaction, operationalized by institutional satisfaction; and (c) student engagement, operationalized by faculty/student engagement.

The dependent variables represented three forms of academic outcomes: (a) academic achievement, consisting of academic development, classroom engagement, and GPA satisfaction; (b) student satisfaction, measuring institutional satisfaction; and (c) student engagement, measuring faculty/student engagement. The study included two types of independent variables: (a) inputs/background (primary variables), which included student demographics and parents' background and (b) college environment/experiences (secondary variables), which included obligations/responsibilities, goals/aspirations, and socialization.

Blocked stepwise multiple regression analysis was used, with all significant levels set at $p < .001$. Variables conceptually identified as "inputs/background" independent variables and "college environment/experiences" independent variables entered as blocks in the regressions, respectively. The blocks were defined as Block 1: AAPI ethnicity; Block 2: student characteristics; Block 3: parent demographics, socioeconomic and income levels; Block 4: hours allocated per week to academic and nonacademic activities; and Block 5: peer interaction. A final block, Block 6: reasons for selecting a major, was provided only to upper division students, as no comparable item existed for lower division students. Since the upper division sample contained 11,906 cases and had a good representation among all AAPI subgroups, the item was used in this study but in a separate regression that controlled for size and student status.

RESULTS

Three major findings that emerged from the study revealed the extent to which Filipina/o and AAPI student factors and college experiences influence their college outcomes. First, among AAPIs overall, including Filipina/os, there appeared to be similarities with respect to the inputs/background variables. However, a closer examination indicated that significant differences existed between the subgroups with respect to their student characteristics and parental and familial demographics. Second, for Filipina/o respondents, several positive predictors emerged in the analyses relative to academic achievement, student satisfaction, and student engagement, including socioeconomic status, incoming student status, parents' nativity, time allocated for work and studying, peer interaction, and major selection.

Finding One: Similarities and Differences of AAPI and Filipina/os

The aggregated AAPI respondents had the following overall characteristics. Gender data showed 59% of AAPI respondents were female, and 41% were male. Data indicated that 65% of AAPI students were U.S.-born, while 12% arrived in the United States in 1991 or earlier, 7% arrived between 1992 and 1995, and 16% arrived in 1996 or later. English skills data indicated 44% of the respondents were native English speakers, while 31% learned English before they were 5 years old, 16% between 6 and 10 years old, 8% between 11and 15 years of age, and 2% after they turned 16 years old. The data on AAPI respondents who were not the first in their family to attend college indicated 74% of parents had some college and 21% of parents had no college.

With respect to AAPI parents' characteristics, 10% of mothers and 13% of fathers were born in the United States. Individual results on mothers and fathers' educational levels indicated both parents had received some formal education. More specifically, for mothers, 22% had no high school or some high school/high school degree, 12% had some college, 9% had a 2-year college degree, 32% had a 4-year college degree, and 14% had partial or completed postgraduate work. For fathers, 26% had no high school or some high school/high school degree, 11% had some college, 6% had a 2-year college degree, 28% had a 4-year college degree, and 28% had partial or completed postgraduate study. Finally, the data on income levels indicated 38% of AAPI families had income levels of less than $10,000–$49,999, there were 20% at $50,000–$79,999, a total of 36% at $80,000–$199,999, and 6% at $200,000 or more. For socioeconomic status, 25% of AAPI families were low/working-class/poor, 39% middle class, 23% upper class, and 13% wealthy.

For the group that is the focus of this chapter, Filipina/o respondents, the disaggregated data revealed somewhat different characteristics. For gender, 61% were female and 39% were male. A total of 74% of Filipina/o students were born in the United States, while 14% arrived in the United States in 1991 or earlier, 5% arrived between 1992 and 1995, and 7% arrived in 1996 or later. The rate of Filipina/os who were native English speakers was 47%, while 31% learned English before they were 5 years old, 14% learned between 6 and 10 years old, 6% learned when they were 11 to 15 years old, and 2% learned after they had turned 16 years old. The data on Filipina/o respondents who were not the first in their family to attend college revealed that 90% of Filipino parents had obtained some college education compared to 5% of parents who had not attended college at all.

Filipino parent characteristics included 9% of mothers and 16% of fathers who were born in the United States. With respect to the individual statistics for parental education levels, the data indicated both parents had attained formal education. Only 10% of Filipino mothers had no high school or some high school/high school degree, while 13% had some college, 7% had a 2-year college degree, 59% had a 4-year college degree, and 4% had some or completed postgraduate study. For Filipino fathers, 13% had no high school or some high school/high school degree, 18% had some college, and 8% had a 2-year college degree, 46% had a 4-year college degree, and 15% had some or completed postgraduate work. Family income data indicated that 18% of Filipino families had an income level of less than $10,000 to $49,000, that 23% had a level of $50,000–$79,000, that 46% had a level of $80,000–$199,999, and 4% had a level of $200,000 or above. The socioeconomic levels of Filipino families were 28% low/working class/poor, 44% middle class, 19% upper class, and 1% wealthy.

Overall, Filipino mothers had higher rates of 4-year college degrees and postgraduate study than either Filipino fathers or the general AAPI sample did. Ironically, for Filipina/o students, the positive influence typically assigned by research to the mother's higher education level is not fully realized (Okamura, 1998). Okamura found this was due in part to institutional barriers, including the lack of recruiting and outreach programs specific to Filipina/o students. The lack of support systems in place to address the specific needs of Filipina/o students is also problematic.

Finding Two: Predictors of Filipina/o College Outcomes

In light of the background and parent characteristics of Filipina/o students, distinct from the AAPI aggregate group, this study conducted further analysis to determine the factors and experiences affecting the college outcomes of Filipina/o students. College environment and experiences can either directly or indirectly effect college outcomes (Weidman, 1989).

Predictors of Academic Achievement

Predicting academic development. In predicting academic development, two sets of regressions were performed, controlling for Filipina/o only. The first set of regressions included Blocks 2–5. To accommodate for the reduced group size, the threshold was set at .05 for entry. Based on existing literature and research, the expected result was that the predominant factors influencing the academic development of Filipina/os would be the input/background variables; interestingly, that was not what the analysis showed (see Table 5.4.).

The results from the multivariate regressions revealed the R^2 accounted for 10% of the variance and indicated a moderate relationship between the input and outcome variables. A total of 21 variables entered the regression and 8 remained in the equation and kept their statistical significance at the $p < .05$ level. Among the "input" variables that entered the regression, socioeconomic status and income levels remained in the model and kept their predictive power ($\beta = .112$ and *p*-value = .00; $\beta = .074$ and *p*-value = .01, respectively). Of the "experience" variables in the regression, six variables emerged: time allocated for working in an academically related position (.075), paid employment (.097), and studying (.067) as well as peer in-

TABLE 5.4 Predictors of Academic Development for Filipina/os, Blocks 2–5

Block #/At Entry	Source	Beta	*t*	Sig.
5/Step 8-FINAL	Socioeconomic status	0.112	4.837	0.00*
	Income level	0.074	3.214	0.00*
	TA: Paid employment (related to academic interests)	0.075	3.303	0.00*
	TA: Paid employment total	0.097	3.181	0.00*
	TA: Study and other academic activities outside of class	0.067	3.271	0.00*
	PI: different political opinions	0.104	4.601	0.00*
	PI: different sexual preference	0.101	4.477	0.00*
	PI: different nationality	0.077	3.480	0.00*

Note: $R^2 = .101$, Adj. $R^2 = .098$. Socioeconomic status; 4-pt. scale: 1 = low-/working-class/poor to 4 = wealthy. Income level; 4-pt. scale: 1 = less than a $10,000 to $49,999 to 4 = $200,200 or more. Time Allocation (TA) = hours allocated per week to 4-pt. scale: 1 = 0–10 hrs., 2 = 11–20 hrs., 3 = 21–30 hrs., 4 = more than 30 hrs. Peer Interaction (PI) = interacting with students with...; 6-pt. Likert scale: 1 = Never to 6 = Very often.

* $p < .05$

teraction with students from different political opinions (.104), different sexual orientation (.101), and different nationality (.104). This suggested the amount of time allocated to work and study as well as peer interaction may be more positively related to Filipina/os' academic development, and it may be more influential than previously acknowledged factors such as culture, student characteristics, and parent-related factors.

Predicting classroom engagement. Predicting classroom engagement centers on student participation, particularly as it relates to participating in class discussions, selection of course assignments, subject integration, and class presentations. While the regressions in this area tested fewer variables, the predictors emerging from the analysis indicated Filipina/o students were more likely than not to be actively engaged in the classroom. For the regressions using Blocks 2–5, the R^2 accounted for almost 8% of the variance. Father's nativity entered the model and had a predictive power of .126, while gender entered the model with a β of –.087. Both variables remained statistically significant at the $p < .05$ level. The results suggested that in general, Filipina/o students with U.S.-born fathers were more likely than not to be actively engaged in the classroom, and that Filipinos were more likely than Filipinas to be actively in engaged in the classroom (see Table 5.5).

In the results for the regression using Blocks 2–6, which included reasons for major (RFM), 29 variables entered the regression and 7 remained in the equation and kept their statistical significance at the $p < .05$ level. The results were similar to the regressions utilizing Blocks 2–5, with the exception of including RFM choice. With respect to this variable, prestige (.083) was the only item that remained in the equation at the $p < .05$ level as a predictor of academic development.

Predicting GPA satisfaction. In assessing grade point average satisfaction as part of academic achievement, two issues emerged. For regressions using Blocks 2–5, the R^2 accounted for 2% of the variance, with the variables statistically significant at the $p < .05$ level. The results further indicated Filipina/o students who participated in precollege outreach programs

TABLE 5.5 Predictors of Classroom Engagement by Pilipino/Filipino

Block #/At Entry	Source	Beta	*t*	Sig.
2/Step 2-FINAL	Gender	–0.087	–1.989	0.05*
	Father's nativity	0.126	2.872	0.00*

Note: R^2 = .078, Adj. R^2 = .070. Gender: Dichotomous scale: 0 = male, 1 = female. Parent's nativity: Dichotomous scale: 0 = Foreign born, 1 = U.S. born.

* $p < .05$

were less satisfied with their GPA than students who did not (–.072). Other factors that related to GPA satisfaction were nativity of both mothers (.076) and fathers (.063) as well as fathers with higher levels of education (.051). Finally, the data indicated a positive relationship between students' GPA satisfaction and interactions with students with a different sexual orientation.

For regressions incorporating Blocks 2–6, the R^2 accounted for almost 4% of the variance, which reflected a weak relationship between the UWC GPA satisfaction and the independent variables. The results indicated that mother's nativity (.069) as well as interacting with students with different religious beliefs (.064) were both positive predictors (see Tables 5.6 and 5.7).

TABLE 5.6 Predictors of UC GPA Satisfaction for Filipina/os, Blocks 2–5

Block #/At Entry	Source	Beta	*t*	Sig.
5/Step 5-FINAL	Participate in ANY Outreach Program	–0.072	–3.427	0.00*
	Mother's nativity	0.076	3.331	0.01*
	Father's nativity	0.063	2.780	0.00*
	Father's education	0.051	2.449	0.01*
	PI: different sexual orientation	0.047	2.243	0.02*

Note: R^2 = .024, Adj. R^2 = .022. Participate in ANY outreach program: Dichotomous scale: 0 = no, 1 = yes. Parent's nativity; Dichotomous: 0 = Foreign born, 1 = U.S. born. Parent's education: 6-pt. scale: 1 = no high school to 6 = Post-graduate study. Peer Interaction (PI) = interacting with students with...; 6-pt. Likert scale: 1 = Never to 6 = Very often.

* $p < .05$

TABLE 5.7 Predictors of UC GPA Satisfaction for Filipina/os, Blocks 2–6 with RFM

Block #/At Entry	Source	Beta	*t*	Sig.
5/Step 6-FINAL	Mother's nativity	0.069	2.237	0.01*
	PI: different religious beliefs	0.064	2.153	0.03*
	RFM: parental desires	–0.128	–4.297	0.00*
	RFM: intellectual curiosity	0.082	2.728	0.01*
	RFM: easy	–0.067	–2.239	0.02*

Note: R^2 = .039, Adj. R^2 = .035. Parent's nativity; Dichotomous: 0 = Foreign born, 1 = U.S. born. Peer Interaction (PI) = interacting with students with...; 6-pt. Likert scale: 1 = Never to 6 = Very often. Reason for Major (RFM) = reason for selecting major...; Dichotomous: 0 = no, 1 = yes.

* $p < .05$

Predictors of Student Satisfaction and Student Engagement

Predicting institutional satisfaction. In measuring institutional satisfaction, respondents were asked to rank their overall academic and social experiences, the value of their education with respect to cost, and campus climate. In the regressions using Blocks 2–5, the R^2 accounted for 7% of the variance, and it indicated a weak relationship between the predictor variables and the outcome variable. A total of 19 variables entered the regression, and 6 remained in the equation and kept their statistical significance at the $p < .05$ level. Socioeconomic status (.072) was the only "input" variable that remained in the regression at the $p < .05$ level.

With respect to the "experience" variables, time spent studying and other academic activities (.053) and attending classes, sections, or labs (.035) were positively related to Filipina/os' institutional satisfaction. Interaction with students of different religious beliefs (.112) and different sexual orientation (.93) were also positive and statistically significant. However, interacting with students from a different social class had a negative correlation to institutional satisfaction, suggesting that for Filipina/o students, social class was not a contributing factor in their institutional satisfaction. This also suggests that Filipina/o students are more apt to benefit from social aspects related to student interaction when it comes to their overall academic and social experiences and their sense of belonging on their campus (see Table 5.8.). Regressions using Blocks 2–6 produced results similar to the previous regressions.

Predicting faculty/student engagement. With respect to faculty/student engagement, this variable measured how actively engaged students were

TABLE 5.8 Predictors of Institutional Satisfaction for Filipina/os, Block 2–5

Block #/At Entry	Source	Beta	t	Sig.
5/Step 7-FINAL	Socioeconomic status	0.072	3.468	0.00*
	TA: Study and other academic activities outside of class	0.053	2.367	0.02*
	TA: Attend classes, sections, or labs	0.035	1.556	0.12*
	PI: different religious beliefs	0.112	4.723	0.00*
	PI: different sexual orientation	0.093	3.758	0.03*
	PI: different social class	–0.070	–2.749	0.01*

Note: $R^2 = .055$, Adj. $R^2 = .052$. Socioeconomic status; 4-pt. scale: 1 = low-/working-class/poor to 4 = wealthy. Time Allocation (TA) = hours allocated per week to...; 4-pt. scale: 1 = 0–10 hrs, 2 = 11–20 hrs, 3 = 21–30 hrs, 4 = more than 30 hrs. Peer Interaction (PI) = interacting with students with...; 6-pt. Likert scale: 1 = Never to 6 = Very often.

* $p < .05$

with their faculty, through either in- or out-of-class contact, e-mail, or by taking a research-oriented seminar.

The results of the regression on faculty/student engagement tested fewer variables. The R^2 accounted for almost 3% of the variance, indicating a weak relationship between the outcome and predictor variables. Father's education was also influential (.134) in the model as well as student status (freshman versus transfer student) (.108). The results suggest Filipina/o students who had transferred into the UWC system and students whose fathers had higher levels of education were more likely to engage their faculty.

DISCUSSION AND RECOMMENDATIONS

The results of this study revealed that Filipina/o college students could not be considered as simply a homogeneous extension of their AAPI counterparts. The study also revealed that college environment and experience factors might be more significant to outcomes than previously thought, and perhaps more than student background and parent characteristics. In some instances, response variation was minimal, indicating a certain amount of homogeneity across the subgroups, particularly with respect to student characteristics and parents' demography.

In this study, influences on academic achievement were by no means standard. According to studies, parents and parents' educational background are significant contributors to students' academic achievement (Inkelas, 2006a, 2006b). Studies on Filipina/os in higher education cite parents' education and socioeconomic status as influencing factors on college outcomes (Monzon, 2003). However, in this study, such factors did not emerge as significant for Filipina/o students. For example, with respect to academic development, parent's education level did not emerge as a predictor. The same held true for student nativity, gender, generational status, and parents' nativity. Predictors of classroom engagement included gender, which had a negative association, as well as parents' nativity, which had a positive association. Positive predictors of GPA satisfaction included major selection and parents' nativity. Institutional satisfaction was positively associated with socioeconomic status, time allocation (for work and studying), peer interaction (with students from different religious backgrounds, different sexual orientation, and different race/ethnicity), and major selection. Faculty/student engagement was positively associated with only two variables, incoming student status and parents' education.

Finally, while it was expected that the aggregated results would be comparable in the comparisons made between the AAPIs, including Filipina/os, it was surprising to find similarities when the data were disaggregated. This may be due to the selectivity of the UWC system and its recruiting and admission policies. It may also be a function of the self-selection process occurring prior to students entering the UWC system.

IMPLICATIONS AND FUTURE RESEARCH

Although this is only a single study with inherent limitations such as the lack of qualitative data to add depth to the quantitative data, the results have implications for how we think about the academic achievement, student satisfaction, and student engagement of AAPIs and Filipina/os, and potentially for minority student groups in general. Common notions about academic outcomes based on sheer representation continue to promote stereotypes about AAPIs "outwhiting" Whites. This study demonstrates the importance of considering the context in which AAPIs are studied and demonstrates the importance of disaggregating data in order to study AAPIs and other minority student populations. The UWC survey exemplifies how the collection and use of disaggregated data can more accurately portray its diverse AAPI student population and subgroups such as Filipina/os.

The UWC survey can serve as a model for the type of research that can be used by policymakers to identify and plan for the differences and unique needs of minority groups and subgroups. By adopting policies that promote diversity, higher education institutions and systems will increase the likelihood of diverse peer interactions that, as the data suggest, favor positive effects on both student performance and student satisfaction. Additionally, using research policies that foster collection and analysis of disaggregated data, postsecondary institutions and systems will promote the interests of AAPI students and create the likelihood that the institution recognizes the differences between minority groups, especially AAPIs.

Using disaggregated data in future research on URMs, including AAPIs and Filipina/os, can help determine what factors and experiences influence college outcomes not currently captured from existing research. Disaggregating data promotes the creation and use of different frameworks to study ethnic and racial minority groups, including AAPIs, in higher education. Recommendations for future research include creating new models/frameworks using disaggregated data to determine if homogeneity is real or simply the result of aggregation and using data from surveys such as the UWC to help promote data collection and analysis of AAPIs, including Filipina/os. Future research should consider the intersections of culture, generational status, immigration patterns, and parent influences, and it should consider how college experiences impact college outcomes for AAPI and Filipina/o students.

REFERENCES

Agbayani-Siewert, P. (2004). Assumptions of Asian American similarity: The case of Filipino and Chinese American students. *Social Work, 49*(1), 39–51.

Agbayani-Siewert, P., & Revilla, L. (1995). Filipino Americans. In P. G. Min (Ed.), *Asian Americans: Contemporary trends and issues* (2nd ed., pp. 134–168). Thousand Oaks, CA: Sage.

Alvarez, A. N. (2002). Racial identity and Asian Americans: Supports and challenges. *New Directions For Student Services, 97,* 33–43.

Astin, A. W. (1970). The methodology of research on college impact, part one. *Sociology of Education, 43*(3), 223–254.

David, E. J. R., & Okazaki, S. (2006a). The Colonial Mentality Scale (CMS) for Filipino Americans: Scale construction and psychological implications. *Journal of Counseling Psychology, 53*(2), 241–252.

David, E. J. R., & Okazaki, S. (2006b). Colonial mentality: A review and recommendation for Filipino American psychology. *Cultural Diversity and Ethnic Minority Psychology, 12*(1), 1–16.

Espiritu, Y. L. (1994). The intersection of race, ethnicity, and class: The multiple identities of second-generation Filipinos. *Identities: Global Studies in Culture and Power, 1*(2/3), 249–273.

Espiritu, Y. L. (1995). *Filipino American lives.* Philadelphia, PA: Temple University.

GAO. (2007). *Higher education: Information sharing could help institutions identify and address challenges that some Asian American and Pacific Islander students face* (Report to Congressional Requesters). Washington, DC: U.S. Government Accountability Office.

Hune, S., & Chan, K. S. (1997). Special focus: Asian Pacific American demographic and educational trends. *American Council on Education,* (Special ed.), 39–63.

Inkelas, K. K. (2006a). Overview of literature. In K. Kurotsuchi (Ed.), *Racial attitudes and Asian Pacific Americans: Demystifying the model minority* (pp. 21–44). New York, NY: Routledge.

Inkelas, K. K. (2006b). Problem and context. In K. Kurotsuchi (Ed.), *Racial attitudes and Asian Pacific Americans: Demystifying the model minority* (pp. 1–20). New York, NY: Routledge.

Maramba, D. C. (2008a). Immigrant families and the college experience: Perspectives of Filipina Americans. *Journal of College Student Development, 49*(4), 336–350.

Maramba, D. C. (2008b). Understanding campus climate through voices of Filipino/a American college students. *College Student Journal, 42*(4), 1045–1060.

Maramba, D. C., & Museus, S. D. (in press). Examining the impact of environmental and behavioral factors on Filipino American college students' sense of belonging at a predominantly White institution. *Journal of College Student Retention, 15*(1).

Monzon, R. I. (2003). *Integration and persistence of Filipino American college students: The mediating effects of family obligation and reputation.* (Unpublished dissertation). Claremont Graduate University and San Diego State University, Claremont, CA, and San Diego, CA.

Museus, S. D., & Maramba, D. C. (2011). The impact of culture on Filipino American students' sense of belonging. *Review in Higher Education, 34*(2), 231–258.

Nadal, K. L. (2004). Filipino American identity development model. *Journal of Multicultural Counseling and Development, 32*(1), 44–61.

Okamura, J. Y. (1998). Filipino Americans as the marginalized minority. In F. Ng (Ed.), *Imagining the Filipino American diaspora* (pp. 31–58). New York, NY: Garland.

Pascarella, E. T. (2006). How college affects students: Ten directions for future research. *Journal of College Student Development, 47*(5), 508–520.

Posadas, B. M. (1999a). Contemporary issues among Filipino Americans. In B. Posadas (Ed.), *The Filipino Americans* (pp. 99–124). Westport, CT: Greenwood.

Posadas, B. M. (1999b). Filipino American identity as American identity. In B. Posadas (Ed.), *The Filipino American* (pp. 139–150). Westport, CT: Greenwood.

Strobel, L. M. (2001). *Coming full circle.* Quezon City, Philippines: Giraffe.

Teranishi, R. T., Ceja, M., Antonio, A. L., Allen, W. R., & McDonough, P. (2004). The college-choice process of Asian Pacific Americans: Ethnicity and socioeconomic class in context. *Review of Higher Education, 27*(4), 527–551.

U.S. Census. (2000). *2000 census brief: The Asian population.* Washington, DC: U.S. Bureau of the Census Government Printing Office.

Vea, B. B. (2008). *The college experiences of Filipina/o Americans and other AAPI subgroups: Disaggregating the data.* (Unpublished dissertation). Claremont Graduate University, Claremont, CA.

Weidman, J. C. (1989). Undergraduate socialization: A conceptual approach. In J. C. Smart (Ed.), *Higher education: Handbook of theory and research* (Vol. 5, pp. 289–322). New York, NY: Agathon.

Wolf, D. L. (1997). Family secrets: Transnational struggles among children of Filipino immigrants. *Sociological Perspectives, 40*(3), 457–482.

Yeh, T. L. (2002). Asian American college students who are academically at risk. *New Directions for Students, 97,* 61–71.

CHAPTER 6

COUNSELING FILIPINO AMERICAN COLLEGE STUDENTS

Promoting Identity Development, Optimal Mental Health, and Academic Success

Kevin L. Nadal
City University of New York

There has been a vast amount of literature that argues that people of color are often misdiagnosed, misunderstood, and receive ineffective psychological treatment because most research and training in the mental health fields tend to utilize White, middle-class, American values as norms (for a review, see Sue & Sue, 2008). Because of this, in 2003, the American Psychological Association (APA) published the "Guidelines on Multicultural Education, Training, Research, Practice, and Organizational Change for Psychologists," which emphasize the ethical responsibility for clinicians to be culturally competent in working with various cultural groups. Specifi-

The "Other" Students, pages 103–119

cally, psychologists and other practitioners must demonstrate cultural competence through knowledge (e.g., maintaining a breadth of information about various cultural groups), awareness (e.g., recognizing one's cultural attitudes and biases as well as how one's identity affects counseling dynamics), and skills (e.g., applying culturally effective interventions when working with different clients).

One of the difficulties in promoting cultural competence among counselors and clinicians is that many cultural groups are often overlooked or misrepresented in mental health training programs. For example, most studies in psychology that focus on Asian Americans tend to centralize around East Asian Americans, namely, Chinese, Japanese, and Korean Americans (David & Okazaki, 2006; Nadal, 2011; Root, 1997). Consequently, many Asian American ethnic groups are ignored, are falsely assumed to adhere to East Asian American values, or both. Moreover, because of the Model Minority Myth, Asian Americans are often stereotyped as being highly educated and not having any mental health problems, leading to a lack of urgency in understanding or advocating for this population. Thus, many practitioners may not receive the proper training in working with Asian American populations, resulting in the potential for ineffective or inappropriate mental health treatment for this group, particularly non–East Asian American ethnic groups.

One ethnic group that is often ignored in mental health literature is Filipino Americans. Although they are projected to become the largest Asian American population, there is disproportionately less mental health literature written on this population than any of the other major Asian American ethnic groups (David, 2010). This lack of representation of Filipino Americans is daunting for a number of reasons. First, Filipino Americans encounter a number of health and educational disparities that are opposite of the Model Minority Myth. For example, Filipino Americans tend to have a prevalence of cardiovascular disease, diabetes, gout, and obesity, while also having higher rates of high school dropouts and teen pregnancy than most other East Asian Americans (Nadal, 2011). Thus, when clinicians assume that all Asian Americans fit such stereotypes, specific needs of Filipino Americans may not be met or addressed. Second, because of the unique colonial history of the Philippines, Filipino Americans may adhere to cultural values that are different than other Asian Americans; specifically, most Filipinos tend to be Catholic and share several similar family values and systems as Latinos (Nadal, 2004). Therefore, training practices based on knowledge of East Asian American values and experiences may not be applicable or effective in working with Filipino American clients. Third, because Filipino Americans may have a phenotype that may be different than other East Asian Americans, in that they are often mistaken as Latinos, Pacific Islanders, or other racial/ethnic groups (Nadal, 2011; Nadal, Escobar, Prado, David, & Haynes, 2012; Rumbaut, 1995; Uba,

1994), their encounters with racism and discrimination may differ from what people typically assume as Asian Americans' experience. Furthermore, there have been many studies that suggest Filipino Americans may underutilize mental health services or drop out of psychotherapy earlier than other Asian American groups, suggesting the need for more education and outreach for this group (David, 2010). Finally, while Filipino Americans tend to have lower rates of treatment of mental illness than the general population, those who do seek treatment have more severe or dysfunctional psychological disorders (Sanchez & Gaw, 2007). Thus, two likely conclusions can be drawn: there may be many more Filipino Americans who do have mental health problems but do not seek treatment, and Filipino Americans with mental health problems are seeking help when it may be too late.

There are a number of barriers that may prevent Filipino Americans from seeking mental health treatment. One study found that they tend to utilize health services at low rates as a result of limited healthcare access and a lack of culturally sensitive or linguistically able service providers (Ziguras, Klimidis, Lewis, & Stuart, 2003). This trend is similar to other ethnic communities, including other Asian Americans, African Americans, and Latina/os. Thus, it is clear that there are numerous institutional barriers that prevent all people of color from seeking mental health treatment. Cultural stigma is often cited as the main reason why Filipino Americans do not seek mental health services (David, 2010; Sanchez & Gaw, 2007). Because of the Filipino cultural value of *hiya* (shame), many Filipino Americans may avoid seeking mental health treatment as it may be viewed as a sign of weakness or as a disgrace to one's family. A Filipino American individual may always feel the pressure to represent her or his family well, while avoiding bringing embarrassment or dishonor to the family. If others in the community were to discover that an individual had mental health problems, an individual may feel an overwhelming guilt, feeling that she or he is representing her or his family in a negative way. When a person has psychological problems, it may somehow be depicted as a result of a bad family system, poor parenting, a punishment from God, or as a lack of strength or spirituality (Nadal, 2011).

There are some studies that have illustrated the ways in which Filipino Americans' experiences in mental health treatment may be different than other Asian American groups. For example, while many Asian Americans (particularly East Asian Americans) are more likely to prefer directive counseling, whereby the clinician gives the client solid and practical advice, Filipino Americans are more likely to prefer an emotionally close and warm relationship with their clinicians (Nadal, 2011). Moreover, while East Asian American groups are more likely to admit to only educational and vocational concerns in counseling, Filipino Americans are more likely to discuss more personal and emotional problems (Tracey, Leong, & Glidden, 1986). So while there is indeed a stigma of mental health treatment in the Filipino American community, when an individual finally does enter mental health treatment, it may be easier for them to talk about emotional problems than other Asian Americans. The desire for emotionally close therapy relationships is preferred more often for Latino clients, signifying that Filipino Americans may have similar cultural values as Latinos, due to the 400 years of Spanish colonial rule shared by both Filipinos and Latinos (Nadal, 2011).

Instead of seeking traditional mental health treatment, Filipino Americans may be more comfortable seeking help from other lay persons, specifically general practitioners, religious leaders, or other folk healers (Gong, Gage, & Tacata, 2003). Some individuals may turn to their primary care physicians and report psychosomatic symptoms instead of mental health concerns. For example, sometimes Filipino Americans may feel stomach pains, headaches, and other ailments, which are usually due to psychological distress more so than they are to actual physiological illness. Thus, when they go to their physicians, they may be referred to mental health treatment, however, because of cultural stigma, they may not feel able to act on the referral. Similarly, some Filipino American individuals may turn to religious leaders or spiritual healers to assist them during times of distress. Filipinos who are Catholic may turn to pastoral counseling with their local priests, while others may turn to shamans and indigenous healers who may practice various nontraditional methods to assist in their mental health problems (Nadal, 2011).

MENTAL HEALTH OF FILIPINO AMERICAN COLLEGE STUDENTS

While there is a dearth of research involving Filipino Americans in general, there is even less literature involving the experiences of Filipino American college students. There have been some reports that second-generation Filipino Americans achieve lower rates of college admission and retention than East Asian Americans and that Filipino Americans tend to attain college degrees at half the rate of some East Asian American groups (Nadal, 2011; Okamura, 1998). Nadal, Pituc, Johnston, and Esparrago (2010) suggested that racial discrimination (on both interpersonal and institutional levels) might be one reason that may prevent Filipino Americans from achieving higher levels of education, in comparison to their East Asian American counterparts.

There have been even fewer studies that have focused on the mental health experiences of Filipino American college students. One study reported that Filipino American college students hold differing levels of "Asian Cultural Values" than Chinese, Korean, and Japanese American college students (Kim, Yang, Atkinson, Wolfe, & Hong, 2001). Specifically, Filipino American students indicated significantly fewer adherences to emotional self-control, family recognition through achievement, familial piety, conformity to norms, and collectivism (Kim et al., 2001). Thus, Filipino Americans may maintain cultural values that are unique to East Asian Americans, potentially impacting many factors, including their mental health, coping mechanisms, and identity development. One study revealed how gender role expectations for Filipina American female college students impact their abilities to achieve academically as well as their identity development and mental health (Maramba, 2008). A study with Filipino American graduate students emphasized how Filipino Americans often feel isolated, discriminated against, and misunderstood, which may lead to many psychological stressors and difficulty in academic success (Nadal et al., 2010). These studies support the idea that practitioners who work with Filipino American college students must be mindful of the various psychological stressors affecting this population, while considering the many ways that their experiences are unique to other Asian American groups. These studies also report that there are a number of factors that may affect academic performance, suggesting the need for further outreach and support for Filipino American students.

Some studies concentrating on Filipino American youth may provide additional insight into the experiences of Filipino American college students. One major study, which analyzed Asian American and Pacific Islander high school students through in-school interviews (N = 90,118) and in-home interviews (N = 20,745), reported that Filipino Americans exhibited more problem behaviors (i.e., aggressive and nonaggressive delinquent offenses, sexual behaviors, and substance abuse) than Chinese, Korean, and Vietnamese American youth (Choi, 2008). Furthermore, the same study reported that Filipino Americans held lower grade point averages and higher amounts of drinking and smoking than did Chinese, Korean, Vietnamese, and Native American youth. Results from this study match previous literature describing how Filipino Americans experience more educational disparities than these subgroups as well (Nadal, 2011). These findings also match previous reports that indicate that Filipinos tend to smoke and drink more than East Asian Americans and that cultural factors (e.g., alcohol abuse as a norm in Filipino culture) and experiences with racism may influence substance abuse behaviors (Nadal, 2000). As a result, practitioners who work with Filipino American students (both high school and college) must remain cognizant of potential substance abuse in this population, providing the proper prevention and rehabilitation resources if needed.

Another study involving Filipino and Chinese American high school students reported that Filipinos felt less encouraged by their teachers and counselors, while also perceiving more racial discrimination than their Chinese

American counterparts (Teranishi, 2002). Specifically, these Filipino American youth described how they were stereotyped as being "gangsters" who would not be interested or successful in college. This finding aligns with a study involving Filipino and Chinese Americans' perceptions of racial microaggressions, or subtle forms of discrimination toward people of color (Nadal, 2008). In this study, Filipino American participants reported significantly higher amounts of microaggression experiences involving being treated like a criminal or as an intellectual inferior—types of discrimination not typically experienced by Asian Americans, but rather reported by African Americans and Latinos. Similarly, a study with Filipino Americans also found that Filipino Americans are mistaken as members of different racial or ethnic groups, which often leads to microaggression experiences in which they are treated as criminal deviants, second-class citizens, and exoticized objects (Nadal et al., 2012). Accordingly, practitioners working with Filipino American college students must be aware of the unique experiences of race and racism that these students may encounter, particularly validating that their experiences may be unique to other Asian American groups. Moreover, educators must be aware of the ways that Filipino American college students may encounter racism in the classroom and on campus as well as the ways that these experiences may negatively impact academic performance.

Through these studies, it is evident that future research examining the experiences of Filipino American college students is necessary. Moreover, it is clear that there is a need for research on the mental health of Filipino American college students. Thus, the purpose of this chapter is twofold. First, the chapter will explore how various factors may affect the mental health of Filipino American college students. Specifically, we will focus on the unique racial and ethnic identity development of Filipino Americans, cultural values and conflicts experienced by this group, and how these variables affect psychological processes and development. Second, the chapter will discuss various counseling techniques that may be effective in working with Filipino American college students, including various theoretical orientations from psychology. In learning about all of these concepts, it is hoped that practitioners of all sorts (e.g., psychologists, counselors, administrators, and student affairs professionals) can develop the knowledge, awareness, and skills that are needed to be multiculturally competent in working with this population.

RACIAL AND ETHNIC IDENTITY DEVELOPMENT

There has been a growth in literature that has described how Filipino Americans may experience a racial and ethnic identity development that is different from other Asian American groups (Nadal, 2004, 2011). Some authors have noted that Filipino Americans often feel marginalized within the general Asian American community (Espiritu, 1992; Nadal, 2004, 2011; Okamura, 1998). Filipino Americans have reported that they are often viewed as the bottom of the Asian American hierarchy, and that they are often viewed as "not Asian enough" (Nadal et al., 2012). Many Filipino Americans have continued to feel discriminated against by other ethnic groups, often serving as targets of ethnic jokes as well as being underrepresented in Asian American leadership positions and allocations of funds (Okamura, 1998). This discrimination by Asian Americans has often led Filipinos to separate themselves from other Asian Americans, often affiliating themselves with Pacific Islanders, Latinos, or even their own specific racial group (Espiritu, 1992). In fact, because many Filipinos have found it to be most beneficial to identify themselves as an individual racial or ethnic group, Filipinos in the state of California successfully lobbied for California Senate Bill 1813 in which all Filipinos must be recognized as "Filipino" and not as "Asian" or "Hispanic" in state personnel surveys or statistical tabulations (Espiritu, 1992). This ethnic-specific political activism has led Filipinos to distinguish themselves from other Asian groups (e.g., civic organizations, ethnic studies departments) and might contribute to their unique identity development. For example, Filipino American children living in California would never have to identify with a racial group other than "Filipino" on statistical forms or censuses. This ethnic-specific identity can be positive, as it encourages the Filipino American individual to be aware of oneself as an ethnic being with a unique history and culture separate from other racial groups. At the same time, this identity can be perceived as less positive, as it might elicit segregation of Filipino Americans from Asian Americans completely (Nadal, 2004).

Considering all of these factors, an ethnic identity development model was proposed to examine the unique experience of Filipino Americans from other Asian American groups (Nadal, 2004, 2011). The 6-status model was modified from the Racial/Cultural Identity Development Model (Atkinson, Morten, & Sue, 1998) and the Asian American Identity Model (Sue & Sue, 1971). Newly developed statuses that can be applied specifically to Filipino Americans were added. The model is meant to be nonsequential and nonlinear, suggesting that the statuses may not transpire chronologically and that various statuses may be revisited throughout one's lifetime. Such a model may serve as a framework for counselors to understand the ethnic identity of Filipino American clients in order to provide the best therapeutic treatment for them.

Status 1: *Ethnic Awareness,* which tends to occur during childhood, is exhibited by an individual who understands that she or he is Filipino, based upon the people, traditions, and languages that she or he is surrounded by. During this time, an individuals have neutral feelings about their ethnicity;

being Filipino is simply the norm. Status 2: *Assimilation to Dominant Culture* takes form when Filipinos realize that they are different from Whites. This often results from watching mainstream television or meeting school or neighborhood friends of different ethnic backgrounds. In this status, individuals may attempt to assimilate into the dominant culture by chastising their parents' accents, rejecting Filipino foods, and associating only with White Americans. Status 3: *Social Political Awakening* arises when individuals become actively aware of how racism (on interpersonal and institutional levels) affects their life as a person of color. This status may be triggered by something negative (e.g., hearing a racial slur or being discriminated against) or even something positive (e.g., learning about the history of Asian Americans in an Ethnic Studies class). In this status, individuals may want to separate themselves from Whites and may choose to associate only with other Filipino Americans and other people of color. Status 4: *Panethnic Asian American Consciousness* is a status in which Filipino Americans adopt an Asian American identity. They associate with other Asian Americans and feel a sense of pride in being part of the general Asian American community. Status 5: *Ethnocentric Realization* occurs when a Filipino American learns or experiences the marginalization of Filipino Americans within the Asian American community. This status may be triggered by a discriminatory experience by an East Asian American or by learning of the historically marginalized experience of Filipinos within the Asian American diaspora. During this status, an individual may disassociate with all other Asian Americans (and continue to separate oneself from Whites), while choosing to explicitly form relationships with other Filipino Americans. With this status, this individual may also feel connected to African Americans, Latinos, and Pacific Islanders because of the recognition that these groups may share similar experiences with discrimination and marginalization as well as sense of pride in being "Brown." Finally, Status 6: *Introspection* reflects a time when Filipino Americans have learned to commit their life to advocating for social justice, particularly for Filipino Americans. During this time, they may be comfortable with an Asian American identity while recognizing the importance of developing alliances with Whites. Individuals in this status realize how tiresome it is to remain angry and instead utilizes their energy toward proactive positivism.

Clinicians must understand how identity impacts their Filipino American clients in order to provide the most culturally competent treatment for them. For example, if a Filipino American is assimilated and adheres to the norms of dominant culture, a goal in psychotherapy might be to assist the individual to understand how one's internalized racism may impact one's self-esteem, self-efficacy, or life satisfaction. Similarly, if a Filipino American is in a social political awakening status, it may be important for clinicians to remain cognizant of how racial issues may be a salient part of treatment.

Furthermore, clinicians must also be aware of their clients' ethnic identity development because of the potential dynamics that may occur in psychotherapy. For example, cultural mistrust (or patient suspicion toward mental health services) has been found to negatively impact Filipino Americans' inability to seek and stay in mental health services (David, 2010). If a Filipino American upholds an ethnocentric status, she or he may feel distrustful of a White or East Asian American therapist, signifying a need for such a therapist to build a stronger rapport and appease a client's doubts. Conversely, if an individual is highly assimilated, she or he may have lower levels of cultural mistrust, but they might view White therapists as being superior or all-knowing. In this type of scenario, a therapist may encourage a client to examine how such perceptions affect counseling dynamics while reflecting one's internalized oppression.

CULTURAL VALUES

There are a few cultural values that may influence a college student's mental health and their ability to address their mental health problems. First, there are many indigenous Filipino values that are said to have existed prior to colonization. As mentioned before, *hiya* describes the idea that Filipinos attempt to avoid bringing shame to themselves and their families. However, other values include *kapwa* (fellow being), *utang ng loob* (debt of reciprocity), and *pakikasama* (social acceptance). *Kapwa* refers to the connection that Filipinos may feel with one another as well as the collectivist nature of the Filipino community. *Utang ng loob* refers to the notion that Filipinos are kind and generous toward each other, particularly because they know that others will do the same for them. *Pakikasama* can be defined as one's desire to get along well with others, which sometimes means avoiding conflict. Because of all of these values, it may be difficult for many Filipino Americans to seek mental health services or to even discuss their psychological problems with any practitioner. For example, the values of *hiya* (shame) and *pakikasama* (social acceptance) may lead to the stigma of mental health services in the Filipino American community. Because individuals want to represent their families well, it may be difficult for them to ask for help. They do not want their peers to know that they are struggling with any psychological problems, so they may pretend that there is nothing wrong in their lives.

Second, because of Spanish colonization, the Philippines became a predominantly Catholic country, which has influenced various traditions and beliefs. Because of this, there are some other values that may influence views of mental health as well. One value that Filipinos may uphold is *bahala na*, which translates to "leave it up to God." Similar to many other Latino ethnic groups, many Filipinos believe in this value of fatalism. Accordingly, there are many Filipino Americans who may perceive mental health problems as a "sign" or "punishment" from God. Thus, many individuals may choose to pray instead of seeking counseling or talking about their problems with others. Others may accept their perceived "fate" from a higher power and not believe that they have any power to solve their problems or take control of their lives. Second-generation Filipino American college students may not necessarily identify with this value on a conscious level, but they may have learned and internalized this value from their immigrant parents.

Additionally, because of Spanish and American colonial rule, Filipino Americans are said to experience a colonial mentality, or the denigration of one's self and culture, which may then negatively impact an individual's psychological processes and mental health (David, 2008; David & Okazaki, 2006). Previous authors have cited that the four levels that colonial mentality can impact an individual include the following: denigration of one's self, denigration of one's culture, discrimination against those who are less acculturated, and tolerance and acceptance of contemporary oppression of one's ethnic group (David & Okazaki, 2006).

Denigration of one's self includes the ways that an individual may self-deprecate or gain low self-esteem because she or he does not fit the image or characteristics of the colonizer. Denigration of one's culture includes the ways that an individual develops negative feelings toward one's culture because the group's values, culture, or traditions do no match those of the colonizer. Discrimination against those who are less acculturated includes how individuals may judge others based on how similar their acculturation level is to the colonizer. Finally, tolerance and acceptance of contemporary oppression of one's ethnic group includes how individuals may be forgiving of oppression of one's group because she or he learned to be grateful to the colonizer.

Colonial mentality can affect both Filipino nationals (those born in the Philippines) and second-generation Filipino Americans (those born in the U.S.) on various levels, and there are many ways that colonial mentality can be harmful to one's mental health. For example, if a college student wishes she had lighter skin or a differently shaped nose, she might develop self-hatred, low self-worth, or even body image issues. Furthermore, David (2008) found that higher levels of colonial mentality were correlated with higher levels of depression. Thus, it is important for practitioners to be cognizant of the ways in which colonial mentality may manifest in their students' lives in order to protect them from potential mental health problems. Moreover, it may be necessary for higher-education practitioners to educate their students on the negative impacts of colonial mentality in order to promote healthy identities, academic success, and optimal mental health in the community.

An individual's level of acculturation or assimilation may also potentially cause an individual's psychological stress. Acculturation is defined as the systematic process wherein one cultural group comes into contact with another group and experiences changes in attitudes, values, and beliefs as they adhere to the values of the dominant society (Nadal & Sue, 2009). On the other hand, assimilation refers to a process in which members of one cultural group abandon their beliefs, values, and behaviors and fully adopt those of a new host group (Nadal, 2004). Both acculturation and assimilation may cause some distress for Filipino American college students. For instance, many Filipino American college students may struggle with acculturating into the dominant culture. An example may include a Filipina college student who may have recently immigrated to the United States and may have difficulties in speaking English in class or among her peers. She may feel discouraged, frustrated, or ashamed, which may then lead to potential mental health problems like anxiety or depression. Similarly, assimilation may also lead to psychological distress; if a student is unhappy with being Filipino, she or he may develop low self-esteem or other mental health disorders. This distress may also cause a strain on one's ability to achieve optimal academic success.

COUNSELING TECHNIQUES

As previously mentioned, it is necessary for a practitioner to become a culturally competent clinician in working with her or his clients by demonstrating one's knowledge, awareness, and skills. So far, this chapter has provided an overview of the types of mental health problems that Filipino American college students may encounter, introducing the "knowledge" component of cultural competence. This next section will highlight recommendations for practitioners to attain the "awareness" and "skills" components in working with this population. Counseling theories and interventions from the field of psychology will also be introduced in order to promote the most effective cultural approaches in working with Filipino American college students.

First, in order to gain multicultural awareness, it is essential for counselors and clinicians to be conscious of one's own attitudes, beliefs, biases, and assumptions as well as how all of these might affect a therapeutic relationship with a Filipino American client. Counselors or clinicians of any racial or ethnic background may have cultural biases, which may then influence the type of interventions and guidance they use in psychotherapy. For example, a Filipino American male college student might decide to speak with his college counselor or other higher-education practitioner about wanting to change his major from pre-med to fine arts, but the student is concerned about what his parents might say. A practitioner who may not be aware of her or his biases may automatically tell this student that it is his decision and not to worry about what his parents think. However, a practitioner who is aware of her or his biases may recognize that, while it may be acceptable in her or his culture or family to make independent decisions, it would be culturally insensitive to assume it would be acceptable in a client's culture or family.

Second, practitioners must be aware of how their race, ethnicity, gender, age, and other identities impact their work with Filipino American college students. Some Filipino American clients may have difficulty trusting or building rapport with counselors of other racial or ethnic backgrounds. David (2010) found that some Filipino Americans may have cultural mistrust toward mental health services, which aligns with previous research that has reported that people of color in general are distrustful of the mental health field. For psychotherapy specifically, it may be important for clinicians (particularly non-Filipino clinicians) to make extra efforts in building rapports with their clients in order to ensure their comfort and their likeliness to continue with therapy. Similarly, practitioners of all sorts must pay attention to how gender or age may impact interpersonal dynamics with their students as well. For example, many Filipino American men may have difficulties in expressing their emotions due to the gender-role expectations that exist in Filipino culture (Nadal, 2011). Many Filipino American men are taught (explicitly and implicitly) the importance of being masculine, strong, and emotionally restrictive. Therefore, it would be necessary for practitioners to remain cognizant of how this gender role norm might prohibit a Filipino American man from openly sharing his feelings or talking about his problems.

To become culturally competent, one must also be able to use skills that are effective with various populations. In order to do this, many counselors, clinicians, and other practitioners may turn to theoretical orientations in psychology to assist in conceptualizing their clients' or students' problems and planning clinical interventions. This next section will introduce three main theoretical orientations that may serve as a guide for working with Filipino American students. These three approaches include: Psychodynamic Theory, Cognitive Behavioral Theory, and Humanistic Theory.

Psychodynamic therapies are derived by Sigmund Freud's Psychoanalytic Theory. Using this approach, the goal of therapy is to make the unconscious conscious; this is accomplished by allowing clients to recognize ways that they may have repressed negative feelings in their life. For instance, many individuals may repress traumatic or unpleasant memories that may have an impact on their adult lives. An example may include a female student who felt emotionally neglected by her parents when she was a child; as an adult, she finds herself needing a lot of attention in order to feel validated. Another example may include a male student who always felt berated by his father throughout his life; as an adult, he develops a great deal of anxiety that impacts his academic abilities. With both of these examples, a psychodynamic clinician may use a variety of tools to assist the clients in connecting to these repressed feelings so that both can resolve some of these issues, which would hopefully lead to some improvements in their lives. Some of the tools that may be used include dream exploration (i.e., searching for meaning and symbolism in a person's dreams) or free association (i.e., allowing a client to talk openly about any topic that comes to mind, without any interruptions).

Utilizing Psychodynamic Theories, clinicians may also attempt to identify defense mechanisms that clients may use to cope with their problems. For example, it may be very common for Filipino Americans to rationalize that everything is going well in their lives, when in fact they are feeling sad, frustrated, angry, or hurt (Nadal, 2011). Furthermore, it can be common for Filipino Americans to use humor as a way of distracting themselves from their feelings in order to cover the pain that they are really feeling. This can be demonstrated by a Filipino American student who talks with an academic advisor but who laughs and makes jokes as she talks about her academic failures. Her advisor may want to address the student's humor and attempt to discover if there are other issues that the student is trying to conceal.

Finally, using the psychodynamic model, clinicians may also explore "transference" and "countertransference" in order to understand other repressed feelings and unresolved business. Transference is the set of feelings that clients hold toward their therapists, and countertransference is the set of feelings that therapists have toward their clients. Usually explorations of transference and countertransference serve as opportunities for clients to understand repressed feelings about other people in their life. For example, if a Filipino American male client has transference issues with an older female clinician, it may be possible that he perceives her as a mother figure; thus, his feelings about his mother may manifest somehow in the therapy session. Accordingly, if this clinician notices the dynamics of this relationship, she may encourage the client to talk about his feelings about their therapeutic relationship in hopes of uncovering some repressed thoughts and emotions.

Cognitive Behavioral Therapies (CBT) are a combination of approaches that focus on cognition (i.e., how one thinks) and behavior (i.e., how one behaves). This approach has been found to be very useful working with many Asian American clients who prefer more structured and directive counseling/psychotherapy (Uba, 1994). In using this theoretical orientation, the clinician may first focus on the various ways of thinking that individuals have learned throughout their life. Oftentimes, the sources of many people's problems are the faulty cognitions that they have developed. For example, if a Filipina woman grew up in a family in which she was always compared to her sisters or her cousins, she may develop the cognition that she isn't good enough or that she would never be as good as her sisters or cousins. The first step of CBT would be to help the client identify these defective thoughts and to provide her tools to counter such cognitions. Some examples of CBT approaches that she can learn include cognitive restructuring (i.e., refuting and reframing her cognitive distortions) or thought-stopping (i.e., halting one's faulty thinking immediately).

In utilizing CBT, the second step is to focus on one's behaviors. For instance, sometimes people turn to alcohol or substance abuse as a way of coping with their problems. Perhaps they do this in reaction to some of the other faulty cognitions that they have developed. There is much research that supports the finding of alcohol abuse among Filipino men, primarily because it is the socially acceptable way for them to cope with their life stressors (Nadal, 2000, 2011). If a Filipino individual's drinking is problematic and interfering with his social and occupational functioning, one goal would be to decrease his alcohol use (or to eliminate it altogether). In order to accomplish this, the CBT therapist would examine the client's cognitions as the source of the problem and provide tools and techniques to help him in reaching his goal.

Humanistic Therapies are derived from the work of Karl Rogers, Abraham Maslow, and many other psychologists in the mid-1900s. These therapies concentrate on several core concepts, including empathy, genuineness, unconditional positive regard, and self-actualization. Empathy refers to a counselor's ability to convey one's complete understanding of a client's perspective, while genuineness can be defined as a clinician's capacity to be one's real and honest self in the therapy session. Unconditional positive regard is the notion that counselors will care for their clients regardless of the situation. Finally, self-actualization is the idea that every human has the ability to reach their fullest potential psychologically, physically, spiritually, and emotionally. Clinicians will use a variety of tools in order to guide their clients in achieving this self-actualization in psychotherapy.

Humanistic Therapies may be very effective in working with Filipino Americans, particularly college students. First, demonstrating unconditional positive regard and genuineness may help to build rapport with a client who may not be accustomed to attending counseling sessions or who may not be comfortable in talking about their feelings. Because of the stigma of mental health services in the Filipino American community, these two constructs may be very important because these individuals may need the extra encouragement to feel at ease in therapy. Furthermore, humanistic therapists can be useful because they can help to validate their clients and normalize their experiences, which can be very important, because many of them often feel isolated and alone. Finally, Humanistic Therapies may especially be helpful because of the aforementioned desire for Filipino Americans to develop emotionally close and personal relationships with their therapists. Because of the values of *kapwa* (fellow being) and *pakikasama* (social acceptance), building a warm and accepting relationship may be a basic requirement in working with Filipino American college students.

CONCLUSION

This chapter explored myriad considerations for counseling Filipino American college students. First, by exploring the experiences of Filipino Americans in mental health treatment, the chapter cited the numerous obstacles that may hinder Filipino Americans in seeking mental health treatment. Concepts like racial and ethnic identity development and cultural values were introduced as potential influences of mental health problems with Filipino American college students. Finally, culturally competent counseling methods (including theoretical approaches from the field of psychology) were provided as potential guides for working with this population. It is expected throughout the chapter that individuals may have gained basic knowledge of Filipino American culture and Filipino American college students. It is hoped that the reader gains further self-awareness and develops the skillsets that will be most effective in working with this population. In doing so, various practitioners (e.g., psychologists, counselors, administrators, professors, and student affairs professionals) will be able to work with Filipino American college students in culturally competent ways.

REFERENCES

American Psychological Association. (2003). Guidelines on multicultural education, training, research, practice, and organizational change for psychologists. *American Psychologist, 58*(5), 377–402.

Atkinson, D. R., Morten, G., & Sue, D. W. (1998). *Counseling American minorities: A cross-cultural perspective.* Dubuque, IA: W.C. Brown.

Choi, Y. (2008). Diversity within: Subgroup differences of youth problem behaviors among Asian Pacific Islander American adolescents. *Journal of Community Psychology, 36*(3), 352–370.

David, E. J. R. (2008). A colonial mentality model of depression for Filipino Americans. *Cultural Diversity and Ethnic Minority Psychology, 14*(2), 118–127.

David, E. J. R. (2010). Cultural mistrust and mental health help-seeking attitudes among Filipino Americans. *Asian American Journal of Psychology, 1*(1), 57–66.

David, E. J., & Okazaki, S. (2006). Colonial mentality: A review and recommendation for Filipino American psychology. *Cultural Diversity and Ethnic Minority Psychology, 12*(1), 1–16.

Espiritu, Y. L. (1992). *Asian American panethnicity: Bridging institutions and identities.* Philadelphia, PA: Temple University Press.

Gong, F., Gage, S. L., & Tacata, L. A. (2003) Helpseeking behavior among Filipino Americans: A cultural analysis of face and language. *Journal of Community Psychology, 31,* 469–488.

Kim, B. S. K., Yang, P. H., Atkinson, D. R., Wolfe, M. M., & Hong, S. (2001). Cultural value similarities and differences among Asian American ethnic groups. *Cultural Diversity and Ethnic Minority Psychology,* 7(4), 343–361.

Maramba, D. C. (2008). Immigrant families and the college experience: Perspectives of Filipina Americans. *Journal of College Student Development, 49*(4), 336–350.

Nadal, K. L. (2000). Filipino American substance abuse: Sociocultural factors and methods of treatment. *Journal of Alcohol and Drug Education, 46*(2), 26–36.

Nadal, K. L. (2004). Filipino American identity development model. *Journal of Multicultural Counseling and Development,* (32), 44–61.

Nadal, K. L. (2008). Ethnic group membership, phenotype, and perceptions of racial discrimination for Filipino and Chinese Americans: Implications for mental health. (Unpublished doctoral dissertation). Teachers College, Columbia University, New York, NY.

Nadal, K. L. (2011). *Filipino American psychology: A handbook of theory, research, and clinical practice.* New York, NY: John Wiley & Sons.

Nadal, K. L., Escobar, K. M., Prado, G., David, E. J. R., & Haynes, K. (2012). Racial microaggressions and the Filipino American Experience: Recommendations for counseling and development. *Journal of Multicultural Counseling and Development, 40,* 156–173.

Nadal, K. L., Pituc, S. T., Johnston, M. P., & Esparrago, T. (2010). Overcoming the model minority myth: Experiences of Filipino American graduate students. *Journal of College Student Development, 51*(6), 1–13.

Nadal, K. L., & Sue, D. W. (2009). Asian American youth. In C. S. Clauss-Ehlers (Ed.), *Encyclopedia of cross-cultural school psychology* (pp. 116–122). New York, NY: Springer.

Okamura, J. Y. (1998). *Imagining the Filipino American diaspora: Transnational relations, identities, and communities.* New York, NY: Garland.

Root, M. P. P. (1997). Introduction. In M. P. P. Root (Ed.), *Filipino Americans: Transformation and identity* (pp. xi–xv). Thousand Oaks, CA: Sage.

Rumbaut, R. G. (1995). The new Californians: Comparative research findings on the educational progress of immigrant children. In W. A. Cornelius & R. G. Rumbaut (Eds.), *California's immigrant children.* La Jolla, CA: Center of U.S.-Mexican Studies, University of California, San Diego.

Sanchez, F., & Gaw, A. (2007). Mental health care of Filipino Americans. *Psychiatric Services, 58*(6), 810–815.

Sue, D. W., & Sue, D. (2008). *Counseling the culturally diverse* (5th ed.). New York, NY: John Wiley & Sons.

Sue, S., & Sue, D. W. (1971). Chinese American personality and mental health. *Amerasian Journal, 1,* 36–49.

Teranishi, R. T. (2002). Asian Pacific Americans and critical race theory: An examination of school racial climate. *Equity & Excellence in Education, 35*(2), 144–154.

Tracey, T. J., Leong, F. T., & Glidden, C. (1986). Help seeking and problem perception among Asian Americans. *Journal of Counseling Psychology, 33*(3), 331–336.
Uba, L. (1994). *Asian Americans: Personality patterns, identity, and mental health.* New York, NY: Guilford.
Ziguras, S., Klimidis, S., Lewis, J., & Stuart, G. (2003). Ethnic matching of clients and clinicians and use of mental health services by ethnic minority clients. *Psychiatric Services, 54,* 535–541.

PART III

FILIPINO AMERICAN STUDIES AND PEDAGOGIES

CHAPTER 7

STRUGGLING TO SURVIVE

Poverty, Violence, and Invisibility in the Lives of Urban Filipina/o American Youth

Allyson Tintiangco-Cubales
San Francisco State University

> Maya walked into the room like she was pissed off at the world. She measured four feet, ten inches, but she stood tall. She wore burgundy lipstick on her pierced lips and thick jet-black eyeliner drawn to accentuate her almond shaped lids. She held her hands stuffed in the pockets of her extra-large puffy jacket and wore tight faded jeans rolled up above her ankles with socks tucked into her spotless white Pumas. Immediately, she fired off a number of questions. "Who the hell are you? Why did I get called in this time? Are you gonna call my mom and dad? You probably won't get them anyway, they're always working cause they got hella jobs... Do you speak English or are you going to try to counsel me in Tagalog?" I began to introduce myself and describe the purpose of the interview. I assumed she was going to loosen up, but rather she came forth with rolling eyes and more suspicion.

After this first of several meetings with Maya, it became clear that low-income Filipinas/os in San Francisco are not only defying the "Model Minority Myth," but they are also greatly suffering from being neglected, underserved, and understudied. Maya was living in the Excelsior neighbor-

The "Other" Students, pages 123–143

hood,[1] the largest population of Filipinas/os in San Francisco. Sadly, at the time of our interviews, there were few services geared toward Filipinas/os in her community.

The information presented here should not be interpreted as a holistic view of the lives of Filipina/o American urban youth; rather, it is a discussion on the challenges that affect their academic success. Although one of my initial intentions for this project was to focus on the resiliency of Filipina/o American youth rather than presenting them as "victims," I realized through my interactions with the youth that it is necessary to first uncover their struggles before proceeding to engage their survival. Students' descriptions of their lives not only defy the misconceptions that Filipina/o Americans youth are "model minorities," they counter that "culture" is the cause of their problems. Rather, cultural practices can be viewed as a coping mechanism that many of them use to deal with economic hardship. The main purpose of this chapter is to share the experiences of urban Filipina/o American high school students and explore how poverty affects their academic lives.

Before I present my findings, I will share some general experiences of Filipina/o American youth, outline my methods for this chapter, and describe the neighborhood in which this particular population lives. I will then present, in the students' own words, descriptions of their economic hardships in their school and at home. I will end with the development of Pin@y Educational Partnerships, a teacher apprentice pipeline that aims to address the lack of Filipina/o American teachers, curriculum, and culture in the lives of urban Filipina/o American youth.

FILIPINA/O AMERICAN YOUTH

Although some researchers and policymakers point to "culture" as the reason why Filipinas/os and other Asian Americans "succeed," the same culture is often blamed for the myriad issues facing youth. These stereotypes are persistent among researchers, funders, and providers of social service programs. When I began to inquire about funding available for Filipina/o American youth services, many insisted that Filipinas/os did not need culturally specific programming. An administrator told me, "Filipino American students are doing pretty well in school, so they really do not need educational programs." With regard to mental health issues, one service provider told me that in comparison to other races, "Filipinos in America do not have that many mental health issues, and those that do, don't seek help."

In the San Francisco Bay Area, there are approximately 316,877 Filipinas/os, and about 45,793 of them reside in San Francisco County. More than a third of San Francisco's Filipina/o population resides in the district that is the subject of this study. This district has the lowest per capita income in the city and the lowest educational attainment at 71% of residents having earned less than a BA or associates degree. More than half of the residents, approximately 52%, are foreign born, and 8% are below the federal poverty level. In this same district in San Francisco, 32% speak an Asian/Pacific Island language and speak English "not well" or "not at all" (Filipina/o Community Center, 2005).

According to Zhou (2004), the key predictors of student performance that are often associated with immigrant schooling show that immigrant status, language, and class factors alone cannot explain the dropout rates of students across national-origin groups. In schools located in lower-income areas with high populations of Filipinas/os, their dropout rate greatly surpasses the general dropout rate recorded for the district, county, and state. Dropout rates are usually an indication that there is much more going on with the students themselves and the types of environments and situations to which they are exposed. These rates were the catalyst for my inquiry into the psychosocial ecology of Filipina/o students to include their experiences in their neighborhood, in their community, and at home. There is a clear need to connect the effects of poverty on these sites to their academic lives.

In the schools, students are often blamed for their failures, and this in turn can create severe internalized inferiorities and psychological trauma. These mental health issues can relate directly to the experiences of Filipina/o students, especially when measured against what is expected of them as "Asian American model minorities." Along with issue of high dropout rates, Filipinas/os are also facing other mental health–related dilemmas, such as suicide and depression.[2] Unfortunately, there has been a lack of research conducted on the reasons why Filipinas/os have these mental health issues. Some researchers problematize Filipina/o American "culture," and in some cases, this puts the blame on the parents without taking an in-depth look at the social conditions that contribute to or create the issue (Lau, 1995).

In "Family Secrets: Transnational Struggles Among Children of Filipina/o Immigrants," Wolf (1997) explores the intergenerational conflict and the role of family ideology in serving "to keep problems within the circle of immediate kin" as well as the impact of this ideology, which limits the "practice of children turning to their parents for help." Wolf points to the role of the family in influencing suicidal thoughts by creating high educational expectations, along with religious and moral restrictions on girls. As part of the problem, she also points to the resistance of Filipina/o parents to seek outside help. These difficulties result in potential neglect, and parents often getting blamed for their children's issues. Like the youth in Wolf's article, the youth in this study are searching for acceptance and recognition from their parents, teachers, and society.

Many studies about Filipina/o Americans explore very interesting questions about identity formation, group identity, family histories, labor, transnationalism, and immigration, but most of them focus on Filipina/o Americans from suburban communities (Bonus, 2000; Espiritu, 2003; Wolf, 1997). There has yet to be a comprehensive community-based research project on the lives of urban Filipina/o youth. Consequently, issues of poverty and violence are not at the center of the conversations happening in these contemporary studies.

METHODS

In this study, I used two methods of data collection: in-depth semistructured interviews and journal entries of students in a Filipina/o American studies high school course. To protect the students in the study, I have changed all of their names to pseudonyms.

Interviews

With sensitivity toward experiential knowledge, the findings in this chapter are partly based on in-depth interviews with 30 Filipina/o American youth at a high school in San Francisco. The interviews took place over 10 weeks. The interviews were conducted in two sessions (about 30 minutes each). I contacted key individuals who knew students who would best fit the criteria or list of attributes for inclusion in this study. The main criteria were to find low-income Filipina/o youth who were in their second or third year of high school and who were performing below their academic potential. The informants referred to these students as "at-risk." Out of the 30 students, 17 were immigrants and 13 were American-born. With the help of eight research assistants, each high school student was interviewed, mostly in English (some students preferred to use Tagalog words or phrases to describe certain occurrences) for about 30 minutes. The interviews were structured around the following three questions:

1. What are the main issues or problems that Filipina/o youth face today?
2. How do these issues affect your performance at school?
3. What do you feel are some ways that these problems can be solved?

Journals

To triangulate the study and to test the reliability of the interviews, I felt the need to utilize another method of data collection to confirm the emerging findings. At the same high school where I conducted the interviews, I worked with a Filipina/o American studies course to develop a journal-writing project to find out the main issues affecting their lives. The students in the class were assigned to write about the following topics: family, neighborhood/community, youth culture, gender/sexism, race/racism, school life, gangs, and poverty.

Journaling proved to be a way for the youth to share their innermost thoughts on the issues that they face, and it served as a way to document their living stories. I was inspired by methods developed by Hilary Carlip and historian Dorothy Cordova. In *Girl Power* (1995), a book of young women's writing, Carlip quotes a young woman on the introductory page: "I write because the page is the only thing that will listen to me" (p. 1). In Nomura's (2003) description of Dorothy Laigo Cordova's path-breaking creation of journal-writing groups for pioneer-generation Filipina Americans, she wrote that "journal writing can be a powerful tool in recovering personal and community history" (p. 138). In one of the first journal entries in this project, a Filipina wrote,

> I could really use this time to just sit and write and write... I think it's the best way for me to express feelings that I have inside, in a manner which I like... For a while now I've been feeling neglected.

The criteria for recruiting students to be in the course were similar to that of the interviews. The course was created for low-income Filipina/o American students who were considered "at-risk." Out of the 25 Filipinas/os in the class, 10 were interviewed for this study during the previous semester. There were 14 females and 11 males, all of whom came from low-income families. About 70% of the students were immigrants, and all of their parents were born and raised in the Philippines. Consequently, none of the students in the course had parents who attended college in the United States. Several languages other than English were spoken in their homes, including such Filipina/o languages as Ilokano, Kapangpangan, Visayan, and Tagalog.

The students wrote seven or eight journals each. After looking at nearly 200 journal entries, I noticed that there were major themes that kept reemerging in their writing: there was a connection between poverty and academic achievement. With the combination of the in-depth interviews and the journals, I also spent about 3 days a week for over a year at the school and in their neighborhood doing participant observations to supplement the interviews and journals. In the following section, I present a brief ethnography to contextualize the students' home and school lives.

"LIVING IN DA HOOD": FROM HOME TO SCHOOL

When it was new, Maya's school was the city's pride, but has since fallen on hard times. Tall metal gates circle the unmanicured grass of the football field. Faded blue and orange paint flakes off of shabby bleachers. Secret urban manifestos and signs of claimed territory, newly crafted and tagged in spray paint, are scrawled on walls and windows. The prison-like 12-foot cast-iron bars outline the school's perimeter from the front to the side entrances. From the sidewalk that surrounds the pasty-peach-colored structure, the school's storied past can be seen and almost heard. Voices of ghosts and memories live in the hallways. Blood, sweat, and tears remain in the crevices of the cracked asphalt and stain the grout of the beautiful Mexican tile that accents the moldings and the stairs. Despite its humble and aged demeanor, it stands as an edifice of San Francisco history. This high school holds the history of many people, many generations, many families, and many students from a variety of racial, ethnic, and cultural backgrounds, including Filipinas/os.

Unlike many urban high schools, this school is tucked away in the middle of a residential neighborhood. Its central location caters to young San Franciscans from the low-income areas of the Excelsior, Outer Mission, Crocker Amazon, Visitation Valley, and Sunnydale housing projects. Some students, particularly those who are Filipina/o, travel from as far as the working-class streets of the SoMa (South of Market) district in downtown San Francisco, and they ride three or four buses just to get to school. This high school prides itself on the ability to serve diverse populations and students who live in these working-class neighborhoods. Despite the school's long history of struggle, survival, and success, its reputation has been tainted by negative media portrayals, gang violence, multiple attempts at teacher reconstitution, low test scores, lack of district funding, poor faculty retention, and high student dropout rates.[3]

"IT'S HARD TO MAKE MONEY HERE": THE IMPACT OF ECONOMIC HARDSHIPS ON HOME LIFE

When school ends, Maya waits outside. She is usually picked up by her uncle. Maya comes home to a house that is not really hers. After school, she is the sole caretaker of her brother and her three cousins until around 10 p.m., when her mom comes home. Between 4 and 10 in the evening, she is the babysitter, the cook, and the maid. After she makes sure everyone is fed, she talks to her boyfriend on the phone until her mom gets home. When her teachers ask her why she doesn't do her homework, Maya has plenty of excuses: her home life does not allow her any time.

Upon meeting these students, one cannot immediately discern the nature of their home lives. They are often able to hide their family's adjustment issues and financial struggles from their teachers and friends. In some cases, their home lives have a direct impact on their academic performance and their social adaptation. Often, parents or families are blamed for their economic hardships. However, this research project, which describes the challenges faced by Filipina/o American youth with regard to home life, should not be interpreted as an attack on the Filipina/o American family. In *Homebound*, Espiritu (2003) points out that Filipina/o immigrant parents came to the United States to provide a better life for their children. All of the families in this study came to the United States to live better lives. In this pursuit, they have found themselves confronted with unbearable conditions such as poverty, occupational downgrading, and discrimination. This is the context of their living conditions.

Economic hardship is one of the most prevalent challenges facing these youth. In describing the experiences of these Filipina/o American urban youth, there is a great need to discuss the quality of their "home life." In this section, I analyze two major themes that emerged from the writings and interviews that are a result of economic hardships: overcrowding as a result of the large number of people living in their households and home-life responsibilities as a consequence of parents/guardians with multiple jobs.

Family Consolidation

After the Immigration Act of 1965, Filipina/o families in the United States began to grow in record numbers as a result of many families in the Philippines being sponsored by immigrants who had preceded them. But what happens when, in the process of migration and as a result of the high price of housing in San Francisco and other urban areas, rooms are shared and houses are full to bursting? In this chapter, I name the phenomena of overcrowding in low-income Filipina/o American households a result of "family consolidation." Family consolidation is rooted in the history of chain migration and refers to more than one nuclear family living under the same roof. Although this may not seem uncommon to the Filipina/o American experience, its effects on the family and the individual have yet to be studied.

The concept of family consolidation can be seen as a coping mechanism for Filipina/o American immigrant families. It can also be seen as being "culturally specific" and having roots in the Filipinas/o's practice of a "tribal system" versus a nuclear family system in which "the whole tribe or community is the family" (Dearing, 1997, p. 288). Although it is important to contextualize family consolidation as a "cultural" means to address the economic hardships faced by immigrant families, an analysis of the economic conditions that force these families to live together should not be overlooked. The focus on cultural explanations for multiple Filipina/o families in a single-family home can easily put the blame of overcrowding on Filipina/o cultural practices. In this discussion of "cultural deficiency," the economic root of the problem gets lost. Moreover, the cultural explanation alone does not allow for a complete understanding of how overcrowding may affect the lives of those who live in these consolidated households, because it reduces it to a cultural practice. There is a great need to look at how class creates the overcrowding situation in which Filipina/os respond with the practice of family consolidation.

When asked about their home life, students were generally open about their living conditions, and they told us that sharing crowded quarters often caused them stress and created a lack of space needed for studying and doing homework. In most cases, there were more than 10 persons living in their household. Many of the students were residing in multiple-family households in single-family homes. In *Where We Stand: Class Matters*, bell hooks writes, "Living with many bodies in a small space, one is raised with notions of property and privacy quite different from those of people who have always had room" (2003, p. 10).

When too many people live in one house, resentment and tension arise. In most cases, overcrowding is result of chain migration, resulting in multiple-family households. Some of the American-born students or those who immigrated as children find their immediate families "hosting" some of their more recently arrived relatives. Immigrant students find themselves in situations in which their immediate family is staying temporarily with relatives until they are able to rent or purchase a home of their own. One student described her home life as a "war zone." Another student, Tina, told us,

> We came last year and I live with 13 people. My auntie, uncle, their five kids, my lola (grandmother), my three brothers, my mom, and me. We stay at my auntie and uncle's 3 bedroom house in San Francisco. My auntie and uncle can act like we don't really belong. Actually, no one really knows this but we (grandmother, brothers, mom, and me) stay in the one room. It used to be the family room but they changed it to be more like a bedroom, except we sleep on the floor and because it is wood, I don't sleep well. It's sometimes kind of hard to take it, I really don't do my homework because there is nowhere to do it, but I know we don't have a lot of money to get our own place.

As we can see, Tina's family just immigrated and they are living with another family. Probably due to the lack of room in the house, the family room has been designated as their sleeping quarters. This short quote from the student's interview shows how a great deal of home-life stress could in turn affect her academic performance. She mentioned the difficulty that she faced trying to complete her assignments due to the lack of space. There is also a sense that the student feels unwanted and ashamed of her situation. This can greatly impact her self-esteem and therefore affect how she presents herself at school. Also through an interview, Tony described his situation:

> My four cousins and their parents stay with us from the Philippines. It's all weird 'cause my dad is younger than his sister but they just got here to San Francisco last year. We were pretty cool before they got here but now there is no place to think. Everywhere I go, there is one of them in front of me. I don't want to be mean and all, but they gotta hurry up and find their own place. My mom gets pissed off that I'm getting bad grades and compares me to my girl cousin who speaks English with an accent and who just came here and we go to [high school] together and she's doing better than me.

This student is part of the "host" family, and as described in his interview, he is also negatively impacted by overcrowding. Tony seemed very frustrated to have his father's sister and her family staying with them. There is a sense that before they came to stay, his home life was more stable and the space was more comfortable. It is also clear that his mother compares him to one of his cousins, and this causes some anger regarding the competition between the two teenagers.

Along with the issues of overcrowding, some of the students shared their feelings of neglect by their parents, or the lack of acceptance by relatives with whom they were currently living. In several of the interviews, students expressed feeling unwanted at home. In two of the interviews, students presented cases of feeling resentful toward their parents' decision to send them to the United States to get a "better education." Regardless of their parents' intentions, students do not feel accepted by their host families, and this can cause them to not do well in school, which undermines the real purpose of their move to the United States. During a follow-up interview, a student named Jonathan told me that over the course of 6 months, he had tried to run away five times since he had been living with his uncle. This could be due to overcrowding, but it could also have been a result of feeling neglected and not feeling accepted by his uncle.

Although there can be challenges living with so many people, many Filipina/o American immigrant families have had to resort to living with relatives out of necessity. In my own personal history, my parents lived with my father's brother, his wife, and their three children when they first arrived in the United States. When they were able to afford to buy their own home, my parents sponsored more of their siblings and their families. They in turn stayed at our home. Throughout my youth, there were between 10 and 12 people living in our house. These multiple-family households are also common among these students. Roderick said, "All my friends live with lots of their relatives. We have four families in our small place." Although he did acknowledge that his house was "small," he did not seem to believe that his situation was worse than anyone else.

On the Job(s)

An overcrowded household is only one of many consequences of the economic hardships caused by the urban economy, the lack of affordable housing in the San Francisco Bay Area, and Filipina/o immigration patterns. Many of the students' parents work more than one job. In an interview, Jemalyn stated, "We are not poor; we just have some hard times. I know my mom works two jobs and sometimes another one on the weekends, but it's because my dad doesn't want to work. He gets pains in his feet when he tries to walk."

Filipina/o employment has also been affected negatively by the souring California economy. While most Filipinas/os come to this country expecting to find more and better economic opportunities for themselves and their families, globalization as well as domestic policies, such as the Homeland Security Act and the Aviation and Transportation Security Act, are reducing the number of opportunities for Filipinas/os, according to a report by San Francisco's Filipino Community Center (2005). For example, the Filipina/o American community was particularly affected throughout the Bay Area when hundreds of airport security screeners, the majority of whom were Filipina/o, were fired in the wake of 9/11.

In some families, only one parent is working and is forced to work more than one job. Even when more than one parent is working, they are often holding down multiple jobs. These parents find work mainly in the service sector, and they are the city's janitors, housekeepers, clerks, and cooks. Many of these parents face occupational downgrading. Some have college educations from the Philippines, but they are often in positions in the United States that are not commensurate with their degrees and credentials. Reasons for this include language difficulties, racism, and the lack of curricular articulation between foriegn universities and American institutions.

Maryclaire journaled about her mother, who earned a nursing degree in the Philippines, and upon her arrival, took a job in maintenance and in a restaurant. She wrote,

> My mother works at a restaurant in the daytime and she cleans buildings at night. I don't really see her that much. I end up cooking for my little brothers when I get home. She is crazy tired when she gets home at night and sometimes doesn't even take off her uniform or her shoes when she sleeps. We don't really see her, but she says she doesn't want me to work 'til I finish high school so I just help her at home... My mom went to college in the Philippines. She has a nursing degree, but she doesn't use it here.

In her interview, Maryclaire told me that "In [our] one-bedroom apartment, I take care of my grandmother after school, plus I have to cook dinner, some meat and always rice for my two brothers. I don't know when I'll ever finish my homework." According to Maryclaire, the lack of a place, and adequate time, to do homework was detrimentally affecting her academic achievement. Many students like Maryclaire, particularly the young women, often have familial responsibilities wherein they are caring for their siblings, grandparents, and other relatives. This is often gendered reproductive labor that takes a toll on their capacity to complete academic requirements.

Because of occupational downgrading, the high cost of living in San Francisco, and low wages paid for service work, parents are often overworked and do not have an adequate amount of time to spend with their children. Many of the youth in this project have parents who work several jobs. This sometimes forces youth to be their own caregivers. They are forced to cook for themselves, and the older children are sometimes responsible for taking care of the younger siblings. This is common practice in families with parents with multiple jobs. In some cases, the students suffer academically or get stressed out about having to balance their responsibilities at school with their responsibilities at home. Due to occupational downgrading and low pay, the parents are forced to work so hard that it doesn't always allow them the time to take care of family home life. In his journal, Chris writes about his resentment toward his mom, "She [mother] doesn't know what's up. I just take off when I want. She [is] always working at the [thrift] store and at night she goes to her other job."

Unfortunately, these youth feel neglected when parents are not around. There were students who felt resentful toward their parents' inability to spend more time with them. In several of the interviews, students mentioned that they do not get any school help from their parents, not so much because of their intellectual inability but rather the lack of time that their parents had to devote to their children's schoolwork.

In some cases, the youth felt as though their parents needed help or services to deal with their problems, which included substance abuse. In one of his journals, Alan discussed his mother's drug problem and how it affects his life:

> My mom is on drugs. She left me with her sister while she gets clean and she [the sister] just [had] a baby. I sometimes don't go to school because I have to take care of my cousin when my auntie goes to work. She works all the time. Sometimes when people call her to work in the middle of the day she calls me out of school to take care of my cousin.

Because of his mother's substance abuse problem, he is forced to be in a situation in which his guardian, his auntie, works a lot. He is often left to take care of his sister and his auntie's baby. His school life becomes secondary to his responsibilities at home.

The consequences of economic hardships and poverty have a direct impact on how these students view themselves and their existence. The students' lack of space leads me to believe that the students did not feel ownership of their space and felt disenfranchised and displaced. Along with this lack of space, students shoulder adult responsibilities. Students in these circumstances may sometimes feel that they must grow up faster than their peers. It was difficult to ascertain whether or not shouldering adult responsibilities makes students more resentful or more responsible.

Acculturative Stress or Purpose

Recent studies on "acculturative stress" highlight the "mismatch" between Asian American familial obligations and the demands of American society (Fuligni, Yip, & Tseng, 2002; Zhou, 1997). Some reports have suggested that this "mismatch" creates anxiety among immigrant students. Other studies have pointed out that a developed connection to familial obligations can provide immigrant students with a sense of identity and purpose (Fuligni, 1998). This tension between acculturative stress versus familial responsibilities and its potential to have a positive effect on one's identity allows for a fruitful discussion on the role of culture among Filipina/o American students who are coping with economic hardship.

In the journals and in a discussion with the youth about their economic hardships, the question of "culture" was at the center of how they understood their parents' commitments to their families and how they responded to economic hardships they experienced. In most of the interviews, the students mentioned frustrations with their parents' or guardians' absence from home, but the students also understood the need for their parents to work, oftentimes in multiple jobs, to survive financially. In her interview, Adrienne expressed, "Filipina/o culture comes from sacrifice, but it's not the blame for why my parents sacrifice. It's hard to make money here." In her statement, she distinguishes between the economic pressure and the cultural sacrifice. Adrienne goes on to share some of her own familial strategies on how they cope with the economic hardships,

> We take care of one another and do it because that's what we have to do to be okay . . . I'm not sure if it's all about Filipino culture, but that's how my family fixes the problems that we have. Sometimes money's just really hard, and we have to do what we have to do . . . even though they're [my parents] not always around to help me with school stuff, I have their backs and they have mine.

Regardless of how culture is used to understand their experiences, many of the students like Adrienne made connections between their parents' sacrifices and pursuit of a better life for their children in the United States. In this study, it also became clear that the economic challenges they faced compromised this pursuit.

"I'M NOT IN A GANG, BUT I SEE FOLKS GETTING ALL JACKED UP": EXPOSURE TO VIOLENCE AND GANG CULTURE

Maya and her brother are not the only Filipinas/os dropped off by their parents or family members. Just standing in front of the school at 7:45 a.m., it is easy to notice that there is a trend. Maya laughs about her mother's concern for her welfare, but she doesn't mind being chauffeured to school. She feels like she can take care of herself. She says she used to be part of a gang before she moved to San Francisco. She claims that there are "girls" after her and if they ever "front" her she would not hesitate to "fuck them up." She does recognize that it is scary in the neighborhood for her brother. She shared a story about having to beat up a boy who was picking on her brother when he was in junior high. She has often made it clear that she is always ready to defend herself and her family from any type of attack.

The issue of violence constantly appeared in the students' journal entries. Many of the youth described violence as a daily occurrence, and some have become somewhat desensitized to the impact that it has on how they deal with their personal issues. In this section, I outline the experiences of these youth according to three sites of violence: in their neighborhood, at their school, and in their homes. I conclude this section with a discussion on the gangs and their relationship to violence and Filipina/o American youth culture.

Violence in the streets where these students live is commonplace. A student mentioned to me that he sees police cars around his neighborhood every day. He describes his understanding of violence in his neighborhood in the following manner:

> I see police on my street all the time because they are always trying to stop this guy from killing his wife or girlfriend. There is also a drug house only a block away, and the cops hang out on my street to keep watching them.

The student's parents keep telling him that they are going to move someday when they have enough money.

In addition, students are both witness to and perpetrator of violent acts. One Filipina journaled about the day she cut class:

> We went to drive by a ghetto place called... There [I saw] my old enemy but they still recognize me. So they hit the window [on the] passenger [side of the] car, where I was sitting... I got mad, I got out of the car and we start[ed] fighting and my homegirl was just yelling and telling me to come on. I don't know who lost; all I know is I got one hit in the face and threw a lot of hit[s]. I got [into] the car and bounc[ed] with my homegirl.

In this story, and in other journals, she talked about how violence is a means to protect oneself from being deemed "weak." She felt that the reason to engage in violence was to prevent others from imposing violence on her. In relation to this fight, she stated, "You know, that's the way we [Filipinos] are; always fighting each other." She has accepted the fact that this is a way of life and that it is inherent in being Filipina. The rationalization of these acts of violence through an internalization of stereotypes of the young woman's ethnic identity, culture, and gender gave a sense that she felt powerless in this cycle of violence. She also admitted to me that she really wishes that it did not have to be this way.

Similar to what is happening in their neighborhoods, the students are also faced with confronting violence at school. One Filipina wrote in her journal,

> School is supposed to be safe. You would think it was, with all the security guards on all the floors and at the front of the school. Yeah, and we have this huge gate around the school. Violence is not suppose [sic] to happen here but it still does.

As mentioned in Maya's story, her parents and family feel that it is unsafe for her to take the bus or walk to school. This is not an uncommon feeling among all parents and guardians of the students at this school. There have been many attempts to prevent the violence at this school by creating such rules and procedures as dress codes to eliminate students wearing their gang colors. Some students do not feel like the rules really protect them. In an interview, a Filipino student said,

> I'm not sure if you heard about the boy who got shot the other day. I heard that the one who shot him had his gun all day long at school. It sucks that we get in trouble for wearing red, but they didn't even know that guy had a gun. What's worse?

One Filipina student writes, "Our school is like a prison with gates, lots of cops, lots of fights." Another student also mentioned that he felt like his school was like a prison, and he felt that this makes students feel untrusted, and it also creates an environment that makes "kids feel crazy and just want to bust out and do something crazy." Students also say that they feel powerless when it comes to school violence. It has become so common for them that they see it as part of their school culture.

Beyond the violence that students face in their neighborhoods and in their schools, Filipina/o Americans are also experiencing violent situations in the home. Although there were only a few who admitted to either witnessing or being victim of domestic violence, it is significant to mention. I also got a sense that the students were not as willing to talk about potential violence in their homes as they were in detailing their stories in their neighborhoods and school. In one of his most compelling journals, a student writes, "My mother left that jerk because he hit her a lot. He wasn't even my dad, and I think she left because he tried to hit me when I came home late one night."

Although they did not directly present evidence of current violence in their own households, there were a few stories of "family members" that were extremely disturbing. One of the Filipina students remembers,

> When we were little I will never forget how my uncle used to take my cousin in the room and make her cry. I think he used to beat up on her. I don't think I will ever know because they moved backed to the Philippines last year.

Another Filipina mentioned having to call the police on her mother's boyfriend because he gave her mom a black eye. "I don't know why she brings guys like that into our life; they're no good for her."

Although violence occurs in many different sites for them, students in this study automatically associated violence with gangs. It was not that they thought that violence in the Filipina/o American community was rooted in gang culture. More importantly, they felt that gangs are often unfairly blamed for being the root of neighborhood and school violence. Many of the students in the class had a very oppositional view to the perspectives presented in popular media. One student journaled,

> Joining a gang is like having new brothers. They are always there for you [during] any problem. They are right there to depend [on when] you have any troubles. Gangs are just out there and some of them are against each other. Members are sometimes get killed . . . I still remember my cousin's friend used to be in gang, but he didn't die because he was in a gang. He died because like Rudy [Rudy Corpuz, from United Playaz, a gang prevention program in San Francisco] says, it's because of how many guns are out on our streets.

In contrast to the focus of the popular media on gang violence and their criminal or illegal activities, Alsaybar (1999) argues against the demonization of Filipina/o gang members. He writes, "Gangs and other youth groups interact in everyday life, bound together by participation in a social network cutting across ethnic, spatial, and class boundaries." While much of the early literature on Filipinas/os focuses on gang membership, it is interesting and important to note that the violence in the lives of the youth in this study had little relationship with gangs or membership in a gang. Furthermore, most of the youth in this study, like those in Alsaybar's study, view gangs as being similar to a *barkada,* "the indigenous peer grouping suffused by an egalitarian orientation emphasizing mutual caring, loyalty, and friendship that often tends to run deeper than blood relationships" (p. 132).

Whether gang-related or, in most cases, not, we must not ignore violence that occurs in the lives of these youth. The Services and Advocacy for Asian Youth (SAAY) report (2004) notes that among all Asians, it was the Chinese, Vietnamese, and Filipino youth who had the highest arrest rates between 1990 and 2000. During 1999, Chinese, Samoan, and Filipina/o youths constituted the largest numbers among all API groups receiving institutional placement outside of their homes. In their 2002 community needs assessment, San Francisco's Department of Children, Youth, and their Families (DCYF) recognized Filipina/o youth along with African Americans, Latinos, and Vietnamese youth as having an inequitable amount of resources and services despite their great need.

"MOST OF OUR TEACHERS ARE WHITE AND WE'RE NOT IN THE HISTORY BOOKS": THE LACK OF FILIPINO/A AMERICAN TEACHERS AND CURRICULUM

> After a couple of months, Maya really loosened up and began to share with me her thoughts about education. She told me she hated school because it was boring. I asked her why it was boring, and she basically said that there was nothing for her at school. She admitted that she looked forward to our conversations because she liked talking to an adult that kind of looked like her and was interested in her future. I asked her if she learned anything in school about her identity as Filipina American and she stated, "Hell no, we just learn about White folks and maybe a little about Blacks and Mexicans but never about being Filipino. It's kinda messed up, but I guess that's the way it is. Maybe that's why I hate going to school. Yeah, most of our teachers are White and we're not in the history books, but I guess that's the way it is."

Maya's comments on the lack of Filipina/o American teachers and curriculum represent the perspectives of many of the students in this study.

When asked if it matters to their academic success to have Filipino teachers, students overwhelmingly said yes, but interestingly, students were more descriptive about what type of Filipino teacher they needed. One student said, "It's not just having them [teachers] be Filipino, they have to about care about Filipinos too." This same student when on to say that "It takes more than having them just speak Tagalog to relate to us; they need to understand what we go through."

Teacher identity is an understudied variable in Filipino student achievement, but for the students in this study, it seems to be a major factor in how they view schooling. When asked if they wanted more Filipino teachers, almost all the students raised their hands to say yes. When asked why they felt like they needed Filipino teachers, Jonathan said, "We need Filipino teachers. It's like TV, we need hella more Filipinos on TV, so we could know we could be like them. You know, be able to be somebody or do something with ourselves."

Linda quickly followed up and pointed out that there were Filipino teachers at their school but, "If they hire Filipinos, they only hire the ones from the Philippines." This poses a very complex dilemma in finding teachers who can best serve Filipina/o American students. Regardless of being Filipina/o, it may be challenging for someone who received their schooling from the Philippines to know how to effectively teach Filipinas/os in the United States without training that helps them learn about the issues that the Filipina/o American youth face. In a journal entry, Allan, a senior who was born in the United States, described his favorite teacher:

> I know it might sound weird but he's like a father to me. I have a dad, but then I never see him 'cause he is always out gambling. Mr. Lopez is tough on me and everything, but I can talk to him. He's like Filipino but he's like American born like me and knows how it is... He's like always there when you need him, and he likes to talk to us about being Filipino.

Students in the study seem to value the need to have teachers who reflect their identity, regardless of whether the teacher was born in the United States or in the Philippines. What would help the students the most is teachers getting to know the issues that the students face and be willing to find ways to address them.

Along with the lack of effective Filipino teachers, there is also a lack of curriculum that reflects the Filipina/o American experience. During one of our research sessions, Angel stated, "I wish we could learn about Filipino stuff in our classes. Why can't we have classes that talk about us?" This simple request began an extensive discussion between my research assistants and me about how we planned on using all of our data and how we wanted to address the issues that our subjects were facing. Through negotiation and partnership, we were able to work with the school to pilot one of the first Filipina/o American studies courses in the school district.

PIN@Y EDUCATIONAL PARTNERSHIPS

Maya, along with many of the Filipina/o students in San Francisco, inspired me to create Pin@y Educational Partnerships (PEP) in the fall of 2001. PEP piloted a mentorship program in which students from San Francisco State University went to Balboa High School in the Excelsior neighborhood during lunchtime to meet with students to assess both their personal and academic needs. PEP also provided lunchtime activities and workshops that focused on Filipina/o American history and culture. By the end of the fall semester, PEP asked the students what they wanted, and they spoke loud and clear. They wanted PEP to be a class in their master school schedule. After a bit of negotiation with Balboa's administration, they agreed to allow PEP to pilot a class in the spring 2002 semester. The Filipino American experiences course that began with 11 teachers and 30 students was both challenging and transformative.

PEP has become an educational pipeline that has created a "partnership triangle" between the university, public schools, and the community. PEP's partnership triangle includes San Francisco State University's Asian American Studies Department, San Francisco public schools; the Filipino Community Center; and the Filipino American Development Foundation.

As Terrance Valen, the organization director of the Filipino Community Center, PEP's community home, eloquently describes,

> The Pin@y Educational Partnerships (PEP) Program has been instrumental in transforming the underserved and marginalized Filipino community in the Excelsior neighborhood of San Francisco. The integration of undergraduate and graduate students from San Francisco State University with low-income, recent immigrant, and US-born Filipino students from elementary, middle school, high school, and now City College students has created a community of conscious youth, who better understand their place in the world and are poised to be part of transforming their own communities, wherever their individual paths may lead them.

Now 10 years later, PEP provides Filipina/o American Studies/ethnic studies courses for credit at Balboa and Burton High Schools, along with Denman Middle School, San Francisco City College, and an enrichment program at Longfellow Elementary School. PEP currently has 56 teachers and serves over 200 students. About 95% of PEP teachers have gone on to become educators in schools and/or in the community in some capacity. Many of them have gone on to pursue teaching credentials, master's degrees, and doctoral degrees in fields such as education, ethnic studies, social studies, history, social work, and public policy. As part of PEP's educational pipeline, some of the students from PEP have also come full circle and become PEP teachers and coordinators of school sites. We have also developed a curriculum that infuses both critical Filipina/o American studies and critical pedagogical praxis (Tintiangco-Cubales, 2007, 2009). Through Youth Participatory Action Research, PEP students research problems in their communities and propose ways to change them. Although it began as just a simple mentorship program, PEP has become a place of transformation for both students and teachers and a genuine pursuit of social justice.

NOTES

1. This chapter is about a community of Filipina/os who live in and around the Excelsior District, a working class neighborhood in San Francisco that borders Daly City. According to the 2000 Census, San Francisco is home to over 40,000 Filipina/os. Today, the greatest concentration of Filipina/os in San Francisco live in the southeastern neighborhoods of the city, particularly in the Excelsior/Outer Mission, Visitation Valley, and Portola neighborhoods.
2. According to a study by the Services and Advocacy for Asian Youth (SAAY) consortium, Filipina/o and Pacific Islander youth have the second-highest percentage of San Francisco middle-schoolers who have had thoughts of suicide. SAAY also reported that almost a third of Filipina/o and Pacific Islander youth report having depression, the third-highest percentage. In 2000, suicide was the leading cause of death for API youth nationwide, second only to unintentional injuries.

   In early February 1995, a front-page story in the San Diego *Union-Tribune* sent shock waves through the local Filipina/o American community. The newspaper reported that almost half of all Filipina girls surveyed by the local school district had been "seriously considering suicide." Using a questionnaire on suicide developed by the Centers for Disease Control and Prevention, the district found that rates for Filipina American high school students were extremely high at 45.6%, compared to Latinas at 26.2%, Whites at 26.2%, and 25.3% among Blacks. A news article offered few reasons for this alarming statistic and only vaguely pointed to "cultural" explanations as the reason for these high suicide rates (Lau, 1995).
3. According to the SFUSD High School Accountability Reports, "Dropouts are defined as students who are absent without reason for 45 days or more." The overall SFUSD high school dropout rate was 3.6% for the 1999–2000 school year. This school's dropout rate for that same year was 9.2%. This was an "improvement" from the 17.1% of the 1997–1998 school year and the 15.8% rate of 1998–1999. For the past 5 years, the three major groups that have the highest numbers of enrollment and dropout at this particular school are Latinos, African Americans, and Filipinas/os. Interestingly, Filipinas/os reached over of 30% of the entire school population compared to the 6.7%

of the entire district; they were the largest ethnic group at this school during the 1997–1998 school year. During that same year, out of the 415 Filipina/o students at the school, 53 dropped out (about 12.8% of Filipina/o student enrollment). Many of these students who dropped out were only in 9th grade (17 students). This phenomena has only gotten worse. During the 1998–1999 school year, Filipinas/os began to dropout at a rate of 15.1%. This rate was significantly high for that school year compared to the Filipina/o high school districtwide dropout rate of 5.2%, the county rate of 5.3%, and the California State total of 2.2%. Actually, the overall dropout rate for this particular school has decreased, but the dropout rate for Filipinas/os has increased. These statistics defy the stereotypical "model minority" image that has been imposed on Asian American students. This image has made it difficult to convince American educational institutions that Filipinas/os are in dire need of assistance. These rates pose a challenge to those of us in the fields of education and Filipina/o American Studies to develop new ways to look at the complexities embedded in the experiences of these youth.

REFERENCES

Alsaybar, B. D. (1999). Deconstructing deviance: Filipina/o American youth gangs, "party culture," and ethnic identity in Los Angeles. *Amerasia Journal, 25*(1), 116–138.

Bonus, R. (2000). *Locating Filipina/o Americans: Ethnicity and the cultural politics of space.* Philadelphia, PA: Temple University Press.

Carlip, H. (1995). *Girl power: Young women speak out!* New York, NY: Time Warner.

Dearing, E. G. (1997). The family tree: Discovering oneself. In M. P. P. Root (Ed.), *Filipina/o Americans: Transformation and identity* (pp. 287–298). Thousand Oaks, CA: Sage.

Espiritu, Y. L. (2003). *Homebound: Filipina/o American lives across cultures, communities, and countries.* Berkeley: University of California Press.

Filipina/o Community Center of the Excelsior. (2005). *A community needs assessment.* An unpublished report on Filipinas/os in the Excelsior District of San Francisco, California.

Fuligni, A. (1998). The adjustment of children from immigrant families. *Current Directions in Psychological Science,* (7), 99–103.

Fuligni, A. J., Yip, T, & Tseng, V. (2002). The impact of family obligation on the daily behavior and psychological well being of Chinese American adolescents. *Child Development, 73,* 306–318.

hooks, b. (2000). *Where we stand: Class matters.* New York, NY: Routledge,

Lau, A. (1995, February 11). Filipina/o girls think suicide at no. 1 rate. *San Diego Union-Tribune.*

Nomura, G. (2003). Filipina American journal writing: Recovering women's history. In. S. Hune & G. Nomura (Eds.), *Asian/Pacific Islander American women: A historical anthology* (pp. 138–154). New York: New York University Press.

San Francisco Department of Children, Youth and Their Families. (2002). Snapshot: San Francisco's Children and Youth Today. *National Child Care Informa-*

tion and Technical Assistance Center. Retrieved from http://occ-archive.org/node/24275

Services and Advocacy for Asian Youth (SAAY) Consortium. (2004, March). *Moving beyond exclusion: Focusing on the needs of Asian/Pacific Islander youth in San Francisco.* Retrieved from http://www.policyarchive.org/handle/10207/bitstreams/5970.pdf

Tintiangco-Cubales, A. (2007). *Pin@y educational partnerships: A Filipina/o American studies sourcebook. Volume I: Philippine and Filipina/o American history.* Santa Clara, CA: Phoenix Publishing House International.

Tintiangco-Cubales, A. (2009). *Pin@y educational partnerships: A Filipina/o American studies sourcebook. Volume II: Filipina/o American service, activism, and identity.* Santa Clara, CA: Phoenix Publishing House International.

Wolf, D. L. (1997). Family secrets: Transnational struggles among children of Filipina/o immigrants. *Sociological Perspectives, 40*(3), 457–483.

Zhou, M. (1997). Growing up American: The challenge confronting immigrant children and children of immigrants. *Annual Review of Sociology,* (23), 63–95.

Zhou, M. (2004). Coming of age at the turn of the twenty-first century: A demographic profile of Asian American youth. In J. Lee & M. Zhou (Eds.), *Asian American youth: Culture, identity, and ethnicity* (pp. 33–50). New York, NY: Routledge.

CHAPTER 8

THEORIZING FROM PAIN, PASSION, AND HOPE

The Making of Filipino American Curricula and Pedagogy

Patricia Espiritu Halagao
University of Hawai'i, Manoa

> *I longed passionately to teach differently from the way I had been taught since high school.*
>
> —hooks, 1994, p. 7

It has taken me almost 15 years to write about my work in Filipino American curricula and pedagogy. As curricularists, we oftentimes get so lost in developing and implementing the curriculum that we neglect taking the time to reflect and write about its personal story, theoretical background, and outcomes before we move on to the next project. The first part of this chapter steps back in time to critically analyze the inspiration, theoretical underpinnings, and impact of my first curriculum, Pinoy Teach, which was co-developed with artist and community activist Timoteo Cordova. I spend a considerable amount of time analyzing Pinoy Teach because it laid the foundation for all future curricula. I share how its development was organic

The "Other" Students, pages 145–163

and its theoretical framework grew from deep-seated pain and passion. The remainder of the chapter focuses on translating my imagination and hope into action through the development and partnerships of our latest two curricula. It is during this period that the purpose of curricula moves more toward transformation, equity, access, social justice, and, ultimately, educational achievement.

I conclude this introduction with an important point about the names of our curricula. The names deliberately reflect our identities as Filipinos, conscientiously drawing from the strength of our past and are symbolic of the overarching mission of the curricula. For Pinoy Teach, the term *Pinoy* is a shortened term coined by the early Filipino settlers to self-describe themselves. It pays tribute to our Pinoy/Pinay ancestors who struggled and persevered under oppressive conditions to make a better life for themselves within an environment in which "being Filipino was a crime" (Bulosan, 1996). As Freire (1989, p. 39) purports, "the pedagogy of the oppressed cannot be developed or practiced by the oppressors... the oppressed must be their own examples in the struggle for their redemption." In naming our curriculum Pinoy Teach, Cordova and I were also upfront about our "positionality" as Filipino Americans who researched, conceptualized, and developed the curriculum as well as the need for our own people to go forth and teach the curriculum.

For iJeepney.com, we named the curricula after the converted World War II jeeps, which are now a popular mode of transportation in the Philippines. The name signifies our colorful, resilient past and our innovative abilities as Filipinos to make something our own. As an online curriculum, iJeepney.com becomes "the vehicle" for curricula to be accessible and the means to connect our community. Finally, the Sistan C. Alhambra Filipino American Education Institute is named after the first Filipina teacher and later principal of Hawaii so we may honor and emulate her trailblazing spirit and contextualize our work to Hawaii. Our decision to call it an institute moves us from the limitations of a single curriculum to creating a movement in the schools to impact mainstream curricula and pedagogy.

METHODOLOGY

In this chapter, I use critical autoethnography to explore my journey of curricular making. This approach is a critical and reflexive account of one's own experiences situated in a broader context. This form of inquiry serves as a counternarrative to the traditional mainstream Eurocentric construction of curricula. As cited in Afonso and Taylor (2009), critical autoethnography is a response to a "colonizing or 'othering' discourse" (Burdell & Swadener, 1999, p. 22)—the discourse in which one's story is written (understood, interpreted, and represented) by another person as a counter-narrative to the colonial stories (p. 276).

Using this methodology inquires what makes up Filipina/o curricula and pedagogy from our own perspective: How has our past, specifically colonialism, shaped Filipina/o American curricula and pedagogy? What kinds of common themes and approaches do we see across the different curricula? Is there growth in the development of the three curricula (Pinoy Teach, iJeepney.com, and the Sistan C. Alhambra Filipino American Education Institute)? What is specific and unique to Filipina/o curricula?

Subjectivity is central to critical autoethnographies; the story becomes the foreground. But the story is not shared merely for the story's sake. Not only does the researcher make sense of his or her individual experience, but autoethnographies are political in nature as they engage their readers in important social issues. Therefore the purpose of this inquiry is also to shed light, change perceptions, and challenge ideas around educational issues for Filipino Americans. So I concluded by asking, What is the social significance of this narrative inquiry? What implications does this inquiry have on Filipino American curriculum development and society?

THEORIZING FROM PAIN

In my narrative, I point to pain, passion, and hope as emotions that guided our theoretical models, content, and pedagogy. When we theorize, we make sense of the world around us and our place within it to oftentimes overcome pain and to find meaning in life. Theory doesn't come out of nowhere. In 1994, bell hooks wrote about theorizing as a liberatory practice:

> I came to theory because I was hurting—the pain within me was so intense that I could not go on living. I came to theory desperate, wanting to comprehend—to grasp what was happening around and within me. Most important, I wanted to make the hurt go away. I saw in theory then a location for healing.

Much like hooks, I turn to theory to explain my life and as a location for healing through my curricular work. Throughout much of my youth, I battled issues regarding my ethnic identity as a Filipina American. Like many Filipino Americans, I suffered from the legacy of colonialism. Over 350 years of Spanish and U.S. colonialism in the Philippines created a "colonial mentality," which attributes everything positive and desirable to the colonizers and reinforces the belief that the colonized peoples are psychologically and intellectually subordinate (Memmi, 1967). This attitude results in cultural inferiority, inability to articulate one's ethnic identity, and lack of ethnic pride (Strobel, 2001). Lott (1980, p. 133) finds that, "The Pilipino community in the United States has been and continues to be shaped by the influences of a mentality that had its origins in the Philippines." It has had a negative affect on Filipino American ethnic identity and academic achievement (Nadal & Halagao, 2010).

For example, when I was growing up, my mother would tell me to gently stroke the bridge of my nose upward and say "tall nose, tall nose" before I was to go to bed (Espiritu, 2003). I did what she said, believing that my nose would transform from pugness to pointedness. But deep down, I always wondered why I was doing this. Was there something wrong with me? I have come across other Filipinos who tell me that their mothers have told them to do the same. Little acts such as these symbolize the self-denigration prevalent in the mindset of Filipino Americans. I do not blame my mom for thinking like this, but rather the legacy of colonialism that made her unconsciously pass these negative attitudes on to her children.

In looking back, another contributing factor to my self-denigration was the absence of positive Filipino roles models in school and the K–12 curriculum. I became even more aware of our Eurocentric curriculum during my 2-year commitment as a Teach for America teacher in the Oakland public schools. I noticed that my largely Latino and Cambodian 1st-grade students were unable to connect to what I was required to teach. Before I knew about the theories of multicultural education, I innately recognized the need to develop culturally relevant curriculum that affirmed and connected my students' identities and backgrounds to what they were expected to learn. This interest resulted in pursuing a master's degree and PhD in multicultural education and social studies. It was only at this time did I learn about my history and culture as a Filipino and became empowered to make a difference in Filipino American education.

In order to move our Filipino community forward, we need to unlearn our colonial mentality. If Filipinos are colonized, they need to be decolonized. Decolonization is the process of humanizing the dehumanized as well as moving from self-denigration and ethnocentrism to accepting self and others at a multicultural and global level. When I reflect on my journey, I see the development of Pinoy Teach as the vehicle for my decolonization. Strobel (2001, p. 188) writes, "Decolonization means to reconnect with the past to understand the present and to be able to envision the future." Pinoy Teach kept me looking backward to challenge the roots of my colonial mentality and pushed me forward to translate my liberation into professional practice.

Laenui (2000) developed a decolonization framework based on his experiences as a Native Hawaiian and sovereignty activist to describe the unique experiences that colonized peoples undergo when shedding the yoke of colonialism. He described five stages: (a) rediscovery/recovery, (b) mourning, (c) dreaming, (d) commitment, and (e) action. Decolonization begins with the individual's "rediscovering" one's history and "recovery" of ethnic roots by way of an accident, curiosity, or anger. This rediscovery and recovery then becomes an epiphany of awareness. In the second stage, formerly colonized people "mourn" or are in a state of longing for what was taken away from them. According to Laenui, it is important for people to move on to the "dreaming" stage when they can imagine a world free from self-denigration. At a political level, they imagine a social order that includes their people as equals who can reexamine their history and advance as a people. He also cautions people not to rush out of this stage because they need to be given the opportunity to think outside the box without replicating colonial model solutions. The next two stages advance people into making a "commitment" to a focused direction after considering all possibilities and finally in taking "action" toward realizing the dream and vision.

Based on Freire's (1989) model, Strobel (2001) offered a condensed version of decolonization founded on her research study of post-1965 Filipino Americans. She characterized the stages simply into naming, reflecting, and acting. Naming the oppression and articulating its impact on one's identity (i.e., loss of "cultural memory" and "loss of language") are the first steps to healing (Strobel, 2001, p. 122). The next stage of reflection is for an individual to look deeply and think critically of one's position. However, unless the individual is moved to action, the reflection stage can be self-consuming and nonproductive. The final step is to become a leader and to "give back to the Filipino American community" by ongoing questioning and spreading "one's story" (p. 123.). As Freire (1989) agrees, "Only power that springs from the weakness of the oppressed will be sufficiently strong to free both" (p. 28).

While the process of decolonization may be similar, each stage may manifest differently, depending on one's background and experiences. For example, Cordova moved through decolonization quickly and early in life. He is a third-generation Filipino American, raised by foremost Filipino American historians, Drs. Fred and Dorothy Cordova. He benefited from positive role models and was surrounded by notions of social justice and empowerment. Cordova translated his ideals and thoughts through his revolutionary musical plays and community work with the nonprofit organization, Filipino Youth Activities. On the other hand, my path to decolonization occurred later in life. I am the daughter of two physicians who immigrated to the United States in 1969. I grew up in the Midwest where I experienced self-rejection as a result of racism, marginalization, and disconnect from a largely White community. I later became a teacher, graduate student, and professor committed to issues of social justice. While Cordova's work challenged the status quo from outside the mainstream, I advocated for change from the inside. Ultimately, our contrasting backgrounds and perspectives created a curriculum grounded in theory, activism, practicality, and pedagogy.

When reflecting on our life histories, it was not easy to name our pains and to theorize from our two different locations. Pinoy Teach underwent many changes that reflected our movement on the journey of decolonization. Without realizing we were moving through Laenui's (2000) decolonization framework, Cordova and I set out to develop a curriculum that "rediscovered and recovered" our roots. This meant mourning for what had been lost. When you examine early covers of Pinoy Teach, you see a prominent picture of an aboriginal man, which represents our nostalgia for the past. During the curriculum's early stages, we focused on an ethnic studies approach to compensate for the lack of Filipino content in social studies.

However, as we began to move into the "dreaming" stage, we experienced conflict over its direction. We began to imagine a curriculum that located the dynamic Filipino American *experience*—not merely history and culture—within a more multicultural and global context. Being of a more alternative mindset, Cordova realized the importance of moving away from a single studies ethnic approach. We employed the highest multicultural principles of Bank's (2008) stages of multicultural reform, the transformative and social actions approach. The transformative approach places universal concepts at the center to be viewed from multiple perspectives.

In Pinoy Teach, concepts preceded content. It was important for us to begin our lesson with concepts to give students a framework to understand their own cultural experiences, the Filipino experience, and other ethnic group experiences. For example, when students study the concept of revolution, they first experience the stages of revolution in the classroom, helping them sympathize with actors and events of the Philippine Revolution. Next, students compare the stages of revolution to the American Revolution or to another revolution like the women's movement or Civil Rights movement.

While all concepts are universal and timeless, some can apply more particularly. Concepts in Pinoy Teach were deliberately chosen and relayed in a specific order to tell the story of Filipinos. Our curriculum focused on the concepts of diversity, multiculturalism, perspective, revolution, imperialism, immigration, racism, and identity. We began with diversity and multiculturalism to celebrate the beauty of our diverse culture. In formerly colonized cultures, it was important to recognize the indigenous and precolonial influences and confront inaccurate notions that we were uncivilized. The curriculum then focused on the concepts of perspective, revolution, and imperialism to tell the story of a resilient, strong, and dynamic culture. Its concluding emphasis on immigration, racism, and identity teaches about the harsh realities and universal struggles of immigrant communities.

Questioning does not come without pain and discomfort. On the one hand, it was liberating to teach differently than what I experienced, but on the other hand, it was uncomfortable challenging previously held assumptions and knowledge. Because we thought it was important to critically examine whatever we learned, we wanted to similarly empower students to do so as well. An important aspect of Pinoy Teach is to encourage students to question what they learn, even our curriculum. We were not interested in merely replacing one master narrative with another. We were more interested in fostering critical historical thinking (Wineberg, 2001).

HARNESSING THE PASSION

When I was in graduate school at the University of Washington, Seattle, I took my first class on Filipino American history and culture by Filipino American historians Drs. Fred and Dorothy Cordova. Everyday I sat like a sponge soaking up information that had been denied to me all my life. I felt pride when I learned our forefathers and foremothers did not sit back and accept colonialism, but revolted against Spanish and American domination. Before the class, I had never viewed Spanish or U.S. colonialism negatively. I now began to understand the roots of our colonized mentality and feelings of inferiority.

When the course ended, I felt like I had been lifted to enlightenment and then forced to come back down. I was not ready for it to end. Like many inspired students, I had a strong desire to do something with what I learned. I moved into Laenui's (2000) "commitment" phase when I realized that as an educator, I wanted to do everything in my power to make sure that students would not wait until college to learn about their ethnic history and culture. It became my mission to create a curriculum conceived by Filipinos, about Filipinos, and for Filipinos to liberate them from the shackles of ignorance.

PINOY TEACH

I often compare the conception and creation of Pinoy Teach to childbirth, because it represents an emergence of something new—something that liberated me from the confines of what existed. Freire (1989, p. 33) says liberation "is thus a childbirth and a painful one. The man who emerges is a new man." I drew from my passion of experience (hooks, 1994, p. 91) to give birth to a new kind of Pinoy pedagogy.

Freire (1989, p. 33) poses the key question, "How can the oppressed, as divided unauthentic beings, participate in developing the pedagogy of their liberation?" Our answer was to put our own people into positions in which they were empowered to teach their ethnic history and culture to others. Pinoy Teach exemplified Banks' (2002) "social actions" approach, which encourages "taking action related to the issues, concepts, and problems they are studying" (p. 25). After naming our internalized oppression and reflecting on the construction of these colonial narratives, the final step in decolonization is to take action and give back to the Filipino American community (Strobel, 2001). Strobel states that "decolonization is a source of courage and agency to choose and act in ways that uplift the Filipino American community" (2001, p. 118).

The idea of using college students to mentor and teach younger students is not new. But 15 years ago, linking service learning, teaching, multiculturalism, and ethnic content was a new combination. What better way to spread these principles than to use eager, energetic, and intelligent college students to take their recently claimed knowledge and spread it to the younger generation. After all (and understandably), teachers were too tired, too overwhelmed, and too ignorant to pass on this specific knowledge. Our slogan, "Knowledge is power, but teaching is empowerment," represented the power of harnessing the passion and knowledge of college students for the betterment of our community.

Cordova and I taught a two-quarter teacher-education course at the University of Washington's College of Education, where college students first learned the principles and content of Pinoy Teach. They learned about their history, the curriculum, and teaching skills to develop multicultural unit plans. The following quarter, teams of three college students were placed in 7th grade public and private classrooms where they taught Pinoy Teach to students once a week for 10 weeks. Pinoy Teach college students engaged middle-school students in learning about concepts that related to themselves while subversively including Filipino and Filipino American content. The classroom, with all its limitations, became a "location of possibility" (hooks, 1994, p. 207).

Just after 4 years of implementing Pinoy Teach in eleven middle schools in Seattle and Bellevue, Washington, and recruiting over 85 college students to teach the curriculum, I conducted a research study that examined the college student's experiences with Pinoy Teach (Halagao, 2004a). Using Siedman's (1998) phenomenological interviewing, I interviewed six diverse Filipino American college students from the course to understand their experiences with Pinoy Teach. Several patterns emerged, which reflected the complexity of learning about one's ethnic self in history. These patterns fell into three major categories: collisions, connections, and co-agency. Students experienced collisions between their prior knowledge of a colonial mentality and the curriculum's push for transformative thinking. They also found a new sense of community with other Filipino American peers. However, an unexpected finding was the significance of teaching Pinoy Teach to youth. The act of teaching one's ethnic history to others and not just learning about it resulted in ethnic pride and empowerment. One student synthesized:

> The Philippine Revolution was a reason to be proud, but I didn't personally fight the revolution... It's not the history that makes you proud so much as that I know I am taking the time to learn this material, to know it, use it, and to spread it. (Halagao, 2004a, p. 472)

Kreisberg (1992) argues that individual consciousness is not enough; true empowerment comes from social engagement. Empowerment is not an individual act of advancement but rather a social and collective act.

The lessons of Pinoy Teach extended past the classrooms and schools. Participants practiced lessons on their brothers and sisters. The controversial nature of Pinoy Teach also provoked dialogue between participants and family members. When transformative knowledge spilled into the homes of the participants, it broke the cycle of "colonial mentality" prevalent in the Filipino American community, thus enacting Strobel's (2001) final step in decolonization, "acting." One student explained that when she shared her knowledge with her siblings, "they were all so in awe of what I know that they were encouraged to read the Pinoy Teach book. They saw my confidence and became inspired to do something" (Halagao, 2004a, p. 478).

While Pinoy Teach does not live on in its original form anymore, it lives on in other ways. In a long-term study, I surveyed past participants on the effects the curriculum has had on their personal and professional lives (Halagao, 2010). Data was collected through the use of a questionnaire survey, which covered demographic information and included five open-ended questions, to understand the memory and impact of Pinoy Teach on past college student teachers in the present. A total of 40% of past Pinoy Teach participants responded through an e-mail survey. Of those who responded, 51% are currently working as teachers, with 17% of these pursuing or completing advanced degrees in education. This finding revealed an important tangential outcome of the curriculum, which is that it served to recruit more teachers of color. The study revealed the following long-term outcomes among respondents:

1. Deeper love and appreciation of ethnic history, culture, identity, community.
2. Feelings of empowerment (to realize fully one's potential) and self-efficacy (power to produce an effect)—belief in self.
3. Life commitment to philosophies of diversity and multiculturalism.
4. Continued activism in the teaching profession and/or involvement in social and civic issues in the community.

Although Pinoy Teach was not designed with a decolonization framework in mind, this study confirmed that the participants underwent decolonization, which continues into their present lives. The four themes above showed that Pinoy Teach became the catalyst for moving students through the journey of decolonization. During and after their experience with Pinoy Teach, these participants continued to cycle through a decolonization framework of naming, reflecting, and acting (Strobel, 2001). The research study contributes to the field of decolonization educational theory and shows the potential of a decolonizing curriculum such as Pinoy Teach.

CRITICAL HOPE FOR OUR FUTURE

Even though Pinoy Teach was transformative and met Banks' (2002) criteria of social action, there was still more work to be done in the field of Filipino American curricula and pedagogy. Laenui (2000) encourages spending time in the "dreaming" stage to imagine and further think outside of the box, so as to challenge a colonial curricula that was top-down, glossed over struggle, and focused on a singular narrative and male-perspective, didactic approach to history. But in this attempt to present a more complex story of oppression and struggle of history, there must also be messages of hope and change. How do we find hope, imagine solutions, and reconstruct a more responsive and just world for our students? We turn to Freire's (1989) call for "critical hope," a hope grounded in careful analysis and understanding of a historical situation and a move to action to affect the sociopolitical, economic, and cultural realities that shape our lives (Entin, Rosen, & Vogt, 2008, p. 171).

IJEEPNEY.COM

My work with Pinoy Teach and other ventures continued to open up other avenues of curriculum exploration and challenging traditional boundaries of curriculum. In 2006 and in honor of the Filipino centennial immigration to the United States, I received a grant from the Smithsonian Institution to develop the nation's first online Filipino American curriculum, which we nicknamed iJeepney.com and can be found at www.ijeepney.com. I assembled a Hawaii-based curriculum design team of University of Hawaii Filipino American studies professor Dr. Theodore Gonzalves, middle-grade-level teacher Rodrigo Acoba, elementary teacher Judith Miguel, high-school teacher Katrina Guerrero, Master of Arts communications student Farzana Nayani, Web designer David Goldberg, and Disney artist Josie

Trinidad to create a fresh and accessible curriculum that represented the wave of the future.

It was exciting to combine the latest information on Filipino American history, culture and issues, multicultural theories, and technology. When we sat down to create the curriculum, it was important to create an interactive and engaging curriculum that our Filipino youth could relate to. With so few Filipino role models, we deliberately told the story through the perspective of a Filipino girl and boy who embark on an introspective and investigative journey of the Filipino American experience. Knowing that Filipinos tend to be visual learners (Park, 1997), we involved a Filipino American Walt Disney artist with the approval of middle-school students to design and bring to life two Filipino characters, Marissa and Jordan.

The online curriculum centers on four major goals: increasing ethnic pride, establishing cultural connections, cultivating critical thinking, and empowering the community. The curriculum begins with Unit 1, "Journey Filipinas," in which students are invited on a journey through the Philippines. Youth jump aboard a jeepney and sail on a *balangay* (sailboat) to see the colorful heritage of the Philippines' history. Here, students see a vibrant picture of the rich diversity of the land and people. In Unit 2, "Challenge History," critical thinking is placed front and center. It draws on lessons from Pinoy Teach, which highlights the concepts of perspective, revolutions, and imperialism. Represented in Filipino native warrior garb, Marissa and Jordan provoke critical questions while telling Philippine history through famous artwork.

In Unit 3, "Brown America," we look at the shaping of America from the Filipino perspective. Examining the "Browning" of America expands students' notions of history beyond the traditional White and Black canon. Students learn about the different waves of Filipino migration and the three "L" reasons for leaving: labor, love, and learning. One of the critiques of learning history is that students cannot relate to what happened in the past. In order to get youth to empathize with the past, the Disney artist drew Marissa and Jordan into the historical photographs. Youth were able to see and imagine themselves in historical settings and situations. Finally, in Unit 4, "Kick it Up! Make History," we challenge students to do social action. Using the metaphor of sipa, the Philippine national sport and popular game in America's schools, we ask students to imagine them playing sipa and to keep the ball moving forward by doing something with what they've learned. We provide examples from the past, showing Filipino Americans active in social causes and issues. Ultimately, we leave students with the message that they are responsible for uplifting our community.

Finally, technology afforded us the opportunity to connect the Filipino American community locally, nationally, and globally. In providing our curriculum online for free, we placed it in the hands of teachers and students.

However, we did not want to stop there. In order to keep advancing our community, we encouraged ongoing dialogue about education between Filipino American researchers, teachers, administrators, policymakers, and youth. Therefore, we added an online community feature to our curriculum that will hopefully ignite conversation and networking among Filipino Americans.

These two social networking features consist of a site for teachers entitled "Tsismis.edu," and for students entitled "My Balangay Journal." Tsismis.edu serves as a search engine for teachers to find, upload, and comment on Filipino curriculum resources. Why reinvent the wheel when others have already developed lessons? My Balangay Journal is an interactive online journal for students, with four activities that connect their learning to the past, present, and to one another. Our Balangay Library allowed students to share their work with classmates and youth across the nation. It then becomes a springboard to discuss concepts of diversity, geography, and culture. Through these multiple spaces, we intend the topics of Filipinos, curriculum, and education to become commonplace in children's homes, schools, and communities across the nation.

CRITICAL REVIEW OF K–12 FILIPINA/O[1] AMERICAN CURRICULA

By 2009, there was a growing body of Filipina/o American curricula, pedagogy, and scholarship in the nation. In taking Freire's call for hope grounded in careful analysis, historical reflection, and action, we realized that we needed to take stock of what curricula we had and where we were heading. I collaborated with Dr. Joanie Cordova, historian and president of Filipino American National Historical Society (FAHNS), and Dr. Allyson Tintiangco-Cubales, Director of Pin@y Educational Partnerships (PEP), to publish a critical review of 33 Filipina/o American curricula. One of the major findings was the long-standing history of "community and academic partnerships since the 1960s that are grounded liberatory theoretical frameworks and practices of community knowledge production" (Halagao, Tintiangco-Cubales, & Cordova, 2009, p. 13). We also found the growth and proliferation of Filipina/o pedagogy. In the end, we recommended the need to apply the curricula and pedagogy in the schools to diminish the "severe opportunity gaps in the K–12 schools." Working on this review with Dr. Cordova and Dr. Tintiangco-Cubales challenged my own understanding and construction of Filipina/o curricula and pedagogy and had a profound impact on my future curricula.

THE SISTAN C. ALHAMBRA FILIPINO AMERICAN EDUCATION INSTITUTE

Living in Hawaii and teaching as a professor at the University of Hawaii at Mānoa has encouraged me to look at my scholarship differently. I realize that what worked in Washington State will not necessarily work in Hawaii. For one, while Filipinos talk about colonialism as a legacy in our community, the indigenous people of Hawaii are living colonialism every day in lands that were stolen from them. I am acutely aware that I am an Asian settler making colonialism take on a different meaning to me. I strive to understand the causes and issues of Native Hawaiians and draw parallels with the Filipino history and experience. I also aim to learn from the progressive teacher-education models that Native Hawaiians have developed to empower their own people in education.

In 2010, I received a United States Federal Department of Education (DOE) "Improving Teacher Quality" grant and support from the University of Hawaii Diversity and Equity Initiative to establish the Sistan C. Alhambra Filipino American Education Institute, (www.filameducation.com). Inspired by University of Hawaii's Hoʻokulāiwi: ʻAha Hoʻonaʻauao ʻŌiwi (Center for Native Hawaiian and Indigenous Education), the mission of our Institute is to critically engage professors, teachers, and community members to meet the academic, social, cultural, and language needs of Filipino immigrant and local-born students, many who are failing in the state's public schools.

In Hawaiian public schools, Filipino Americans are considered an "invisible majority." They represent the second-largest ethnic group in public schools (21%), and they hold the negative distinction of being ranked second to the bottom on Hawaiʻi State Assessments (HSA) in reading and math achievement. Ogilvie's (2008) compiled national report on Filipino Americans and schooling found that schools in Hawaii, where Filipinos represent over 30% of the population, had higher rates of poverty, students needing special education, and/or students needing ELL (English-language learners) services. No professional development for teachers exists to target and raise the educational achievement of this student population in Hawaii. Low academic achievement has led to lower graduation rates, with a little over half of high school students pursuing a college education (Okamura, 2008).

An ambitious task of challenging Hawaii's education system takes an ambitious approach, requiring innovation and collaboration. To achieve this task, we drew up the principles of community of practice and critical pedagogy. Lave & Wenger (1991) described community of practice as a group of people who share a passion and collaborate together for a common goal. Wenger (1999) outlined three criteria of community of practice:

(a) its identity is defined by domain of interest; (b) the community works together in joint discussions and interactions to pursue the domain of interest; and (c) community members are practitioners who develop a shared experience with stories, tools, and resources to address issues. Each member contributes and learns from other members.

Although the University of Hawaii can boast of leading scholarship in Philippine studies, Filipino American studies, and languages and literature, there was little collaboration among the departments and limited outreach and impact on K–12 schools. The Institute finally created an organized partnership among scholars, educators, and community members in the name of K–12 education. As a community of practice, the Institute consists of four partners: the University of Hawai'i, Mānoa's (a) College of Education, (b) College of Arts & Sciences, (c) Leeward Community College, and (d) Department of Education's Farrington Complex, which includes four schools (Farrington High School, Kalakaua Middle School, Fern Elementary School, and Kalihi Kai Elementary School).

A major goal of the Institute is to eliminate oppression and systemic injustice in the Filipino American community using critical pedagogy. Shaw (2008) believes critical pedagogy strives for teaching practices that encourage understanding and combating problems. This social action approach connects to Freire's (1989) notion of critical praxis or informed acts of consciousness that follows a cyclical process of theory, practice, and reflection. The structure of the Institute reflects critical praxis with its three phases of curriculum-making, curriculum-exchanging, and curriculum-applying.

During curriculum-making, Institute members (referred to as *Partners*) collaborated to create the curriculum from the ground up. While it would have been easy to have used Pinoy Teach and iJeepney.com curriculum and other existing curricula, we wanted to create a community in which professors of Philippine and Filipino American history, culture, languages, and literature and pedagogy partnered with practicing teachers selected by their principals to develop Institute curricula. Teams developed F2F and online modules (which can be found at www.filameducation.com) using new technologies and media on the following topics: (a) art, culture, and identity; (b) language, culture, and literature; (c) memories, perspective, and colonialism; (d) immigration, local culture, and stereotypes; and (e) pop culture, issues, and social action.

During curriculum-exchanging, 24 teachers from the Farrington Complex (referred to as *Participants*) enrolled in a 3-week summer professional development/graduate course (EDCS 640M) to engage with Institute partners to learn about Filipina/o curriculum and pedagogy. Throughout this phase, teachers reflected on learning, application, and development of a multicultural, standards-based unit plan.

In the final phase of curriculum-applying, teacher participants taught their unit plans and studied an inquiry question around a problem/issue in their classroom. Institute partners and teacher participants reconvened in October and November to reflect on their practices and implications.

A number of different forms of assessment examined the impact of the Institute: course evaluations, partner focus-group interviews, pre- and posttest online surveys, and teacher artifacts (i.e., online comments, assignments, and unit plans). A composite of these evaluations revealed that we met the goals and outcomes of the Institute. Partners emphasized the importance of collaboration, equal validation of each of the partner's unique knowledge and skills, the necessity of context in involving teachers from the schools so that professional development is "done with" versus "done on" teachers, ownership or "buy-in" by all partners, flexibility and structure in creating content, and personal and professional outcomes. Our artist partner stated, "The Institute work is exponentially appreciated. As I have learned about my Filipino culture, I will continue it tenfold to my son and others."

The overall evaluations of the participants in the Institute revealed positive outcomes with scores of 5/5. Teachers valued the collaboration among multiple and diverse partners to develop and teach the curriculum. Many commented on the usefulness of the website to make materials accessible, cutting-edge, and interactive. They also wrote about an enlarged and deeper understanding of their students. One teacher expressed, "I am a changed teacher as a result of this Institute."

Pre- and posttest online surveys were administered prior to the start of the Institute, after the 3-week Institute concluded, and after the completion of the course, which was 4 months into the school year. Gains were made in all areas from the baseline survey. Questions surveyed teacher attitudes toward the content knowledge and attitudes toward the importance of Philippine and Filipino American culture, history, and issues; as well as integrating multicultural content, radical pedagogy, and social action approaches into their classrooms. The most positive attitudes toward the Institute were immediately after the conclusion of the Institute. However, when school started, teachers shared challenges incorporating newfound knowledge, skills, and pedagogy amid the reality of other pressures, and they commented on the need for continued support and community.

When I reflect on the development of the Institute compared to Pinoy Teach and iJeepney.com, I see three major differences. We developed a curricula and pedagogy that was more critical, was more focused on academic achievement, and impacted education at the institutional and systemic levels. We made confronting our oppressive educational system a priority. We addressed the lack of communication and partnerships among the University of Hawaii and K–12 schools and within these school complexes. We targeted specific content areas of languages and math to improve educational outcomes of Filipinos. We improved in-service teachers' understanding, knowledge, and attitudes toward their Filipino students and moved them into advocacy. We achieved what we describe as "critical communities of praxis," wherein we critiqued how content was constructed from our different vantage points as professors, cultural specialists, and teachers. We created educational partnerships that confront systems of oppression. Partners and participants reach a state of conscientization about their teaching, wherein they have the ability to analyze, problematize, and affect the sociopolitical, economic, and cultural realities that shape all of our lives. Freire (1989) believes that praxis requires "reflection and action upon the world in order to transform it" (p. 36).

CONCLUSION

The process of decolonization can be both a painful and liberating process, with hope and action. Pain can be a powerful motivator to move through the stages of decolonization as well as being an inspiration for change. In my case, pain came with the conviction to challenge the norm and create transformative and empowering Filipino American curricula. In analyzing the making of Pinoy Teach, iJeepney.com, and the Sistan C. Alhambra Filipino American Education Institute, I hope to contribute to the growing scholarship on Filipino American curriculum within the fields of decolonizing and multicultural education.

The field of Filipina/o American curriculum and pedagogy was slim 15 years ago. Those of us in this field of education began with few models. In some sense, this allowed curriculum to develop without preconceived notions and be based on innate and organic needs informed by educational theories. When imagining and committing to the curriculum framework, we had our Filipino American audience in mind. We realized it was not enough to deliver content, but we were interested in fostering and strengthening the whole child and our community.

In order to be successful in school, students need to believe in themselves and their abilities to achieve. This is tied into their ideas of self-concept and self-esteem. For students from formerly colonized groups, curriculum needs to address the pain and self-denigration from the legacy of colonialism (Halagao, 2004b). An effective curriculum should develop love for oneself, critical thinking, empowerment, self-efficacy, and co-agency. This means creating a curriculum based on libratory and critical pedagogy, which enables students and teachers to "transgress" across internal, racial, sexual, and class boundaries that can prevent us from being all that we can (hooks, 1994).

Part of affirming oneself has to do with seeing yourself positively in relation to others. The curriculum's emphasis on teaching universal concepts from multiple perspectives, including the Filipino's viewpoint, allows Filipino students to see their histories and cultures alongside other cultural groups. It is important for students to see themselves similar, yet different from their peers. This acknowledges our uniqueness, but it also shows the commonalities among humankind.

Now when our story is contrasted with other racial groups, the concept story might be different. When I presented our curriculum at an international conference in Canada, one British scholar compared the different story of concepts he would present. He believes the story of the British people would be the opposite of Filipinos, with the concepts of homogeneity and imperialism in the beginning. The emphasis on issues of racism and identity would perhaps not be as prevalent and emotional to their story.

Like other minority and marginalized youth, Filipino American students have the additional responsibility of uplifting their Filipino American community. A Filipino American curriculum must include a social-actions component, which pushes students to take what they've learned and apply it to make the world a better place. Students gain hope and inspiration that they can contribute positively to their futures.

It is also important that we tap into technology to modernize our curriculum's accessibility and applicability. By providing curriculum online, we deliver it directly to teachers and youth. We provide modules to students that engage their multiple senses and present teachers with standards-based lessons and unit plans. But again, our work does not stop in merely supplying knowledge. In our online curriculum, we established an "online community," which encourages teachers and students to dialogue over Filipino Americans and education. Knowledge is not enough to improve our community, but again, it is about empowering the constituents to network, develop, and share curriculum. Instead of becoming consumers of history, students then become history makers. Instead of teachers becoming curriculum implementers, they then become curriculum developers.

Finally, ethnic pride, representation in the curriculum, community empowerment, and technology are not enough if we are to challenge and transform the educational system that oppresses our very own students. We need to create curricula and pedagogy that taps into organized partnerships across all levels of education, including social and political systems like our model of "critical communities of praxis" in Hawaii, where we work together to focus on the goal of raising the educational achievement of our Filipino American youth. Only then can we hope for and enact a more social and just world for all of our children and community.

NOTE

1. When we use "Filipina/o" the "a/o" recognizes that "Filipina/o" is derived from gendered language (Spanish), as well as the gendered experiences of Filipinas/os. Filipinas are female, Filipinos are male. Using "a/o" is an attempt to be inclusive of both male and female experiences.

REFERENCES

Afonso, E. Z., & Taylor, P. C. (2009). Critical autoethnographic inquiry for culture-sensitive professional development. *Reflective Practice: International and Multidisciplinary Perspectives, 10*(2), 273–283.

Banks, J. (2002). *Introduction to multicultural education* (3rd ed.). Boston, MA: Allyn & Bacon.

Bulosan, C. (1996). *America's in the heart.* Seattle: University of Washington Press.

Burdel, P., & Swadener, B. B. (1999). Critical narrative and autoethnography in education: Reflections on a genre. *Educational Researcher, 28*(6), 21–26.

Entin, J., Rosen, R. C., & Vogt, L. (Eds.). (2008). *Controversies in the classroom: A radical teacher reader,* New York, NY: Teachers College Press.

Espiritu, P. C. (2003) Uniting mind and soul through cultural knowledge and self-education. In G. Gay (Ed.), *Becoming multicultural educators:Personal journey toward professional agency* (pp. 194–220) San Francisco, CA: Jossey-Bass

Freire, P. (1989). *Pedagogy of the oppressed.* New York, NY: Continuum.

Halagao, P. E. (2004a). Holding up the mirror: The complexity of seeing your ethnic self in history. *Theory on Research and Social Education, 32*(4), 459–483.

Halagao, P. E. (2004b). Teaching Filipino American students. *Multicultural Review, 13*(1), 42–48.

Halagao, P. E. (2010). Liberating Filipino Americans through decolonizing curriculum. *Race, Ethnicity & Education, 13*(4), 495–512.

Halagao, P. E., Tintiangco-Cubales, A., & Cordova, J. M. (2009). Critical review of K–12 Filipina/o American curriculum. *AAPI Nexus: Asian Americans and Pacific Islanders Policy, Practice and Community, 7*(10), 1–23.

hooks, b. (1994). Teaching to transgress. New York, NY: Routledge.

Kreisberg, S. (1992). *Transforming power: Domination, empowerment, and education.* Albany: State University of New York Press.

Laenui, P. (2000). Process of decolonization. In M. Battiste (Ed.), *Reclaiming indigenous voice and vision* (pp. 150–160). Vancouver: University or British Columbia Press.

Lave, J., & Wenger, E. (1991). *Situated learning: Legitimate peripheral participation.* Cambridge, UK: Cambridge University Press.

Lott, J. T. (1980). Migration of a mentality: The Pilipino community. In R. Endo (Ed.), *Asian Americans social and psychological perspectives* (Vol. 2, pp. 132–140). Palo Alto, CA: Science and Behavior.

Memmi, A. (1967). *The colonizer and the colonized.* Boston, MA: Beacon.

Nadal, K., & Halagao, P. E. (2010). *"I am Spanish, Chinese, Filipino": The influence of Filipina/o American identity and colonialism on school achievement.* Paper presented at the annual meeting of the American Educational Research Association, Denver, CO.

Ogilvie, T. (Ed.). (2008). *Filipino American K–12 public school students: A study of ten urban communities across the United States.* Washington, DC: National Federation of Filipino American Association.

Okamura, J. (2008). *Ethnicity and inequality in Hawaii,* Philadelphia, PA: Temple University Press.

Park, C. C. (1997). Learning style preferences of Asian American (Chinese, Filipino, Korean, and Vietnamese) students in secondary schools. *Equity and Excellence in Education, 30*(2), 68–77.

Shaw, A. (2008). *What is "Possibilities?"* Retrieved from http://www.21stcenturyschools.com/Possibilities.htm

Siedman, I. (1998). *Interviewing as qualitative research: A guide for researchers in education and social sciences.* New York, NY: Teachers College Press.

Strobel, L. M. (2001). *Coming full circle: The process of decolonization among post-1965 Filipino Americans.* Quezon City, Philippines: Giraffe.

Wenger, E. (1999). *Communities of practice: Learning, meaning, and identity.* Cambridge, UK: Cambridge University Press.

Wineburg, S. (2001). *Historical thinking and other unnatural acts.* Philadelphia, PA: Temple University Press.

CHAPTER 9

INVISIBLE SUBJECTS

Filipina/os in Secondary History Textbooks

Roland Sintos Coloma
University of Toronto

According to the 2004 American Community Survey Report, there are over 2.1 million Filipina/os living in the United States. Filipina/os comprise the third-largest Asian ethnic group in the country, and the Philippines is the third top country of birth of immigrants in the United States (U.S. Census Bureau, 2007, 2002a, 2002b).[1] Some of the well-known Filipina/o figures in U.S. politics, military, arts, sports, and business include former Hawai'i governor Benjamin Cayetano; army major general Antonio Taguba; Tony award-winning actress Lea Salonga; former Los Angeles Rams quarterback Roman Gabriel; and the CEO of TLC Beatrice International, Loida Nicolas Lewis. Given our increasing numbers and prominence, how are Filipina/os and the Philippines represented in the formal school curriculum in the United States?

This chapter investigates the ways in which Filipina/os and the Philippines are depicted in U.S. secondary history textbooks, particularly those that focus on U.S. and world histories. It specifically analyzes school textbooks as

The "Other" Students, pages 165–182

discursive and material sites of curricular construction, circulation, and contestation. In *Social Studies for the Twenty-first Century*, Jack Zevin (2007) asserts that textbooks are a "fact of life" and "mainstay of instruction" in schools that are fortified by state requirements, mandated courses and tests, and an influential publishing lobby. Although Zevin recommends that teachers should utilize textbooks as anchors to organize content, he concedes that teachers remain heavily dependent upon textbooks and the supplementary materials provided by publishers since these resources are concrete, manageable, and readily available. Given the strong reliance on textbooks by social studies teachers, examining these materials is particularly important since textbooks actively participate in ontological, ideological, and corporal regulation that adjudicates what is deemed as legitimate knowledge, transmits historical and cultural truths, and disciplines bodies. As bearers and mediators of officially sanctioned school curriculum, textbooks function as "gatekeepers of ideas, values and knowledge" (Foster, 1999, p. 253) and as trainers for normative U.S. citizenship (Chappell, 2010).

My study draws from a robust body of research that investigates the multicultural content of school textbooks (Banks & Banks, 2004; Gay, 2000). It is also inspired by studies that examine the depictions of other marginalized groups and issues in the curriculum, such as Latino/a communities and lesbian, gay, bisexual, and transgender topics (Cruz, 2002; Macgillivray & Jennings, 2008). Unfortunately, curriculum research that analyzes the histories, cultures, and contributions of Asian Americans and Pacific Islanders in general and of Filipina/os in particular in school textbooks remains lacking (Coloma, 2006; Pang & Cheng, 1998). Ultimately, I aim to address a major void in curriculum research regarding Filipina/os in school textbooks. These issues are particularly salient and timely to raise in light of the recent curriculum controversy in Texas. On May 21, 2010, the Texas State Board of Education adopted a social studies and history curriculum that dilutes the teaching of U.S. civil rights, religious freedoms, and foreign affairs. The curriculum contest in Texas mirrors previous and ongoing struggles to define what ought to be taught in schools and how history ought to be interpreted. It also signals future challenges to other official curricula. Addressing concerns over curriculum and textbook content will enable us in the fields of education and ethnic studies to grapple with long unresolved issues of injustice, suffering, and interpretation that, I contend, need to be addressed before racial reconciliation and healing in the United States can occur.

RESEARCHING SCHOOL TEXTBOOKS

My study analyzes eight secondary history textbooks that were published from the years 2001 to 2005. The textbooks are distributed by three of the leading textbook publishers in the United States—Glencoe of McGraw-Hill, McDougal Littell of Houghton Mifflin, and Prentice Hall of Pearson. They were written by university faculty members and professional historians, including prominent scholars such as Joyce Appleby of UCLA, Alan Brinkley of Columbia University, and Andrew Cayton of Miami University. As the listing of various advisory and technical boards indicates, the textbooks were reviewed for their substantive and multicultural content by other university academics, curriculum specialists, and school teachers.

Out of the eight textbooks, five focus on United States history and three address world history. The U.S. history textbooks are the following: *The American Republic* (Appleby, Brinkley, Broussard, McPherson, & Ritchie, 2003) and *American History: The Modern Era Since 1865* (Ritchie, 2001), both published by McGraw-Hill's Glencoe; *The Americans* (Danzer, Klor de Alva, Kireger, Wilson, & Woloch, 2003) and *Creating America: A History of the United States* (Garcia, Ogle, Risinger, Stevos, & Jordan, 2003), both by Houghton Mifflin's McDougal Littell; and *America: Pathways to the Present* (Cayton, Perry, Reed, & Winkler 2005) by Pearson's Prentice Hall. The world history textbooks are the following: *World History: Patterns of Interaction* (Beck, Black, Krieger, Naylor, & Shabaka, 2003), published by McDougal Littell; *World History: Connections to Today* (Ellis & Esler, 2005) and *World Cultures: A Global Mosaic* (Ahmad, Brodsky, Crofts, & Ellis, 2004), both by Prentice Hall.

My study does not claim to be a comprehensive survey of all secondary history textbooks that have been published since the year 2000 and that are used in school classrooms throughout the United States. As a preliminary investigation, it intends to determine patterns and gaps in school materials that will be utilized for a larger research project on Filipina/os in the curriculum, which includes analysis of Canadian historical texts for secondary, university, and general readerships (Coloma, in press). My study also does not assert that the inclusion of specific content about the Philippines and Filipina/os constitutes actual lessons implemented in schools. In fact, educators may skip or exceed certain textbook content for a variety of considerations, including curriculum focus and design, teacher expertise, student interest, and time allocation. As Michael Apple and Linda Christian-Smith (1991) point out in *The Politics of the Textbook*, teachers and curriculum play a significant role in determining not only *what* knowledge is of the most worth but also *whose* knowledge is of the most worth.

A significant factor in the use of textbooks in school classrooms within the past decade was the passage and implementation of the No Child Left Behind (NCLB) Act of 2001. For many educators, NCLB facilitated the detrimental emphasis on curriculum standardization and high-stakes testing. They were alarmed by the increasing pattern in school curriculum development that limited subject-matter content predominantly based on what was being tested (Leonardo, 2007; Meier & Wood, 2004). For publishing companies, according to Marcy Baughman, the director of academic research for Pearson Education, NCLB posed "great challenges," including "difficulty in conducting experimental research in schools, timing the research along with the states' proposed adoption cycles, and using research to meet the needs of a diverse group of stakeholders invested in producing high-quality curricula for students" (Baughman, 2008, p. 86). Baughman noted that the push for scientific research and funding on product *effectiveness* "may lead to fewer resources available for product *development*" (p. 93, my emphasis). In short, educators and publishers were concerned that federal regulations, such as NCLB, may curtail the potential expansion in the content of U.S. and world history textbooks that were needed to prepare all students for our multicultural and global society.

Given the broader pedagogical and political contexts of textbook use, I utilize three approaches to investigate the representations of the Philippines and Filipina/os in secondary history textbooks: a quantitative method, a content analysis, and a gap examination. These approaches are driven by three questions: How much textbook space is allocated for Philippine and Filipina/o content? What types of information are included? What details are left out? I conclude by highlighting the interventions of Filipina/o scholars in addressing the virtual invisibility of Filipina/os in the school curriculum.

MARGINALIZATION IN SCHOOL TEXTBOOKS

My quantitative examination addresses the following question: How much textbook space is allocated for Philippine and Filipina/o content? To determine space allocation, I analyzed each textbook by looking at its index for references to the term "Philippines" (since the term "Filipino" is not an index category) and turning to the referenced pages. Then I made a distinction between how many times Philippines and/or Filipina/os are referred to (marked as "References") and how much space is allocated for content on the Philippines and/or Filipina/os (marked as "Content"). For *References*, I tallied the actual number of pages that Philippines and/or Filipina/os appear; thus, an actual page that refers to them one or five times counted as only one page in this accounting. For *Content*, I calculated the number of full and partial pages that the content or topic of the Philippines and/or Filipina/os is addressed. For instance, a three-quarter page description of the Philippine-American War counted as 0.75 page in this accounting. Finally, I looked at the *Total* number of textbook content pages, not including the front matter materials of introduction, acknowledgment, and table of contents as well as the back matter materials of references, appendix, and index. To determine the *Percentage* of Philippine and Filipina/o content in each textbook, I divided the number of Content pages on the Philippines and Filipina/os by the Total number of textbook content pages.

My quantitative analysis reveals the virtual invisibility of Filipina/os in secondary U.S. and world history textbooks. In 5 U.S. history textbooks (see Table 9.1), References to the Philippines and Filipina/os appear in as few as 8 pages and as many as 18 pages. However, the actual Content approximates to a mere 2 to 6 pages in textbooks with total content pages that range from 489 to 1,119 pages. My research reveals that curriculum content on the Philippines and Filipina/os constitute from 0.18% to 0.65% in the five U.S. history textbooks included in the study. Danzer et al.'s *The Americans*, published by McDougal Littel in 2003, has the least quantity of curriculum content on the Philippines and Filipina/os with 2 pages out of 1,119 total pages, amounting to 0.18%. Cayton et al.'s *America: Pathways to the Present*, published by Prentice Hall in 2005, has the largest quantity of curriculum content on the Philippines and Filipina/os with 6 pages out of 923 total pages, amounting to 0.65%. Although Ritchie's *American History: The Modern Era Since 1865*, published by Glencoe in 2001, has the most number of references to the Philippines and Filipina/os, which appears in 18 pages, its actual curriculum content approximates to 3 pages out of 801 total pages, thereby amounting to 0.35% and placing third in the list of five textbooks. This last finding shows that more quantitative references to the Philippines and Filipina/os do not automatically mean more substantive

TABLE 9.1 U.S. History Secondary Textbooks

Textbooks and Authors	Publishers	Year	Refs.	Content	Total	Percentage
The Americans (Danzer et al.)	McDougal Littell (Houghton Mifflin)	2003	8	2 pages	1,119	0.18%
The American Republic Since 1877 (Appleby et al.)	Glencoe (McGraw-Hill)	2003	9	3 pages	921	0.33%
American History: The Modern Era Since 1865 (Ritchie)	Glencoe (McGraw-Hill)	2001	18	3 pages	801	0.37%
Creating America: A History of the United States (Garcia et al.)	McDougal Littell (Houghton Mifflin)	2003	9	3 pages	489	0.61%
America: Pathways to the Present (Cayton et al.)	Prentice Hall (Pearson)	2005	8	6 pages	923	0.65%

curriculum content in the textbooks. In other words, how references are used and explained actually matters in considering the amount and substance of the curriculum content.

My quantitative analysis of the world history textbooks reveals a similarly dismal pattern. In the three textbooks examined (see Table 9.2), References to the Philippines and Filipina/os appear in as few as 5 pages to as many as 20 pages. The actual Content, however, approximates to only 2 to 4.5 pages in textbooks with total content pages that range from 773 to 969 pages. Beck et al.'s *World History: Patterns of Interaction*, published by McDougal Littell in 2003, has the least number of references and the least quantity of content pages regarding the Philippines and Filipina/os, which amounts to 0.21% in 969 total textbook pages. On the other hand, Ahmad et al.'s *World Cultures: A Global Mosaic*, published by Prentice Hall in 2004, has the most number of references and the largest quantity of content pages, which amounts to 0.58% in 773 total textbook pages. In the case of materials that deal with world history, unlike those that deal with U.S. history, the textbook with the most number of references to the Philippines and Filipina/os has the most substantive content as well.

These findings indicate that curriculum content on the Philippines and Filipina/os in formal school-sanctioned textbooks is very little. Consistently constituting less than 1% of the total textbook content pages, Filipina/os are virtually invisible in the narration of U.S. and world histories. The relegation of Filipina/os to curricular obscurity has dire consequences in the education of both Filipina/o Americans and all Americans about Filipina/o history and culture in the Philippines and in the diaspora. The extremely marginal position occupied by Filipina/os in U.S. and world history textbooks situates them as historically unimportant or worse, as a people with no history at all.

TABLE 9.2 World History Secondary Textbooks

Textbooks and Authors	Publishers	Year	Refs.	Content	Total	Percentage
World History: Patterns of Interaction (Beck et al.)	McDougal Littell (Houghton Mifflin)	2003	5	2.0 pages	969	0.21%
World History: Connections to Today (Ellis & Esler)	Prentice Hall (Pearson)	2005	11	2.5 pages	959	0.26%
World Cultures: A Global Mosaic (Ahmad et al.)	Prentice Hall (Pearson)	2004	20	4.5 pages	773	0.58%

REPRESENTATION AND INTERPRETATION IN SCHOOL TEXTBOOKS

My second approach in investigating secondary history textbooks draws from content analysis research (Commeyras & Alvermann, 1994; Gordy & Pritchard, 1995; Kelevh, 2002). It is guided by the following question: Given the limited space allocated for content on the Philippines and Filipina/os, what type of information is actually included in the textbooks? In this section, I foreground three general themes in the representation of the Philippines and Filipina/os in secondary U.S. and world history textbooks.

The first theme depicts the Philippines and Filipina/os within the historical contexts of U.S. international affairs. In all eight history textbooks, the inclusion of the Philippines and Filipina/os in historical narratives derives from two contexts: the Spanish-American War and the emergence of the United States as a global power at the turn of the 20th century; and the Second World War and the culmination of the United States as one of the world's superpowers by the middle of the 20th century. Consequently, the Philippines in mainstream narrations merely serve as a geographic stage on which the United States and other imperialist nations like Spain and Japan enact their battles as history's primary actors. The maps included in the textbooks always position the Philippines in relation to larger global wars. For instance, *The Americans* textbook shows a map of East Asia, Southeast Asia, and the Pacific to depict U.S. military activities during the Second World War (Danzer et al., 2003, p. 786). With the title "World War II: The War in the Pacific, 1942–1945," the map uses bold arrows and explosions to delineate the movements and victories of the U.S.-led Allied Forces. In this visual representation, the Philippines was one of the sites, but not the center, of the global action. Even the accompanying "Geography Skillbuilder" inset that asks students to explore the map further does not mention or focus on the Philippines. Similar versions of this map appear in the other U.S. and world history textbooks (Ahmad et al., 2004, p. 407; Appleby et al., 2003, p. 636; Beck et al., 2003, p. 828; Garcia et al., 2003, p. 369; Ritchie, 2001, p. 594).

Since the Philippines functions in mainstream histories primarily as a geographic stage for U.S. global involvement, it is no surprise that the lead actors in these narratives are Americans. The textbooks invoke U.S. political and military figures like President William McKinley, the U.S. civilian governor of the Philippines and eventual U.S. president William Howard Taft, navy admiral George Dewey, and army general Douglas MacArthur as heroes who saved the Philippines from the imperialist clutches of Spain and Japan. MacArthur in particular receives special attention in the textbooks in the form of biographical details (Ritchie, 2001, p. 618) and photographs depicting the fulfillment of his promise to return and rescue the Philippines in 1944 (Appleby et al., 2003, p. 637). The only Filipina/os marked specifically by name in the textbooks are the revolutionary leader Emilio Aguinaldo, national hero Jose Rizal, former president Ferdinand Marcos, slain reformer Benigno Aquino, and Aquino's widow and eventual president, Corazon Aquino. Of these five Filipina/o figures, only Aguinaldo is featured in all eight textbooks included in the study. Since U.S. historical narratives include the Philippines only during the Spanish–American and Philippine–American Wars at the turn of the 20th century as well as during World War II, Rizal, Marcos, and the Aquinos do not fit within the predetermined storylines of the U.S. history textbooks; these Filipina/o figures appear only in the world history textbooks.

As mostly supporting cast, Filipina/os therefore serve as nameless actors in the U.S.-centered global stage. To illustrate their marginal position further and to bring in historical interpretation in content analysis, I utilize an early 1900s photograph of 2 Filipina women, one of whom is carrying a child, which appears in three of the U.S. history textbooks. The captions for the same photograph reveal differing historical interpretations of the impact of U.S. military action on Filipina/os. The first caption states, "Two Filipino women nervously converse with American troops in the Philippines. Filipino civilians suffered many hardships while Filipino guerrillas fought American troops. Thousands perished from sickness, starvation, and other indirect effects of war. What American policy contributed to civilian hardships in the Philippines?" (Appleby et al., 2003, p. 404). The second caption states, "U.S. military action in the Philippines resulted in suffering for Filipino civilians. About 200,000 people died as a result of malnutrition, disease, and such guerrilla tactics as the burning of villages" (Danzer et al., 2003, p. 561). The third caption states, "As in most wars, the civilians suffered many hardships. Thousands of Filipinos perished from sickness, starvation, and other indirect effects of war. The Philippines gained independence in 1946. When was Puerto Rico granted territorial status?" (Ritchie, 2001, p. 385). While one textbook directly points to U.S. military action as the major cause of Filipina/o suffering, the other two are unclear in determining the main culprit. The last caption even dismisses death and destitution as the inevitable collateral damage of war and shifts attention to the eventual independence of the Philippines. Through the use of images and captions in textbooks with limited content on the Philippines and Filipina/os, such historical narrations only incidentally mention Filipina/os as people who endured imperialist and global wars, thereby reinforcing their position as nameless supporting characters in U.S. and international affairs. More significantly, the textbooks' ambivalent interpretations of U.S. imperialist activities in the Philippines erase U.S. complicity and responsibility for Filipina/o death and suffering.

Related to the first theme of the appearance of Filipina/os in U.S. and world history textbooks within the context of U.S. global affairs is the second theme of U.S. imperialism and benevolence in the Philippines. All eight secondary textbooks acknowledge the U.S. acquisition and occupation of the Philippines after the Spanish–American War. Yet only one of the three world history textbooks and all five U.S. history textbooks use the terms "empire," "imperialism," and "colonialism" to describe U.S. policies and activities in the Philippines (Appleby et al., 2003; Beck et al., 2003; Cayton et al., 2005; Danzer et al., 2003; Garcia et al., 2003; Ritchie, 2001). The other textbooks use the terms "annexation," "rule," and "control" (Ahmad et al., 2004; Ellis & Esler, 2005). Perhaps the *American History: The Modern Era Since 1865* textbook best captures the various discourses of U.S. imperialism:

> Senator Henry Cabot Lodge spoke for those who wanted a larger American role in world affairs. Business interests thought of new markets and fields of investment. Public opinion was excited by the prospect of acquiring an empire. Patriotism merged with belief in social Darwinism, or the belief in the "survival of the fittest." If the United States was the most fit to govern the Philippines, why should it haul down the Stars and Stripes and allow Japan or Germany or some other power to step in and take them.
>
> For others, like Revered Josiah Strong, there was a sense of mission based on racial and religious bias. Strong, in his book *Our Country,* blended social Darwinism with his interest in spreading Christianity. He felt the nationality groups were in a competition from which Anglo-Saxons were destined to emerge victorious. (Ritchie, 2001, p. 381)

This textbook's articulation of the various political, economic, religious, and racial discourses that undergird the project of U.S. imperialism is consistent with the academic scholarship on the history of U.S.–Philippine relations (Go, 2008; Kramer, 2006; Miller, 1984). It also supports the significance of mobilizing empire as a relevant category of analysis in U.S. educational research (Coloma, 2009).

My content analysis reveals that the eight textbooks depict ambivalent perspectives on U.S. imperialism. As the previous paragraph suggests, certain U.S. sectors favored the acquisition of the Philippines. All eight textbooks also include the rebellion of Filipina/os, led by Emilio Aguinaldo, who "expected the Americans to recognize their independence" but became "bitterly disappointed" when the Treaty of Paris in 1898 between Spain and the United States "placed the islands under American control" (Ahmad et al., 2004, p. 269). The textbooks certainly address the violence of wars and foreign rule. Two of the world history textbooks mention the hundreds of thousands of Filipina/o deaths due to the Philippine-American War (Ahmad et al., 2004, p. 269; Ellis & Esler, 2005, p. 652), and two of the U.S. history textbooks mention the United States using the same draconian military practices, such as forcing Filipina/os to live in designated zones, that "America[ns] had condemned Spain for using in Cuba" (Appleby et al., 2003, p. 404; Danzer et al., 2003, p. 561). Perhaps to counter the violence of U.S. colonialism, a considerable amount of textbook coverage discusses U.S. opposition to imperialism. Four of the U.S. history textbooks include sections on the Anti-Imperialist League and various American resistances to the annexation of the Philippines for moral, political, racial, economic, and labor grounds (Appleby et al., 2003; Cayton,et al., 2005; Garcia et al., 2003; Ritchie, 2001). While the *America: Pathways the Present* textbook devotes two full pages to U.S. anti-imperialism under the section "Debating America's New Role" (Cayton et al., 2005, pp. 372–373), not a single world history textbook addresses U.S. anti-imperialism.

In spite of their narration of ambivalent responses to U.S. occupation and control, the textbooks are unanimous in depicting the overall benevolent intentions and benefits of U.S. colonialism in the Philippines. Two U.S. history textbooks and one world history textbook specifically invoke the words of President William McKinley, who envisioned the benign U.S. foreign policy in the archipelago: "There was nothing left for us to do but to take them all, and to educate the Filipinos, and uplift and civilize and Christianize them" (Appleby et al., 2003, p. 404; Beck et al., 2003, p. 708; Cayton et al., 2005, p. 361). The other textbooks offer improvements in education, health, communication, transportation, and other infrastructure like dams and ports as manifestations of U.S. goodwill. Yet only two textbooks contextualize these improvements and reforms as U.S. efforts to pacify and win over Filipina/os (Appleby et al., 2003, p. 404; Ritchie, 2001, p. 383). In addition, a significant benefit of U.S. rule highlighted in the textbooks is the training of Filipinos for self-government. One textbook even points out that "Unlike the European imperial powers, the United States allowed Filipinos to hold high government office" (Ahmad et al., 2004, p. 269). The textbooks discuss the establishment of the bicameral legislative bodies, the U.S. promise for eventual Filipina/o self-rule, and the independence of the Philippines in 1946. Yet only one textbook acknowledges the role of "Filipino nationalists [who] continued to make demands for freedom" (Ahmad et al., 2004, p. 270); the rest of the textbooks gloss over details in the Philippines between the early 1900s and the Second World War as if nothing significant took place during that time period.

The third theme addresses the general context of the Philippines. Whereas all eight textbooks situate the Philippines in relation to U.S. global affairs, only the world history textbooks provide a somewhat more comprehensive contextualization of the history, culture, and politics of the Philippines. Although the world history textbooks also discuss the Spanish-American and Philippine-American Wars in the late 1890s as well as the Second World War in the 1940s, their interpretive treatment includes Spain and Japan, and it is not exclusively focused on the United States. In addition, two world history textbooks frame these major events and time periods within the broader categories of "Imperialism" and "World Wars" (Beck et al., 2003; Ellis & Esler, 2005). For instance, the *World History: Patterns of Interactions* textbook has a section entitled "Western Powers Rule Southeast Asia," which narrates how "The Philippines Changes Hands" in a little over one third of a page (Beck et al., 2003, p. 708–709). As part of a chapter on "The Age of Imperialism, 1850–1914," the wars over the Philippines are situated within the broader history of imperialism in which Western powers fought over and occupied Asia, Africa, and the Middle East.

Whereas two of the world history textbooks employ a topical approach in organizing their units and chapters, the third textbook utilizes a comparative and geographical approach that treats regions and countries more fully. As the tables in the previous section on quantitative analysis indicate, the *World Cultures: A Global Mosaic* textbook has the highest number of references on the Philippines and Filipina/os among all eight textbooks in the study and has the largest quantity of content pages among the three world history textbooks (Ahmad et al., 2004). Discussed throughout three chapters on the Southeast Asian region, the history, geography, climate, culture, religion, politics, and economy of the Philippines receive both separate and comparative attention in relation to other Southeast Asian nations. The Philippines is even briefly mentioned in a chapter on Latin America, which underscores the first global circumnavigation by the remaining crew of Ferdinand Magellan in 1521. It must be noted that there is no discussion of the "discovery" of the Philippines by Magellan. This particular textbook also has more information about postindependence Philippines. It tackles critical issues in the country, including the persistent gap between rich and poor, government corruption, social movements such as the Huk rebellion and the Muslim separatists, anti-American sentiments that led to the closing of the U.S. military bases in 1992, and the struggle against terrorism that was exacerbated by the September 11, 2001, attacks. In my examination of the eight secondary history textbooks, the *World Cultures* by Iftikhar Ahmad and his colleagues has the most extensive coverage on the Philippines and Filipina/os.

INTEGRATION IN SCHOOL TEXTBOOKS

With less than 1% of the secondary history textbook content devoted to Philippine and Filipina/o topics, it is quite an understatement to say that there are significant gaps in the formal curriculum. I highlight three aspects in response to the question, What details are left out?: Filipina/os in the United States, Filipina/o perspectives, and comparative histories.

All eight textbooks in the study focus on Filipina/os in the Philippines, but never *in the United States.* It is understandable that the world history textbooks situate Filipina/o history in the Philippines; however, it is intellectually and pedagogically irresponsible for U.S. history textbook authors to not present Filipina/o lives and experiences in the United States. The consequences of omitting Filipina/o American history in secondary textbooks are the reinforcement of Filipina/os as "forgotten Asian Americans" (Cordova & Cordova, 1983) and the implication of Filipina/os as not having history in the United States at all. The virtual absence of Filipina/o American history in U.S. history school textbooks also fails to integrate the growing critical mass of scholarship in this area (e.g., Baldoz, 2011; Choy, 2003; Espiritu, 2005; Fujita-Rony, 2002). Since Filipina/o American topics are severely lacking in the P–12 school curriculum, students and teachers are introduced to Filipina/o American history in colleges and universities that offer courses in Asian American and ethnic studies. However, there are three problems to this curricular strategy of teaching and learning about Filipina/o Americans exclusively at the postsecondary level: (a) not all students attend colleges and universities, (b) there is a limited number of colleges and universities that offer Asian American studies in general and Filipina/o American studies courses in particular, and (c) courses in history and multicultural education do not adequately integrate Filipina/o American topics. Consequently, the lack of knowledge and understanding of Filipina/o American history, culture, and politics becomes a form of miseducation for both Filipina/o Americans and the U.S. community at-large. It is often through independent reading outside of the formal school curriculum that students and teachers learn about Filipina/o American history. These readings can include the pan–Asian American history books of Sucheng Chan (1991) and Ronald Takaki (1998) as well as the Filipina/o American history books of Fred and Dorothy Cordova (1983) and Barbara Posadas (1999).

The previous section on content analysis reveals that the history of Filipina/os is primarily framed within U.S. and Western international affairs. It confirms the major finding in a comprehensive survey of U.S. history textbooks: "Textbooks underscore the conviction that the experiences of ethnic groups are only important in so far as they contribute to the larger story of an American history dominated by white society" (Foster, 1999, p. 271). So how do we integrate Filipina/o perspectives in the narration of U.S. and world history? Following John Walter's (2001) survey of the African American history in U.S. history textbooks and inspired by the Cordovas' (1983) immigration wave framework, I delineate four Filipina/o American time periods and corresponding topics that need to be included in the secondary curriculum. The first time period focuses on the pre-20th-century migration of Filipina/os to the Americas, including the Philippine-Mexico galleon trade between the mid-1500s and the early 1800s; the first Filipinos in North America who arrived in Morro Bay, California, in 1587; and the first Filipino settlements in North America, established in southern Louisiana in 1763. The second time period spans from the 1890s until 1940, including the Spanish-American and Philippine-American Wars, the migration of students and workers to the United States, the labor organizing of Filipina/o workers, anti-Filipina/o discrimination and violence, and the 1934 Tydings-McDuffie Act. The third time period is from the 1940s until 1965, including the Second World War, the enlistment of Filipino soldiers in the U.S. military, the arrival of the wives and children of Filipino veterans, the independence of the Philippines in 1946, and the 1965 Immigration and Nationality Act. The fourth time period focuses on the post-1965 era, including labor strikes and organizing, the struggle for ethnic studies, the anti–martial law movement in the United States, and the 2003 Citizenship Retention and Re-acquisition Act. These time periods and topics foreground the experiences and perspectives of Filipina/os in U.S. history to counter the normative frameworks and narratives that prevail in secondary school curriculum.

Given the already voluminous amount of details packed into secondary history textbooks, how can these Filipina/o American topics be included in the curriculum? I suggest that, along similar directions taken by Iftikhar Ahmad and his colleagues (2004) in their *World Cultures* textbook, an integrated approach that seriously mobilizes multicultural, comparative, and transnational perspectives is a helpful strategy in incorporating Filipina/o American topics in the curriculum. For instance, lessons on the pre-1900 diaspora can include the arrival of Filipinos in 1587; discussions of U.S. imperialism can connect the U.S. annexation of the Philippines with the immigration of Filipina/o students and workers as U.S. nationals in the early 1900s; and a unit on the Great Depression can direct attention to the violence perpetrated against Filipinos who were perceived as economic and racial threats. Other curricular possibilities include studying the independence of the Philippines alongside other African and Asian countries in the 1940s and 1950s; teaching the coalition building and solidarities between Filipina/os and other communities of color in their struggles for better working conditions in the agricultural fields and for better and more inclusive education; and learning about the post-1965 growth of various Asian ethnic communities throughout the United States. The curriculum integration that I propose simultaneously works within and against the conventional frameworks and narratives of U.S. history. It refers to major events in U.S. history, such as the emergence of the United States as a global power in the early 1900s, the Great Depression in the 1930s, the Second World War, and the increasing demographic diversity in the latter third of the 20th century. However, I do not take a simple additive approach that sprinkles decontextualized details about Filipina/os in the Philippines and the United States. To fill in the large gaps in our school curriculum, what I ultimately propose is an equitable integration of racialized minority lives and experiences that represents and interprets U.S. and world histories in multicultural, comparative, and transnational ways.

FILIPINA/O INTERVENTIONS IN P–12 SCHOOL CURRICULUM

In conclusion, I want to highlight community and academic efforts to diversify the curriculum. Local community members have certainly been at the forefront of working with educators. Teachers often rely on Filipina/o parents and elders as presenters in classrooms and professional development workshops. In fact, the Filipino American National Historical Society (FANHS) was founded in Seattle, Washington, in 1982 by community activists and pioneering historians Dorothy and Fred Cordova "to preserve, document, and present Filipino American history and to support scholarly research and artistic works which reflect that rich past."[2] With over two dozen chapters, national and regional conferences, rich archival collections, and public programs, FANHS has become a significant resource on Filipina/o American history for primary and secondary schools. Its 54-minute video *Filipino Americans: Discovering Their Past for the Future* is an accessible curriculum material that can be used by teachers and students alike (Wehman, 1994).

A number of community-minded academics and educators have made concentrated efforts to work with schools. In Seattle, Washington, Patricia Espiritu Halagao and Timoteo Cordova created Pinoy Teach in 1996 "to address the absence of curriculum about Filipino Americans in schools." It has grown to become a multifaceted curriculum that includes a textbook, an activity booklet, a teacher's manual, and a resource kit (Cordova & Espiritu, 2001; Espiritu & Cordova, 1999, 2002). Since her move to University of Hawai'i as an Education professor, Halagao has expanded her work to establish Global Teach, which aims "to broaden teacher perspectives of the global society we live in and provide them tools to build multicultural curricula that foster sensitivity, equity, and inclusion of diverse cultures and peoples." In 2006, she led a team of university faculty, school teachers, and artists to develop the online Filipino American Curriculum Project for the Washington, DC-based Smithsonian Institution in order to mark the 100th anniversary of Filipina/o immigration to the United States (see Halagao, this volume).[3]

In California, Filipina/o academics and educators have also created and disseminated educational materials on Philippine and Filipina/o American issues. Allyson Tintiangco-Cubales, an Asian American studies professor at

San Francisco State University, has developed Pin@y Educational Partnership, which initiated the first high school Filipino American Studies course in the San Francisco public schools in 2001 and published a sourcebook on Philippine and Filipina/o American history in 2007 (Tintiangco-Cubales, 2007; see Tintiangco-Cubales, this volume). Through the support of the University of California Consortium for Language Learning and Teaching, UC Berkeley lecturer Irma Peña and her collaborators created the Filipino Curriculum Project, a 15-unit online resource for Filipino heritage language learners at the high school and university levels. Moreover, Leny Mendoza Strobel, an American multicultural studies professor at Sonoma State University, organized a multicultural conference for K–12 educators in 2007 entitled "KAPWA: You and I are One, Infusing Filipino and Filipino American Content in the Curriculum." Through the auspices of the North Bay International Studies Project, the conference offered workshop sessions on the integration of Filipina/o and Filipina/o American content in elementary and secondary subjects, including art, humanities, language arts, math, music, social studies, and theater.[4]

Admittedly, this listing is not comprehensive by any means; however, I foreground these intellectual, pedagogical, and activist interventions to recognize and honor the daunting efforts of Filipina/o academic and community educators in bringing together theory, research, and practice, and building bridges between the university and the community. These interventions are significant and necessary praxis to diversify the curriculum and to prepare students and teachers for a multicultural and global society. My larger concern, however, is that, although Philippine and Filipina/o American studies have been flourishing in U.S. higher education, it has made little impact in the formal school curriculum. The invisibility of Filipina/o content in secondary history textbooks suggests that the growing and vibrant Philippine and Filipina/o American studies scholarship has not been taken up by textbook authors and teachers and as a result, has neither effectively contributed to nor challenged what and whose knowledge is taught and learned in schools. The question of to what degree and in what ways our scholarship impacts the schooling of Filipina/o Americans and the general student body, is a crucial issue that theorists, researchers, and educators need to continue wrestling with politically, empirically, and pedagogically.

NOTES

1. The two largest Asian ethnic groups in the United States are the Chinese and Asian Indian communities. The top two countries of birth of immigrants to the United States are Mexico and China.
2. Filipino American National Historical Society website: www.fanhs-national.org

3. Pinoy Teach website: www.pinoyteach.com; Global Teach website: www.globalteach.com; Smithsonian Institution's Filipino American Curriculum Project website: www.filam.si.edu/curriculum
4. University of California Filipino Curriculum Project website: www.language.berkeley.edu/ucfcp/index.php; KAPWA Conference website: www.sonoma.edu/projects/nbisp/philippines/kapwa_agenda.html

REFERENCES

Ahmad, I., Brodsky, H., Crofts, M. S., & Ellis, E. G. (2004). *World cultures: A global mosaic.* Upper Saddle River, NJ: Prentice Hall.

Apple, M. W., & Christian-Smith, L. K. (Eds.). (1991). *The politics of the textbook.* New York, NY: Routledge.

Appleby, J., Brinkley, A., Broussard, A. S., McPherson, J., & Ritchie, D. A. (2003). *The American republic since 1877.* New York, NY: Glencoe.

Baldoz, R. (2011). *The third Asiatic invasion: Migration and empire in Filipino America, 1898–1946.* New York: New York University Press.

Banks, J. A., & Banks, C. A. M. (Eds.). (2004). *Handbook of research on multicultural education.* San Francisco, CA: Jossey-Bass.

Baughman, M. (2008). The influence of scientific research and evaluation on publishing educational curriculum. *New Directions for Evaluation, 117,* 85–94.

Beck, R. B., Black, L., Krieger, L. S., Naylor, P. C., & Shabaka, D. I. (2003). *World history: Patterns of interaction.* Evanston, IL: McDougal Littell.

Cayton, A., Perry, E. I., Reed, L., & Winkler, A. M. (2005). *America: Pathways to the present.* Upper Saddle River, NJ: Prentice Hall.

Chan, S. (1991). *Asian Americans: An interpretive history.* Woodbridge, CT: Twayne.

Chappell, D. (2010). Training Americans. Ideology, performance and social studies textbooks. *Theory and Research in Social Education, 38*(2), 248–269.

Choy, C. C. (2003). *Empire of care: Nursing and migration in Filipino American history.* Durham, NC: Duke University Press.

Coloma, R. S. (2006). Disorienting race and education: Changing paradigms on the schooling of Asian Americans and Pacific Islanders. *Race Ethnicity and Education, 9*(1), 1–15.

Coloma, R. S. (Ed.). (2009). *Postcolonial challenges in education.* New York, NY: Peter Lang.

Coloma, R. S. (in press). Abject beings: Filipina/os in Canadian historical narrations. In R. S. Coloma, B. McElhinny, E. Tungohan, J. P. Catungal, & L. Davidson (Eds.), *Filipinos in Canada: Disturbing invisibility.* Toronto, Canada: University of Toronto Press.

Commeyras, M., & Alvermann, D. E. (1994). Messages that high school world history textbooks convey: Challenges for multicultural literacy. *The Social Studies, 85*(6), 268–274.

Cordova, F., & Cordova, D. L. (1983). *Filipinos, forgotten Asian Americans: A pictorial essay, 1763–circa 1963.* Dubuque, IA: Kendall/Hunt.

Cordova, T., & Espiritu, P. C. (2001). *Pinoy Teach: A multicultural curriculum exploring Filipino history and culture* (4th ed.). Seattle, WA: Filipino Youth Activities.

Cruz, B. C. (2002). Don Juan and rebels under palm trees: Depictions of Latin Americans in U.S. history textbooks. *Critique of Anthropology, 22*(3), 323–342.

Danzer, G. A., Klor de Alva, J. J., Krieger, L. S., Wilson, L. E., & Woloch, N. (2003). *The Americans.* Evanston, IL: McDougal Littell.

Ellis, E. G., & Esler, A. (2005). *World history: Connections to today.* Upper Saddle River, NJ: Prentice Hall.

Espiritu, A. F. (2005). *Five faces of exile: The nation and Filipino American intellectuals.* Palo Alto, CA: Stanford University Press.

Espiritu, P. C., & Cordova, T. (1999). *Pinoy Teach activity booklet.* Seattle, WA: Filipino Youth Activities.

Espiritu, P. C., & Cordova, T. (2002). *Teacher manual for Pinoy Teach: A multicultural curriculum exploring Filipino history and culture* (4th ed.). Seattle, WA: Filipino Youth Activities.

Foster, S. J. (1999). The struggle for American identity: Treatment of ethnic groups in United States history textbooks. *History of Education, 28*(3), 251–278.

Fujita-Rony, D. B. (2002). *American workers, colonial power: Philippine Seattle and the transpacific west, 1919–1941.* Berkeley and Los Angeles: University of California Press.

Garcia, J., Ogle, D. M., Risinger, C. F., Stevos, J., & Jordan, W. D. (2003). *Creating America: A history of the United States.* Evanston, IL: McDougal Littell.

Gay, G. (2000). *Culturally responsive teaching: Theory, research, and practice.* New York, NY: Teachers College Press.

Go, J. (2008). *American empire and the politics of meaning: Elite political cultures in the Philippines and Puerto Rico during U.S. colonialism.* Durham, NC: Duke University Press.

Gordy, L., & Pritchard, A. M. (1995). Redirecting our voyage through history: A content analysis of social studies textbooks. *Urban Education, 30*(2), 195–218.

Kelevh, N. (2002). Theoretical dimensions of multicultural education and curriculum development: A content analysis of multicultural textbooks. (Unpublished doctoral dissertation). Teachers College, Columbia University, New York, NY.

Kramer, P. A. (2006). *The blood of government: Race, empire, the United States, and the Philippines.* Chapel Hill: University of North Carolina Press.

Leonardo, Z. (Ed.). (2007). Special symposium: No Child Left Behind. *Race Ethnicity and Education, 10*(3), 241–321.

Macgillivray, I. K., & Jennings, T. (2008). A content analysis exploring lesbian, gay, bisexual, and transgender topics in foundations of education textbooks. *Journal of Teacher Education, 59*(2), 170–188.

Meier, D., & Wood, G. (2004). *Many children left behind: How the No Child Left Behind Act is damaging our children and our schools.* Boston, MA: Beacon.

Miller, S. C. (1984). *"Benevolent assimilation": The American conquest of the Philippines, 1899–1903.* New Haven, CT: Yale University Press.

Pang, V. O., & Cheng, L. L. (Eds.). (1998). *Struggling to be heard: The unmet needs of Asian Pacific American children.* Albany: State University of New York Press.

Posadas, B. M. (1999). *The Filipino Americans.* Westport, CT: Greenwood.

Ritchie, D. A. (2001). *American history: The modern era since 1865.* New York, NY: Glencoe.

Takaki, R. (1998). *Strangers from a different shore: A history of Asian Americans.* Boston, MA: Back Bay.

Tintiangco-Cubales, A. (2007). *Pin@y educational partnerships: A Filipina/o American studies sourcebook, Volume 1: Philippine and Filipina/o American history.* Manila, Philippines: Phoenix Publishing House International.

U. S. Census Bureau (2002a). *A profile of the nation's foreign-born population from Asia* (2000 update). Washington, DC: U.S. Department of Commerce.

U. S. Census Bureau (2002b). *A profile of the nation's foreign-born population from Latin America* (2000 update). Washington, DC: U.S. Department of Commerce.

U. S. Census Bureau. (2007). *The American community—Asians: 2004, American community survey reports.* Washington, DC: U.S. Department of Commerce.

Walter, J. C. (2001). The influence of African American history on U.S. history survey textbooks since the 1970s. In J. E. Butler (Ed.), *Color-line to borderlands: The matrix of American ethnic studies* (pp. 65–100). Seattle: University of Washington Press.

Wehman, J. (Director). (1994). *Filipino Americans: Discovering their past for the future.* Seattle, WA: Filipino American National Historical Society.

Zevin, J. (2007). *Social studies for the twenty-first century: Methods and materials for teaching in middle and secondary schools.* Philadelphia, PA: Lawrence Erlbaum.

CHAPTER 10

KUWENTO AND KARAOKE

Literacy Perspectives on Culture and Education

Korina Jocson
Washington University in St. Louis

What is *kuwento*? What is karaoke? What do they have to do with literacy? And why is it important to consider them in rethinking possibilities in education? This chapter offers some insights into *kuwento* and karaoke specifically as practiced by Filipina/os and Filipina/o Americans. Such cultural ways are key in the lives of those in the Philippines, the United States, and elsewhere in the diaspora. Both *kuwento* and karaoke exemplify what has been termed "literacy practice"; that is, from a sociocultural perspective on literacy, they are recurring and goal-oriented activities in the lives of participants. In this view, literacy manifests as situated, localized, and dependent upon context. What follows is a discussion largely of *kuwento* as a tool for learning in a Filipino Heritage social studies classroom (or Filipino Heritage Studies, for short).[1] In the end, I provide some thoughts on both *kuwento* and karaoke as a social practice, with implications for literacy development. Interestingly, in the world of boxing, Filipino fighter Manny

The "Other" Students, pages 183–196

Pacquiao has demonstrated the cultural use of *kuwento* to tell his life story in various media interviews, rising from poverty in the Philippines; he has also revealed (if not popularized) to the world karaoke as his choice of entertainment while in training at home or abroad.[2] Both *kuwento* and karaoke are cultural phenomena worthy of examination. First, a definition of literacy is key to our understanding.

DEFINING LITERACY AND LITERACY PRACTICE

Earlier arguments distinguished between orality and literacy, implying who was considered "literate" and who was not. Certain junctures in theory have posited a much broader conceptualization of the meaning of literacy beyond its relationship to intellectual development, higher thinking skills, and reading and writing. Research in literacy studies have further challenged current frameworks and interrogated the nature in which literacy functions in various communities and also manifests in various forms. It is to these works that link literacy to complexities of social and cultural processes that I turn.

Studies employing a cross-cultural approach offer a particular framework for understanding and defining literacy. In their work on the Vai people of Liberia, Scribner and Cole (1981) found that certain patterns in the use(s) of language as well as reading and writing systems achieve specific *purposes* in people's everyday practices (e.g., letter writing, recordkeeping, communicating with others). They suggest that such purposes depend on the notion that literacy had certain functions organized around the Vai's "particular systems of knowledge" and more importantly, the application of this knowledge in "contexts of use." As I will point out, *kuwento* offers classroom participants "systems of knowledge" that allow not only for the co-construction but also the reconstruction of history.

Along with uses and functions, literacy is also seen as a communicative practice. Hymes' (1964, 1974) "ethnography of communication" focused on examining communicative patterns and language use within communities. Building on this work, Heath's (1983) examination of three communities in the Piedmont Carolinas showed that each community had its own ways with words as established by its respective members. In similar fashion, Street (1984) asserted the need to expand the conceptualization of literacy to include social *context* and to explore literacy as embedded in the practices of everyday life. For Street, literacy *is* a social practice mediated and produced by the very contexts it occupies; it is not and cannot be defined as being removed from context. Literacy is more than one's ability to read and write; it is one's ability to manipulate certain kinds of texts (written, oral, visual, or otherwise) that are situated within social contexts. Literacy practices, then, are cultural ways associated with reading and/or writing upon which people draw in their lives. These works within literacy studies provide a helpful frame for treating *kuwento* and karaoke as practices in everyday life. In the next section, I will discuss how *kuwento* becomes a tool for learning in the classroom and how karaoke becomes a tool for tapping into available resources—human, material, cultural—for the purposes of maintaining a sense of community.

WHAT IS *KUWENTO*?

The Tagalog word *kuwento* is derived from the Spanish *cuento*, meaning "story." Its spelling reflects the presence of consonants (k and w) to take the place of the letter "c" and create similar "ue" vowel sounds (i.e., "koo-wento") in the Philippine alphabet, respectively. Over 300 years under Spanish rule resulted in the amalgamation of people, cultures, and languages. The latter is of interest here as *kuwento*, drawn from Philippine oral traditions, continues to be a cultural and sociolinguistic practice among Filipina/o Americans. The concept of *kuwento* is best described both as a noun (story) and a verb (telling/listening/participating in a story). To be clear, *kuwento* is not about simply sharing or listening to stories themselves, but also about the nature in which stories take place. This is similar to cultural practices of "talk story" in Hawaiian communities (Au & Jordan, 1981). To understand *kuwento* is to understand story.

A story is an abstraction of history, that is, one that transforms experience into a chronological sequence of events. It is an "account" consisting either of the past, present, or future and is based on temporal events that are of key importance to individuals who choose to tell them (Bloome, Champion, Katz, Morton, & Muldrow, 2001). Variations in the construction of a story abound as each teller has her/his own individual experience, an experience that is co-constructed by many experiences. In other words, a story is produced, reproduced, and recycled as a consequence of social interactions.

Many Filipinos retain a rich oral tradition, transmitting significant human experience (Eugenio, 1981). *Kuwento* (story) or *kuwento-kuwentohan* (the act of sharing story) becomes part of everyday life for children, youth, and adults. Abundant in folk literature, it is a tool for communicating experiences with family and community (Eugenio, 1981). It is neither gossip nor rumor; rather, it is based on (aspects of) actual events retold and reconstructed in the presence of others. Creativity in the telling may result in exaggeration or imagined worlds, but the basis of *kuwento* holds some truth value. Passed on from one generation to the next, *kuwentos* find their way into the lives of those who hear and live through them. From a Bakhtinian perspective, we learn from others, and in the process of interaction, also learn to incorporate others' words or voices into our own. Borrowed and reconciled stories shape, if not make up, the ones we tell with our own voice(s) and intentions (Bakhtin, 1981). It is in this kind of manipulation or "owning" of such words that personal stories are born. In constructing them, stories as participant structures also expand to incorporate the multiplicity of voices surrounding the teller (Goodwin, 1990; Phillips, 1972). As children, we are socialized by stories told to us by our parents, grandparents, and other kin. Endless stories have amused us, stimulated our imaginations, and taught us about ourselves. When these stories become our own, they reflect our inner thoughts, feelings, beliefs, aspirations, values, goals, expectations, and creativity. In short, stories represent a construction of our reality (Bruner, 1991), and as we come to understand the experiences in the world we live in, stories shape how we see ourselves as well as the identities we take on (Baquedano-López, 1997; Ochs & Capps, 1996; Ochs, Taylor, Rudolph, & Smith, 1992).

Salient in stories is the context of social events in which they are constructed. Stories are not simply the result of what the speaker has produced, but also the result of a sort of co-authorship between the speaker and listeners (Ochs, 1997). In a classroom context, the co-construction of story is mediated by interaction with classmates and the teacher. "Footings" or roles such as introducer(s), primary recipient(s), problematizer(s), and evaluator(s) shape the nature of the story being told (Goffman, 1981). Further, stories take oral, visual, spatial, or written forms, an imagined space to voice out relevant tales. They are central to the process of meaning making to understand how present events in our lives are shaped by a historical past. Through the telling of stories, both the teacher and students in a classroom, for example, can learn about each other's diverse experiences and make connections to understand the sociocultural world in which they live. They open up avenues for building social relationships with the larger school community as well as place value on encounters with the outside world.

In conceptualizing stories for use in the classroom, Michaels (1981) and Cazden (1994) assert that during sharing time, stories provide teachers and students official time to speak about out-of-school experiences. Doing so offers unlimited pedagogical possibilities and encourages the active construction of newer understandings. In sharing stories, students are free "from the dreariness of fact-driven curriculums, find power in re-thinking and re-formulating ideas," and realize the complexity of the world "in which multiple perspectives exist" (Brooks & Brooks, 1993, p. 22). The classroom becomes more than a traditional place of learning; it becomes an unbounded space for elevating students' potential beyond the norm and for accommodating their diverse stories. In the case of paucity in classroom material, the teacher can also engage students in learning through her/his own writing (Vascellaro & Genishi, 1994) and her/his own construction of oral stories. As I will illustrate, the teacher and students of Filipino Heritage Studies used multiple stories to convey present-day realities that in large part shape the very subject they were studying. *Kuwento* functioned as a pedagogical tool to construct as well as challenge existing forms (or lack) of knowledge about Filipina/o American history in the classroom. *Kuwento* established cultural continuity and legitimized students' sense of knowing. On the one hand, it was a major source of knowledge (Nieto, 1998, 2000); on the other, it served as a means for students to communicate who they are, represent relevant experiences, and take charge of their circumstances (Sleeter & Grant, 1991). Additionally, *kuwento* was central to providing alternative narratives to dominant discourses, in particular through counter-storytelling, which recognizes a collective history of marginalization based on race and other forms of oppression (Solórzano & Yosso, 2000; Tate, 1997). *Kuwento* was key in (re)shaping larger discourses relevant to multicultural education.

KUWENTO IN THE CLASSROOM

In a study conducted at a racially diverse high school in northern California, I found that *kuwento* was abundant in a variety of instances. Below are examples of *kuwento* from a Filipino Heritage social studies classroom for co-constructing and reconstructing history. While I recognize that there are different types and styles, *kuwento* is mainly represented here as (a) monologic (individual speaker); (b) occurring in the past and present (subject matter spanning a historical continuum); and (c) oral (versus written or visual) in form. In the following excerpts, Mr. Q, the teacher, addressed Filipina/os' crucial role in the Spanish-American War, beginning with a description to contextualize the larger U.S. colonial occupation of other countries. As indicated by bold italicized text, Mr. Q used *kuwento* in his lectures to incite *empathy* for understanding the subject matter.[3] He explicitly asked students to pay attention and "hear two (of his) stories" as one means of demonstrating how history is constructed through narrative. According to Mr. Q, one of those stories was about the Americans' arrival and eventual presence *in* the Philippines to help Filipina/os fight against Spaniards. The other was Filipina/os' determination to keep Americans *out* of the Philippines. Mr. Q placed emphasis on the latter and, again, explicitly asked students to note which version of history is common knowledge and often depicted in textbooks. The *kuwento* is as follows:

Mr. Q: The Philippines resembles Puerto Rico. The war started when the Philippines was under Spain (.) Americans decided *not* to get involved ( ) first with Cuba then Puerto

Rico ( ) in 1898. When all this time, ***I'm telling you***, the Intramuros had Spaniards on the run ( ) *that's* when the Americans joined in. Aguinaldo decided to come back to the Philippines with Dewey ( ) when the Americans came. They came by ship (.) landed in Manila ( ) then the Spanish surrendered. The story, ***I'm telling you***, is full of cheating and deceit (.) like the action movies you see these days . . .

[Students were attentive and focused on Mr. Q's words; many were taking notes and writing in their notebooks.]

Mr. Q: War is the reason why probably ***you and I*** are here today. Official relationship between U.S. and the Filipinos was like the Vietnamese in the Vietnam War. Understand this, Filipino American War really starts talking about Filipino Heritage Studies, but we'll take our time with this, probably will take three weeks or something.[4]

In this classroom episode, Mr. Q used personal statements (in bold italics) to pull the attention of students toward a specific time of war and struggle, which he further described in an interview as "a time often blurred and forgotten in our lives." Notably, Mr. Q also referred to the traditionally named "Spanish-American War" in history books as the "Filipino-American War" in his lecture. According to him, "it was important for students to see it and name it differently." Shifting the focus away from Spaniards and on to Filipina/os fighting against imperialism was part of reconstructing history, part of an engaged pedagogy that is potentially empowering and emancipatory (Banks, 1991; Darder, 1995; hooks, 1994; Shor, 1992). Central to Filipino Heritage Studies is everyday people's resolve and resistance against foreign forces to keep their independence, their freedom, and their nation. Mr. Q affirmed this by saying, "Yes, *even* against the Americans who originally set out to *help* Filipinos in their battle against the Spaniards" (emphasis in original).

Critical of how the war's events are usually told in mainstream history texts, it was important for Mr. Q to express his counterviews about the role of the United States in decolonizing and separating the Philippines from Spain. He utilized *kuwento* to illustrate history, not simply as facts but rather as relevant life instances affecting them collectively (Bruner, 1991; White, 1980). *Kuwento* became a means of imagining alternative ways of seeing the world and themselves differently. Mr. Q admitted the use of story in his lecture as purposeful and inviting. He noted, "I wanted stories to help students see what I'm talking about, to learn about themselves. *That's* my job." Mr. Q called upon empathy and, as he prefaced accordingly, identified for his students the deliberate consideration of "two stories" prior to beginning his lecture. In the above excerpt, he illustrated the war's events in such a way that drew upon his own connection with students (i.e., "I'm telling you" and "you and I"), as well as knowledge of popular culture (i.e., "movies you see today") to offer complex perspectives about history. Mr. Q elaborated on his approaches to teaching and learning, specifically through *kuwento,* as "wanting [my] students to appreciate who they are and where they come from." Central to this teaching and learning process were illustrative accounts about nationalism, resistance, Filipino army soldiers, and guerrilla fighters in the Philippine Revolution. Mr. Q admittedly did not paint the usual patriarchal image of the United States as "savior of third world peoples" as present in traditional texts. Instead, he drew on *kuwento* to offer a more balanced perspective and to counter grand narratives found in mainstream history books (Solórzano & Yosso, 2000; Tate, 1997). Mr. Q also positioned himself as a cynic, evident in his calling of the Philippines-U.S. relationship as "full of cheating and deceit."

In the following excerpt from the next-day lecture on the Filipino-American War, Mr. Q appropriated vivid details in order to generate further empathy from his students. He prefaced this part of *kuwento* by situating the war through its effects on communal living conditions, making his empathetic tone and human sensibilities more evident.

> **Mr. Q:** A lot of good stuff in this story. ((smiles)) At that time, about 9 million Filipinos were alive. Over a million Filipinos died in that war. 1 out of 9 or maybe something like 1 out of 8. *Killed.* ( ) people died by the hundreds, by really unsavory means. One time, ***I was*** ( ) reading from a friend of mine's book who's a soldier in the military. His friend was a White guy ( ) master's thesis writing about military campaign ( ) in the Filipino-American War ( ). Men went into a village and wiped EVERYTHING out, killed everything, and burned everything. I mean, chickens, dogs, everything, all animals (.) *nothing* was left.

Here, Mr. Q's use of imagery and personal association to describe the killings was bracing. It humanized the war and uncovered unique aspects of Philippine history, which, according to him, "have been excluded from mainstream texts." Throughout his lecture, Mr. Q pointed out to students the importance of the continuous resistance of Filipina/os against these killings. Using storytelling to reconstruct history, he was arming students with atypical knowledge about the Philippine Revolution; that is, it began before the close of the 20th century *and* lasted for more than 2 years. Speaking from the same lecture on the war, Mr. Q shifted his talk from deaths to national heroes, starting with General-turned-president Emilio

Aguinaldo, along with Antonio Luna and other Filipino military soldiers, and ending with revolutionary leaders such as Andres Bonifacio and other *Katipuneros* who were instrumental in ousting Spanish rule in 1896. Key in Mr. Q's message was that the Philippine Revolution took place *prior* to the Spanish–American War. This shift in focus, according to him, was necessary to juxtapose the casualties against the triumphs of war and vice versa. He also wanted to "provide a sense of Filipino strength and unity" through the recognition of a secret society called *Katipunan* to reaffirm the power of common folk and to convey to students the long-standing resistance of Filipinos against colonization. It was important to name *Katipunan* (short for *Kataastaasan Kagalang-galang na Katipunan nang manga Anak nang Bayan*) as a revolutionary group made up of mostly poor working-class Filipina/os whose aims included freeing the Philippines from Spain by force and serving and treating all people as equal.[5] When asked about his instructional style, Mr. Q noted that "the lesson was not only about who fought, who died, what happened, but it's also about students getting a sense of their history, to know their lineage, that they were, they *are* heroes." The collective struggle and resistance against colonialism (in old and new forms) are indeed as much a part of present-day realities as they were over a century ago. Mr. Q pointed out the relevance of deconstructing the past in order to imagine different possibilities for the present and future. Toward the end of this particular lecture, Mr. Q alluded to the uncertainty of the so-called Spanish-American War's end as recorded in history books. He implied that once again, some information found in mainstream texts is incorrect and that "it is really important for us to question them and find better explanations." He then wrote several dates on the board before pointing to the map on the wall and directing students' attention to the southern island of Mindanao.

> **Mr. Q:** In Mindanao ((pointing to the map)) there was *still* fighting going on but, you know, there are different dates that people say the Filipino-American war ended. 1901, because Aguinaldo got captured. 1902 because in Leyte some of whom considered insurgents surrendered, ***you remember?*** President Roosevelt declared it a safe place to be. *But 1916*, because until 1916, Americans were STILL in Mindanao. They were fighting Moros there. They were fighting against being kicked out of their own land.

Harking back to an earlier point about the duration of the war, Mr. Q and his continued *kuwento* reinforced the significance of critical thinking in the learning of history. Mr. Q's emphasis here was the construction of knowledge toward empowerment. He provided students with the more popular dates that supposedly marked the end of the so-called Spanish-American War. At the same time, he provided them with a sequence of events, altering the dominant discourse about who and what is left out in mainstream history texts. Indeed, if war ended in 1902, then why were Americans "STILL in Mindanao" in 1916? The question seemed rhetorical. For Mr. Q, it reaffirmed the point in the lesson and why Filipino Heritage Studies exists as part of social studies. He noted, "If there is anything they [students] take away from this, it's questioning *that* [chronology], and if they question *that,* then they would question a *whole* lot of other things."

KUWENTO AS LITERACY AND MULTICULTURAL EDUCATION

Kuwento, as delivered by Mr. Q in lecture, was one way of shaping the subjects that make up Filipino Heritage Studies. One the one hand, it built on the cultural ways of students; *kuwento* as a literacy practice present in homes was key to information exchange in the classroom. On the other, *kuwento* served as a tool to promote cultural relevancy while challenging dominant texts and discourses about Filipina/os. *Kuwento* was a way of naming a collective history—present, past, and future—which also served as an opportunity to explore what it means to be "Filipina/o American." There were numerous *kuwentos* that I found within students' textual production and conversations with each other as well as interactions with Mr. Q, both in small and large groups. It is not enough to rejoice in the development of Filipino Heritage Studies as multicultural education; the complexities of the teaching and learning process are many. The focus here has been the use of *kuwento* in a whole-group lecture, with an emphasis on temporal events and details related to the Philippine-American War. Teachers who work with Filipina/o American students in similar contexts might consider adopting *kuwento*-related practices (as well as other relevant literacy practices of students) to invigorate the teaching of social studies.[6] There are myriad ways of employing *kuwento* in the classroom; the challenge is how to link *kuwento*'s potential to the construction of knowledge, not as separate, but as embedded within larger discourses in school and in society.

KARAOKE AND SOME IMPLICATIONS FOR LITERACY

Another notable cultural practice among Filipina/os and Filipina/o Americans is karaoke. Karaoke (also known as sing-along) originated in Japan in the 1960s and spread across different parts of Asia in the 1970s and 1980s. Briefly, karaoke in the initial years took the form of cassette tapes of popular music from various eras and genres, which were played on a sing-along machine and accompanied by lyric books. Now, karaoke is an interactive entertainment system that allows amateur singers to sing along with recorded music; song lyrics appear on a video screen, and singers follow the text as the song progresses. At the end of the song, a score on a scale of 100 is provided based on the performance. Whether in the privacy of one's home or in public venues such as restaurants and bars, karaoke provides its participants an opportunity to select a song of choice and invent a singer-self during the performance. In the Philippines and in the United States, karaoke became popular upon the development of a Filipino patent of the "minus one" machine in the 1980s. When I was growing up in Los Angeles, I remember the minus one machine being the primary form of entertainment at every family gathering (i.e., birthdays, holidays, etc.). Even today, karaoke is ever-present at every special occasion. While "videoke" and "magic mic" as new technologies have taken the place of the traditional karaoke or minus one machine, its social function as a form of interactive entertainment remains the same. According to Sarmiento (2008), it functions in several ways: to de-stress from a busy work schedule, to briefly escape reality, and to bond with others. Such functions parallel responses to a 2008 survey I conducted in the Philippines (rural and urban) as well as in southern California. In that survey, I found that 90% of karaoke/videoke users (N = 325) prefer to sing songs among family and friends—during special occasions, after work, and other social events. While there is variation in the setting and frequency of use, I also found that 65% of karaoke/videoke users choose both Tagalog and English songs; 26% prefer English and 9% prefer Tagalog/Other or did not respond. In either case, it is clear that language is embedded in karaoke/videoke. The text that appears on the video screen (and the interaction with that text) can influence one's language development. What might happen if that interaction were to be sustained over time? If such were the case, how might it influence learning, specifically to improve reading, acquire language, or develop fluency of children (and perhaps adults)? For many Filipina/os and Filipina/o Americans, the availability of both English and Tagalog songs affirms a complex history of Americanization and migration, as well as a strong influence of American media and popular culture. Songs in both languages are readily accessible and offer a wider range of selection for participants.

From a sociocultural perspective, these trends suggest relevant and nuanced ways that literacy manifests in particular contexts. The interactive use of karaoke or videoke machines at home or other settings among family and friends implies some possibilities for literacy development. A recent study in Khodi in the state of Gujarat, India, suggests that karaoke assists in reading and improves the likelihood of rural children staying in school. The "karaoke for literacy" program broadcast by India's national television network introduced karaoke-style subtitles in popular Bollywood films and other programs using the language that stars sing in (Shah, 2010). Captions on the bottom of the screen serve as text for viewers to follow, and sometimes it is copied to a piece of paper. Effects of this unique study in India include higher rates of newspaper reading and participants becoming more proficient readers in the Khodi and Hindi languages. As other studies are underway, it is these possibilities in literacy that are key in education. Similar uses of karaoke are prevalent among Filipina/os around the world. It is important to pay attention not only to cultural trends but the specific cultural ways in which literacy practices such as karaoke can further develop language and literacy skills. The reading of text on the video screen is only the beginning. While the pairing of written and visual text has become common in karaoke, it is outside the scope of this chapter to address the uncomplimentary nature of some images that may require a type of media literacy. However, it is my hope that this brief treatment of karaoke spurs discussion about other possibilities in literacy, both in research and in practice. Indeed, the next time boxing champion-turned-politician Manny Pacquiao (or anyone for that matter) takes the mic to sing a song in front of family and friends, careful note should be given to the singer's multiple interactions with text, the role of language in that text, and depending on the setting, the different audience responses during the performance. There is no doubt that it will be more than a cultural phenomenon.

CONCLUSION

In this chapter, it has been my charge to discuss *kuwento* and karaoke from a sociocultural perspective of literacy. Each represents a unique set of literacy practices specific to many Filipina/os and Filipina/o Americans. Yet these practices are also relevant to other racial and ethnic groups across the globe. What I have highlighted here are key functions of *kuwento* in a multicultural classroom as well as karaoke in social settings to offer some insights into literacy and to suggest possible directions for research in education. There are numerous possibilities for examining situated literacies in school and out of school. It is in our hands to guide and carry out such investigations.

NOTES

1. Parts of this chapter have appeared in a different argument (Jocson, 2008, 2009).
2. The Home Box Office (HBO) cable network runs a boxing documentary series called "24/7" to feature the training and life experiences of boxers like Manny Pacquaio during the weeks leading up to a specific scheduled fight.

Included in the shows are instances of Pacquiao performing songs among family and friends.

3. Elsewhere (Jocson, 2008), I note the different manifestations of *kuwento* in teaching and learning, including empathy, entertainment, and empowerment. The latter is key to multicultural education and the struggle for ethnic studies in K–16 education.
4. The transcribed symbols used for the segments are: *italics* for pronounced emphasis; colons for elongated sound of the previous letter; period in parentheses for noticeable pause; brackets for observer's added commentary; empty parentheses for unintelligible words or phrases; ((double)) parentheses for nonverbal behavior; (single) parentheses for clarifying notes and other information; CAPITALIZED words for increased volume; and ellipsis points for omitted data. Conventional punctuation marks are used to indicate ends of utterances or sentences, usually indicated by slight pauses on the audiotape. Commas refer to pauses within words or phrases. Also, **bold *italicized*** words or phrases are used to direct the attention of the reader for textual understanding.
5. Loosely translated, the formal name of *Katipunan* means "the most highly respected society of the nation's children."
6. Recommended texts for teachers and other educators include Halagao & Cordova's *Pinoy Teach* (2004) and Tintiango-Cubales's *Pin@y Educational Partnerships* (2007).

REFERENCES

Au, K., & Jordan, C. (1981). Teaching reading to Hawaiian children: Finding a culturally appropriate solution. In H. Trueba, B. P. Guthrie, & K. H. Au (Eds.), *Culture and bilingual classroom: Studies in classroom ethnography* (pp. 139–152). Rowley, MA: Newbury.

Bakhtin, M. M. (1981). *The dialogic imagination: Four essays by M. M. Bakhtin.* Austin: University of Texas Press.

Banks, J. A. (1991). A curriculum for empowerment, action, and change. In C. E. Sleeter (Ed.), *Empowerment through multicultural education* (pp. 125–141). Albany: State University of New York Press.

Baquedano-López, P. (1997). Creating social identities through *doctrina* narratives. *Issues in Applied Linguistics, 8*(1), 27–45.

Bloome, D., Champion, T., Katz, L., Morton, M. B., & Muldrow, R. (2001). Spoken and written narrative development: African American preschoolers as storytellers and storymakers. In J. Harris, A. G. Kamhi, & K. E. Pollock (Eds.), *Literacy in African American communities* (pp. 46–76). Mahwah, NJ: Lawrence Erlbaum.

Brooks, J. G., & Brooks, M. G. (1993). *In search of understanding: The case for constructivist classrooms.* Alexandria, GA: Association for Supervision and Curriculum Development.

Bruner, J. (1991). The narrative construction of reality. *Critical inquiry, 18,* 1–21.

Cazden, C. B. (1994). What is sharing time for? In A. H. Dyson & C. Genishi (Eds.), *The need for story: Cultural diversity in classroom and community* (pp. 72–79). Urbana, IL: NCTE.

Darder, A. (1995). Buscando America: The contributions of critical Latino educators to the academic development and empowerment of Latino students in the U.S. In C. Sleeter & P. McLaren (Eds.), *Multicultural education, critical pedagogy, and the politics of difference* (pp. 319–347). Albany: State University of New York Press.

Eugenio, D. L. (1981). *Philippine folk literature: An anthology.* Diliman, Quezon City: The University of the Philippines Folklorists.

Goffman, E. (1981). *Forms of talk.* Philadelphia: University of Pennsylvania Press.

Goodwin, M. H. (1990). *He-said-she-said: Talk as social organization among black children.* Cambridge, MA: Harvard University Press.

Halagao, P., & Cordova, T. (2004). *Pinoy Teach: Teachers manual.* Seattle, WA: Filipino Youth Activities.

Heath, S. B. (1983). *Ways with words: Language, life, and work in communities and classrooms.* Cambridge, UK: Cambridge University Press.

hooks, b. (1994). *Teaching to transgress: Education as the practice of freedom.* New York, NY: Routledge.

Hymes, D. (1964). Introduction: Toward ethnographies of communication. In J. Gumperz & D. Hymes (Eds.), *The ethnography of communication* (pp. 1–34). Washington, DC: American Anthropological Association.

Hymes, D. (1974). *Foundations of sociolinguistics.* Philadelphia: University of Pennsylvania Press.

Jocson, K. M. (2008). Kuwento as multicultural pedagogy in high school ethnic studies. *Pedagogies: An International Journal, 3*(4), 241–253.

Jocson, K. M. (2009). Whose story is it anyway?: Teaching social studies and making use of kuwento. *Multicultural Perspectives, 11*(1), 31–36.

Michaels, S. (1981). "Sharing time": Children's narrative styles and differential access to literacy. *Language in Society, 10,* 423–442.

Nieto, S. (1998). Fact or fiction: Stories of Puerto Ricans in U.S. schools. *Harvard Educational Review, 68*(2), 133–163.

Nieto, S. (2000). *Affirming diversity: The sociopolitical context of multicultural education* (3rd ed.). New York, NY: Longman.

Ochs, E. (1997). Narrative. In T. A. Van Dyjk (Ed.), *Discourse as structure and process* (pp. 181–204). London, UK: Sage.

Ochs, E., & Capps, L. (1996). Narrating the self. In W. Durham, E. Daniel, & B. Schieffelin (Eds.), *Annual review of anthropology* (pp. 19–43). Palo Alto, CA: Annual Reviews.

Ochs, E., Taylor, C., Rudolph, D., & Smith, R. (1992). Storytelling as a theory-building activity. *Discourse Processes, 15*(1), 37–72.

Phillips, S. (1972). Participant structures and communicative competence: Warm Springs children in community and classroom. In C. Cazden, V. John, & D. Hymes (Eds.), *Functions of language in the classroom* (pp. 370–394). New York, NY: Teachers College Press.

Sarmiento, P. (2008, March 25). Conquered by videoke. *pcij.org.* Retrieved from http://www.pcij.org/i-report/2008/videoke.html

Scribner, S., & Cole, M. (1981). *The psychology of literacy*. Cambridge, MA: Harvard University Press.

Shah, R. (2010). Watch and learn: How music videos are triggering a literacy boom. *boston.com* Retrieved from http://www.boston.com/bostonglobe/ideas/articles/2010/09/19/watch_and_learn

Shor, I. (1992). *Empowering education: Critical teaching for social change*. Chicago, IL: University of Chicago Press.

Sleeter, C., & Grant, C. A. (1991). Mapping terrains of power: Student cultural knowledge versus classroom knowledge. In C. Sleeter (Ed.), *Empowerment through multicultural education* (pp. 49–67). Albany: State University of New York Press.

Solórzano, D., & Yosso, T. (2000). Toward a critical race theory of Chicana and Chicano education. In C. Tejeda, C. Martinez, & Z. Leonardo (Eds.), *Charting new terrains in Chicana(o)/Latina(o) education* (pp. 35–66). Cresskill, NY: Hampton.

Street, B. (1984). *Literacy in theory and practice*. Cambridge, UK: Cambridge University Press.

Tate, W. (1997). Critical race theory and education: History, theory and implication. In M. Apple (Ed.), Review of research in education (pp. 195–247). Washington, DC: American Educational Research Association.

Tintiango-Cubales, A. (Ed.). (2007). *Pin@y educational partnerships: A Filipina/o American studies sourcebook series*. Quezon City, Philippines: Phoenix.

Vascellaro, S., & Genishi, C. (1994). "All things that mattered": Stories written by teachers for children. In A. H. Dyson & C. Genishi (Eds.), *The need for story: Cultural diversity in classroom and community* (pp. 172–198). Urbana, IL: NCTE.

White, H. (1980). The value of narrativity in the representation of reality. *Critical Inquiry, 7*(1), 5–27.

CHAPTER 11

REFLECTIONS ON THE CONTOURS OF AND TRAJECTORY FOR A CRITICAL FILIPINO STUDIES

Antonio T. Tiongson, Jr.
University of New Mexico

> But there is also a violence committed, in the name of "community," when critical class issues are deleted from Filipino American community formations. For instance, while the National Association of Filipino American Associations (NaFAA) supported the airport screeners by launching a class-action lawsuit contesting the ATSA's citizenship requirement, it simultaneously supported Philippine President Gloria Macapagal Arroyo's call for global Filipino "unity" which included here support of the Bush administration's global war on terror. A progressive community politics, however, must recognize that the violence suffered by Filipino communities, whether through racist lay-offs or gay baiting, is linked to a larger history of gendered U.S. imperialism and collusion with the Philippine neocolonial state.
>
> —Robyn Rodriguez and Nerissa S. Balce (2004)

The Philippines has been variously articulated through Puerto Rico in turn-of-the 20th century legal debates, as part of the Latin American borderlands

The "Other" Students, pages 197–209

> in early-twentieth-century popular literature, and with Hawai'i and the Pacific Islands in mid-century cinema.
>
> —Allan Punzalan Isaac (2006)

> Strident and open Filipino negrophobic racism notwithstanding, it may well be that the only possibility for serious *political* kinship between blacks and Pinoys (locally and diasporically, beyond liberal, culturalist, or compensatory Filipino negrophilia) exists in the proximity and familiarity that can only be shared as we approach our differently produced—though somehow still stubbornly *common*—identifications with the horror of collective vulnerability to sudden mortality and bodily subjection to higher forces (whether "God," "nature," the US state, or officially sanctioned white supremacist violence).
>
> —Dylan Rodriguez (2007)

I begin this chapter with the foregoing epigraphs as a way to put into focus a body of work that compels us to rethink the way we frame and approach the study of Filipino social formations.[1] I consider these epigraphs as part of an emergent literature that raises significant questions concerning the contours and trajectory of Filipino American studies. Written from a range of disciplinary and theoretical perspectives, they represent a body of work that does not thread well-worn pathways for the study of Filipino social formations. Instead, these epigraphs speak to a body of work that provides a space for reconsidering conceptual frameworks and dominant narratives that have historically informed the study of Filipino social formations. I look to this body of work as a possible point of departure, expanding the grounds from which to consider Filipino social formations and in the process, generating new theoretical insights and new lines of inquiries.

Collectively, this emergent literature opens up new avenues of critical engagements that do not easily translate into existing paradigms and narratives. It speaks to how a field such as Filipino American studies can no longer be mapped according to conventional cartographies or through the use of a familiar set of organizing tropes based, for example, on the frame of nation and the narrative of immigration, settlement, and assimilation or on the logic of multiculturalism if it is to serve as a space for radical critique. To continue to rely on such conventional frames is to reproduce parochialisms that have become the sine qua non of "area studies" and "ethnic studies" disciplinary formations (Campomanes, 2006). In contradistinction, this recent literature provides a compelling case that Filipino social formations as an object of study can no longer be taken for granted. At the same time, it gestures toward a possible direction in terms of how Filipino American studies might be practiced and what an alternative cartography might look like. Thus, it lays the basis for a remapping of the conceptual terrain of Filipino American studies.

In the first epigraph, Robyn Rodriguez and Nerissa S. Balce (2004) address the question of what constitutes a "progressive community politics," the kind of politics that grapples with the legacies of empire but also accounts for its multiple and varied articulations and permutations in particular historical contexts. Focusing on colonial/postcolonial crossings and convergences involving Filipinos and other colonized subjects, Allan Punzalan Isaac (2006) gestures toward a critical comparative approach that does not simply recognize and acknowledge "similarities and differences" but delves into the ways the histories of these groups are mutually constitutive without collapsing distinct dynamics into one another. In the third epigraph, Dylan Rodriguez (2007) addresses the question of Black/Brown imbrications, exploring the potential for political identifications predicated not on liberal pluralist notions of "multiculturalism" or "solidarity" but on the recognition of shared familiarity with and vulnerability to global White supremacy.

This chapter maps out the implications—theoretical, pedagogical, and political—of this emergent body of work in terms of how we approach the study of Filipino social formations. Taking up the question of empire in a post-9/11 context, colonial/postcolonial crossings, and Black/Brown imbrications, these works serve to broaden the scope of Filipino American studies and remap what are considered the disciplinary boundaries of the field. I am particularly interested in the kinds of questions these works raise concerning the continuities and ruptures of empire across time and space, the convergence of colonial/postcolonial histories and legacies, and the emergence of a critical common sense that can serve as the basis of identification for Black and Brown subjects. Therefore, my aim is neither to provide a survey of contemporary Filipino American scholarship nor to reflect on the current state of the field. Rather, it is to begin to elucidate the parameters of what I consider a critical Filipino American studies based on the consideration of a few select works that, collectively, raise significant questions about the contours and trajectory of Filipino American studies.

ON EMPIRE WITHIN A POST-9/11 CONTEXT

For those of us who grapple with the question of empire in our teaching, scholarship, and activism, the notion that U.S. imperialism is implicated in the everyday realities of millions around the world has become almost axiomatic. Of course, this is not a particularly novel insight. A cohort of Pinoy/Pinay scholars, including E. San Juan Jr. (1992), Steffi San Buenaventura (1998), Oscar Campomanes (1992, 1995, 1997), and Rick Bonus (2000), have all asserted this point in compelling and powerful ways. In many ways, their works have established the bounds for the study of empire and Filipinos. For this cohort of scholars, imperialism is not a social phenomenon of the past but instead a phenomenon that looms large in the lives of Filipinos across the globe despite the disavowal of U.S. imperial history. Although the era of formal U.S. imperialism has ended, U.S. presence in the Philippines created ties—cultural, military, economic, and political—between the two nations, ties that structure the lives of Filipinos today. This is evident, for example, in the continued large-scale migration of Filipinos to the United States and U.S. military presence in the Philippines (even after closure of U.S. bases) in the form of military-related assistance including technical support in the so-called global war on terror.

As exemplified by the foregoing scholarship, Pinoy/Pinay scholars have worked hard to expose the centrality of empire-building to U.S. nation-building and challenge the official narratives of the nation predicated on the disavowal of empire and more specifically the notion that empire has never occurred (and could never occur) within the United States. Empire-building, in other words, does not constitute a "tragic but exceptional" episode in U.S. history but rather a project inextricably linked to nation-building. These scholars have done much to decenter the United States, troubling claims of U.S. exceptionalism, and claims of the nation-state as the seemingly logical and inevitable object of study. They look to empire as a historical phenomenon necessitating a full accounting of its evolving dynamics and discourses. Accordingly, Pinoy/Pinay scholars have been at the forefront of raising the spectre of empire in disciplines such as Asian American studies and ethnic studies, and putting into focus the complicity of these disciplinary formations in perpetuating the illegibility of empire in academe (Campomanes, 1992, 1995, 1997). Therefore, Pinoy/Pinay scholars ought to figure crucially in debates revolving around empire, particularly given the current political and historical moment.

Scholars like Amy Kaplan (2004) and Neferti Tadiar (2004) characterize the contemporary period as no longer marked by simply a denial and disavowal of empire. Instead, these scholars make the point that there has been a dramatic shift in the way policymakers, academics, and journalists talk and think about empire in the wake of 9/11. They put forth this notion that there seems to be a shift in the discourse surrounding U.S. imperialism, a shift marked not only by avowal but also a resignification of "empire." In other words, denial and disavowal no longer seem to characterize imperial discourse. Instead, there now seems to be an open embrace of empire. In both media and political discourse, "America" and "empire" are no longer seen as antithetical or as mutually exclusive categories. Moreover, empire seems to have taken on new inflections in relation to other words that have entered the political discourse, such as "terrorism" and "homeland."[2] The focal point of debates and discussions no longer revolves around the question of whether the United States is an empire but on "what kind" of empire it is. In contrast to pre-9/11 imperialist discourse, it now revolves around the question of whether or not the United States is beneficent or self-interested and whether or not it is an empire on the rise or on the decline (Kaplan, 2004; Tadiar, 2004).

If it is indeed the case that we are seeing a shift in the discourse surrounding U.S. imperialism, then what are the implications for those of us who have always been interested in the question of empire? What does it mean that the invocation of "American empire" is no longer taboo but commonplace? What kind of challenge does this present to the work we are doing? What are the implications in terms of our engagement with empire? How does it complicate our approach to the study of empire? What does it mean to fully account for empire—its varied articulations and permutations—at this historical moment? How do we ensure that our approach to the study of empire accounts for the contingent nature of imperial discourse?[3] What of the term "empire" itself? Should its utility and viability as a category of analysis and explanatory framework be up for discussion? Has it outlived its utility and viability as a category of analysis and explanatory framework? What do we make of Kaplan's (2004) contention that "all this talk about empire conceals more than it reveals" (p. 3) and Tadiar's (2004) assertion that we need to be cognizant of the kinds of lines of inquiry that are foreclosed through the continued usage of "empire?" What these scholars are alluding to is the need to account for the resignification of empire and at the same time, the need to develop theoretical frames and analytical tools better suited for the contemporary moment.

In a co-authored essay published in the *Peace Review*, Robyn Rodriguez and Nerissa S. Balce (2004) take up the question of empire in a post-9/11 context and more specifically, how the war on terror is very much rooted in U.S. imperial history. They reflect on the implications of the war on terror for Filipinos, examining the case of Filipino airport screeners who were summarily fired in the wake of 9/11 and the case of a gay, half-Filipino Marine reservist who was punished and disciplined by the government for his open admission of his sexuality and his antiwar views. Balce and Rodriguez (2004) make the claim that we need to be attentive to the variegated consequences of the so-called war on terror, particularly on immigrant communities and how these consequences are mediated by race, class, and sexuality. In the case of the Filipino screeners, the presumption was that they could never be part of the nation's line of defense against terrorism precisely because of their location outside the bounds of both legal and extralegal or popular notions of Americanness. Their legal and class status rendered them particularly vulnerable to changes in requirements for airport workers post-9/11. As Rodriguez and Balce (2004) point out, these changes encompass stipulations for citizenship, English proficiency, and high school education.

The plight of Lance Corporal Stephen Eagle Funk speaks not only to the racism and homophobia of the U.S. military but also to the ways sexuality serves to exclude individuals like Funk from the logic of national belonging. His service speaks to the long history of Filipino involvement in the U.S. military. At the same time, Funk embodies what Rodriguez and Balce (2004) describe as "a counter-narrative of patriotism" (p. 136), which resonates with a kind of Filipino radicalism that cuts across national boundaries by linking various issues facing Filipinos in different parts of the globe. By counternarrative of patriotism, Rodriguez and Balce (2004) mean not only the kind of patriotism that is predicated on peace rather than war but also the kind of patriotism predicated on love and respect for human life rather than love of country. Both cases speak to the limits of legal citizenship brought to sharp relief in moments of crises and the need to rethink notions of belongingness, particularly state-sanctioned categories and definitions.

Rodriguez and Balce (2004), I believe, engage in the kind of scholarly intervention that serves to illuminate the current political and historical moment. It is the kind of scholarship that gestures toward what it would mean to engage with the question of empire within a post-9/11 context in a nuanced manner. These scholars provide the kind of analysis that does not lose sight of the variegated consequences of the post-9/11 period for Filipinos, on the need to be attentive to issues of class in the case of the fired Filipino immigrant workers (who were of working-class background), and on the need to be attentive to the collusion between race and sexuality in the case of Funk. They provide the kind of analysis that speaks of empire neither in abstract terms nor in terms that conceive of it as monolithic or unchanging. Rather, their work speaks to the need to consider empire as a heterogeneous and historically specific set of phenomena precisely because of shifts in the signification of "empire" that has taken place.

What is significant about Rodriguez and Balce's (2004) work is their attempt to elucidate the genealogy of a post-9/11 Filipino radical politics at a time, as these authors point out, when (hyper)patriotism is seen as the appropriate response to war and terror. According to these authors, we should not lose sight of what they term as "radical Filipino community politics," borne out of the post-9/11 social order. And by "radical Filipino community politics," Rodriguez and Balce (2004) mean community formations that "link contemporary struggles with seemingly disparate campaigns that U.S. Filipinos and Filipinos in the Philippines have faced in the past" (p. 132).

They contend that this emergent form of politics is part of a longer and larger history of Filipino radical movements, which look at Filipino struggles in the Philippines, the United States, and the diaspora as inextricably linked to one another. It is the kind of politics marked by a critical engagement with U.S. imperialism and conventional understandings of U.S. citizenship and patriotism. The Filipinos for Global Justice Not War Coalition, for example, is one of those organizations engaged in precisely this kind of work, recognizing the necessity of organizing across national borders and the inextricable link between U.S. domestic policy and U.S. imperialism. Formed in the wake of 9/11, the organization comprised an array of organizations including campus and community-based organizations as well as immigrant worker organizations (Rodriguez & Balce, 2004).

ON COLONIAL/POSTCOLONIAL CROSSINGS AND CONVERGENCES

Another point of departure converges around the shared histories of subjugation under U.S. imperial rule and shared histories of enduring the legacies of empire and more specifically, that formative moment at the turn of the 20th century when the United States possessed an empire that stretched from the Caribbean into the Pacific. At the time, the U.S. empire included the Philippines, along with Hawaii, Puerto Rico, and Guam. Like these other island territories, the Philippines was considered "unincorporated," which meant, among other things, that it was "subject to the plenary power of the U.S. Congress but not subject to the full protection of the American constitution" (Go, 2005, p. 215). And like the inhabitants of these other island territories, Filipinos were rendered racially intelligible through the use of the same racial logic deployed to make sense of America's domestic others. Stereotypical attributes projected onto Native Americans, for example, were also projected onto Filipinos. Imperialists considered Filipinos, like Native Americans, savages as well as children in need of U.S. tutelage and guidance (San Buenaventura, 1998).

Notwithstanding the gravity and import of these crossings and convergences, they remain unspecified or underspecified. And in fact, only recently have we seen works interrogating the broad theoretical and political implications and significance of these crossings and convergences. So what does it mean to come to terms with this formative historical moment? What does it mean to fully account for these shared histories of subjugation to U.S. imperial rule in a way that does not lose sight of the distinctiveness in the historical trajectories of these island territories? In what ways were these colonized subjects constituted in relation to one another, and what are the broader implications in terms of our understanding of the contours of the history of each group?

A challenge has been the existing institutional arrangements that have served to preclude a critical interrogation of the foregoing questions. Given the institutional absorption of Filipino American studies within Asian

American studies, for example, Oscar Campomanes raises the question of the viability of this kind of alignment in light of the Philippines' imperial history. He makes the point that Filipino and Filipino American social formations are

> probably best and more fully understood through comparisons with and new insertions into alternative accounts, such as those developed for Chicanos/as, Puertorriquenos/as, Hawaiians, and Pacific Islanders (and what binds all of them is the common subjection to a history of U.S. imperial expansion; we belong to this history more than to the history of Asian Americans). (Campomanes, 2006, p. 40)

If it is indeed the case that, as Campomanes asserts, we belong to this history more than to the history of Asian Americans, then what are the theoretical and pedagogical implications in terms of the way we frame and approach the study of Filipino social formations?

In *American Tropics: Articulating Filipino America,* Allan Isaac (2006) engages a number of the foregoing questions in his critical consideration of a complex set of colonial/postcolonial crossings and convergences through what he terms "American tropics," a physical and discursive space subjected to U.S. imperial rule. In his consideration of the various forms of contact in this particular kind of space, Isaac illuminates the ways the Philippines was rendered intelligible only in relation to other geopolitical sites also subjected to U.S. imperial rule. One of the things he does is juxtapose his readings of Filipino American texts such as Carlos Bulosan's *America is in the Heart* and Jessica Hagedorn's *Dogeaters* with Puerto Rican and Hawaiian texts such as Piri Thomas's *Down These Mean Streets* and John Dominis Holt's *Waimea Summer* as way to flesh out U.S. imperial discourse and the question of national belonging for colonized subjects. Isaac goes on to raise the following questions: "By connecting these American island spaces, what can Asian American literary studies learn from Pacific and Hawaiian studies and Latino and Puerto Rican studies? How can one rearticulate the colonial/postcolonial convergence and contestation to bear upon the battles on the Asian American cultural and literary front?" (Isaac, 2006, p. xxix).

Isaac's work is the kind of scholarship that recognizes that U.S. imperialism exerted its power throughout the Caribbean, Asia, and the Pacific, linking the various territories that make up the U.S. imperial archipelago in deep and profound ways. He raises the question of how these linkages might be more fully represented and rendered intelligible, especially given existing institutional arrangements that dissuade such practices. Through his readings of a wide array of literary, legal, and filmic texts, including texts that are not generally subsumed under the rubric of "Filipino American studies," Isaac engages in the kind of scholarly work that attempts to come to terms with the ways "histories and communities are mutually complicated and constitutively related, open to mutual illumination" without resorting to a facile side-by-side juxtaposition of divergent social formations (Shohat, 2002, p. 75).

Isaac offers the kind of scholarship that places disciplinary formations with distinct histories, imperatives, and concerns in critical dialogue with one another, which ultimately serves to illuminate the particularities of Filipino social formations. In opening up these disciplinary conversations, Isaac challenges the parochialisms and conventions of disciplinary formations. His careful consideration of the U.S. imperial archipelago—particularly his use of American tropics—establishes the parameters for a critical comparative race studies approach and broadens the ground from which to consider the contours of ethnic and national history, identity, and racial formation.

ON DISASTERS AND BLACK/BROWN FORMATIONS

A third point of departure converges around the interconnections between Black and Brown formations. Much of this literature takes as its starting point the U.S. occupation of the Philippines at the turn of the 20th century as a lens through which to examine the convergences between America's domestic "others" and its overseas colonial subjects. To illustrate, Steffi San Buenaventura (1998) looks to U.S.–Philippine encounters at the turn of the 20th century as an important site to interrogate what she describes as "earlier and little-known ethnic and racial intersections between Filipinos and other Americans" (p. 2). She posits that U.S. overseas expansion across the Pacific was marked by the association of America's domestic "others" with its overseas colonial subjects. For San Buenaventura, a full accounting of the Filipino American experience necessitates coming to terms with the interconnectedness of Filipinos "with the American ethnic others" (p. 22). In a similar vein, Rene G. Ontal (2002) looks to African American involvement in the Philippine-American War as a critical locus for examining affinities forged between two marginalized groups. Despite acknowledgement of the complications posed by the presence of Blacks in the Philippines, Ontal characterizes the identifications forged in the war as a crucial moment of "anti-imperialist alliance between African Americans and Asians" (p. 130).

From this vantage point, Dylan Rodriguez's work seems to be an extension of this body of writing. But rather than look to U.S. occupation of the Philippines as a context to explore the interconnections between Black and Brown social formations, Rodriguez (2007) looks to a social disaster like hurricane Katrina. He makes the point that a social disaster like hurricane Katrina may very well register in Filipino diasporic consciousness given their familiarity with disasters such as the 1991 explosion of Mt. Pinatubo. For a majority of Filipinos, the kind of devastation, damage, and dislocation evident in the wake of Katrina is not something altogether unfamiliar or alien given the Philippines' intimate familiarity with disasters of all sorts and its status as one of the most impoverished countries in Asia. For Rodriguez, then, Katrina and Mt. Pinatubo constitute "linked formations of global white supremacy and racism that can forge the basis for some sort of collective identification between the two groups predicated on the elaboration of a critical common sense resonant with a critical black common sense" (p. 144).

More substantively, however, Rodriguez's work represents a marked departure from the literature on empire and Black-Brown imbrications. While Rodriguez raises the question of how Filipinos should understand themselves in relation to Black people in the wake of hurricane Katrina, he does so without resorting to simplistic and reductive notions of "cross-racial identification" or "common ground." More to the point, Rodriguez recognizes the potential for identification between Blacks and Filipinos but without losing sight of the complications; the possibility for serious political kinship between the two groups that go beyond facile expressions of cross-racial solidarity. In other words, Rodriguez provides a critical interrogation of the very terms—theoretical and political—through which historical and contemporary Black-Brown encounters have been rendered illegible. To borrow from Helen Jun in another context, Rodriguez's work is not characterized by "a teleological investment in 'interracial solidarity'—a notion that relies heavily on the premise of identification" that can sometimes obscure the complexities and contradictions that mark the terrain of Black/Brown imbrications (Jun, 2006, p. 1051).

Rodriguez also makes the point that notwithstanding Filipino familiarity with disasters, Filipino diasporic consciousness is not seamless or without its own set of contradictions, particularly in relation to those hardest hit by the Mt. Pinatubo devastation—Philippine indigenous groups like the Aetas and the Negritos—given their positioning outside the Philippine national, racial, and diasporic imaginary as inauthentic national subjects. And here, Rodriguez is getting at the need to account for racialized hierarchies in the way Filipinos imagine themselves; racialized hierarchies very much implicated in the destruction and devastation that befell these indigenous groups as well as in the relief efforts in the wake of the eruption. Rodriguez (2007) notes, for example, how a state official was aghast at the refusal of the Aetas to consume canned goods and at the same time, views this refusal as a marker of distinction between "indigenous/Aetas/Negritos and 'straight'/lowlander Filipinos" (p. 141). As Rodriguez points out, this kind of distinction recapitulates the racialized logic of a discipline like anthropology at the turn of the 20th century.

BROADER IMPLICATIONS

So what does all this mean to Filipino American studies at this particular historical moment? What does it mean in terms of the conceptual boundaries and underlying assumptions of the field? How does the foregoing works complicate our task as educators, scholars, and activists? What are the implications in terms of the way we approach the study of Filipino social formations? How do we begin to heed their call for critical analysis? What does it mean to grapple substantively with the kinds of challenges and complications they raise?

On the surface, the works I have considered here seem to represent disparate intellectual projects. Yet, what binds them together is their refusal to take for granted disciplinary orthodoxies and boundaries. Rather than simply integrating Filipinos as objects of study into preexisting disciplinary paradigms, these works call into question the coherence of a disciplinary formation such as Filipino American studies. They do so by not simply integrating Filipinos as objects of study into preexisting disciplinary paradigms but by also questioning the terms of their production and inscription. Additionally, these works account for historical shifts that have made it increasingly necessary to reassess the constitutive basis of disciplinary formations.

In the case of Rodriguez and Balce (2004), they direct our attention to the multivalent nature of empire. These scholars make a compelling case that if the term "empire" is to have any analytical utility, we need to account for its historical specificities rather than think of it as an unchanging phenomenon. As for Isaac (2006), he articulates a point of departure for a critical comparative race studies approach, the kind of approach cognizant of the inherent complications and challenges of comparative work. In the case of Rodriguez (2007), his work touches on the need to consider identifications between marginalized groups in relation to uneven histories that have structured relations between groups such as Blacks and Filipinos. In short, the significance of the foregoing projects may be precisely their capacity to open up a space for a different kind of praxis—pedagogical, scholarly, and political—that can begin to account for the complex and varied articulations of Filipinoness (including its imbrications with other social formations) across time and space in a nuanced and precise manner.

NOTES

1 By "social formations," I'm alluding not only to the ways Filipinos have been historically constituted—fashioned into a particular kind of subject in order to fulfill U.S. imperialist, White supremacist, patriarchal, and capitalist imperatives—but also to the contradictory ways Filipinos themselves have ne-

gotiated the very terms through which they have historically been defined, acknowledged, and recognized.

2. Kaplan makes the point that the embrace of empire in the contemporary moment has taken on two forms: In neoconservative discourse, U.S. exercise of hegemony power on a global scale is seen as the realization of its Manifest Destiny, while in liberal discourse, the United States is seen as a reluctant imperial power compelled to intervene in world affairs in order to bring order and stability.
3. Kaplan raises the point that current moment calls for a critical interrogation of the ways American studies scholars approach the question of empire. More specifically, she makes the point that the seemingly open embrace of empire speaks to the need to expand our repertoire of engagement with empire beyond what she terms as a "method of exposure." In other words, Kaplan makes the point that the thrust of our scholarly inquiries can no longer be organized primarily or exclusively around rendering visible the workings of empire.

REFERENCES

Bonus, R. (2000). *Locating Filipino Americans: Ethnicity and the cultural politics of space.* Philadelphia, PA: Temple University Press.

Campomanes, O. V. (1992). Filipinos in the United States and their literature of exile. In S. G. Lim & A. Ling (Eds.), *Reading the literatures of Asian America* (pp. 49–78). Philadelphia, PA: Temple University Press.

Campomanes, O. V. (1995). The new empire's forgetful and forgotten citizens: Unrepresentability and unassimilability in Filipino-American postcolonialities. *Critical Mass: A Journal of Asian American Cultural Criticism, 2*(2), 145–200.

Campomanes, O. V. (1997). New formations of Asian American studies and the question of U.S. imperialism. *Positions, 5*(2), 523–550.

Campomanes, O. V. (2006). On Filipinos, Filipino Americans, and U.S. imperialism. In A. T. Tiongson Jr., E. V. Gutierrez, & R. V. Gutierrez (Eds.), *Positively no Filipinos allowed: Building communities and discourse* (pp. 26–42). Philadelphia, PA: Temple University Press.

Go, J. (2005). Modes of rule in America's overseas empire: The Philippines, Puerto Rico, Guam, and Samoa. In S. Levinson & B. H. Sparrow (Eds.), *The Louisiana Purchase and American expansion, 1803–1898* (pp. 209–229). Lanham. MD: Rowman & Littlefield.

Isaac, A. P. (2006). *American tropics: Articulating Filipino America.* Minneapolis: University of Minnesota Press.

Jun, H. H. (2006). Black orientalism: Nineteenth-century narratives of race and U.S. citizenship. *American Quarterly, 58*(4), 1047–1066.

Kaplan, A. (2004). Violent belongings and the question of empire today: Presidential address to the American Studies Association, October 17, 2003. *American Quarterly, 56*(1), 1–18.

Ontal, R. G. (2002). Fagen and other ghosts: African-Americans and the Philippine-American war. In A. Velasco Shaw & L. H. Francia (Eds.), *Vestiges of war:*

The Philippine-American war and the aftermath of an Imperial dream 1899–1999 (pp. 118–133). New York: New York University Press.

Rodriguez, D. (2007). The meaning of "disaster" under the dominance of White life. In The South End Press Collective (Eds.), *What lies beneath: Katrina, race, and the state of the nation* (pp. 133–156). Cambridge, MA: South End.

Rodriguez, R., & Balce, N. S. (2004). American insecurity and radical Filipino community politics. *Peace Review, 16*(2), 131–140.

San Buenaventura, S. (1998). The colors of manifest destiny: Filipinos and the American other(s). *Amerasia Journal, 24*(3), 1–26.

San Juan, E., Jr. (1992). *Racial formations/critical transformations: Articulations of power in ethnic and racial studies in the United States.* Amherst, NY: Humanity Books.

Shohat, E. (2002). Area studies, gender studies, and the cartographies of knowledge. *Social Text, 20*(3), 67–78.

Tadiar, N. X. M. (2004, January 8–10). *Cultures against empire: Keynote address.* Covering U.S. Empire Conference, University of Michigan, Ann Arbor.

PART IV

FILIPINO AMERICANS AND POLICIES IN EDUCATION

CHAPTER 12

FILIPINO AMERICAN ACCESS TO PUBLIC HIGHER EDUCATION IN CALIFORNIA AND HAWAI'I

Jonathan Y. Okamura
***University of Hawai'i,* Mānoa**

In 1998, Filipino American students were party to a class-action federal lawsuit (*Rios et al. v. Regents of the University of California*), which charged that the admissions policies of the University of California (UC), Berkeley violated federal antidiscrimination laws. The suit was submitted in March of that year before the substantial declines in African American and Latino freshmen became apparent in the fall as a result of the prohibition of race-based affirmative action in UC admissions through the passage of Proposition 209. The suit was filed by the Asian Pacific American Legal Center of Southern California, the NAACP Legal Defense and Education Fund, and the Mexican American Legal Defense and Education Fund on behalf of African American and Latino students besides Filipino Americans.[1] These organizations maintained that Berkeley's admissions process discriminated against and violated the civil rights of Filipino American, Latino, and Afri-

The "Other" Students, pages 213–235

can American past and future applicants in several ways, including giving "unjustified preferential consideration to applicants who have taken certain courses [Advanced Placement] that are less accessible in high schools attended largely by African American, Latino, and Pilipino American students" and placing "undue and unjustified reliance upon standardized test scores to make judgments based on educationally insignificant differences in test scores" (as cited in U.S. Commission on Civil Rights, 2000). While some of the reasons for the lawsuit still remain valid, during the years since it was filed in 1998, Filipino Americans (and Latinos) have diverged from African Americans in their increased admissions and enrollment at UC Berkeley and (with Latinos) have significantly expanded their representation in the UC system.

In this chapter, I focus on access to public higher education of Filipino Americans in California and Hawai'i, the states in which they have their greatest number and percentage of the population, respectively. An analysis of the enrollment in college of Filipino American undergraduates in those two states may have relevance for them in other states where they represent a significant proportion of the population, such as Washington, New York, and Illinois. My concern is with how state policies in higher education have impacted Filipino American access and enrollment, particularly the elimination of race-based affirmative action in California and the implementation of substantial tuition hikes in Hawai'i, both of which occurred in 1996. For California, I focus on the University of California system, particularly UC Berkeley, UCLA, and UC Irvine, because the two former campuses are the most academically selective of the nine undergraduate UC institutions,[2] and the latter has the highest number and percentage of Filipino Americans in the UC system. For Hawai'i, my concern is with the University of Hawai'i system, especially UH Mānoa, its flagship doctoral-degree granting campus that has the largest number of Filipino American undergraduates.[3] It might be argued that these universities are not readily comparable since the UC institutions have higher admission standards than those at UH Mānoa, but the latter is the premier public university in Hawai'i as are UC Berkeley and UCLA in California.

As I discuss below, the access and enrollment in public higher education of Filipino Americans in California and Hawai'i during the 12-year period from 1997 to 2009 are quite divergent, with much more positive outcomes in the former state than in the latter. This finding seems somewhat anomalous given the much greater proportion of the population and political power of Filipino Americans in Hawai'i than in California. In both states, I compare the representation of Filipino American undergraduates with that of other ethnic and racial groups, including Asian Americans, African Americans, and Latinos in the latter state, and Native Hawaiians and Whites in the former, in order to have an understanding of how their enrollment status and trends compare to both majority and minority groups.

POST–AFFIRMATIVE ACTION, UNIVERSITY OF CALIFORNIA

In 1995, the UC Board of Regents passed the SP-1 resolution that eliminated race-based affirmative action in university admissions.[4] The next year, California voters approved Proposition 209, the so-called Civil Rights Initiative, which prohibited race and gender-based affirmative action in college admissions and in hiring and contracting by public institutions.[5] Since the end of affirmative action, Filipino Americans have significantly increased their enrollment in the UC system and at the Berkeley and Irvine campuses but not at UCLA. Since 1997, the year before the ban on affirmative action became effective in undergraduate admissions, Filipino American enrollment in the UC system expanded by more than 39%, or more than 2,200 students, from that year (5,700) to fall 2009 (7,900).[6] During this same period, their representation among UC undergraduates remained at 4.4%, one reason being UC enrollment increased by nearly 38% to almost 178,000 students. Compared to their proportion of California public high school graduates (3.3%) and of the California state population (3.3%), Filipino Americans thus are slightly overrepresented in the UC system (California Postsecondary Education Commission, 2010d). At an annual average of about 5% between 1997 and 2009, Filipino Americans are also somewhat overrepresented among first-time freshmen enrolling in the UC system (California Postsecondary Education Commission, 2010e). Besides entering a UC campus as freshmen, Filipino Americans also enroll as community college transfers and comprised less than 3% of such transfer students from 1997 to 2009 (California Postsecondary Education Commission, 2010a). More than four times as many Filipino Americans are admitted each year as first-time freshmen than as community college transfer students, which enhances their persistence and graduation from a UC institution.

At UC Berkeley, Filipino Americans increased by 62%, or more than 300 students between fall 1997 (500) and fall 2009 (800), thus comprising 3.3% of undergraduates. Contrary to expectations, their numbers steadily grew immediately after the prohibition on affirmative action took effect, perhaps an early indicator that their enrollment experiences would be more like those of other Asian American students than those of African Americans and Latinos. Contributing to the growth in Filipino American undergraduates has been their progressive increase in the number of first-time freshmen admitted at Berkeley between fall 1997 (86) and fall 2006 (143). These enrollment gains reversed the previous downswing of nearly 200 students among Berkeley undergraduates between the late 1980s and 1996, which was due to their elimination from affirmative action recruitment and admissions programs in 1986, their being negatively affected by changes in admissions policies initiated in 1991, and their lower retention rate compared to other student groups (Okamura & Agbayani, 1997, p. 190).

In contrast, the expanded enrollment of Filipino Americans at UC Berkeley after 1997 can be attributed especially to the concerted recruitment and retention efforts by Filipino American student organizations because UC campuses have transferred these functions to such groups after affirmative action was eliminated (Horn & Flores, 2003, p. 54). One of these organizations at Berkeley is PASS, or Pilipino Academic Student Services, which is entirely student-operated, primarily through voluntary efforts. Fortunately, perhaps in response to the enormous reductions in African American and Latino admissions in the UC system resulting from the ban on affirmative action, in 1999, California voters passed Proposition 3, which allows for a portion of the annual fees ($6 per student) paid by students to be used to support student-organized racial and ethnic minority recruitment and retention programs such as PASS.[7] In terms of recruitment activities, PASS students conduct outreach visits to high schools and community colleges with significant numbers of Filipino Americans in the San Francisco Bay Area and Southern California to provide them with information on preparing for or transferring to a university. Each fall, they hold Filipino Empowerment Day, which brings Bay Area Filipino American high school students to the Berkeley campus, where they meet with representatives of area community colleges and universities to learn about college life and receive assistance with the application process. PASS students also offer day-long or overnight campus visits, which include information workshops and tours for high school and community college students, including newly admitted high school seniors. As for retention services, PASS organizes activities for transfer students to become acquainted with one another and campus life. Similar student-directed Filipino American recruitment and retention programs at UCLA, UC Davis, UC San Diego, and other campuses have contributed to increasing their enrollment at their respective institutions. Buenavista (2007) conducted her doctoral dissertation research with "1.5" generation Filipino American student "activists" involved in such a program, which she called the "Pilipino Recruitment and Retention Center," at a large, academically selective university in California. She found that students initiated "culturally affirming educational experiences," such as discussions on family issues concerned with college choice, multilingual activities, and a graduation ceremony for Filipino American students. Given the relative scarcity of Filipino American faculty and staff in the UC system, such student organizations must be recognized as highly significant resources in recruiting and retaining Filipino American students. They also serve as models for other universities in expanding Filipino American and other minority student enrollment.

UCLA had a different Filipino American enrollment experience than at UC Berkeley insofar as enrollment slightly declined between fall 1997 (1,100) and fall 2009 (1,050), when Filipino Americans comprised 3.9% of students, with a low of 951 students as recently as 2006. This decrease reversed the trend of their growing numbers during the 1990s of more than 200 students. The University of California, Irvine is well known (at least in its home state) for its majority Asian American undergraduate population, perhaps the only major university in the nation with this distinction. Perhaps as a result, Filipino Americans have their highest absolute (1,700) and proportional representation (7.6%) in the UC system at Irvine. Their number grew by 52%, or nearly 600 students, between fall 1997 (1,100) and fall 2009 (1,700), which continued a progressive trend that began in the 1980s. A possible contributing factor to this gain was that during the same 12-year period, undergraduate enrollment at UC Irvine expanded dramatically by 57%, or more than 8,000 students, thus creating greater opportunities for Filipino American students.

Another possible reason for the increase in Filipino American enrollment in the UC system may be the Eligibility in Local Context (ELC) program that was initiated with the fall 2001 freshman class, following the prohibition of affirmative action. Through the ELC program, the top 4% of graduates (as determined by cumulative grade point average in the tenth and eleventh grades) of each comprehensive public and private high school in California are guaranteed admission to a UC campus (Horn & Flores, 2003, p. 17).[8] Such "percentage plans" for college admissions were also established in Texas and Florida in the aftermath of the elimination of race-based affirmative action in those states. Under the California program, students are not granted admission to the UC institution of their choice, and this has resulted in the criticism that it channels racial minority students to the less selective UC campuses (Selingo, 1999, as cited in Horn & Flores, 2003, p. 17). In a critical report, the U.S. Commission on Civil Rights (2000) contends that "The percentage plans are experimental responses to the attacks on affirmative action. But they are no substitute for strong race-conscious affirmative action in higher education." Other critics of the ELC program maintain that it should be expanded to between 6% and 9% of each high school class in order to foster "both UC's democratic and meritocratic ideals" (Hayashi & Kidder, 2004). Another reason for expanding the program is that, while it has increased the access of African American and Latino students, they still remain greatly underrepresented in the UC system (see below).

The steady gains in Filipino American undergraduate enrollment in the UC system, and particularly at UC Berkeley and UC Irvine between 1997 and 2009, can be correlated with the overall undergraduate growth at those institutions, especially at Irvine. Such expansion appears to have created admission spaces for Filipino Americans that may seem a matter of common sense, but enrollment increases at UCLA and UH Mānoa (see below) did not result in corresponding gains for Filipino American students. Conversely, the cap on UC admissions in fall 2004 (because of budget cutbacks) resulted in decreases in Filipino American enrollment at all UC campuses. These outcomes indicate the direct impact on Filipino American (and other) students from state policies in higher education, including those concerning termination of affirmative action, tuition hikes, enrollment limits or increases, and 4% admissions programs. However, at least some of these policies may have greater negative consequences for Filipino Americans because of their racialized minority status. To address the loss of more than $800 million in state funding since 2008, the UC Board of Regents raised tuition (or "fees," as it is called in the UC system) by 32% in two installments, with the first beginning in January 2010, which was met by student protests and demonstrations at several UC campuses. It remains to be seen if this huge increase will reduce Filipino American enrollment. Like UH Mānoa a decade earlier (see below), the University of California in 2010 began to increase its recruitment and admission of out-of-state students (who pay $23,000 more than state residents for annual tuition) as another means to generate revenues. More than 8% of the projected 37,200 UC freshmen enrolling in fall 2010 were expected to be nonresidents, up from 6% in the previous year, with UC Berkeley and UCLA having the greatest gains (Gordon, 2010a). In 2010, for the first time ever, UCLA admissions officers went to 10 U.S. cities, including Honolulu, Boston, and Chicago, as well as to China, Japan, Korea, Hong Kong, and Singapore, to recruit nonresident students, while UC Davis, Irvine, and Santa Barbara also initiated "serious" out-of-state recruitment efforts for the first time (Gordon, 2010b). According to Thomas Lifka, UCLA associate vice chancellor of student academic services, the university planned to increase its proportion of nonresident undergraduates from 11% to 18% during the next 3 to 5 years without decreasing the number of students from California (Gordon, 2010b).

Another recent development that may affect the access of Filipino Americans to the UC system is the proposed change in admissions policy that will eliminate SAT subject tests on which Asian Americans tend to "excel" (Krieger, 2009). Adopted by the UC Regents in 2009 following a faculty study, this change is scheduled to take effect for freshmen entering in fall 2012 and is intended to make UC more accessible to low-income students, a laudable goal that is contradicted by the enormous tuition hike in 2010. According to an analysis by the UC Office of the President based on freshman admissions in 2007, the admissions policy change will result in a potential decline in Asian American freshmen from 36% to approximately

29%, while increasing White admissions from 34% to approximately 44%. Not surprisingly, the proposed change has been strongly criticized by Asian American educators and community leaders, including retired UC Berkeley ethnic studies professor Ling-chi Wang, who remarked, "It's affirmative action for whites. I'm really outraged and profoundly disappointed with the institution" (as cited in Krieger, 2009). Under the new admissions policy, the two most underrepresented racial minorities in the UC system, African Americans and Latinos, which both have substantial proportions of low-income families, nonetheless, are estimated to augment their freshmen minimally: from 4% to approximately 5% for the former group and from 19% to approximately 22% for the latter. These projected results have led to the strong suspicion in the Asian American community that the real intent behind the admissions policy change is to reduce the number of Asian Americans for the benefit of Whites. Such a deliberate reduction occurred in the mid-1980s through changes in admissions policy that disadvantaged Asian American applicants at UC Berkeley, UCLA, and other academically highly selective universities on both the East and West Coasts (Takagi, 1993). Insofar as Filipino Americans have expanded their representation in the UC system, like other Asian American students following the termination of affirmative action, they may be similarly negatively impacted by the proposed admissions policy change.

The rise in Filipino American undergraduate enrollment in the UC system is consistent with the hefty addition of more than 23,000 Asian American students since affirmative action ended. In the UC system, Asian American undergraduates grew from 37% in fall 1997 to 40% in fall 2009; they thus greatly exceed their percentage of the California population (13%). At 37%, they constitute the largest racial group in UC freshman admissions and are almost one-half (46%) of Berkeley freshmen (Krieger, 2009). In 2002, Asian Americans became the largest group among UC undergraduates when they exceeded Whites for the first time, even though Whites have also gained nearly 7,000 students in the UC system since 1997. Nonetheless, the proportion of White students has been steadily dropping since 2000 and is currently less than one third of UC undergraduates. Thus, with the exception of those at UCLA, the post–affirmative action enrollment experiences of Filipino Americans in the UC system is more comparable to that of Asian Americans than of disadvantaged racial minorities such as African Americans (see below). As had been predicted before the elimination of race-based affirmative action, Blacks have suffered huge enrollment depletions at Berkeley and UCLA, while Asian Americans and Whites have gained the most. In contrast, as will be discussed below, the enrollment experiences of Filipino Americans at UH Mānoa during approximately the same 12-year period were those of a marginalized minority rather than of model minority Asian Americans.

Beyond the UC system, Filipino Americans have their greatest absolute and proportional undergraduate representation at San Francisco State University. In fall 2009, some 2,141 Filipino Americans comprised almost 10% of students and ranked second to Chinese Americans (13%) among Asian Americans (Office of University and Budget Planning, 2010). Their considerable numbers can be attributed to the significant Filipino American communities in San Francisco, nearby Daly City, and the San Francisco Bay area in general. In addition, following the 5-month long student strike in 1968–1969 at what was then San Francisco State College, it was the first university to offer courses in Asian American studies, beginning in 1969, through the new Ethnic Studies Department. San Francisco State currently provides courses in Filipino American studies in its Department of Asian American Studies, which includes three Filipino American faculty. Clearly, having sufficient numbers of Filipino American faculty who can develop and offer courses on Filipino American history, literature, and contemporary culture and community, and serve as advocates and role models for students, is another important means to advance Filipino American representation.

According to the 2000 U.S. Census, Filipino Americans in California have relatively high rates of college completion among persons 25 years and older, as evident from the percentages of both females (44%) and males (37%) with a bachelor's degree or higher (U.S. Bureau of the Census, 2003). These figures are somewhat higher than those for White women (27%) and men (33%) in the state. The Filipino American percentages are very comparable to those for the more highly educated Asian American groups in California, such as Chinese Americans and Japanese Americans; however, to a significant extent, they can be attributed to the immigration of Filipinos with college degrees rather than to educational mobility over the generations. Nonetheless, Filipino American females (55%) and males (50%) have quite high levels of college or graduate school enrollment among persons 18 to 24 years old, which are considerably greater than those for White women (41%) and men (33%). The above percentages for college completion and enrollment of Filipino Americans in California are also much higher than for their counterparts in Hawai'i (see below).

In marked contrast to Filipino Americans and Asian Americans in general, African Americans have experienced minimal gains in their undergraduate enrollment in the UC system since affirmative action was prohibited, with the exceptions of UC Berkeley and UCLA. At the UC campuses, Black enrollment increased by 1,100 students between fall 1997 (5,000) and fall 2009 (6,100), such that they constituted only 3.4% of UC undergraduates in the latter year, far less than their 7% proportion of California public high school graduates (California Postsecondary Education Commission, 2010d). Beginning in 1998, their UC total underwent four consecutive years of losses of about 550 students before starting to increase in 2002, possibly due to the implementation of the ELC program the previous year. The recovery in African American representation can be correlated with their growing presence at UC Riverside, where they have nearly tripled in number by almost 800 students since 1997, their greatest addition at any of the UC campuses. This substantial gain may be due to the channeling of racial minority students under the ELC program to the less prestigious UC campuses such as Riverside and Santa Cruz.[9]

Quite differently, at UC Berkeley, African American undergraduate numbers steadily dropped by nearly 27% between fall 1997 (1,300) and fall 2009 (900) and, while they seem to have gained since 2006, they have not yet reversed their overall decline. A major factor in their enrollment loss was the sharp decrease in Black freshmen entering Berkeley between 1997 (257) and 2006 (152), with a low of 108 as recently as 2004 (Office of Student Research, 2007). Similarly, at UCLA, the number of African American undergraduates plummeted by 30% between fall 1997 (1,400) and fall 2009 (1,000) but has been increasing since 2007. This decline also can be attributed to a continuing decrease in Black freshmen enrolling each fall. In fall 1997, they comprised 5.6% of freshmen but within 3 years of the end of affirmative action, had dropped to 3.4% in fall 2001, while the freshman class expanded by 400 students during this period (Horn & Flores, 2003, p. 49). Thus, the post–affirmative action admissions of Filipino American students in the UC system have been much more positive than that of African Americans.

In contrast to African Americans, Latinos gained more than 12,300 undergraduates in the UC system between fall 1997 (17,200) and fall 2009 (29,500), a huge upsurge of 72%, such that they comprised 17% of undergraduates. While these additions are impressive, Latinos are still greatly underrepresented in the UC system compared to their proportion of California public high school graduates (38%) (California Postsecondary Education Commission, 2010f). As predicted, the termination of affirmative action resulted in initial declines beginning in 1998, but the numbers have steadily expanded since then. At Berkeley, Latinos increased by nearly 280 students between fall 1997 (2,800) and fall 2009 (3,000), and their enrollment has been on the upswing since 2002 after 4 consecutive years of losses. At UCLA, Latinos also gained almost 160 students between fall 1997 (3,900) and fall 2009 (4,100) after initially declining for 3 consecutive years; however, their enrollment has been expanding since then. Similar to African Americans, Latino undergraduates have their greatest number and representation (25%) in the UC system at Riverside, which also may be due to their being directed to that university under the ELC program, although they also have a significant presence at the Santa Barbara, Davis, and Irvine campuses. Since the ELC program began in 2001, Latinos have increased their annual number of first-time freshmen entering the UC system by 45% to more than 6,200 students in fall 2009 (California Postsecondary Education Commission, 2010c). Projected figures for fall 2010 for first-time freshmen from California enrolling in the UC system indicate that Latinos (23%) follow closely behind Whites (26%) and thus, besides Asian Americans, may constitute another reason why UC administrators have proposed changing admissions policies (Gordon, 2010a).[10]

Given their considerable gains, the post–affirmative action admissions and enrollment of Filipino Americans in the UC system can be considered highly positive, especially at UC Irvine and UC Berkeley. As noted above, at the latter campus in 1998, they had joined African American and Latino students in their class-action lawsuit, charging the university with racial discrimination, but have since reversed their previous declining numbers. Filipino Americans have been very much part of the overall escalation in Asian American students in the UC system following the end of affirmative action rather than advancing only minimally like African Americans. Filipino American enrollment expansion can be attributed to the recruitment and retention efforts of their own student associations at the various UC campuses, which have organized activities and services targeting Filipino American high school and community college students.

POST–TUITION HIKES, UNIVERSITY OF HAWAI'I[11]

In the 1990s, the University of Hawai'i at Mānoa attained national distinction as the only public university to undergo 7 consecutive years of budget cuts. According to a report by the UH Office on Planning and Policy, state funding for the university decreased by 19% during that decade (as cited in Altonn, 1999). Those budget reductions can be directly attributed to the recession in Hawai'i during most of the 1990s, particularly in the dominant tourism industry, which resulted in less tax revenue from the state legislature for the university's budget allocation. To compensate for the budget cuts, the UH Board of Regents raised resident and nonresident tuition at all campuses in 1996 and 1997. These hikes were the largest at UH Mānoa: a whopping 50% in the first year, followed by another 23% the next year for resident undergraduate students. Consequently, UH Mānoa enrollment dropped from 19,800 in 1995 to 17,000 students in three years, and UH system enrollment, including at the less costly community colleges, plummeted from nearly 50,000 to 45,000 students during the same 3-year period (Institutional Research Office, 1999a).

All ethnic groups in the UH system were impacted negatively by the tuition increases, but ethnic minorities, particularly Filipino Americans, were hurt to a much greater extent than other groups. As a socioeconomically disadvantaged minority, Filipino Americans generally lacked the financial resources to meet the drastically raised tuition compared to the more privileged ethnic groups, and so their enrollment dropped. In contrast, starting in the 1980s, Filipino Americans had been making steady gains throughout the UH system, although they continued to be represented below their percentage of public school students. This ongoing progress continued to the early 1990s, when they became the largest ethnic group in the seven UH community colleges at about 20% of students and the largest group at a few campuses near Filipino American communities. At UH Mānoa, Filipino Americans achieved their highest-ever total of students in 1995 (1,900), including both undergraduate and graduate students (Institutional Research Office, 1995b, p. 15). Supported by these gains, Filipino Americans attained their all-time greatest number in the UH system in 1994 (7,600) and comprised 15% of the total enrollment (Institutional Research Office, 1994, p. 13). While they still were underrepresented in comparison to their proportion of public school students at that time (19%), continued enrollment expansion appeared very likely in the immediate future.

However, the tuition hikes in 1996 and 1997 brought an abrupt end to hard-won Filipino American advancement in public higher education. At UH Mānoa, their undergraduate enrollment dropped six consecutive years between 1995 (1,600) and 2001 (1,200), when the downward spiral finally came to an end (Institutional Research Office, 2001b). Since then, their number increased to nearly 1,400 students in fall 2009 but still was about 200 fewer than what it was before tuition was raised (Institutional Research Office, 2010b). Furthermore, at 10% of Mānoa undergraduates, Filipino Americans constitute less than half of their proportion of Hawai'i public high school students (21%). In the UH system, Filipino American enrollment declined 20% over 6 consecutive years from 1995 (7,500) to 2001 (6,000), before finally starting to rebound the following year (Institutional Research Office, 2001a). The last time their total number in the UH system was that low was in 1990; thus, the tuition hikes had eliminated a decade of progressive growth. As of fall 2009, Filipino Americans had regained their 1995 total in the UH system, but it took almost 15 years and a worldwide economic crisis to do so (Institutional Research Office, 2010a).

One of the major factors in the recovery of Filipino American enrollment in the UH system is the substantial escalation of community college enrollment beginning in 2007 as a result of the global recession. Filipino Americans and other Hawai'i residents who had lost their jobs entered the community colleges to retrain or to resume their education, which resulted in record highs in overall UH enrollment from 2008 through 2010, when it exceeded 60,000 students for the first time ever. Since 2006, Filipino Americans in the UH community colleges (5,300) have risen by almost 800 and comprise 17% of the students (Institutional Research Office, 2010b). The only UH campus that has not gained in students is UH Mānoa, where enrollment has shrunk since 2005, the year before a 6-year cycle of tuition hikes began (see below). If not for the global economic downturn and the consequent increases in their community college students, Filipino Americans still might be below their 1995 total in the UH system.

Native Hawaiians are another underrepresented minority at UH Mānoa that underwent initial enrollment decreases as a result of the 1996 and 1997 tuition hikes, although to a lesser extent than Filipino Americans. The reason for their different experience is because Native Hawaiian students have access to financial assistance through a scholarship foundation of the privately financed Kamehameha Schools, the federal Native Hawaiian Higher Education Act, and UH tuition waivers for Native Hawaiians. In 1995, the approximately 6,400 Native Hawaiian students in the UH system initially declined over the next 3 years, but their number had expanded by 63% by fall 2009 (10,400) (Institutional Research Office, 2010a). Like Filipino Americans, they have had huge gains in their community college enrollment (7,200 in 2009) due to the recession. Another possible reason for their increase is that starting in 2005, applicants were asked on the UH admissions application form to indicate if any of their ancestors were Hawaiian, in addition to being asked their "race." The data subsequently reported by the university on Native Hawaiian enrollment is an aggregate number of those who indicated Hawaiian ancestry (who may not necessarily claim Native Hawaiian as their identity) or who selected Native Hawaiian as their "race." At UH Mānoa, unlike Filipino Americans, Native Hawaiian undergraduate enrollment rose between 1995 (1,200) and fall 2009 (1,500) (Institutional Research Office, 2010b).

Since tuition was raised in 1996 and 1997, Whites have gained the most numerically in the UH system although, like the other groups, they had an initial loss. The 9,700 White students in the UH system in 1995 dropped to less than 8,100 by 1998, but they began an upswing in 1999 and had more than recovered by fall 2009 (11,400) when Whites were 20% of the total UH enrollment (Institutional Research Office, 1995a, 2010a). As a result of these advances, Whites became the largest ethnic group in the UH system in 1999 and at UH Mānoa in 2002, a distinction they probably last held sometime during World War II, before Japanese American veterans began enrolling in large numbers using their "GI Bill" educational benefits (Institutional Research Office 1999b, 2002).

The enrollment expansion of White students beginning in the late 1990s is due to UH Mānoa recruiting and admitting greater numbers of undergraduates from the continental United States, because as nonresidents their annual tuition is almost three times higher ($21,024 in 2010–2011) than that paid by state residents. At UH Mānoa, the percentage of White undergraduates increased from about 14% in 1995 to more than 21% in fall 2009, and during this period, their numbers expanded by 60% to 2,900 (Institutional Research Office, 2010b). This growing number of Whites has been particularly evident among first-time freshmen at UH Mānoa, where their proportion has almost tripled from 8.8% in 1998, to 17% in 2000, and to 25% in 2003, when they became the largest group among freshmen, exceeding Japanese Americans for the first time in several decades (Institutional Research Office, 2003b). However, White enrollment has been declining since 2007, very likely because of the considerable proportion of them who pay nonresident tuition, which has dramatically risen beginning the previous year. This downturn, which is part of the recent decrease in out-of-state students, is significant insofar as, in justifying the tuition hikes, UH administrators stated that a portion of the additional tuition revenues would be used to provide financial assistance to needy students such as Filipino Americans. However, declining enrollment at UH Mānoa makes the planned provision of such assistance questionable. The larger issue is that in the process of admitting more White and other students from the continental United States to UH Mānoa, the percentage of first-time freshmen who are Hawai'i residents plummeted from 88% in 1998 to 69% in 2003, thus further reducing the opportunity for Filipino American and other local ethnic minority students to receive a college education.

The university policy to increase the recruitment and enrollment of nonresident students because they pay higher tuition marginalizes ethnic minority students from Hawai'i, particularly Filipino Americans, who have become less of a policy priority to recruit and admit. Consequently, Filipino Americans continue to be grossly underrepresented at UH Mānoa, as they have been for decades, despite being the second-largest group in Hawaii's public schools. Furthermore, in pursuing out-of-state students, UH Mānoa has violated UH Board of Regents policy established in 2002, which caps their enrollment at 30%, when it exceeded that limit in 2003 (Gima, 2007). As is evident, Filipino Americans (and other ethnic minority students from Hawai'i) have become the sacrificial victims of the university's initiative to address its budget cutbacks by focusing on the recruitment and admission of nonresident students.

Despite the previous enrollment losses after tuition was raised drastically, in 2005 the UH Board of Regents unanimously approved substantial tuition increases at all UH campuses from 2006 through 2011. One of the principal reasons advanced by university administrators for the tuition hikes was that they would double annual tuition revenues to $198 million during a period of stagnating appropriations from the state legislature (Vorsino 2005). At UH Mānoa, tuition for resident undergraduates increased by 140% ($816) each academic year for 6 consecutive years. While the tuition hikes apply to everyone, Filipino Americans are being denied equal educational opportunity because, being socioeconomically disadvantaged, they have less financial means to pay the higher tuition and thus are differentially impacted by it. Raising tuition thus clearly contradicts the "mission" of the university as stated in its *University of Hawai'i System Strategic Plan* to "Provide all qualified people in Hawai'i with equal opportunity for high quality college and university education and training" (University of Hawai'i, 2002, p. 4).

From the above discussion, it can be seen that during periods of fiscal crisis, the university administration responds in the same way as the Hawai'i state government, that is, by seeking to attract transient outsiders to the islands as a major means to alleviate their common problem of declining revenues. The university recruits and accepts more students from the continental United States, while the state seeks to attract greater numbers of tourists from the same locale and abroad; in both cases, the people of Hawai'i ultimately are marginalized. More nonresident students mean fewer places for chronically underrepresented ethnic minorities from Hawai'i who will continue to be denied equal access to public higher education. More tourists mean the continued dependency on the highly undependable tourism industry as the mainstay of the economy and the continued underfunding of public higher education, let alone the perpetuation of low-wage and low-mobility service and sales jobs.

Besides lesser access to UH Mānoa, Filipino Americans also have lower graduation rates from the university. A longitudinal study of first-time freshman cohorts from fall 1990 to fall 2007 as of 2008 reported that the average graduation rate after 6 years for Filipino Americans (52%) was lower than for Chinese Americans (71%) and Japanese Americans (65%), although it was higher than for Native Hawaiians (42%) (Institutional Research Office, 2009). The lower Filipino American graduation rate from UH Mānoa is evident in their lesser percentage of persons 25 years and older with a bachelor's degree or higher (15%) in Hawai'i (Okamura, 2008, p. 87). According to the 2000 U.S. Census, this figure was considerably lower than for Whites (31%), Japanese Americans (30%), and Chinese Americans (27%), but higher than for Native Hawaiians (13%). Previous U.S. censuses from 1970 to 1990 in Hawai'i have shown that Filipino Americans had much lower levels of college completion and enrollment than for Whites, Japanese Americans, and Chinese Americans (Okamura, 1982, 1990, 1998).

Besides graduation, Filipino Americans (35%, 27%, females first) have lower college or graduate school enrollment among persons 18 to 25 years old in Hawai'i according to 2000 census data (Okamura, 2008, pp. 87–88). Filipino American representation in college or graduate education was less than for Japanese Americans (51%, 45%, respectively) and Chinese Americans (44%, 37%, respectively) but higher than for Whites (34%, 22%, respectively) and Native Hawaiians (30%, 22%, respectively). The seemingly anomalous relatively low enrollment status of Whites is due to 18 to 24 year olds associated with the U.S. military as enlisted personnel or their dependents because a high proportion of them are not in college.

Through a discussion of the access and enrollment of Filipino Americans at UH Mānoa, I have demonstrated how they participate and benefit unequally in public higher education in Hawai'i. I also have argued that the consequent disparities in the educational attainment of Filipino Americans are primarily the result of discriminatory policies and practices against them. These policies and practices include the long-term underfunding by the state government of both the University of Hawai'i system and the public schools as well as the nonimplementation by the university of its equal educational opportunity, nondiscrimination, and affirmative action policies, which have much greater detrimental consequences for ethnic minorities such as Filipino Americans than for the socioeconomically advantaged ethnic groups. At UH Mānoa, budget cutbacks by the state legislature through most of the 1990s gave rise to huge tuition hikes in 1996 and 1997 and to a recruitment initiative directed at nonresident students in the continental United States, which severely reduced Filipino American admissions and enrollment. The tuition increases of 140% from 2006 through 2011 also have limited Filipino American enrollment from regaining its 1995 level at Mānoa. Clearly, public higher education does not provide equal opportunity for Filipino Americans and in fact contributes to their lower educational status by restricting their access to a college degree.

DISCUSSION

In this chapter, I have sought to compare the access and enrollment of Filipino Americans in the University of California system following the prohibition of race-based affirmative action in college admissions with that of their counterparts in the University of Hawai'i system since the implementation of substantial tuition hikes, both of these major policy changes occurring in 1996. As evident from the above, these policy decisions in public higher education had very different consequences for Filipino American undergraduates in the two university systems during the ensuing 12-year period to 2009. In the UC system, after the passage of Proposition 209 in 1996, Filipino Americans have increased their overall numbers, especially at UC Berkeley and UC Irvine, and can be said to be overrepresented in comparison to their proportion of California public high school graduates. Thus, an argument could be made that their post–affirmative action experiences have generally been positive, at least in terms of admissions and enrollment, and more like those of Asian Americans in general than those of aggrieved racial minorities such as African Americans, who have suffered considerable enrollment declines at Berkeley and UCLA. These advances in higher education are noteworthy since there is a common perception that Filipino Americans, unlike Chinese Americans, Japanese Americans, and Korean Americans, do not generally conform to the model minority stereotype of Asian Americans as academically high achieving students (see below). Nonetheless, their advances in the UC system should not be allowed to obscure the fact that Filipino Americans continue to encounter problems in gaining admission and persisting in college.

Thus, while I have reported some positive outcomes in enrollment in the UC system, other scholars emphasize the continued marginalization of Filipino American students in higher education. Summarizing the work of other researchers on the barriers faced by Filipino Americans, higher education scholar Tracy Lachica Buenavista (2010, p. 117) notes that Filipino immigrant and second-generation youth face high "push-out" rates in secondary education, have lower levels of retention and participation in postsecondary education, and enroll in less selective colleges if they pursue higher education. Applying critical race theory (CRT) to the educational experiences of Filipino Americans, she contends that the intersection among race, immigration, and socioeconomic status particularly structures the obstacles to postsecondary education they encounter insofar as they are a non-White, primarily immigrant community of low socioeconomic status (p. 123).

Also employing a CRT framework, Buenavista, Jayakumar, and Misa-Escalante (2009, p. 78) maintain that, as a result of being racially categorized as Asian American by universities and colleges, Filipino Americans are racialized as "liminal and invisible" minorities in higher education. They occupy a liminal, or in-between, status because while their experiences in college are similar to those of underrepresented racial minorities, as Asian Americans they are stereotyped as model minority students and thus not in need of targeted outreach and retention services. Filipino American students and their specific issues and problems in college hence become invisible to higher education institutions insofar as they are obscured by their racialization as high achieving Asian Americans, and colleges "consequently fail to provide the recognition and invest the resources to address their concerns" (Buenavista et al., 2009, p. 77). Nonetheless, Buenavista (2010, p. 123) remarks that Filipinos also have been viewed as distinct from other Asian American groups as an "outlier" to the model minority stereotype, particularly in areas where they comprise a concentrated population. In such locales, Filipino American youth are racialized as gang members, criminals, and social deviants (Alsaybar, 2002; Teranishi, 2002; Tintiangco-Cubales, 2007; as cited in Buenavista 2010, p. 121), which results in their not being perceived and treated as concerned with education by their teachers and counselors.

Based on her qualitative research study of Filipina American undergraduates at a public research university in southern California, Maramba (2008, p. 344) found that three "themes" were most significant in understanding their college experiences: family and parental influence, home obligations and gender differences, and maintaining and negotiating their Filipina American identity within the context of their home and college environments. To address these themes, Maramba (p. 347) argues that university administrators, faculty, and student affairs staff need to have an understanding of the Filipino American student experience so that they can develop both cultural and gender-appropriate programs and services to foster their recruitment and retention.

Focused on the social relationships, especially family ties, of Filipino American students, these issues certainly also affect their enrollment and persistence in college in addition to those pertaining to institutionalized policies and practices discussed in this chapter and by Buenavista and her colleagues.

In the UH system, after tuition was drastically raised in 1996 and 1997, Filipino American enrollment plummeted, particularly at UH Mānoa. It took nearly 15 years for enrollment to reach its previous levels, but it is still down at Mānoa. In 2005, substantial tuition hikes were again authorized for 2006 through 2011, despite three Filipino Americans serving on the UH Board of Regents, who voted with the other nine board members for their unanimous approval. Thus, somewhat paradoxically, the arguably greater political power of Filipino Americans in Hawai'i compared to their counterparts in California, with their much lower percentage of the state population, does not necessarily translate into an ability to protect themselves from the negative consequences of state policies, at least in public higher education. This situation can be explained by the relatively lower socioeconomic status of Filipino Americans in Hawai'i, which results in their financial inability to meet the higher cost of tuition and thus their numerical decreases at UH Mānoa. Another major factor that constrains their enrollment in the UH system is Hawaii's chronically underfunded K–12 public school system, in which Filipino Americans are the second-largest ethnic group (after Native Hawaiians) and hence suffer the disadvantages of the inadequate education being provided (Okamura, 2008, p. 70). As a notable recent example, a severe state budget deficit caused by declining tax revenues (due to declining numbers of tourist arrivals) forced the public schools of Hawai'i, which has the only statewide school district in the nation, to close for 17 days during the 2009–2010 school year. This incredible situation resulted in Hawai'i having the shortest school year (163 days) in the United States, if not in the developed world.[12]

The divergent experiences in public higher education of Filipino Americans in California and Hawai'i can also be considered anomalous in terms of the larger political and educational context for them in their respective states. Since the mid-1990s, California has led the nation in the anti–affirmative action and anti-immigrant movements, including another voter-approved proposition (Proposition 227), which eliminated bilingual education in its public schools in 1998. In contrast, Hawai‘i had a Filipino American governor from 1994 to 2002, a period in which their numbers in the UH system dropped precipitously, and there are far more Filipino American university regents and state legislators in Hawai‘i than in California, including the president of the state Senate between 1998 and 2006. Furthermore, UH Mānoa has courses on Filipino Americans in ethnic studies and American studies, provides instruction in two Philippine languages (Ilokano and Tagalog), offers the only bachelor's degree in Philippine languages and literature in the nation, offered the first degree in Philippine studies, and had the first student service program designated for Filipino Americans (Operation Manong, started in 1972). Nonetheless, these seemingly advantageous political and educational contexts were not sufficient to protect Filipino Americans from the harmful impact of UH policies and practices, such as raising tuition drastically and recruiting out-of-state students.

POST–GLOBAL RECESSION ACCESS TO PUBLIC HIGHER EDUCATION

Since the onset of the global recession in 2008, both the UC and UH systems have faced enormous budget cuts of hundreds of millions of dollars. They, along with many other public universities across the country, have seen their appropriations from state legislatures dwindle in the past two decades. Thus, confronted with the same financial problems, it should hardly be surprising that the University of California has responded in the same way that the University of Hawai‘i did earlier, that is, by admitting more nonresident students and hiking tuition substantially. It is too early to determine the consequences for Filipino American enrollment in the UC system of these policies. However, based on the Hawai‘i experience, they may well derail the progressive advances that Filipino Americans have been making since the end of race-based affirmative action. Another problem they face is the proposed change in UC admissions policies that will eliminate SAT subject tests on which Asian Americans, including Filipino Americans, perform well. It is extremely unfortunate that as Filipino Americans, often through their own efforts, such as student-directed recruitment and retention programs, attain a measure of success and equality, institutionalized means are initiated that restrict them from gaining greater access to public higher education.

NOTES

1. The lawsuit was later renamed *Castaneda et al. v. the Regents of the University of California* and was filed on behalf of more than 750 African American, Latino, and Filipino American students (Nieves, 1999). Those students included three high school organizations, including the Kababayan Alliance. The suit was submitted by the same three organizations as in the previous suit, together with the Lawyers' Committee for Civil Rights and the American Civil Liberties Union of Northern California. Those organizations settled out of court with UC Berkeley after several changes in admissions policies were made, including a "comprehensive review" of the entire file of every applicant, including personal statements and extracurricular activities, and less emphasis given to SAT scores and AP courses (American Civil Liberties Union of Northern California, 2003).
2. In addition to those at Berkeley, Los Angeles, and Irvine, the nine UC campuses that serve undergraduates are at Davis, Merced (opened in 2006), Riverside, San Diego, Santa Barbara, and Santa Cruz. The University of California, San Francisco is primarily for medical students.
3. Besides UH Mānoa, the UH system consists of seven community colleges and two other institutions, both with fewer than 4,100 students, which offer primarily bachelor's degrees.
4. Very likely as a result of their racial categorization as Asian American, Filipino Americans were removed in 1986 from eligibility for student affirmative action programs at UC Berkeley, even though they were not as well represented as other Asian American groups.
5. The proposition stated, "The state shall not discriminate against, or grant preferential treatment to, any individual or group on the basis of race, sex, color, ethnicity, or national origin in the operation of public employment, public education, or public contracting."
6. The data on student enrollment by race and ethnicity in this section are from the Statistical Summary of Students and Staff published each spring by Information Resources and Communications, University of California (2008) at http://www.ucop.edu/ucophome/uwnews/stat/
7. PASS is one of five racial minority recruitment and retention centers organized by students who formed a coalition called "Bridges" in 1996. Besides PASS, these centers include the Black Recruitment and Retention Center, the Native American Recruitment and Retention Center, the Raza Recruitment and Retention Center (for Latino students), and the Asian/Pacific Islander Recruitment and Retention Center. According to its website (http://www.ocf.berkeley.edu/~bridges/), Bridges was established by a group of student leaders who wanted to "work together in solidarity across lines of race and ethnicity."
8. See Horn and Flores (2003, p. 20) for detailed information on the specific requirements and procedures for determining the top 4% of a high school's graduating class.
9. Except for UC Merced, which opened in 2006, the Riverside and Santa Cruz campuses receive the least number of applications for freshman admission,

while UCLA, at more than 60,000, ranks among the highest U.S. universities in number of applicants.

10. Asian Americans were projected to represent 41% of entering freshmen in fall 2010, while African Americans would be only 3.9% (Gordon, 2010b).
11. Some of the material in this section is from Chapter 4 on "Educational Inequality and Ethnicity" in my book *Ethnicity and Inequality in Hawai'i* (2008), but I have updated it to include more recent data and developments in the UH system.
12. This problem was eventually resolved for the next school year by the state legislature in April 2010, shortly before the end of its session, by appropriating monies that were always available from a state "emergency fund" without having to raise taxes or borrow money. But the long delay in dealing with this issue clearly indicates the low policy priority that public education has in Hawai'i.

REFERENCES

Alsaybar, B. D. (2002). Deconstructing deviance: Filipino American youth gangs, "party culture," and ethnic identity in Los Angeles. In P. G. Min (Ed.), *Second generation: Ethnic identity among Asian Americans* (pp. 129–152). Walnut Creek, CA: AltaMira.

Altonn, H. (1999, April 22). Years of neglect cripple UH-Mānoa. *Honolulu Star-Bulletin,* pp. A1, A8.

American Civil Liberties Union of Northern California. (2003, June 17). Settlement reached in suit over discriminatory admissions process at UC Berkeley [Press release]. Retrieved from http://www.aclunc.org/news/press_releases/settlement_reached_in_suit_over_discriminatory

Buenavista, T. L. (2007). *Movement from the middle: Pilipina/o 1.5-generation college student access, retention, and resistance.* (Unpublished doctoral dissertation). University of California, Los Angeles.

Buenavista, T. L. (2010). Issues affecting U.S. Filipino student access to postsecondary education: A critical race theory perspective. *Journal of Education for Students Placed at Risk, 15*(1), 114–126.

Buenavista, T. L, Jayakumar, U. M., & Misa-Escalante, K. (2009). Contextualizing Asian American education through critical race theory: An example of U.S. Pilipino college student experiences. In S. D. Museus (Ed.), *Conducting research on Asian Americans in higher education: New directions for institutional research* (no. 142, pp. 69–81). San Francisco, CA: Jossey-Bass.

California Postsecondary Education Commission. (2010a). *Community college transfers: Filipino as a percent of total, 1995–2009* [table]. Retrieved from http://www.cpec.ca.gov/StudentData/EthSnapshotGraph.asp

California Postsecondary Education Commission. (2010b). *First-time freshmen: Filipino as a percent of total, 1995–2009* [table]. Retrieved from http://www.cpec.ca.gov/StudentData/EthSnapshotGraph.asp

California Postsecondary Education Commission. (2010c). *First-time freshmen: Latino as a percent of total, 1995-2009* [table]. Retrieved from http://www.cpec.ca.gov/StudentData/EthSnapshotGraph.asp?Eth=4&Rpt=FTF_UC

California Postsecondary Education Commission. (2010d). *High school graduates: Black as a percent of total, 1994–2008* [table]. Retrieved from http://www.cpec.ca.gov/StudentData/EthSnapshotGraph.asp?Eth=2&Rpt=Grad_HS

California Postsecondary Education Commission. (2010e). *High school graduates: Filipino as a percent of total, 1994–2008* [table]. Retrieved from http://www.cpec.ca.gov/StudentData/EthSnapshotGraph.asp

California Postsecondary Education Commission. (2010f). *High school graduates: Latino as a percent of total, 1994–2008* [table]. Retrieved from http://www.cpec.ca.gov/StudentData/EthSnapshotGraph.asp

Gima, C. (2007, June 7). UH-Mānoa and Hilo breaking caps on enrollment. *Honolulu Star-Bulletin*, p. A1.

Gordon, L. (2010a, July 15). Out of state? Come to UC. *Los Angeles Times*. Retrieved from http://articles.latimes.com/2010/jul/15/local/la-me-uc-enroll-20100715

Gordon, L. (2010b, November 15). UC campuses move to recruit more out-of-state students. *Los Angeles Times*. Retrieved from http://www.latimes.com/news/local/la-me-ucrecruit-20101115,0,4096476.story

Hayashi, P., & Kidder, W. (2004, July 18). Level UC's unequal playing field. Guest Commentary, *Contra Costa Times*. Retrieved from http://www.equaljusticesociety.org/press_2004_july_19_cctimes.html

Horn, C. L., & Flores, S. M. (2003). *Percent plans in college admissions: A comparative analysis of three states' experiences*. Cambridge, MA: The Civil Rights Project, Harvard University.

Information Resources and Communications. (2008). *Statistical summary of students and staff. University of California*. Retrieved from http://www.ucop.edu/ucophome/uwnews/stat/

Institutional Research Office, University of Hawai'i. (1994). *Fall enrollment report, University of Hawai'i, fall 1994.*

Institutional Research Office, University of Hawai'i. (1995a). *Fall enrollment report, University of Hawai'i, fall 1995.*

Institutional Research Office, University of Hawai'i. (1995b). *Fall enrollment report, University of Hawai'i at Mānoa, fall 1995.*

Institutional Research Office, University of Hawai'i. (1999a). *Fall enrollment report, University of Hawai'i, fall 1998.* Retrieved from http://www.hawaii.edu/cgi-bin/iro/maps?seuhf98.pdf

Institutional Research Office, University of Hawai'i. (1999b). *Fall enrollment report, University of Hawai'i, fall 1999.* Retrieved from http://www.hawaii.edu/cgi-bin/iro/maps?seuhf99.pdf

Institutional Research Office, University of Hawai'i. (2001a). *Fall enrollment report, University of Hawai'i, fall 2001.* Retrieved from http://www.hawaii.edu/cgi-bin/iro/maps?seuhf01.pdf

Institutional Research Office, University of Hawai'i. (2001b). *Fall enrollment report, University of Hawai'i at Mānoa, fall 2001.* Retrieved from http://www.hawaii.edu/cgi-bin/iro/maps?semaf01.pdf

Institutional Research Office, University of Hawai'i. (2002). *Fall enrollment report, University of Hawai'i at Mānoa, fall 2002.* Retrieved from http://www.hawaii.edu/cgi-bin/iro/maps?semaf02.pdf

Institutional Research Office, University of Hawai'i. (2003a). *Fall enrollment report, University of Hawai'i, fall 2002.* Retrieved from http://www.hawaii.edu/cgi-bin/iro/maps?seuhf02.pdf

Institutional Research Office, University of Hawai'i. (2003b). *Fall 2003 preliminary classified first-time freshmen highlights. University of Hawai'i.* Retrieved from http://www.hawaii.edu/iro/maps.htm.

Institutional Research Office, University of Hawai'i. (2009). *Graduation and retention rates, peer and benchmark group comparisons, University of Hawai'i at Mānoa, fall 1990 to fall 2007 cohorts as of 2008.* Retrieved from http://www.hawaii.edu/cgi-bin/iro/maps?gcma08external.pdf.

Institutional Research Office, University of Hawai'i. (2010a). *Fall enrollment report, University of Hawai'i, fall 2009. University of Hawai'i.* Retrieved from http://www.hawaii.edu/cgi-bin/iro/maps?seuhf09.pdf

Institutional Research Office, University of Hawai'i. (2010b). *Fall enrollment report, University of Hawai'i at Mānoa, fall 2009.* Retrieved from http://www.hawaii.edu/cgi-bin/iro/maps?semaf09.pdf

Krieger, L. M. (2009). New UC admissions policy gives White students a better chance, angers Asian-American community. *The Mercury News.* Retrieved from http://www.mercurynews.com/ci_12014954

Maramba, D. C. (2008). Immigrant families and the college experience: Perspectives of Filipina Americans. *Journal of College Student Development, 49*(4), 336–350.

Nieves, E. (1999, February 3). Civil rights groups suing Berkeley over admissions policy. *New York Times.* Retrieved from http://www.nytimes.com/1999/02/03/us/civil-rights-groups-suing-berkeley-over-admissions-policy.html

Office of Student Research. (2007). *New freshman registrants by ethnicity, fall 1996–fall 2006. University of California, Berkeley.* Retrieved from www.osr2.berkeley.edu/newfroshtrend.html

Office of University and Budget Planning. (2010). *Fall 2009 ethnicity report—Undergraduate enrollment. San Francisco State University.* Retrieved from http://www.sfsu.edu/~ubp/clickmap/ethlevl/eth064.pdf

Okamura, J. Y. (1982). Ethnicity and ethnic relations in Hawaii. In D. Y. H. Wu (Ed.), *Ethnicity and interpersonal interaction in pluralistics societies: A cross-cultural study* (pp. 213–235). Singapore: Maruzen Asia.

Okamura, J. Y. (1990). Ethnicity and stratification in Hawai'i. *Operation Manong Resource Papers, No. 1.* Operation Manong Program, University of Hawai'i at Mānoa.

Okamura, J. Y. (1998). Social stratification. In M. Haas (Ed.), *Multicultural Hawai'i: The fabric of a multiethnic society* (pp. 185–204). New York, NY: Garland.

Okamura, J. Y. (2008). *Ethnicity and inequality in Hawai'i.* Philadelphia, PA: Temple University Press.

Okamura, J. Y., & Agbayani, A. (1997). Pamantasan: Filipino Americans in higher education. In M. P. P. Root (Ed.), *Filipino Americans: Transformation and identity* (pp. 183–197). Thousand Oaks, CA: Sage.

Takagi, D. (1993). *The retreat from race: Asian American admissions and racial politics.* New Brunswick, NJ: Rutgers University Press.

Teranishi, R. T. (2002). Asian Pacific Americans and critical race theory: An examination of school racial climate. *Equity & Excellence in Education, 35,* 144–154.

Tintiangco-Cubales, A. (2007). For a while now, I've been feeling neglected...: A preliminary study on urban Filipina/o American high school students. In A. Tintiangco-Cubales (Ed.), *Pin@y educational partnerships: A Filipina/o American studies sourcebook series* (pp. 29–41). Santa Clara, CA: Phoenix.

U.S. Bureau of the Census. (2003). *Summary file 4 of the 2000 U.S. Census.* Retrieved from http://factfinder.census.gov/servlet/DatasetMainPageServlet?

U.S. Commission on Civil Rights. (2000). *Toward an understanding of percentage plans in higher education: Are they effective substitutes for affirmative action?* Retrieved from http://www.usccr.gov/pubs/percent/stmnt.htm

University of Hawai'i. (2002). *University of Hawai'i system strategic plan: Entering the university's second century, 2002–2010.* University of Hawai'i.

Vorsino, M. (2005, January 22). UH tuition might rise by 123%. *Honolulu Star-Bulletin,* p. Al.

CHAPTER 13

COLLECTIVE SELF-ESTEEM AND PERCEPTIONS OF FAMILY AND CAMPUS ENVIRONMENTS AMONG FILIPINO AMERICAN COLLEGE STUDENTS

Reynaldo I. Monzon
San Diego State University

Like many Asian cultures, the Filipino family structure can be characterized as collectivistic in terms of its norms and values (Triandis, 1989). In other words, the well-being of the family carries more weight than the happiness of the individual, a deference of the self for the harmony of the family (Heras & Revilla, 1994). Thus, for the Filipino American student, attending college is not an "individual" activity, but rather a "collective" one, in which the influence of the family affects the student throughout his or her collegiate experience. Furthermore, because of the hierarchical structure of the Filipino family, in which the authority flows downward and respect and gratification of one's elders is expected at all times (Agbayani-Siewert,

The "Other" Students, pages 237–258

1994; Almirol, 1982; Lynch, 1981; Santos, 1983), Filipino American students are not allowed to question their parents as to why they are expected to attend a particular college or pursue a particular academic major. As a result, they enter college with a strong sense of family loyalty and obligation, determined to fulfill their parents' expectations by adhering to their parents' prescribed or strongly suggested choice of institution and educational/career goal. Moreover, the source of this determination is *hiya* or shame (Lynch, 1981) manifested by an awareness that the reputation of the family hinges on whether they succeed or fail. However, once in college, these same students begin to discover who they are as individuals, their likes and dislikes, and what they can and cannot do. Furthermore, they become more aware of educational and career goals that were never considered. It is through this developmental process that Filipino American students, like most college students, gain more certainty about their educational and career goals, which are, more often than not, different from the original goals that their parents expected them to pursue. When this conflict occurs, many Filipino American students, unlike other college students, expend a lot of time and energy in trying to find a way to satisfy both their individual goals and the goals they were obligated to fulfill for the sake of the family. As a result, they lose focus, but more importantly, their sense of identity and level of self-esteem can be negatively impacted. Therefore, the extent to which this conflict impacts the self-esteem of Filipino American college students is the focus of the present study. According to social identity theorists (Tajfel, 1982; Tajfel & Turner, 1986), the self-concept has two distinct components: a personal identity and a social identity. Personal identity consists of an individual's belief about his or her traits and attributes. On the other hand, social identity, or what is called the collective self (Crocker & Luhtanen, 1990), is defined as "that aspect of the individual's self-concept which derives from his knowledge of his membership in a social group (or groups) together with the value and emotional significance attached to that membership" (Tajfel, 1981, p. 255). Social identity theory also posits that individuals are motivated to achieve a high level of self-esteem described as feelings of self-worth (Rosenberg, 1979) and considered a major component of psychological well-being (Taylor & Brown, 1988).

While much of the research on self-esteem has focused on an individual's motivation to maintain a positive personal identity or "personal self-esteem," others have argued that the collective aspects of the self-concept (e.g., social identity) may also contribute to feelings of self-worth (Crocker & Luhtanen, 1990; Crocker, Luhtanen, Blaine, & Broadnax, 1994). For example, Luhtanen and Crocker (1992) argue that increased collective self-esteem should, in turn, enhance personal self-esteem. Moreover, according to Triandis (1989), the collective self is a more salient feature in collectivistic-oriented cultures such as the Philippines. With regard to Filipino Americans, the collective self can refer to their ethnic identity (being Filipino) or their identification with the family. Therefore, collective self-esteem as opposed to personal self-esteem may be a more relevant factor of psychological well-being for Filipino Americans because of an awareness of their ethnic identity. In fact, Phinney (1990) noted that several researchers have argued that ethnic identity is crucial to self-concept and psychological functioning of ethnic group members.

Therefore, a shift in focus from "personal" self-esteem to "collective" self-esteem may shed light on previous studies of Filipino Americans and self-esteem, particularly as it pertains to the academic success of Filipino American college students. For example, in a study of Filipino American college students, Monzon (1984) found no significant relationship between self-esteem and academic performance. The instrument used in that study measured personal aspects of self-esteem. In a later study using the same self-esteem instrument, Monzon (1996) again found no correlation between personal self-esteem and academic performance. Instead, personal self-esteem was related to perceived aspects of the family environment. In other words, collective aspects of the self in terms of family membership were correlated with the psychological well-being or personal self-esteem of Filipino American college students. Furthermore, other studies examining Filipino American college students found aspects of the family environment to be related to academic performance (Chiong, 1997; Heras & Revilla, 1994).

For the present study, it was proposed that for Filipino American college students, collective self-esteem, as opposed to personal self-esteem, would be more related to academic performance. It was further proposed that perceptions of the family environment and campus environment would also be related to collective self-esteem. Therefore, the goals of the present study are to (a) develop and evaluate a Filipino American Collective Self-Esteem Scale; (b) assess the mean differences across three separate campus samples of Filipino American college students with regard to demographic variables, self-esteem (collective and personal), campus variables, and perceptions of the family environment; and (c) examine the interrelationships between collective self-esteem, personal self-esteem, academic performance, and perceptions of the campus and family environments among Filipino American college students.

In terms of the first goal, a Filipino American Collective Self-Esteem Scale based on the work of Luhtanen and Crocker (1992) was developed. Luhtanen and Crocker created a general measure of collective self-esteem (CSE) that included subscales measuring four aspects of CSE. These subscales included (a) membership, (b) private, (c) public, and (d) identity. The CSE Scale is a 16-item scale, with each subscale consisting of 4 items each. The *membership* subscale included items that involved an individual's judgment of how good or worthy they are as members of their social group. Items in the *private* subscale assessed one's personal judgments of how good one's social groups are, and the *public* subscale items measured one's judgment of how other people evaluate one's social groups. For the *identity* subscale, items that measured the importance of one's social group memberships to one's self-concept were used. Finally, Crocker et al. (1994) also assessed personal self-esteem with race specific CSE for White, Black, and Asian college students. They found correlations between the public and private subscales to be near zero for Blacks, moderate for Whites, and strong for Asians. Therefore, similar to the race-specific CSE developed by Crocker et al., for the present study, a Filipino American CSE Scale was created. This was done through slight modification of the wording in the 16 subscale items, substituting the specific category "Filipino American" for the more general "social groups" used by Luhtanen and Crocker (1992). For example, the item "I am a worthy member of the social groups I belong to" was changed to "I am worthy of being a Filipino American."

In order to achieve the second goal, I collected data on Filipino American college students from three different types of college institutions. In California, the system of higher education is organized into three tiers: (a) University of California–UC, (b) California State University–CSU, and (c) community college–CC. These types of colleges vary in terms of their missions, policies, and student characteristics. For example, the UCs are research universities and typically accept the top 10% of all high school graduates. Moreover, it is possible that these institutional differences may have a significant effect on a student's college experience and persistence. Therefore, for the present study, samples were collected from a campus representing one of the three tiers. All in all, three samples were collected, each from a Southern California UC, CSU, and CC.

With regard to the third goal, I examined the relationships among Filipino American CSE, personal self-esteem, and the campus and family environment variables similar to those used in the Monzon (1996) study. Although previous studies have reported significant relationships between personal self-esteem and academic performance (Pascarella & Terenzini, 1991), Monzon (1984, 1996) found no relationship between these two variables for Filipino American college students. Moreover, Markus and Kitayama (1991) suggest that many Asian cultures (e.g., Philippine culture) emphasize the interconnected nature of the self, the importance of feelings and evaluations of others, and the importance of one's public image. Therefore, it was proposed in the present study that collective self-esteem would be a more relevant correlate of academic performance than personal self-esteem. Similar to the Monzon (1996) study, the Moos (1974) Family Environment Scale was used to measure perceptions of the family environment. In addition, two new scales were used to measure perceptions of the campus environment: Cultural Congruity and University

Environment. These two scales were developed and validated by Gloria and Kurpius (1996) utilizing a sample of Chicano/a college students. Their motivation for developing the scales was to underscore the need for continued examination of racial/ethnic students' perceptions of the university environment. According to Gloria and Kurpius, a major factor contributing to the academic persistence of racial/ethnic students is perceptions of cultural congruity. In other words, individuals belonging to two or more cultures may experience cultural incongruity if the cultures are different in values, beliefs, and expectations for behaviors. These scales are described in the next section.

PARTICIPANTS

Filipino American undergraduate students enrolled at two Southern California universities and one Southern California community college were solicited for their participation. The students were recruited from classroom settings and the Filipino campus organizations. Procedures for recruitment were the same at all three campuses.

At the CC campus, surveys were distributed to students at a Filipino American History class and an Asian Studies class. Both classes were over 90% Filipino American. Surveys were given in a Filipino American History and a Filipino American Community Issues class at the CSU campus. In addition, surveys were collected during a meeting of the Filipino American student organization. Similar to the CSU campus, survey data at the UC campus was collected at a student organization meeting and a Filipino American History class. Non-Filipino students who happened to be in the classes or meetings when the data was being collected were asked to participate, however, they were told to mark their ethnicity at the top of the survey. Across all three campuses, a total of 205 surveys were collected. A total of 11 surveys were non-Filipino and were not analyzed for the present study. A final total of 194 surveys were eventually used for the present study. A majority of the surveys were from the CSU campus (91) followed by the CC (70) and the UC (33) campuses.

All participants were given a short questionnaire that consisted of basic demographics and student self-reported variables in addition to the Cultural Congruity Scale, University Environment Scale, Filipino American Collective Self-Esteem Scale, Moos' (1974) Family Environment Scale, and Rosenberg's (1979) Personal Self-Esteem Scale.

PROCEDURE

After a short explanation about the study, the students were asked for their participation. For the classroom participants, the instructors gave the survey at the start of class and allowed all of the students to finish. No incentives or extra credit were given for participation. The questionnaire data were coded and entered into an IBM compatible personal computer. The PC version of the Statistical Package for the Social Sciences (SPSSX/Windows) was used to compute the demographic variables, language difference variables, and generational status. Scale composites for cultural congruity, university environment, Filipino American CSE, personal self-esteem, and family environment were also computed.

MEASURES

Demographic Variables

Demographic information regarding all participants' age, grade level, gender, and years lived in the United States was solicited. Other demographic variables are described below.

Language Items

Four questions related to what languages are spoken in the home were given. In the Monzon (1996) study, only one question asked what language is spoken in the home. The problem with asking a single question about home language is that it doesn't accurately reflect the possible combinations of dual language dyads. For example, when speaking to their parents, most Filipino American students use primarily English, while parents on the other hand, would speak Pilipino to each other. Therefore, for the present study, students were asked what language is spoken to (a) their parents, (b) their siblings and relatives, and (c) others in the home. A fourth question was related to what language their parents speak to each other. The four language variables were measured on a 5-point Likert scale: 1 = Pilipino language all the time, 2 = Pilipino language most of the time, 3 = Pilipino and English equally, 4 = English most of the time, and 5 = English all the time.

Language Difference

The purpose of this variable was to measure the difference between what language students speak to their parents and what language their parents speak between themselves. For example, if a student speaks English all the time to his or her parents, a score of 5 will be given, and if the parents speak Pilipino all the time to each other, then a score of 1 will be given. Thus, the Language Difference variable would be computed as the difference between these two scores, which is 4.

Generational Status

Individuals who immigrate to this country are considered first generation, while children who are born here are considered second generation. Furthermore, the second generation (and future generations) normally spend their entire lives here. Thus, the degree of knowledge and competence of their heritage culture is dependent upon the first generation. Although this is the usual definition of generational status, asking the participants what generation they considered themselves to be (e.g., first or second generation) was not included in the survey. Instead, generational status was estimated by using a mathematical procedure used in previous research on Filipino American college students (Heras & Revilla, 1994). In this procedure, the number of years lived in the United States is divided by chronological age (years lived in U.S./chronological age x 100 = %) to yield a percentage of time a person lived in the United States. The decision to use this approach was based on the rationale that because of the history in the local area, most of the students in the study are from families affiliated with the United States Navy. Furthermore, there is a high probability that these families spent a considerable amount of time in the Philippines via tour of duty. Thus, it is possible for some students to be born in the United States (defined as second generation), yet spend a considerable amount of time (6 to 10 years) in the Philippines as a child, enough time to learn the language, customs, and traditions similar to most first-generation immigrants. On the other hand, students born in the Philippines (defined as first generation) may have resettled in the United States as an infant and hence have no memory of their country of birth. Therefore, I propose that utilizing the percentage of years spent in the United States is a more accurate measure of generation for the Filipino American students in the present study.

Commuter Status

Participants responded either (1 = yes) or (0 = no) when asked whether they commuted to school from their parents' home. Generally, students who commute from home spend less time with campus activities than students who live near or on campus. This may have an impact on the student's rate of social and academic integration into the college.

Self-Esteem Variables

Filipino American Collective Self-Esteem (CSE) Scale

As mentioned earlier, the purpose of the present study was to develop and evaluate a Filipino American CSE Scale. As mentioned in the previous section, this scale is a modified version of the general CSE Scale developed by Luhtanen and Crocker (1992). Thus, for the present study, this scale reflects how one feels about being Filipino American. Responses to the 16 items were made on a 7-point Likert-type format such that, 1 = strongly disagree, 2 = disagree, 3 = disagree somewhat, 4 = neutral, 5 = agree somewhat, 6 = agree, and 7 = strongly agree. Similar to the general CSE, there are four subscales composed of four items each. The subscales are defined as (a) membership—how one feels about being a "member" of Filipino Americans; (b) private—the extent to which one personally evaluates Filipino Americans; (c) public—the extent to which one perceives how the public evaluates Filipino Americans; and (d) identity—the extent to which being Filipino American relates to one's identity.

Rosenberg's Personal Self-Esteem Scale

Because this scale was used in the Monzon (1996) study, it is used again in the present study for purposes of comparison to the Filipino American CSE Scale. In addition, this scale was used for several other reasons. First, since it only has 10 items, it was convenient to administer in a questionnaire form. Second, self-acceptance is measured on a 4-point Likert scale for each item. Finally, in terms of reliability, Silber and Tippett (1965) found a .85 test-retest reliability over a 2-year period.

Campus Variables

College GPA

Respondents were asked to report their current GPA.

Cultural Congruity Scale (CCS)

As mentioned earlier, this scale was developed and validated by Gloria and Kurpius (1996) in order to assess an ethnic student's sense of cultural congruity or cultural fit within the college environment. Six of the items were from Ethier and Deaux's (1990) Perceived Threat Scale, which assessed perception of threat among racial/ethnic minority students at Ivy League colleges. Based on the literature and their own experiences, Gloria and Kurpius developed and added supplemental items. This scale utilized a 7-point Likert-type response format ranging from 1 = not at all to 7 = a great deal. The original scale consisted of 14 items. After eliminating one item because it detracted from the scale's internal consistency, the final 13-item CCS had a Cronbach alpha of .89. A cultural congruity score is computed by summing across all 13 items.

University Environment Scale (UES)

This scale was also developed and validated by Gloria and Kurpius (1996) and focuses on racial/ethnic minority student concerns with regard to the university campus. Originally based on interviews of racial/ethnic minority students reported by Baron (1981) and a review of the literature, Gloria and Kurpius developed 16 items for this scale. During pilot testing, two items dropped out for lack of internal consistency. The final 14-item scale uses a 7-point Likert-type format ranging from 1 = not at all to 7 = very true. A perceived University Environment score is computed by summing across all 14 items, with a score range of 14 to 98. Finally, the 14-item version of the UES yielded a Cronbach alpha of .84 (Gloria & Kurpius, 1996).

Filipino Student Organizational Involvement

Participants responded either (1 = yes) or (0 = no), whether they actively participated in any student organizations.

Family Environment Variables

Moos' Family Environment Scale

This scale was developed to assess the social climate of families of all types (Moos, 1974). Major emphases are on describing the interpersonal relationships among family members, on the direction of personal growth emphasized within the family, and on the organizational structure of the family. The 10 family dimension scales include the following: (a) cohesion, (b) expressiveness, (c) conflict, (d) independence, (e) achievement orientation, (f) intellectual orientation, (g) recreation orientation, (h) religious orientation, (i) organization, and (j) control. For purposes of the present study, the short form of the Family Environment Scale was used. Each item is scored 0 = false and 1 = true; thus, each subscale is computed as an average with scores ranging from 0 to 1.

RESULTS

Summary Statistics

Table 13.1 lists the distribution of surveys across the three campuses broken down by gender, class level, commuter status, and ethnic organi-

TABLE 13.1 Frequency Distributions by College Campus

Variables	CC	CSU	UC
1. Gender			
Female	32	42	17
Male	38	49	16
2. Class Level			
Freshmen	15	13	10
Sophomore	44	12	6
Junior	—	41	5
Senior	—	25	12
3. Do you commute from home?			
Yes	—	60	14
No	—	30	19
No Answer	—	1	—
4. Involved in ethnic organization.			
Yes	—	35	20
No	—	56	13
5. Total Participants (N = 194)	70	91	33

zation involvement. As can be seen in Table 13.1, there appears to be an equal amount of males and females for all three samples. Although only freshmen and sophomores usually attend CCs, the CC sample has an overrepresentation of sophomores relative to the freshmen. For the other two samples, there is an overrepresentation of juniors at the CSU and both freshmen and seniors at the UC. In terms of commuting from home, the CSU sample had a higher number of commuters as opposed to the UC sample. All students in the CC sample commuted from home and thus were considered as missing data on the commuter variable. Finally, a majority of the UC sample participated in the Filipino American student organization, while the opposite was true for the CSU sample. No respondents in the CC sample indicated organizational involvement and thus were considered as missing data on the organizational involvement variable.

Reliability Analysis

As mentioned earlier, the first goal of the present study was to evaluate the reliability of the Filipino American CSE Scale. The other four composite scales (Personal Self-Esteem, Cultural Congruity, University Environment, and Family Environment) utilized in the present study were all used in previous studies with reported reliabilities. However, Cronbach alpha reliabilities were still computed as a safe measure in order to test the consistency of the scales across study samples and particularly, to test the

TABLE 13.2 Reliability Estimates for the Collective Self-Esteem, Personal Self Esteem, Cultural Congruity, University Environment, and Family Environment Scales

Composite Scale	# of Items	Alpha
(1) Collective Self-Esteem Scale		
a. Membership	4	.7004
b. Private	4	.6492
c. Public	4	.6174
d. Identity	4	.6915
e. Total	16	.8060
(2) Personal Self-Esteem Scale (Rosenberg, 1979)	10	.8884
(3) Cultural Congruity Scale (Gloria & Kurpius, 1996)	13	.6761
(4) University Environment Scale (Gloria & Kurpius, 1996)	14	.7626
(5) Family Environment Scale (Moos, 1974)		
a. Cohesion	4	.4781
b. Expression	4	.4737
c. Conflict	4	.6103
d. Independence	4	.4005
e. Achievement Orientation	4	.2322
f. Intellectual Orientation	4	.4945
g. Recreational Orientation	4	.2903
h. Religious Orientation	4	.4896
i. Organization	4	.4070
j. Control	4	.4438

internal consistency of the Filipino American CSE Scale and subscales. Table 13.2 lists the reliabilities for the Filipino American CSE Scale, Personal Self-Esteem Scale, Cultural Congruity Scale, University Environment Scale, and the Family Environment Scale. For these analyses, the samples from all three campuses were treated as a single sample.

As can be seen in Table 13.2, the Personal Self-Esteem Scale had the highest reliability coefficient of .88, followed by the Filipino American CSE Total Scale with a .80 reliability. The reliability for the Personal Self-Esteem Scale was similar to the one reported by Monzon (1996). The reliability reported for the Filipino American CSE Total Scale was considered adequate, considering the fact that Luhtanen and Crocker (1992) reported a .84 for their general CSE Total Scale. Cronbach alphas of .68 and .76 were found with the Cultural Congruity and University Environment Scales respectively. Although these reliabilities appear to be sufficient, they are slightly lower than the ones found by Gloria and Kurpius (1996), in which they reported a .89 for the Cultural Congruity Scale and a .84 for the University Environment Scale. Finally, the reliability coefficients for the 10 Family Environment subscales varied from a low of .23 (achievement orientation) to a high of .61 (conflict). Monzon (1996) also reported a similar range with the same subscales as the lowest and highest. These low reliabilities may be due to the fact that these scales are only 4 items each. Even though more than half of the Family Environment subscales had moderate reliabilities, caution should still be taken with regard to interpreting the results.

Campus Comparisons

For the second goal of the present study, mean scores were computed for each of the variables by campus and are listed in Tables 13.3 through 13.6. In order to test for campus differences, a Oneway Analysis of Variance was computed for each of the study variables. The results are listed in Tables 13.3 through 13.6.

In terms of the demographic variables, campus differences are shown in Table 13.3. The data on this table show significant campus differences in terms of age, $F(2,191) = 13.61$, $p < .001$; years lived in the United States, $F(2,191) = 3.33$, $p < .05$; language difference, $F(2,189) = 5.10$, $p < .01$; and commuter status, $t(121) = 2.47$, $p < .05$. The mean scores suggest that students in the CSU sample are older and a larger percentage of them commute to school, yet the UC students have lived in the United States, on average, longer than those in the CC and CSU samples. Also, students in the CC sample reported larger language differences between what they speak to the parents and what their parents speak to each other.

Mean self-esteem scores by college campus are listed in Table 13.4. As indicated in this table, significant campus differences were found for membership CSE, $F(2,191) = 6.94$, $p < .001$; total CSE, $F(2,191) = 5.88$, $p < .01$;

TABLE 13.3 Mean Demographic Variables by College Campus

Variables	CC		CSU		UC	
	M	SD	M	SD	M	SD
Demographic						
1. Age***	**19.9**	1.5	**22.0**	3.5	**20.2**	1.8
2. Years Lived in U.S.*	**17.2**	4.2	**18.8**	4.9	**19.1**	3.8
3. Language Spoken to Parents	**4.3**	1.0	**4.1**	1.0	**4.2**	1.0
4. Language Spoken to Siblings	**4.4**	0.9	**4.2**	0.9	**4.6**	0.7
5. Language Spoken to Others	**4.5**	0.9	**4.2**	0.9	**4.4**	1.0
6. Language Parents Speak to Each Other	**2.0**	1.2	**2.3**	1.2	**2.6**	1.2
7. Language Difference**	**2.3**	1.3	**1.8**	1.3	**1.6**	1.2
8. Commuter Status*	—	—	**.67**	.47	**.42**	.50
9. Generational Status	**86.6**	20.5	**86.4**	20.8	**94.4**	16.6

* $p < .05$; ** $p < .01$; *** $p < .0001$

TABLE 13.4 Mean Self-Esteem Variables by College Campus

Variables	CC		CSU		UC	
	M	SD	M	SD	M	SD
Self-Esteem Variables						
1. Collective Self-Esteem (Membership)**	**5.38**	1.1	**5.99**	1.0	**5.67**	1.1
2. Collective Self-Esteem (Private)	**5.92**	1.0	**6.25**	0.8	**6.14**	0.8
3. Collective Self-Esteem (Public)	**4.62**	0.9	**4.99**	1.0	**4.73**	1.0
4. Collective Self-Esteem (Identity)	**5.26**	1.3	**5.55**	1.1	**5.61**	1.1
5. Collective Self-Esteem (Total)**	**5.30**	0.8	**5.70**	0.7	**5.54**	0.7
6. Self-Esteem (Personal)**	**3.10**	.53	**3.33**	.49	**3.06**	.51

* $p < .05$; ** $p < .01$; *** $p < .0001$

and personal self-esteem, $F(2,190) = 5.96$, $p < .01$. Further examination of the mean scores indicate that the students in the CSU sample reported higher levels of membership CSE, total CSE, and personal self-esteem over the other two samples.

In terms of the campus variables that are listed in Table 13.5, there were no significant differences across campus samples. The only exception was a small campus difference on organizational involvement, $t(122) = -2.22$, $p < .05$. As indicated by Table 13.5, a higher percentage of the students in the UC sample were involved with their Filipino American student organization as compared to the CSU sample.

Finally, campus differences on the family environment variables are summarized in Table 13.6. As shown in this table, the UC sample perceived higher expression within the family, $F(2,191) = 3.76$, $p < .05$; while the CSU sample reported family environments that were higher in intellectual orientation, $F(2,191) = 3.03$, $p < .05$ and recreational orientation, $F(2,191) = 3.04$, $p < .05$.

TABLE 13.5 Mean Campus Variables by College Campus

Variables	CC		CSU		UC	
	M	SD	M	SD	M	SD
Campus Variables						
1. College GPA	**2.88**	.47	**2.83**	.46	**2.95**	.41
2. Cultural Congruity Scale	**70.8**	9.2	**73.1**	9.9	**69.2**	9.9
3. University Environment Scale	**68.7**	11.5	**65.2**	11.3	**67.2**	13.7
4. Organizational Involvement*	—	—	**.38**	.49	**.61**	.50

* $p < .05$; ** $p < .01$; *** $p < .0001$

TABLE 13.6 Mean Family Environment Variables by College Campus

Variables	CC		CSU		UC	
	M	SD	M	SD	M	SD
Family Environment Variables						
1. Cohesion	**.69**	.28	**.73**	.27	**.79**	.27
2. Expression*	**.27**	.28	**.38**	.28	**.42**	.32
3. Conflict	**.55**	.32	**.49**	.30	**.52**	.35
4. Independence	**.70**	.29	**.74**	.26	**.66**	.24
5. Achievement Orientation	**.68**	.20	**.66**	.20	**.76**	.20
6. Intellectual Orientation*	**.47**	.28	**.58**	.23	**.51**	.33
7. Recreational Orientation*	**.56**	.27	**.67**	.25	**.64**	.32
8. Religious Orientation	**.66**	.24	**.67**	.28	**.71**	.25
9. Organization*	**.72**	.24	**.62**	.30	**.60**	.25
10. Control	**.61**	.30	**.59**	.28	**.64**	.31

* $p < .05$; ** $p < .01$; *** $p < .0001$

Correlational Analysis

As mentioned earlier, the third goal of the present study is to examine the relationships between Filipino American CSE; personal self-esteem; and the same demographic, campus, and family environment variables used in the Monzon (1996) study on Filipino American college students. Similar to the Reliability Analysis, the samples from all three campuses were treated as a single sample.

First, the interrelationships between the Filipino American CSE subscales and the Personal Self-Esteem Scale were examined. A zero-order intercorrelation matrix of the self-esteem variables (CSE and Personal) is presented in Table 13.7. Previous research on the CSE Scale has shown the intercor-

TABLE 13.7 Filipino American Collective Self-Esteem and Personal Self-Esteem Scales Intercorrelation Matrix

Collective and Personal Self-Esteem	1.	2.	3.	4.	5.	6.
1. Collective Self-Esteem (Member)	1.000					
2. Collective Self-Esteem (Private)	.47***	1.000				
3. Collective Self-Esteem (Public)	.33***	.36***	1.000			
4. Collective Self-Esteem (Identity)	.44***	.50***	.08	1.000		
5. Collective Self-Esteem (Total)	.78***	.78***	.59***	.73***	1.000	
6. Personal Self-Esteem	.31***	.32***	.29***	.04	.32***	1.000

*** $p < .001$

relations between the components of the CSE to be moderate and positive, with the strongest correlation between the private and membership subscales and the weakest between the public and identity subscales (Crocker et. al., 1994). As can be seen in Table 13.7, the correlations among the subscales are moderate and positive. In addition, the weakest correlation was between the public and identity subscales, similar to those reported by Luhtanen and Crocker (1992). However, the strongest positive correlation among the pairs was between the private and identity subscales, not the private and membership subscales, as reported in previous research. In terms of the relationship between the Filipino American CSE and Personal Self-Esteem, the private subscale had the highest positive correlation with Personal Self-Esteem, while the identity subscale had the weakest correlation. Again, this is consistent with similar comparisons previously reported (Crocker et. al., 1992; Luhtanen & Crocker, 1992).

Pearson product-moment correlations were computed to test the significance between the self-esteem variables and the demographic variables. These coefficients are listed in Table 13.8. As indicated in this table, Personal Self-Esteem was highly correlated with age, yet none of the CSE components were. The Filipino American CSE subscales were correlated more with the language variables, but in a negative direction, thus indicating that the more English is spoken, the lower the CSE reported by the respondents. Moreover, negative correlations were found between CSE and commuter status. In other words, students commuting from home tended to report lower levels of CSE.

Pearson product-moment correlations were also computed to test the significance between the self-esteem variables and the campus variables, particularly college GPA. These coefficients are presented in Table 13.9. It was proposed that CSE, as opposed to personal self-esteem, would be more relevant to academic performance for Filipino American college students. As can be seen in Table 13.9, none of the self-esteem variables (collective or personal) was correlated to college GPA. The highest correlation with college GPA was with CSE Private. For personal self-esteem, this finding is consistent with those reported by Monzon (1984, 1996). In terms of the Cultural Congruity and University Environment Scales, both collective and personal self-esteem appear to be moderately related. Finally, only the CSE identity subscale and personal self-esteem were significantly correlated with organizational involvement. Since organizational involvement was a dichotomous variable, an independent T-test was also performed to test the mean CSE identity and personal self-esteem differences between those who were involved and those who were not involved with ethnic organizations. The results indicated that involved students reported higher levels of CSE identity, $t(122) = -3.848$, $p < .001$, yet, lower levels of personal self-esteem, $t(121) = 2.002$, $p < .05$, than noninvolved students.

TABLE 13.8 Correlation Matrix of Filipino American Collective Self-Esteem and Personal Self-Esteem Scales With Demographic Variables

Collective and Personal Self-Esteem	A	B	C	D	E	F	G	H	I
1. Collective Self-Esteem (Member)	.02	–.15*	–.20**	–.20**	–.21**	–.18*	–.02	–.17*	–.14*
2. Collective Self-Esteem (Private)	.05	–.00	–.05	–.08	–.05	–.05	.00	–.13	–.00
3. Collective Self-Esteem (Public)	–.00	–.07	.00	–.15*	–.00	.03	–.02	–.07	–.04
4. Collective Self-Esteem (Identity)	–.00	–.08	–.14*	–.22**	–.20**	–.17*	.03	–.16*	–.06
5. Collective Self-Esteem (Total)	.02	–.11	–.14*	–.23***	–.17	–.14	.00	–.19**	–.09
6. Personal Self-Esteem	.24***	–.04	–.08	–.10	–.09	.05	–.10	–.14	–.15*

* $p < .05$; ** $p < .01$; *** $p < .001$

Note: A = Age
B = Years Lived in U.S.
C = Language Spoken to Parents
D = Language Spoken to Siblings
E = Language Spoken to Others
F = Language Parents Speak to Each Other
G = Language Difference
H = Commuter Status
I = Generational Status

TABLE 13.9 Correlation Matrix of Filipino American Collective Self-Esteem and Personal Self-Esteem Scales With Campus Variables

Collective & Personal Self-Esteem	A	B	C	D
1. Collective Self-Esteem (Member)	–.04	.23***	.11	.14
2. Collective Self-Esteem (Private)	–.14	.28***	.25***	.05
3. Collective Self-Esteem (Public)	–.08	.24***	.26***	–.14
4. Collective Self-Esteem (Identity)	.01	.09	.02	.33***
5. Collective Self-Esteem (Total)	–.08	.28***	.21**	.14
6. Personal Self-Esteem	.08	.42***	.28***	–.18*

* $p < .05$; ** $p < .01$; *** $p < .001$
Note: A = College GPA
B = Cultural Congruity
C = University Environment
D = Organizational Involvement (w/Filipino American Organization)

Finally, Pearson product-moment correlations were computed to test the significance between the self-esteem variables and the family environment variables. These coefficients are listed in Table 13.10. The data on this table show that personal self-esteem is moderately and positively correlated with perceptions of family cohesion, expression, and recreational orientation. Moreover, personal self-esteem is negatively correlated with perceived family conflict. Similar to personal self-esteem, the CSE subscales are correlated with family cohesion and recreational orientation. However, unlike personal self-esteem, CSE is highly correlated with perceived family intellectual orientation.

DISCUSSION

The goals of the present study were to (a) develop and evaluate a Filipino American collective self-esteem scale; (b) assess the mean differences across three separate samples of Filipino American college students with regard to demographic variables, self-esteem (collective and personal), campus variables, and perceptions of the family environment; and (c) examine the interrelationships between collective self-esteem, academic performance, personal self-esteem, and perceptions of the campus and family environments among Filipino American college students.

In terms of the first goal, a Filipino American CSE Scale was developed by modifying an existing CSE Scale (Luhtanen & Crocker, 1992) and administered to a sample of Filipino American college students. Consistent with previous findings, the Filipino American CSE Total Scale had an inter-item reliability of .80. However, the reliabilities for the individual subscales

TABLE 13.10 Correlation Matrix of Filipino American Collective Self-Esteem and Personal Self-Esteem Scales With Family Environment Variables

Collective and Personal Self-Esteem	A	B	C	D	E	F	G	H	I	J
1. Collective Self-Esteem (Member)	.14*	.15*	–.07	.02	.08	.32***	.13	.13	–.05	.08
2. Collective Self-Esteem (Private)	.24***	.14*	–.12	.12	.11	.24***	.29***	.10	–.00	–.03
3. Collective Self-Esteem (Public)	.07	.09	–.17*	.02	.13	.20**	.17*	.06	–.01	–.07
4. Collective Self-Esteem (Identity)	.12	.05	–.00	–.06	.09	.17*	.08	.08	–.02	.08
5. Collective Self-Esteem (Total)	.19**	.15*	–.12	.02	.15*	.32***	.22**	.012	–.03	.02
6. Personal Self-Esteem	.25***	.31***	–.27***	.17*	.01	.12	.24***	.03	.10	–.11

* $p < .05$; ** $p < .01$; *** $p < .001$

Note: A = Cohesion; B = Expression; C = Conflict; D = Independence; E = Achievement Orientation; F = Intellectual Orientation; G = Recreational Orientation; H = Religious Orientation; I = Organization; J = Control ranged from .62 to .70, slightly lower than expected. Although, the Filipino American CSE Scale appears to be adequate, it is recommended that it be tested on a larger sample. In addition, test-retest reliabilities should also be collected.

Institutional differences were examined for the second goal. Of the three campuses, CSU was the largest and the most urban. Thus, the results tended to reflect students who commuted and were older. Also, the students in the CSU sample reported higher levels of both collective and personal self-esteem than the students from the other two campuses. However, in terms of the university environment, the CSU students scored lower, yet nonsignificantly, on the University Environment Scale. Again, this is indicative of a large campus environment. In terms of the family environment, only 4 of the 10 subscales were significantly different across the campus samples. Students in the CC sample reported family environments that were less expressive, less intellectually oriented, less recreationally oriented, yet higher in organization. It is possible that social economic factors may be influencing these results. In other words, students attending a UC and even the CSU come from middle- to upper-middle-class homes, where one or both parents are professionals with college degrees. Thus, the home environments would be more intellectually stimulating and expressive.

Finally, with regard to the third goal, correlational analyses indicated that the Filipino American CSE Scale was negatively related to the language variables. In other words, the more English is spoken in the home, the lower the reported collective self-esteem. Therefore, maintaining the native language in the home may facilitate higher collective self-esteem. Moreover, since personal self-esteem is positively related to collective self-esteem, increasing collective self-esteem would also increase one's personal self-esteem. With the exception of the CSE identity subscale, both collective and personal self-esteem measures were positively related to perceived cultural congruity and university environment. However, only the CSE identity and personal self-esteem were related to ethnic organizational involvement. Assuming that the items in the CSE identity subscale are a measure of ethnic identity, the results are consistent with previous research that show students who enter college with high ethnic identity tend to join ethnic organizations (Ethier & Deaux, 1994; Saylor & Aries, 1999). Although for students in the present study, involvement with ethnic organizations may have come at the cost of their personal self-esteem, since it was reported lower than those who were not involved.

Similar to Monzon's study (1984), college GPA was not significantly correlated with personal self-esteem. However, the data also indicated nonsignificant correlations between college GPA and collective self-esteem. It should be noted here that unlike the Monzon (1996) study, which utilized actual college GPAs, the present study relied on reported GPAs. Thus, the findings may be the result of unreliable data. Of the various family environment dimensions, perceived intellectual orientation was significantly related to all CSE subscales, but not personal self-esteem, which was moderately correlated with family cohesion, expression, conflict, and recreational orientation. One explanation for this finding is that personal self-esteem, which focuses on the individual, is related to the individual aspects of the family environment. For example, being in harmony (cohesion) or conflict, or the ability to express oneself, are individual aspects of the family environment. On the other hand, because collective self-esteem is related to perceived family intellectual orientation, it could be that intellectual discussions within the home are reflective of a group process.

LIMITATIONS

The present study is limited in several ways. First, the study focused on a particular ethnic group, thus the results can be generalized to only Filipino American college students. Second, the UC sample was relatively small, thus results of the comparisons by campus samples should be viewed with caution. Finally, although the procedures were similar during the data collection, there may be differences as a result of collecting data in different venues, Filipino studies courses, and through the student organizations.

CONCLUSION

The primary purpose of the present study was to develop and evaluate a Filipino American Collective Self-Esteem Scale and to examine its relationship to campus and family environment variables as perceived by Filipino American college students. In particular, it was proposed that for Filipino American students, collective self-esteem would be more relevant to academic performance than personal self-esteem. In comparing perceptions across institutions, differences were found in terms of personal and collective (membership) self-esteem and perceived family environment (expression, intellectual orientation, recreational orientation, organization). Students at the larger, more urban CSU reported higher personal and collective self-esteem and perceived their family environments to be more intellectually and recreationally oriented. In terms of perceived cultural congruity and campus environment, the CSU sample perceived higher cultural congruity, but a less favorable perception of the campus. However, these results were nonsignificant.

Although the results did not indicate collective self-esteem to be more related to academic performance than personal self-esteem, the findings do suggest that the Filipino American CSE Scale is reliable with the sample of students used. Moreover, it is recommended that more studies utilizing this scale be conducted. For example, use of a test-retest approach, or given an adequate sample size, a confirmatory factor analysis would be appropriate.

REFERENCES

Agbayani-Siewert, P. (1994). Filipino American culture and family: Guidelines for practitioners. *Families in Society: The Journal of Contemporary Human Services, 75*(7), 429–438.

Almirol, E. B. (1982). Rights and obligation in Filipino American families. *Journal of Comparative Family Studies, 13,* 291–306.

Baron, A., Jr. (1981). *Explorations in Chicano/a psychology.* New York, NY: Praeger.

Chiong, N. D. (1997). *Family perception in relation to the generalized contentment in Filipino American female adolescents.* (Unpublished master's thesis). San Diego State University, San Diego, CA.

Crocker, J., & Luhtanen, R. (1990). Collective self-esteem and ingroup bias. *Journal of Personality and Social Psychology, 58,* 60–67.

Crocker, J., Luhtanen, R., Blaine, B., & Broadnax, S. (1994). Collective self-esteem and psychological well-being among White, Black, and Asian college students. *Personality and Social Psychology Bulletin, 20*(5), 503–513.

Ethier, K., & Deaux, K. (1990). Hispanics in ivy: Assessing identity and perceived threat. *Sex Roles, 22*(7/8), 427–440.

Ethier, K. A., & Deaux, K. (1994). Negotiating social identity when contexts change: Maintaining identification and responding to threat. *Journal of Personality and Social Psychology, 67*(2), 243–251.

Gloria, A. M., & Kurpius, S. E. R. (1996). The validation of the cultural congruity scale and the university environment scale with Chicano/a students. *Hispanic Journal of Behavioral Sciences, 18*(4), 533–549.

Heras, P., & Revilla, L. A. (1994). Acculturation, generational status, and family environment of Pilipino Americans: A study in cultural adaptation. *Family Therapy, 21*(2), 129–138.

Luhtanen, R., & Crocker, J. (1992). A collective self-esteem scale: Self-evaluation of one's social identity. *Personality and Social Psychology Bulletin, 18,* 302–318.

Lynch, F. (1981). Social acceptance reconsidered. In F. Lynch & A. de Guzman, II (Eds.), *Four readings on Philippine values* (4th ed., pp. 1–68). Quezon City, Philippines: Institute of Philippine Culture, Ateneo de Manila University.

Markus, H., & Kitayama, S. (1991). Culture and the self: Implications for cognition, emotion, and motivation. *Psychological Review, 98,* 224–253.

Monzon, R. I. (1984). *The effects of the family environment on the academic performance of Pilipino American college students.* (Unpublished masters thesis). San Diego State University, San Diego, CA.

Monzon, R. I. (1996). *Individual and environmental predictors of academic performance among Filipino American college students.* Paper presented at the ninth annual

Statewide Conference of the Filipino American Educators Association of California, Cerritos, CA.

Moos, R. H. (1974). *Family environment scale preliminary manual.* Palo Alto, CA: Consulting Psychologists.

Pascarella, E. T., & Terenzini, P. T. (1991) *How college affects students.* San Francisco, CA: Jossey-Bass.

Phinney, J. S. (1990). Ethnic identity in adolescents and adults: Review of research. *Psychological Bulletin, 108,* 499–514.

Rosenberg, M. (1979). *Conceiving the self.* New York, NY: Basic.

Santos, R. (1983). The social and emotional development of Filipino children. In G. J. Powell (Ed.), *The psychosocial development of minority children.* New York, NY: Brunner/Mazel.

Saylor, E. S., & Aries, E. (1999). Ethnic identity and change in social context. *The Journal of Social Psychology, 139*(5), 549–566.

Silber, E., & Tippett, J. (1965). Self-esteem: Clinical assessment and measurement validation. *Psychological Reports, 16,* 1017–1071.

Tajfel, H. (1981). *Human groups and social categories: Studies in social psychology.* Cambridge, UK: Cambridge University Press.

Tajfel, H. (1982). Social psychology of intergroup relations. *Annual Review of Psychology, 33,* 1–59.

Tajfel, H., & Turner, J. C. (1986). The social identity theory of intergroup behavior. In S. Worchel & W. Austin (Eds.), *Psychology of intergroup relations* (2nd ed., pp. 7–24). Chicago, IL: Nelson-Hall.

Taylor, S. E., & Brown, J. D. (1988). Illusion and well-being: A social psychological perspective on mental health. *Psychological Bulletin, 103,* 193–210.

Triandis, H. C. (1989). The self and social behavior in differing cultural contexts. *Psychological Review, 96,* 506–520.

CHAPTER 14

PILIPINOS IN THE MIDDLE

Higher Education and a Sociocultural Context of Contradictions

Tracy Lachica Buenavista
California State University, Northridge

> I don't think we can expect our parents to help as much as we'd like. It's hard for a parent who completed a college degree in the Philippines or a student whose parents completed college in the Philippines, which I guess maybe isn't as "legitimate" here as it is back in the Philippines... I know a lot of stories of friends whose parents [got] degrees either in engineering or in the sciences, but over here, it doesn't translate into very much. They're still just doing "regular" work. (Sison)

The (neo)colonial relationship between the United States and the Philippines has created and continues to facilitate a Pilipino diaspora, particularly to the United States (Rodriguez, 2010; San Juan, 1998). Since the early 1900s, colonial immigration policies and an American-based education in the Philippines made possible a constant flow of Pilipinos to the United States as global servants, people who are particularly commodified because of an imposed familiarity with the English language and American culture. Initially, Pilipinos in the United States represented a poor and working class, although post-1965 immigrants socioeconomically diversified the U.S. Pili-

The "Other" Students, pages 259–275

pino population with the influx of a highly educated and skilled workforce (Espiritu, 1995; Takaki, 1998). Immigration policies and employment recruitment agencies favored college-educated individuals to fill labor shortages, including positions in health care, domestic service, and technical industries (Choy, 2003; Root, 1997). However, as portrayed through Sison's narrative above, while many Pilipino immigrants were college educated, their degree attainment served only as a mechanism of entering substandard working conditions in the United States, noncommensurate with their education and skill levels.

In this chapter, I discuss how this imposed, historical pattern of underemployment—a vestige of the power differential between the Philippines and United States—not only impacted earlier Pilipino immigrants but also subsequently affected their children in a contemporary context. Despite relatively higher levels of educational attainment, Pilipino immigrants in the United States consistently experience underemployment due to institutional barriers that make it difficult for them to put their degree into practice (Choy, 2003; Madamba, 1998). While immigration and the underemployment of Pilipino immigrants might seem only marginally related to the educational experiences of present-day U.S. Pilipino students, I argue that these conditions serve as the basis of the issues that second-generation Pilipinos experience within higher education.

In this chapter, I present data from a year-long ethnography in which I examined the access, retention, and activism of 12 Pilipino students involved in the Pilipino Recruitment and Retention Center (PRRC) at West Coast University.[1] The PRRC is the first student-initiated project in the United States to focus on the recruitment and retention of Pilipinos in higher education. A project is considered student-initiated if it is student run, student created, and primarily student funded (Maldonado, Rhoads, & Buenavista, 2005). Although student-initiated projects vary in structure, they are bound by a mission to promote education as a site for social justice and tend to adhere to three organizing principles: community consciousness, social praxis, and social and cultural wealth. As Pilipinos often are not eligible for institutional support programs and services that target first-generation, low-income, and/or historically underrepresented students, the PRRC and the students involved in the project served as an important case study of student-of-color organizing within higher education in a post–affirmative action context.

All of the participants in the project were children from households that had one or more post-1965, college-educated, Pilipino immigrant parents. Students revealed how their experiences resulted from the continuous processes of negotiation in which they engaged in order to access higher education. More specifically, I use selected narratives to describe how student pathways to education were shaped by the following sociocultural inconsistencies: (a) one or more Philippine college-educated parents who were underemployed in the United States; (b) lived experiences shaped by the unrealized benefits of parent college degree attainment and the perception that students could eventually reap the benefits of college; (c) parents who went to college but whose educational attainment afforded limited advantages in students' college choice processes; and (d) conflicting priorities, in which parents promoted college but not over family obligations or financial constraints. The (neo)colonial relationship between the Philippines and the United States manifests itself in everyday phenomena such as these, and such conditions have established a context of contradictions that position Pilipinos to occupy liminal spaces in education, or in their words, the "middle"—second-generation college students without the educational benefits traditionally associated with such a status.

COLLEGE-EDUCATED PARENTS AND UNDEREMPLOYMENT

When asked to describe the educational attainment and work backgrounds of their parents, every student revealed that they had at least one parent who was college educated, and for eight students, both parents had bachelor's degrees. However, despite having college-educated parents, every student, with the exception of one, characterized their parents as underemployed. Underemployment status was determined by the students' perceptions of when their parents' work position and/or financial earnings were not commensurate with their educational training and/or skill levels. Further, student perceptions of parental underemployment were shaped by messages communicated by parents to students, as well as the reality of parents holding multiple jobs and/or working hours beyond the traditional 40-hour work week. Although the degree to which parents were underemployed varied among the students' families, students still considered the disjuncture between their parents' education and employment to be a factor in the way they experienced education. Thus, one of the contradictions shaping students' sociocultural contexts was college-educated parental underemployment.

Based on a demographic questionnaire that the students filled out at the start of the interview process, eight students stated that their annual family income was between $75,001 and $100,000 (seven students) or over $100,000 (one student). These eight students also identified themselves as being from a middle-income socioeconomic status. However, it is important to note that five of the middle-income students revealed that at least one parent had supplemental employment beyond their regular day job (e.g., nonlicensed tax preparer or childcare provider). The other four students considered their families to be working class, although their estimated family income varied: three students reported family income between $15,001 and $30,000, and one student estimated a family income of $50,001 to $75,000. Contrary to the middle-income status that most students occupied, every student except one believed that their parents experienced underemployment. Every student also perceived their parents to work more hours than deemed typical, and they simultaneously provided vague descriptions of their parents' education and work histories.

Four students considered themselves from working-class backgrounds and attributed this socioeconomic position to their parents' underemployment. Silanga, who was primarily raised by her single mother, explained the tensions between her mother's underemployment and the lack of time she had to share her college experiences with her daughter:

> I know she went to college and graduated from it, but that's pretty much all I know... In the Philippines, I think she was an accountant but now she works at [a gaming casino] in San Diego. She just keeps telling me she's a clerk or something, but all I know is she works graveyard.

Silanga felt that her mother did not disclose many details about her college or work experiences. Instead, Silanga only expressed certainty regarding her mother's late-night "graveyard" schedule. Similarly, Bonifacia revealed her confusion over her father's inability to utilize his educational training to attain formal employment:

> The thing that I never really understood was my dad had a degree in business, but he never really did anything with it... my dad's just been having jobs like running errands or doing medical records for my aunt and uncle's homecare. Not anything really business-related, although I do want to mention that my dad, he's like a part-time fisherman... Like, he'll go out fishing and then sell the fish to family members, things like that, so I guess in a sense that's a business.

Bonifacia's father's educational attainment did not translate into a stable career in the United States. While Bonifacia's father attempted to make money from an independent fishing endeavor, she questioned his inability to utilize his college degree to resolve his underemployment status. While both students reported income levels of $30,000 and less, working-class students were not the only ones concerned with parental underemployment.

Seven of the eight middle-income students believed their parents did not have jobs that reflected their education or skill levels. They were also critical of the conditions that exploited their parents' training and did not amount to job satisfaction and/or salaries commensurate with their experience. When talking about her mother's educational attainment, Gabriela said,

> She finished a 4-year college as an accountant, but right now my mom works at Rite-Aid, and she's been working there for 25 years... She's the cashier, and she does stock. For my mom, she says that it's for a better opportunity. In the Philippines, there's not an abundance of jobs that she thinks her education will get her, but the education she had in the Philippines doesn't convert to the education out here, and you're placed at a lower position than what you would be if you were in the Philippines. I just find it kind of weird just because, who's to say that another country's education is better than another.

Pablo's description of his mother paralleled Gabriela's account:

> My mom was a certified accountant, but when she came here, she had to start as a temporary accountant. [I] saw how big a sacrifice it was... the work that she does compared to other people who are [certified], I think she earns almost half of what other people earn doing the same work... her education didn't transfer when she went here.

Both Gabriela and Pablo were critical of their parents' underemployment status. Although their parents found work in which accountant training in the Philippines was remotely applicable, both took lower status positions with lesser pay than they would otherwise be earning if they'd received their degrees in the United States.

The students made an important distinction when they alluded to the problematic work conditions in the United States, versus their parents' work ethic, as reason for their parents' employment situations. They noted pay disparities and questioned why Philippine education did not "convert" to commensurate employment opportunities in the United States. In doing so, they challenged the underlying assumption that a U.S. education was "better" than that offered in the Philippines. Instead, students recognized underemployment as an issue larger than personal circumstances, and they understood parental underemployment as a result of a power differential between countries.

Regardless of income status and the severity of underemployment, for the most part, students identified the contradiction in which parents had college degrees from the Philippines but were underemployed in the United States. While students were impacted by their parents' employment status in various ways, in most cases, long and/or late job schedules prevented frequent opportunities for parents to have interactions with children regarding their higher education history, college knowledge, and work status. Therefore, students had vague understandings of why their parents were unable to find work that validated the sacrifice of their economic worth as determined by their schooling. In the context of students' frustration with their parents' underemployment, it is important to see how these experiences then shaped the students' perceptions of the value of higher education.

UNREALIZED BENEFITS AND PERCEPTIONS OF THE EVENTUAL

> She was telling me when she was a kid, she had no idea like, 40, 50 years from [then] she'd be in the States... It was her dream, and the fact that her dream was accomplished through going to school, through obtaining an education, [I realized] it is feasible; it does happen. (Carlos)

One might assume that the inequity that characterized parental underemployment would facilitate negative perceptions of higher education, as the social and economic value of having a college degree was not demonstrated to students. Instead, students still expressed positive perceptions of higher education, and parental immigration and underemployment served as motivation for high academic aspirations. Higher parental educational attainment generally has a positive effect on student aspirations for college and opportunities to attend more selective institutions (Terenzini, Springer, Yeager, Pascarella, & Nora, 1996). As expressed by Carlos, his belief that higher education was a valuable and attainable goal was shaped by his mother's own education serving as the means to achieve her "dream" of U.S. immigration. However, in the context of the immigration "opportunity" afforded to their parents by college degree attainment, students also considered higher education as the main pathway toward achieving the unrealized socioeconomic mobility of their parents. The second contradiction that shaped the sociohistorical contexts of students were their lived realities in which the benefits of college degree attainment were unrealized and their learned perceptions that college represented a realistic mechanism to eventually reap the benefits of higher education that their parents did not receive.

Students perceived the pursuit of college as a normalized practice within their families, as best stated by Carlos when he said, "From kindergarten I knew I was going to go to college. There was no ands, ifs, or buts about it." Bonifacia echoed his sentiments and further demonstrated that the push for higher education was a result of parental underemployment when she shared how her parents had encouraged her academic pursuits. She asserted,

> Education was something that was like, drilled into my head. You have to have an education in order for you to be anyone... My dad was always saying, "You're not going to end up being anything unless you have your education"... I guess because my parents felt like their jobs aren't what they wanted it to be... they always compare [my goals] to their situation like, "You don't want to end up like us."

Bonifacia's parents' employment as a secretary and temporary worker served as the occupational standard that her parents wanted her to surpass with the attainment of a college degree. She recalled how her parents simultaneously espoused the value of higher education and the struggles of underemployment to communicate an overall message that education serves as the key to becoming someone of importance in the United States. While Bonifacia was cognizant of the contradiction between her parents' educational attainment and feelings about their socioeconomic status, she used her parents' situation and support as a platform to develop positive perceptions about the possibilities that college could provide to her family.

Besides higher education serving as a potential means for socioeconomic mobility, the pursuit of college represented the responsibility that students had to fulfill as part of their parents' sacrifice for U.S. immigration. For example, Sison clearly stated the relationship between his parents' expectations for him to pursue higher education and their decision to leave the Philippines:

> [College] was never a decision of "if," it was just "what and where?" . . . Like they already expected me to go to college, because that's why they came here, so anything less wouldn't be acceptable, and when they started seeing that I was doing pretty well in school, they probably knew that it was no question that I'd probably go to college.

Sison described how his parents constructed college as a normalized practice in his family and stated the only question among them was where he would pursue higher education. He understood his role to be a college-going student as part of an unstated family contract in which his parents held up their part of the bargain by immigrating to the United States. Thus, not fulfilling his responsibilities of educational attainment "wouldn't be acceptable." However, he also posited that his college pursuit was contingent upon his academic performance in school. Thus, Sison's experience suggested that college choice was a learned practice that resulted from the connection between parental immigration, parental expectations, and student performance.

Sison recognized a relationship between immigration and education. Further, his experiences highlighted how educational attainment was constructed as a family obligation and not necessarily an individual pursuit. In fact, all 12 students expressed some notion of their educational aspirations as a shared understanding between students and parents regarding students' responsibilities to their families. Through their descriptions of how they perceived higher education, the students articulated the relationship they saw between immigration, parental underemployment, and the manifestation of degree attainment as their familial obligation. In a context of parental underemployment, parents communicated to their children messages of higher education's potential to achieve the socioeconomic mobility that remained elusive to them. Although parents were often vague with their children about the details surrounding their education in the Philippines and work in the United States, they were much more transparent about the educational responsibilities they placed on students as a result of the sacrifices they made. Thus, student college aspirations became normalized through a combination of observed and explicit practices in the family that communicated obligations of students to fulfill their parents' expectations.

However, while students were able to assess and accept their role as college-going family members, they did not do so without question. The contradiction between their parents' educational attainment and subsequent lack of opportunities enabled students to recognize that a college degree did not directly translate to the necessary resources and college-knowledge that parents could provide to help students realize their goals. For example, Pablo expressed, "Honestly, even with my parents graduating and having that social capital, [they] didn't know a lot of things about college." In the following student narratives regarding parental underemployment and perceptions of education as an obligation, students took the opportunity to discuss the contradiction between having supportive, college-educated parents and the limitations of their parents' understanding of and involvement in the college-going process.

LIMITED ADVANTAGES AND INDIRECT INVOLVEMENT

Students with college-educated parents, or second-generation college students, are more likely to utilize their parents as sources of college information (McDonough, 1997; Terenzini et al., 1996). Yet such educational research often does not consider the context of foreign-educated parents with U.S.-educated children. Students in the PRRC described receiving various types of parental support, specifically including direct assistance with academic activities (e.g., school work) during their K–8 experience. Because they were familiar with their parents' educational expectations, students sought whatever assistance they could receive from their parents, but found that assistance was often dependent on parental availability during nonwork hours, as well as their parents' disciplinary knowledge base. In other words, while parents were supportive of children's education, direct parent participation in educational activities was constrained by time and academic subject familiarity. A major contradiction shaping Pilipino experiences was the limited advantages traditionally afforded to second-generation college students by their parents.

For example, because her mother's evening work schedule prevented Vera from seeking her educational advice, Vera often relied on her father for academic assistance. Vera's father earned a bachelor's degree in engineering in the Philippines. When he was at home, Vera was able to benefit from her father's educational attainment, particularly his math expertise. Interestingly, while it is not clear how her father communicated the depth of his educational attainment, one can assume that a degree in engineering required rigorous mathematical capabilities. However, Vera described the limitations of the assistance provided by her father:

> My mom worked during the night and my dad worked during the day, so any help that I could get was from my dad, and he was more the math person, so he'd help me in math a lot... [But] my dad stopped helping me after like, the sixth or seventh grade... and he was an engineer in the Philippines, you know, and he's just like, "Oh, if you ever need help, just ask your teacher," and I was like, "OK," and just a lot of times, you really do have to find information outside of your family.

Vera expressed the irony of her father having an engineering degree and his reluctance to assist her with math classes beyond her middle school years. Moreover, she was critical of her father's advice to not depend on him and to instead seek information sources outside of the family, such as her teacher. She was frustrated that her parents' college education did not equate with her ability to rely on them for a direct source of academic support.

The extent to which students appeared to directly benefit from their parents' college education was most often through homework assistance during the early schooling years, and early on they realized the limitations to which their parents could or would assist. The only other instance in which parents' participation was credited was during the college application process, especially in matters involving family finances. Several students acknowledged that their parents were especially sacrificial in prioritizing expenses related to higher education and helpful in providing the necessary tax information to complete the financial aid application. Through students' stories and sentiments regarding the disconnect between their parents' educational attainment and their subsequent limited support, the students' experiences appeared counterintuitive to traditional notions of knowledge exchange that often occur between second-generation college students and their parents. However, it is important not to dismiss how parents attempted to provide direct support despite work and time constraints.

Overall, students did not name their parents as a primary source of substantive higher education information. Rather, parents served as the students' main source of encouragement for their academic goals. Based on their own educational experiences, the best college-going quality passed on from college-educated parent to college-aspiring student was the very idea of college. When asked to describe the role of his parents in his college-choice process, Pablo discussed in general the limitations of direct parent involvement to explain his parents' contributions:

> I know that for many Filipinos that higher education is really valued in our families; like our parents went to [great] length to provide for us. But at the same time, many of our parents, they don't really know what's going on. When you think about it, all the parents are probably working like one or two jobs at a time... I'm not saying they're being bad parents because obviously [they have] good intentions, but at the same time like, as a support system on a day-to-day basis, it's not really present... But what I have is this notion with my parents telling me that education is really important.

Pablo began by framing his experience with what he perceived was an issue affecting the larger Pilipino community. He pointed out that while parents highly valued educational attainment and had "good intentions" behind their work responsibilities, their "day-to-day" interactions were absent, thus limiting the extent to which parents could assist their children. While Pablo painted a larger picture of how college-educated-parent knowledge could be obscured by underemployment, his point also provided context to emphasize the values instilled by his parents, the "notion" of educational attainment as a significant endeavor in and of itself.

Yet despite Pablo and others' recognition of their parents' unconditional support, their statements were based on the fact that a gap existed between parental encouragement for higher education and the transmission of knowledge related to the mechanics of becoming college-ready. In other words, while the students assumed that their parents' previous college experiences could foster understanding and college-going practices, they realized the contradiction between parental experiential knowledge of college and the limited advantages afforded by their education, and subsequent lack of direct involvement in student lives. From the students' perspectives, parents helped to normalize college-going aspirations, but their tangible assistance was often lacking.

CONFLICTING PRIORITIES

Although college aspirations were normalized for students by parents, the students often described mixed messages they received from parents regarding how to prioritize educational activities. Parents consistently communicated to students that higher education was the number-one priority for students, yet it would often take a backseat when parents deemed other family matters more important. Thus, a fourth contradiction shaping Pilipino student experiences was the practice of parents promoting college, but not over family obligations or financial constraints.

While parents were overwhelmingly supportive of their children's desire to attend college, there were some instances when they encouraged students to choose participation in family practices versus college-going practices. For example, although Vera understood that participation in community service was an unofficial college admissions requirement, her mother felt that she spent too much time on her extracurricular activities:

> My mom especially didn't like me doing extracurricular activities. I was like, "I can't just do school . . . " and it was community service work too and she was like, "Why do you have to go out all the time?" and I'm like, "I'm going to a convalescent home. It's old people . . . How can you say that I can't do this?" and it was because of the ride problem because she hated picking me up because she was always so tired.

Vera had a difficult time when her mother questioned her volunteerism, but she recognized that her mother's disdain had to do with Vera's dependence on her for transportation. Despite being aware of the time constraints it placed on her mother, Vera continued her community work.

All 12 students described instances in which they felt their educational activities imposed on their families. For Gabriela, family was central in her narrative, including when she spoke about barriers to college:

> Whenever my parents tried to persuade me to go visit family and miss school, I was like, "No, I gotta stay home." See, that's one thing, I always put school ahead of everything else, even my family . . . They would make me ditch school to go to some amusement park to hang out with my family and I'd be so mad. I remember always being upset with my family like, "How can you make me go to these places? I have to do school work."

Gabriela recalled situations in which she had to choose between tending to her schoolwork and participating in family gatherings. Her family would portray school as something that she could "ditch," which Gabriela regarded as problematic, considering her academic priorities.

The time that students dedicated to school was often a contentious topic of discussion within their families, particularly when school appeared to take precedence over family commitments. The mixed messages that students received posed emotional barriers that they had to deal with in preparing for college. The most prominent tangible challenge that students discussed concerned financial barriers that materially affected them and their families, especially family income status. Students felt that they were expected to pursue higher education, but they became discouraged when their parents brought up the perceived inability to afford college. Bonifacia, who considered herself as low-income, explained how her family's socioeconomic status impacted her:

> My family was low-income and so my mom would always say, "You know, without scholarships, you probably won't go to college," which is ironic because

> they always pushed me to go to college, but the financial situation just didn't allow it at the time.

She knew that her family's income was limited, yet she did not necessarily consider it a factor in her college aspirations until her parents explicitly made their finances a factor for her to consider.

Similarly, Silanga discussed how her mother cautioned her about affordability. She realized that higher education would not be realistic until she found a way to afford school:

> When I was in middle school, I didn't think I was going to go to college because I know that money was an issue and she always told me, "I don't know, [Silanga], I don't know. We'll see in the future. We'll see in the future." And then I guess the only realization that I actually knew I was going to go to college was probably sophomore or junior year of high school because I found out about financial aid, and I told her about this. I'm like, "Mom, you can't not let me go away for school because there's money out there!"

Since Silanga and her mother did not believe college was attainable on limited finances, the issue was initially put on hold. When Silanga learned about financial aid, however, she used the information as leverage to convince her mother that their socioeconomic status should not prevent her from pursuing higher education.

Furthermore, there were instances in which limited finances dissuaded students from preparing for college in the same ways that other students were preparing. Again, Silanga found herself compromising college-going strategies because of the unavailability of money:

> I was always scared to ask my mom for money [and] that's actually why I held back on SATs... I only took SATs the second half of my junior year, which I regretted because I think I could have done better if I took it again. I always had to hold back because I felt like my mom would get mad or something. It's just a thing you feel like you shouldn't ask for. When it comes to academics, it's like, "Oh, I think I can hold back awhile."

Silanga discussed a common strategy to take the standardized exams more than once in the hope of improving scores; however, she opted not to pursue another exam because she was "scared" to ask her mom to spend more than what she perceived was necessary. Silanga decided to financially "hold back," a practice she acquired based on a sociocultural belief that, although important, academics should not take precedence over general costs of living.

While pursuing college remained a priority among the students' families, the way in which educational practices were deemed less important than family and financial practices created tensions for students. On the one hand, students realized that they had to engage every day in activities that would better prepare them academically. On the other hand, they often felt conflicted about their aspirations when their parents communicated to them that, although college was important, family and immediate socioeconomic stability took precedence. Such seemingly irreconcilable priorities served as another contradiction that shaped Pilipino student experiences.

PILIPINOS IN THE MIDDLE

The overall idea that students operated in a sociocultural context of contradictions is grounded in the disjuncture between parental encouragement for higher education and the transmission of knowledge related to the mechanics of becoming college-ready. It is this gap, or liminal space, in which the educational pathways of students were shaped and negotiated. Whether explicit or implicit, all 12 students described feelings of being in the "middle": although considered second-generation college students by institutional standards, they did not necessarily benefit from such a status and instead experienced education more similar to first-generation college students.

Four students explicitly used the metaphor of being in the "middle" to describe their education generational status. When Bonifacia shared how she wished that her parents were more involved in her college choice process, she followed up with a general discussion regarding how many students who shared this position are marginalized. She explained,

> Our community is kind of left out sometimes because there is a first-generation and second-generation [college student]. That's usually what everyone thinks about when they think of college, but what about the community in the middle? It's important to recognize those students and their struggles and what they had to go through, how different it is for them as opposed to being like a second-generation college [student].

Bonifacia spoke about her education in the context of the larger "struggle" for many Pilipino students to have their experiences recognized. She positioned her and others' experiences as distinct from and between that of first-generation and second-generation college students.

Rizalo elaborated on this notion of marginalization when he explained why he sometimes did not know how to name his experience in regard to education generational status:

> What about the students whose parents maybe went to college in the Philippines but didn't really get the advantages because it was set up differently in the Philippines... they didn't get the resources that typical second-genera-

> tion college students usually get, so they're kind of stuck in the middle in that they are second-generation technically, but they should really be called first-generation because they don't have the resources that the second-generation student normally does have.

Rizalo pointed out two factors that facilitated a disconnect between parents and students: the perceived difference between Philippine and U.S. college education and a lack of college-going resources, although it is not clear if he is referring to resources as transmittable college knowledge or socioeconomic, as might be the case considering the conditions set up by parental underemployment. Based on these two factors, Rizalo established how one might feel "stuck in the middle" between who is typically constructed as first- or second-generation college students.

The middle position that students occupied was the foundation of their educational marginalization. This marginalization extended beyond a feeling of not being recognized by educational institutions, and it manifested into distinct issues that students encountered during the college-choice process. Bonifacia generally described what happened when parent education did not translate into educational experiences with which students could relate:

> Filipino students like myself wouldn't really know what college is aside from what their parents tell them, *if* they tell them, and the whole image that their parents give them. But it's hard because our parents are talking to us about college from their experiences in the Philippines... You can't even compare education in the Philippines and here because it's totally different. So I feel like a lot of students don't have that real idea of what college is about... so they might know that they should go to college, but they don't know how.

Bonifacia highlighted the reality of students either receiving no concrete information regarding parental college experiences or that which was based on an incomparable educational reality. She stressed the incompatibility of the information parents could provide and the information students would need to make the point that students did not always possess a "real idea of what college is about." Thus, she explains why students who have aspirations to attend college might not be familiar with the steps and practices associated with the college-choice process.

A few students made statements that elaborated on Bonifacia's point. Pablo discussed his frustration during the college-choice process when he had to state his parents' educational attainment as an indicator of his educational experiences:

> When people ask me if my parents were college educated, I would say yes... That's one of the biggest things, I'm really kind of pissed off because

> being literal about things, my parents are college educated, but then at the same time . . . their support can only go so much. If I need help with anything, I can't really go to them because they don't know what's goes [*sic*] on. And I know I'm not the only one like that. I would say a lot of [Pilipinos] actually fill out [on applications] that their parents are college educated.

Pablo was upset for having to associate with a category with which he did not comfortably identify, based on the assumption that having college-educated parents equated with notions of privilege he did not believe he had. His frustration was grounded in the perception that Pilipinos were forced to misrepresent themselves during common college-choice practices. He brought up how students had to "fill out" information on college applications, without the opportunity to contextualize their experiences. In this case, his feelings exemplified how students felt most marginalized when assumptions of educational privilege did not materialize.

Similarly, Jose also discussed the limitations of the college application, but went on to challenge institutions to better consider Pilipino student experiences. He said,

> The education system they have [in the Philippines], even though it is based off of and influenced by the U.S. system, it's different than here. Just because they're college educated, their degrees don't always like match up here, or aren't recognized here . . . even when you check the [educational attainment] boxes, you're saying that they had college, but you don't mention that it's not in the U.S., and maybe that should be a box.

Jose outlined the complexity of having an American-based education system in the Philippines, as well as the tangible differences between the systems as demonstrated by the fact that Philippine degrees are not considered equivalent to those earned in the United States. He pointed out the double-bind students found themselves in when identifying one's parents as college-educated. This designation has served as a particular factor that has assumptive notions of being more likely college-going, although this designation does not clearly address that parental education was "not in the U.S.," an indicator that would complicate the topic of categorization on the application. Jose posed that the option should be offered to contextualize one's response, and perhaps more importantly, he historicizes the relationship between colonialism in the Philippines, its impact on his parents, and his subsequent U.S. experiences.

A SOCIOCULTURAL CONTEXT OF CONTRADICTIONS

As demonstrated in the student narratives, there exists a relationship between Pilipino immigration and educational experiences. (Neo)colonial

Philippine education and U.S. immigration policies worked in unison to promote the immigration of the students' college-educated parents to the United States. Parents' college attainment, however, did not translate into work opportunities commensurate with their education and skill levels, a phenomenon observed and described by students. Thus, students were well aware of the underemployment status of their parents and centralized this experience to simultaneously contextualize their parents' educational expectations and their own learned perceptions of higher education.

Students developed a complicated perception of higher education based on the expectations placed on them by parents. Due to their parents' immigration and work struggles, students viewed education as an obligatory family responsibility. At the same time, college also represented opportunities to gain socioeconomic benefits elusive to parents. Thus, students held positive perceptions of college for its potential to better the collective situation of families.

While students developed educational aspirations, they in turn recognized the limited capacity for parents to directly assist in college preparation. Since underemployment and difficult work schedules often did not allow frequent interactions between parents and students, students had vague understandings of the processes involved with pursuing college. Further, because of the devaluing of Philippine college degrees as indicated by underemployment, students and parents alike operated from the notion that parents were limited in their college-going knowledge. They were perceived to not possess the cultural capital often associated with higher education attainment. It is important to note that institutional practices and how they have failed to better inform and involve parents, as well as accommodate the complexity of student lives, should be better interrogated in future research.

The tension between parental college attainment, immigration, and underemployment, and the subsequent student perceptions of and aspirations for higher education led students to position themselves in the "middle" of first- and second-generation college students. Parental educational attainment connotes various advantages afforded to their children during the college-going process. While students recognized that due to their parents' college degrees, they were considered second-generation college students in the United States, their experiences did not reflect the material privileges assumed to traditionally benefit second-generation college students. This conflict played out in various ways, but students focused on the unfair practice of decontextualizing their experiences when they were forced to identify themselves as second-generation college students.

While the transmission of college aspirations and values were a clear result of parent-to-student interactions, the transmission of knowledge regarding college-preparation practices and processes was absent. Pilipinos lived in a sociocultural context of contradictions shaped by (a) college-educated parental underemployment, (b) living with the unrealized benefits of college degree attainment while maintaining eventual hope for the benefits of higher education, (c) little and indirect college-educated-parent involvement in the college choice process, and (d) conflicting family and educational priorities. As contradictions characterized Pilipino educational issues, these sociocultural contexts must be better considered in developing specific advocacy practices to address Pilipino liminal positions within higher education in the United States.

NOTE

1. The Pilipino Recruitment and Retention Center and West Coast University are pseudonyms, as well as the names used to identify participants in the study.

REFERENCES

Choy, C. C. (2003). *Empire of care: Nursing and migration in Filipino American history.* Durham, NC: Duke University Press.

Espiritu, Y. L. (1995). *Filipino American lives.* Philadelphia, PA: Temple University Press.

Madamba, A. B. (1998). *Underemployment among Asians in the United States: Asian Indian, Filipino, and Vietnamese workers.* New York, NY: Garland.

Maldonado, D. E. Z., Rhoads, R. A., & Buenavista, T. L. (2005). The student-initiated retention project: Theoretical contributions and the role of self-empowerment. *American Educational Research Journal, 42*(4), 605–638.

McDonough, P. M. (1997). *Choosing colleges: How social class and schools structure opportunity.* Albany, NY: State University of New York Press.

Rodriguez, R. M. (2010). *Migrants for export: How the Philippine state brokers labor to the world.* Minneapolis: Regents of the University of Minnesota.

Root, M. P. P. (1997). *Filipino Americans: Transformation and identity.* Thousand Oaks, CA: Sage.

San Juan, E., Jr., (1998). *From exile to diaspora: Versions of the Filipino experience in the United States.* Boulder, CO: Westview.

Takaki, Ron. (1998). *Strangers from a different shore: A history of Asian Americans.* Boston, MA: Back Bay.

Terenzini, P., Springer, L., Yeager, P., Pascarella, E., & Nora, A. (1996). First-generation college students: Characteristics, experiences, and cognitive development. *Research in Higher Education, 37,* 1–22.

CHAPTER 15

SEXUAL HEALTH AND RESPONSIBILITY

The Role of Public Schools in Filipina American Teenage Mothers' Lives

Charlene Bumanglag Tomas
University of Hawai'i, Manoa

Sex education in the public schools has been a major source of national and local controversy for decades (Fields, 2008; Irvine, 2004; Luker, 2006). While these debates occur globally to include the Philippines, this chapter focuses on the U.S. context. The battle between abstinence-only education (AOE) and comprehensive sex education (CSE) has influenced health education policies, classroom practices, and sexual health. Political decisions that affect youths rarely incorporate their perspectives in policy development. Instead, proposed solutions about sex education indirectly address youths' concerns, while perpetuating unintended sexual health outcomes such as HIV/AIDS, STDs, and teenage pregnancy.

Filipinos in the United States experience the entire gamut of sexual health (SH) problems regardless of their categorization and stereotypes (model minority, asexual, or hypersexualized) associated with being "Asian," "Asian

The "Other" Students, pages 277–295

American," "Asian Pacific American," or "Asian Pacific Islander." While national reports indicate that Asian Americans/Pacific Islanders have little to no SH concerns, disaggregated data reveals that Filipinos have alarming numbers of HIV/AIDS and teenage pregnancy cases (Chung et al., 2005; Javier, Chamberlain, Rivera, & Gonzalez, 2010; Manalansan, 2003; Nadal, 2011; Qin & Gould, 2006, 2011; Tiongson, 1997). In Hawaii, the Department of Health reports between 2007 and 2011, which do not include people who have not been tested, shows that the number of cumulative diagnosed AIDS cases in 2007 increased seven times by 2011 to include HIV/AIDS cases (State of Hawaii Department of Health, 2007, 2011). HIV/AIDS and other STDs can be asymptomatic for years, and even when diagnosed they can be hidden. Unlike HIV/AIDS and STDs, teenage pregnancy is difficult to hide. Unless the fetus is miscarried or aborted early in the pregnancy, it is a visible SH symbol. Teenage pregnancy (TP) is the most apparent outcome of sexual activity, and it represents the location where intersecting institutions (schools, churches, households) have failed in their attempts to regulate young women's sexuality and reproductive ability. These institutions seek to compartmentalize and constrain sex to the "right" time, place, space, and stage in one's life. Thus, especially for a community like Filipinos, in which traditional Catholic teachings about the importance of abstinence and virginity before marriage are emphasized, TP is often unexpected and doesn't fit the Filipino cultural paradigm. Given this pattern, the typical responses to TP are avoidance, neglect, denial, and silence. These responses continually replicate in Filipino individuals and families experiencing TP, and they have even become a sort of unintended and clandestine norm for the Filipino American community.

In the context of understanding Filipina American teenage mothers' (TMs) *lived* experiences in the high school health education system, this study investigates the unexplored intersections of perceptions of sex and sexuality, school health education, and sex education battles, which have fostered the unintended teenage pregnancy outcome. Specifically, the study takes place in Hawaii, which is an understudied location with a large Filipino population. Through the utilization of complementary research methods, the Filipina American TMs provide deep insight for educational policymakers, school administrators, and health educators in terms of designing and implementing prevention and intervention strategies for the purposes of decreasing the alarming numbers of unintended pregnancy among teenagers.

REVIEW OF THE LITERATURE

Although there is an abundance of literature on TP in the United States, research on TP in the Filipino community is limited in the following two areas: (a) sexual health and teenage pregnancy and (b) sex and sexuality.

Currently, the literature on Filipinos and school health education (HE) does not exist. Further, none of the related studies provide the Filipina American TMs' perspectives and experiences with HE in relation to sex education policies and/or classroom instruction. The following is a review of existing, although still lacking, demographic information about Filipina American teenage pregnancy, sex, sexuality, and school HE.

Filipina American Teenage Pregnancy

The growth of the Filipino American population has caused a demographic shift within the Asian American population, and it contributes to Asian Americans having the fastest population growth rate (Ghosh, 2003; Yoon & Chien, 1996). Historically, Chinese in the continental United States have been the largest Asian subgroup. In California, Filipinas of all ages totaled the highest number of live births (N = 159,329), even compared to Chinese, who had nearly 22,000 fewer live births (Qin & Gould, 2010). This suggests that Filipinos may soon be the largest Asian subgroup in the nation.

Compared to Asian subgroups, Filipinos had the highest incidences of teenage pregnancy. While Filipinos and Chinese youths aged 18 years and under each make up 21% of the Asian population, there are more births to Filipino teens than Chinese teens (Javier, Huffman, & Mendoza, 2007). Filipinos had 8,482 births to teens over a 9-year period, while Chinese had only 804 births (less than one tenth of Filipinos) (Qin & Gould, 2010). Similarly, in an earlier publication, Filipina teens accounted for 5,140 live births over a 5-year period, while Chinese teens had only 537 live births (Qin & Gould, 2006). Additional studies also revealed that Filipinos had the highest number of births to teens compared to other Asian groups (Fuentes-Afflick & Hessol, 1997; Weitz et al., 2001).

A similar trend exists in Hawaii, with Filipino teens having the highest numbers of births. The Guttmacher Institute (2010) revealed that Hawaii ranked third in the nation for teen pregnancy birth rates. A closer look at the Asian Pacific Islander (API) population in Hawaii indicates that the API birthrate is double the rate compared to APIs nationwide at 46 per 1,000 females aged 15–19 (CDC, 2010). The cost of TP in 2004 for Hawaii alone was estimated at $22 million. Moreover, Hawaii data reveal that unintended pregnancy for Asian Americans has primarily affected Filipinos. Between 2003 and 2008, there were 2,878 births to adolescents from ages 10 to 17, many of which were from predominantly Filipino communities (Hawaii Department of Health, 2010). Disaggregated data shows an even more concerning trend. From 2000 to 2010, for teens age 19 and below, there were 3,086 births to Filipinas, 730 births to Japanese, and only 150 for Chinese (State of Hawaii, Department of Health, 2012). Thus, Filipinos in Hawaii average 308 births to teens annually, while Filipinos in California have about 848 births each year. These reports are helpful in understanding the urgent attention required for TP in the Filipino American community.

Filipina Americans' Perception of Sex and Sexuality

Filipino culture values the sexual purity (or virginity) of girls, and Espiritu's (2001) article, "We Don't Sleep Around Like White Girls Do: Family, Culture, and Gender in Filipina American Lives," provides insight into Filipino/as' sexually conservative viewpoints. The study consisted of nearly 100 Filipinos in San Diego and included interviews of Filipino parents. One of the participants shared her frustration with her parents on the topic of romantic relationships:

> Okay, you go to school. You go to college. You graduate. You find a job. Then you find your husband, and you have children. That's the whole timeline . . . If you are not allowed to date, how are you supposed to find your husband? . . . I should get married and I should have children but that I should not date. (Espiritu, 2001, p. 430)

Thus, the young woman articulates knowledge of the expected "timeline" that her parents want her to follow, but she identifies an apparent paradox in it. The timeline does not allow for dating, and the young woman doesn't see how it would be feasible to marry someone without dating them first. The absence of a dating phase in the timeline may not be an accident. One Filipino parent states, "Girls are supposed to be protected, to be clean . . . they know that they are to be virgins until they get married" (Espiritu, 2001, p. 430). This is a clear example of a Filipino parent wanting to do what they feel is best for their daughter in terms of "protecting" her prospects for marriage. The fundamental conflict between the parent and daughter seems to be a catch-22 situation. The daughter knows she is expected to marry, but she cannot marry if she is unable date. The parent wants the daughter to marry, but they also feel obligated to protect the daughter's virginity. While there may be disagreement between parent and daughter in terms of the appropriate time for dating, there does seem to be an understanding between both sides of the idealized and virtuous pathway daughters are supposed to follow about sex and sexuality. In Tiongson's (1997) study with Filipino/a American teenage parents, narratives provide their insight on commitments to parenthood, experiences of discrimination, and sexism. In his study, the teenage mothers suggest that teen fathers have an easier situation. As one teen mother, April, stated, "Nobody made a big deal if a guy got a girl pregnant. It's not their bodies. Women get affected more. It's her experience, her life. He can just walk out and they won't give up their lifestyle" (p. 266). The perception challenges that Filipina girls' experiences are further revealed by Mayeda, Chesney-Lind, and Koo's (2001) study with 58 multiethnic Hawaiian youths. Non-Filipinos said that Filipinas "wear da kine skanky[1] clothes" and "show off everything" (Mayeda et al. 2001, p. 122). Filipinas were even compared to prostitutes who "dress like hoochie mammas, you know, like hookers" (Mayeda et al., 2001, p. 122). Filipina girls in the study, however, described themselves as conservative dressers, consistent with the value system in Espritu's (2001) study. More recent research on Filipino Americans examined parent-child communication about sex. Chung et al.'s (2007) statistical analyses on acculturation and parent-adolescent sex communication revealed that youths spoke about sex with their friends more than with their parents. The adolescents also indicated that their own perceived parental knowledge about sex positively increased parent-child communication.

Sex Education in the Schools

In 2005, Chung et al. utilized focus group discussions with Filipino/a American families to study parent-adolescent communication and sex information. More specifically, values, feelings, and facts about pregnancy, contraception, and STDs were examined. The participants included 85 adolescents, parents, and grandparents. The consensus among the participants was that the schools were the main source for the adolescents' sex education. However, the adults believed that the schools' approach to sex education conflicted with Filipino values primarily because discussion about sex values (e.g., morals) was not emphasized. Parents believed that the schools' approach to sex education diminished their ability as parents to effectively teach their children about sex values. In an attempt to talk with her child about sex, one parent shared her frustration when her child responded, "I've heard that already over and over . . . Mommy, I already learned that in school." In contrast, the adolescents shared a different perspective. They attributed the sex education they learned in school to their willingness and readiness to talk about sex with their parents.

Since sex education is provided in schools, parents often believe that their children are receiving useful information about sex, which promotes healthy sexually abstinent behaviors. While school teachers and administrators may have this intention, time constraints and the depth of information makes it difficult to provide effective sex education. Nationally, HE teachers have eight content areas and national standards to implement in their health education class (see Table 15.1) (Telljohann, Symons, & Pateman, 2009). The standards and content areas work in combination with each other for classroom instruction, each of which should be addressed in the HE

TABLE 15.1 Health Education: Eight Standards and Eight Content Areas

Eight Health Education Standards	Eight Content Areas
1. Core Concepts	1. Mental and Emotional Health
2. Analyze Influences	2. Healthy Eating and Physical Activity
3. Access Information, Products, and Services	3. Personal Health and Wellness
4. Interpersonal Communication	4. Safety and Prevent Unintentional Injury
5. Decision Making	5. Prevent Violence
6. Goal Setting	6. Tobacco-Free Lifestyle
7. Self-Management	7. Alcohol and Other Drug-Free Lifestyle
8. Advocacy	8. Sexual Health and Responsibility

course. The content area, sexual health and responsibility (SHR), is one of eight content area topics provided in the one-semester HE course. Thus, perceptions on the need for sex education, specifically with abstinence-only and comprehensive sex education, have been the source for controversy at the national and local legislative levels. Plus, SHR is crowded into an already overstuffed curriculum that attempts to be an all-in-one HE course.

In Hawaii, SHR education is taught as part of the HE course. In order for students to receive a high school diploma, the State of Hawaii Board of Education (2008) High School Graduation Requirements and Commencement Policy 4540 requires students to earn 24 credits, which includes a half credit for the successful completion of HE. There are two policies that serve to guide schools on SHR content. Policy 2210 Abstinence Based Education is intended to assist students with making decisions that promote healthy behaviors and that result in abstinence from sex in order to prevent HIV/AIDS, STDs, and teenage pregnancy (State of Hawaii, Board of Education, 1995). Policy 2245 Prophylactics in Public Schools allows schools to have discussions about prophylactics (but not distribution), including condoms and birth control, in the context of human reproduction (State of Hawaii, Board of Education, 1994).

In summary, this literature review examined (a) Filipina teenage pregnancy, (b) Filipina sex and sexuality, and (c) sexual health and responsibility education in high school health education classes. These three areas serve as a theoretical framework to understand the phenomenon of Filipina American teenage pregnancy. Based on this review, it is clear that there is the need for further research to understand the impact that HE (or the lack of effective HE) has on understudied areas such as Filipina American teenage pregnancy. In addition, this study contributes to the existing body of literature in the following ways: (a) it provides perspective and experiences of Filipina American teenage mothers; (b) it examines sex education information in the schools and classrooms; and (c) it explores school sex education policies.

METHODS

This study utilizes complementary research methodologies, specifically case studies, surveys, and ethnographic interviews (Green, Camilli, & Elmore, 2006; Merriam, 1998; Spradley, 1979; Yin, 2003, 2009). Case studies (Yin, 2003, 2009) that focus on contemporary phenomenon in a real-life context were suitable to aid in understanding teenage pregnancy in the school environment. The study of TP is important because it is of national public interest, which ultimately influences recommendations for practice and policies for sex education in schools (Yin, 2009).

The study was conducted in Hawaii because of its demographic characteristics. Although the Filipino population makes up 23% (275,728 people) of the entire population in Hawaii (Hawaii Department of Health, 2010), the phenomenon of TP has been minimally explored in this group. This study was composed of 12 Filipina American teenage mothers. Here, Filipina American refers to a girl who has heritage origins from the Philippines (Filipina) and resides in the United States (American). The criteria for research participation were full- or part-Filipina background, public high school attendance, and being pregnant or parenting (see Table 15.2).

These participants were recruited from public high schools located in five communities on the island of Oahu, which had the highest numbers of births to teens, ages 10–17. These communities were predominantly Filipino, and they accounted for the majority (66% or N = 1,165) of births to teens on Oahu from 2003 to 2008. Thus, there is an average of 233 births to teens annually on the island.

TABLE 15.2 Filipina American Teenage Mother Characteristics

Case	Student	Grade	Age	Ethnicit(ies)	GSI	Status
1	Patricia	11	16	Filipina, Japanese	2nd	Parenting
2	Vanessa	10	15	Filipina	1st	Parenting
3	Amanda	10	16	Filipina, Chinese, Indian	3rd	Pregnant
4	Ella	10	15	Filipina, Japanese, Native Hawaiian	4th	Pregnant
5	Marcy	11	16	Filipina, Japanese	2nd	Pregnant
6	Joyce	12	17	Filipina	2nd	Pregnant
7	Kaili	12	17	Filipina	2nd	Pregnant
8	Carla	12	17	Filipina	2nd	Pregnant
9	Lexi	9	16	mixed Filipina	2nd	Parenting
10	Olivia	10	16	Filipina, Japanese, Native Hawaiian	3rd	Parenting
11	Malia	10	16	Filipina, Native Hawaiian, Portuguese	3rd	Parenting
12	Gina	11	17	Filipina	2nd	Parenting

Note: GSI = Generation Since Immigration

The participants provided explanatory multicase studies, which represented "data bearing on cause–effect relationships—explaining how events happened" (Yin, 2003, p. 5). As an insider in the Hawaii community, I utilized "talk stories," an informal style of conversation commonly practiced, as part of my research approach; this was used to capture perspectives from informants in this unique cultural context. To analyze the qualitative data, Miles and Huberman's (1994) causal model and case-ordered metamatrix was employed. The causal model fits well with the case study methodologies, which can serve three functions that demonstrate exploratory, descriptive, and explanatory (causal) "real life" phenomenon.

FINDINGS

The findings in this study describe the role of HE in the lives of Filipina American teenage mothers in public high schools. The following section is divided in two parts: receipt of HE and HE course content experiences. The latter has three segments based on participants' HE status as having completed the course, being currently enrolled, or having never been enrolled. In this section, the TMs also share their perceptions of the HE course content.

Receipt of Health Education and When She Became Pregnant

Table 15.3 displays the school year that the TM should have received health education (HE), became pregnant (P), and gave birth (B). Of the participants, nine girls became pregnant before they were scheduled to receive HE, while three girls became pregnant after they received HE.[2] The nine girls who became pregnant before they were enrolled in HE experienced unplanned pregnancies: four girls became pregnant in the ninth grade (year 1), one during the summer after ninth grade, and four became pregnant in the tenth grade. In all, the participants either gave birth in their first year (N = 1), second year (N = 4), summer before third year (N = 1), or during their third year (N = 3) of high school. These girls were from three different schools, and they were originally enrolled in year 1 or 2 of high school.

Table 15.4 shows the 12 TMs' high school HE enrollment as either completed, current, or never received. Of the 12 mothers, 5 completed their HE course, 3 were currently enrolled, and 4 never received HE, even though they were supposed to take it as part of the school curriculum.

TABLE 15.3 Time-Ordered Matrix: Pregnancy, Birth, and Health Education

	Year 1	1st Summer	Year 2	2nd Summer	Year 3	3rd Summer	Year 4	4th Summer
Patricia	—	P	B	—	HE	—	—	—
Amanda	—	—	P	—	B, HE	—	—	—
Vanessa	P	—	B, HE	—	—	—	—	—
Ella	—	—	P, HE	B	—	—	—	—
Marcy	P	—	HE		P, B		—	—
Lexi	—	—	P, B HE	—	—	—	—	—
Olivia	P, B	—	HE	—	—	—	—	—
Kaili	P		B, HE	—	—	—	—	—
Gina	—	—	P	—	HE, B	—	—	—
Kaili	—	—	—	—	HE	—	P	B
Carla		—	—	—	HE	—	P	B
Joyce	HE	—		—	—		P	B

Note: HE = Health Education; P = Pregnant; B = Birth

TABLE 15.4 Health Education Enrollment

Student	Completed	Current	Never
Joyce	X	—	—
Kaili	X	—	—
Carla	X	—	—
Marcy	X	—	—
Gina	X	—	—
Vanessa	—	X	—
Olivia	—	X	—
Malia	—	X	—
Lexi	—	—	X
Ella	—	—	X
Amanda	—	—	X
Patricia	—	—	X

Health Education Course Content: Completed Health Education

In total, five TMs completed HE (see Table 15.4). Three of these girls (Joyce, Kaili, Carla) were twelfth graders from School 1, and they received HE before they became pregnant. Unlike the other participants, they expressed an interest in becoming pregnant. Therefore, since this chapater

TABLE 15.5 Health Education Enrollment and Sexual Health and Responsibility Content Received

Student	Health Education Enrollment	Content
Gina	Completed	75% worksheets; 25% lecture from teacher
Marcy	Completed	Movies and test about movie
Olivia	Current	Textbook
Malia	Current	Textbook
Lexi	Current	Textbook
Vanessa	None	Assigned classwork to complete at home; School-group work, skit, presentation, lecture
Ella	Never	None
Amanda	Never	None
Patricia	Never	None

serves to discuss reducing unintended pregnancy, their HE experiences are not reported. Table 15.5 shows the nine TMs who became pregnant before they received HE. The table describes their HE enrollment status and the form of SHR content that they received.

Gina and Marcy became pregnant before completing their HE class, and their experiences are described. Marcy attended School 4, and Gina attended School 3. Gina, who was pregnant while in HE class, explained that the teacher used worksheets 75% of the time, and the rest was devoted to lectures. Gina stated that, "When we didn't understand her or if she wanted us to know more about it," the HE teacher would provide lectures. It was through worksheets that she learned about the reproductive system, puberty, organs, and how babies are born. She explained in detail some of the information she learned in HE class:

> I learned a lot from her because it was a surprise to me that they were cells... when I was reading the paper it said like, the reproductive system, and it gave, like, the main topic was how babies develop from stages. So when I was reading it said like, the sperm and the cell they would join. I mean the sperm and the egg would join and turn into a cell and then divides and then it's like, a two. That one is a brain and one is I think a leg or a spine.

Gina learned about reproduction in one class period. She mentioned that "just one" sperm is required to fertilize an egg, which can result in pregnancy. "I was surprised," she stated, "because I thought it would take a lot [of sperm] to just form one baby." Gina went on to say that her teacher also discussed "abstinence and religious people" as well as STDs through a lecture. She also indicated that the teacher explained that, "It's good to wait [to have sex] because we're still young and we have lot of things to do."

Marcy had HE in the tenth grade. She was pregnant in the ninth grade, but miscarried. At the time of the study, she was in the eleventh grade and became pregnant for a second time. She was in her second trimester during the interview. For HE, a typical class pertaining to SHR was watching movies, in which she learned about pregnancy prevention, being pregnant, caretaking, teen parents' struggles (and successes), sex, condoms, and birth control. Marcy also became familiar with the locations of the health clinics in her community.

Health Education Course Content: Currently Enrolled in Health Education

There were three girls (Olivia, Malia, and Lexi) who were currently enrolled in HE, all of whom were already parenting. They all had the same HE teacher at School 4, but during different class periods. Each of these girls indicated that they learned HE from a textbook. Their lessons usually consisted of 10 pages of textbook reading and specified assigned questions at the end of each chapter; for example, of 25 total questions, the teacher requested that students respond to 15. The students worked individually, but sometimes they needed to work collaboratively and share materials because of the limited number of textbooks available. Each lesson took 1 to 2 days, and at the end of the lesson the teacher gave the answers to the questions. Olivia felt that, "He doesn't teach us. We just learn from the book; we do work on our own. Sometimes we share books because people take home books." Olivia described what she learned from the textbook:

> In the pregnancy [lesson], it's about like, teen pregnancy and how you get pregnant, and delivering the baby... about everything like, the puberty is what men go through and puberty is what girls go through and how our bodies change and how all these sex hormones help them and then pregnancy is like, what happens in the first stage of pregnancy and what girls go through, and other stuffs.

Olivia, Malia, and Vanessa attend School 1, where students usually receive HE in the eleventh grade. However, because of her pregnancy, Vanessa was home during the fall semester of tenth grade. The health teacher assigned her work to do while at home. She gave birth in November, and she returned to school in December. In order to accommodate her, school administrators required Vanessa to reenroll in the tenth grade.

Health Education Course Content: Girls Who Did Not Receive Health Education

There were three girls (Amanda, Ella, and Patricia), who never received HE and became TMs during high school. Patricia provided comments on how she believed she might experience HE:

> I don't think Ms. Numa (pseudonym) would get to the point [about] pregnancy... It's probably gonna be more complicated; for her classes we skip, we skip stuff... she teaches... one point, then she jumps to another; she doesn't get to the point.

In her situation, Ms. Numa was her English and Credit Recovery teacher in previous semesters; Patricia was assigned to have Ms. Numa for HE in an upcoming semester. With Patricia's case, she did not feel that she would gain any important information from the class. When it comes to HE, teachers who instruct this course are often responsible for teaching other subjects. Thus, it can be challenging for teachers to provide sex education knowledge and information in a manner that students can apply to their lives.

Amanda, a pregnant tenth grader, did not receive health education. During the interview, she mentioned that she and her boyfriend practiced withdrawal during sex to prevent pregnancy. She was unaware that withdrawal or the "pull-out" could lead to pregnancy, and she stated,

> I don't know the truth, like, if you really pull out can you [become pregnant]?... Joey (pseudonym) would pull it out, like, I don't know sometimes, but sometimes he wouldn't take it out because he would think that nothing would happen.

Given this information, there is a possibility that Amanda became pregnant through the pull-out method. In each of the case studies above, the findings indicate that the majority of the girls in this study became pregnant *before* they received HE. For those participants who completed or were enrolled in HE, the findings show that the SHR instruction methods that the teachers utilized varied from independent learning, reading textbooks, doing worksheets, and attending lectures.

RECOMMENDATIONS

The time has come to listen to youths whose voices are critical for the improvement of sex education policies and classroom practices. In direct response to the U.S. Department of Health and Human Services' *Surgeon General's Call to Action to Promote Sexual Health and Responsible Sexual Behavior*

(2001), this study addresses imperative findings and recommendations from the Filipino American community that contribute to a better understanding of teen sexuality and result in a healthier and more responsible population. Moreover, respectful dialogues on sex education continue and persist, but they demand perspectives from those who are most affected, the youths.

Timely Sexual Health Education: The Missing Link

The abstinence-only education (AOE) and comprehensive sex education (CSE) battles have existed in the continental United States since the 1960s (Fields, 2008; Irvine, 2004; Luker, 2006). These sex education debates, however, are relatively new in Hawaii's legislative bodies. Recently, Senate Bill 922 (State of Hawaii, The Senate, Twenty-Sixth Legislature, 2011) Comprehensive Sex Education states the following:

> Description: Specifies additional elements of Hawaii's existing sexuality health education law and its implementation. Requires the department of education (DOE) to provide certain types of information to the public and to parents. Allows parents to opt out of the DOE's sexuality health education.

Organizations and individuals shared their support or opposition to SB 922 through testimonies. Some of the proponents for SB 922 were representatives from Planned Parenthood, Hawaii Youth Services Network, Healthy Mothers Healthy Babies, and the ACLU. Opponents included the Department of Health, Hawaii Family Forum, Department of Education, and Pro-Family Hawaii. Testifiers have different perceptions on sex education and existing policies. Some believe that Policy 2245 and 2210, which were passed in the 1990s, effectively serve the purpose of educating students about STDs, HIV/AIDS, and teenage pregnancy prevention, so newly proposed bills are unnecessary. The major limitation of these debates, proposed policies, and testimonies are that students, the most critical perspectives, are missing.

From this study, the key finding is that *timely* sex education can benefit all students. Schools can be more effective with preventing unintended pregnancies with timely sex education. The critical cases, Filipina American TMs, who did not intend to become teen parents, received information about SHR in high school health education class *after* they became pregnant in the ninth, tenth, and eleventh grades. Students can benefit by receiving SHR education in middle school and secondary school. Ella, a tenth grader, who hadd not received HE yet, suggests the following:

> They should be teaching it [HE] early because right now there's a lot of teens getting pregnant. It can help them think about their choices. I think they

> should teach it in the eighth grade and then another one, more advanced, in the ninth grade.

Her profound insight can help schools and policymakers make better informed decisions. Currently, there are no policies in place to promote the timely well-being of school youths through HE. Policy 4540 requires students to earn a half credit of HE in order to graduate high school (State of Hawaii, Board of Education, 2008). Policy 2110 and 2245 are about abstinence-based education, HIV/AIDS/STD/teen pregnancy prevention, and prophylactics (State of Hawaii, Board of Education, 1994, 1995). SB 922 mentions the phrase "age appropriate" and requires that public elementary, secondary, and alternate schools provide students with sexual health education (State of Hawaii, The Senate, Twenty-Sixth Legislature, 2011). Because of the lack of emphasis on the appropriate timing for HE instruction, specifically *when* to teach HE, schools have not been as effective as they can be with pregnancy prevention approaches. In the past decade, Hawaii averaged nearly 308 births to Filipina American teenagers (State of Hawaii Department of Health, 2012). A policy about timely health education may be the most significant factor for reducing and eliminating unintended sexual health outcomes.

Moreover, a policy that mandates sex education to a specific grade level can serve a critical role for pregnancy prevention. The TMs were from different high schools with varied HE course enrollments (grades nine, ten, and eleven). Typically for each school, the majority of students will have HE in the same grade level, but this is not always the case. Vanessa and Amanda, for example, attended the same high school, but they had HE in grades ten and eleven, respectively. Moreover, they each became pregnant *before* receipt of HE. Therefore, sex education in the ninth grade (first semester) could prevent TP for future students, but sex education in the ninth grade alone may not be sufficient. Three of the Filipina American TMs became pregnant in the ninth grade. Therefore, sex education in the eighth and ninth grades, as teen mom Ella suggested, may be the more effective solution.

Filipino Americans and the Sex Education Controversy

Controversies over sex education are especially detrimental to minority and low-income youth. Filipino Americans in particular experience complex factors associated with sex education. For example, many Filipinos in Hawai'i live below the federal poverty level, and parents often work two or three blue-collar jobs (such as housekeeping and maintenance) to provide for their families. This heavy commitment to work limits the face-to-face or direct involvement that parents may have in their children's lives. The TMs in this study were from predominantly Filipino communities where up to 38.7% of the population lived below the federal poverty level (Hawaii Department of Health, Family Health Services Division, 2010).

In addition, the immigrant backgrounds (whether first, second, or third generation) of Filipino Americans may lead parents to believe they have little agency or no "right" to participate in the school or political process. Historically, Filipinos in Hawaii have experienced racist stereotyping and have been represented in derogatory ways (Okamura, 2008). Thus, adults may feel inferior or intimidated to engage in the host societies community and political activities. Along with reasons like language barriers, "colonial mentality," and even having anxieties with the topic of sex, Filipino American parents can feel too disempowered and disengaged to demand the appropriate SHR education for their children.

Since schools are supposed to teach about SHR, parents may assume that their children are receiving accurate and sufficient sex information. Often, however, parents are unaware of school limitations (e.g., time, learning style, pedagogy, and materials used). A major constraint for effective education is time; SHR is provided in the context of health education class, which is only one semester. Furthermore, SHR is one of eight content areas that are covered, so SHR is confined to only a slice of time. As a result of these factors, the division between Filipino parents and host society institutions (e.g., schools) breeds the unwanted health outcome of teenage pregnancy. Community-based education sites can help to bridge the gap between health outcomes, policies, schools, communities, and parents.

What Is Important to Teach in Sexual Health and Responsibility

When asked, "What would you teach if you were the health education teacher?" the TMs in this study all responded with topics that fit directly under the *sexual health and responsibility* content area within HE. Their suggestions also align with Policy 2110 on abstinence-based education and Policy 2245 on prophylactics. Congruent with Policy 2110, the TMs specifically mentioned education about pregnancy (e.g., intercourse, how pregnancy occurs, and how babies are formed), human reproduction (e.g., reproductive system, sperm, sex organs, fallopian tube, puberty, adulthood), STDs, and abstinence. Kaili (twelfth grade) stated the following:

> I would just talk about everything about sex and pregnancy. That would interest my students more than nutrients and food that you're not supposed to eat. They're in the stage where they talk about sex; once you get to high school, it's all about sex.

Kaili's response represents a perspective that indicates the need and urgency for sex education, in contrast to the other seven health education content areas. In support of Policy 2245, Carla (twelfth grade) mentioned that if she were a health educator, she would teach about prophylactics (birth control methods, side effects, and contraceptives).

Along these lines, TMs could help to create a sex education handbook to inform HE teachers about useful sex education lessons to help with pregnancy prevention. This student-made handbook could improve or supplement existing sex education lessons and follow HE policies 2110 and 2245. It could also anticipate policies that may pass in the future and include them now. The handbook could have core knowledge about SHR, like the content in Telljohan et al.'s (2009) *Health Education* book, with topic areas further developed by TMs. TMs could provide deeper insight on specific medical terminologies that their peers could better understand. For example, there could be a section on medical terminology aligned with the vernacular language and terminology of youth.

One topic that seems to require special emphasis is human reproduction. Malia, although enrolled in HE, stated that "I would want to know how the baby is actually formed or how to prevent them from being formed. I just don't understand how they're formed, how babies are made." Malia learned SHR from a textbook; she and all students can benefit from sex education discussions in which the teacher provides information and facilitates learning activities (e.g., videos, quizzes, presentations, and learner outcomes). The HE teacher can also serve to dispel myths like sex in the water as an effective way for pregnancy prevention. Amanda, for example, didn't know if the pull-out method worked. Open discussions in the HE classroom can inform students about sex myths, like withdrawal (that it can lead to pregnancy), which is valuable information that can help youths make informed decisions.

CONCLUSION

Public schools in Hawaii have the privilege and responsibility to make a positive impact on underserved minority communities. They have a unique opportunity to work with school-aged youths to promote health education and prevent unintended sexual health outcomes like HIV/AIDS, STDs, and teenage pregnancy. The findings from this study share Filipina American teenage mothers' lived experiences, as a school-aged group, whose lives have been drastically changed from becoming teenage parents. Schools, policymakers, and students can benefit by learning from the teenage mothers' critical voices, those who most needed, but failed to receive, sex education in a timely manner. The knowledge shared by the Filipina American teenage mothers in this study has important and credible solutions that can serve to reduce and eliminate unintended teen pregnancy for the state of Hawaii and communities nationwide.

NOTES

1. Sexy, revealing, tight, short.
2. Kaili, Carla, and Joyce were enrolled in the 12th grade, and they either misused/stopped using birth control and/or intended to become pregnant.

REFERENCES

Centers for Disease Control and Prevention. (2010). *Hawaii success story: Hawaii Youth Services Network—Program adaptation in action.* Retrieved from www.cdc.gov/teenpregnancy/Hawaii.htm

Chung, P., Borneo, H., Kilpatrick, S., Lopez, D., Travis, R. Lui, C.... Schuster, M. (2005). Parent-adolescent communication about sex in Filipino-American families: A demonstration of a community-based participatory research. *Ambulatory Pediatrics, 5*(1), 50–55.

Chung, P., Travis, R., Kilpatrick, S., Elliott, M., Lui, C., Khandwala, S.... Shuster, M. (2007). Acculturation and parent-adolescent communication about sex in Filipino-American families: A community-based participatory research study. *Journal of Adolescent Health, 40*(6), 543–550.

Espiritu, Y. (2001). "We don't sleep around like White girls do": Family, culture, and gender in Filipina American lives. *Signs, 26*(2), 415–440.

Fields, J. (2008). *Risky lessons: Sex education and social inequality.* New Brunswick, NJ: Rutgers University Press.

Fuentes-Afflick, E., & Hessol, N. (1997). Impact of Asian ethnicity and national origin on infant birth weight. *American Journal of Epidemiology, 145*(2), 148–155.

Green, J. Camilli, G., & Elmore, P. (2006). *Handbook of complementary methods in education research.* Mahwah, NJ: Erlbaum.

Ghosh, C. (2003). Healthy people 2010 and Asian American/Pacific Islanders: Defining a baseline of information. *American Journal of Public Health, 93*(12), 2093–2098.

Guttmacher Institute. (2010). *Teen pregnancy rates highest in California, Nevada, Hawaii, Arizona, and New Mexico, new analysis shows.* Retrieved from www.guttmacher.org/media/nr/newsrelease597.html

Hawaii Department of Health, Family Health Services Division. (2010). *State of Hawaii primary needs assessment data book 2009.* Retrieved from http://hawaii.gov/health/doc/pcna2009databook.pdf

Irvine, J. (2004). *Talk about sex: The battle over sex education in the United States.* Los Angeles: University of California Press.

Javier, R., Chamberlain, L., Rivera, K., & Gonzalez, S. (2010). Lessons learned from a community-academic partnership addressing adolescent pregnancy prevention in Filipino American families. *Progress in Community Health Partnership: Research, Education, and Action, 4*(4), 305–313.

Javier, J., Huffman, L., & Mendoza, F. (2007). Filipino child health in the United States: Do health and health care disparities exist? *Preventing Chronic Disease: Public Health Research, Practice, and Policy, 4*(2), 136–157.

Luker, K. (2006). *When sex goes to school: Warring views on sex—and sex education—since the sixties.* New York, NY: W.W. Norton.

Manalansan, M. (2003). *Global divas: Filipino gay men in the diaspora.* Durham, NC: Duke University Press.

Mayeda, D., Chesney-Lind, M., & Koo, J. (2001). Talking story with Hawaii's youth: Confronting violent and sexualized perceptions of ethnicity and gender. *Youth & Society, 33*(1), 99–128.

Merriam, S. (1998). *Qualitative research and case study application in education.* San Francisco, CA: John Wiley & Sons.

Miles, M., & Huberman, M. (1994). *Qualitative data analysis: An expanded sourcebook.* Thousand Oaks, CA: Sage.

Nadal, K. (2011). *Filipino American psychology: A handbook of theory, research, and clinical practice.* Hoboken: NJ: John Wiley & Sons.

Okamura, J. (2008). *Ethnicity and inequality in Hawaii.* Philadelphia, PA: Temple University Press.

Qin, C., & Gould, J. (2006). The Asian birth outcome gap. *Pediatric and Perinatal Epidemiology, 20*(4), 279–189.

Qin, C., & Gould, J. (2010). Maternal nativity status and birth outcomes in Asian immigrants. *Journal of Immigrant Minority Health, 12*(5), 798–805.

Spradley, J. (1979). *The ethnographic interview.* Chicago, IL: Holt, Rinehart, and Winston.

State of Hawaii, Board of Education. (1994). *Policy 2245 Prophylactics in public schools.* Retrieved from http://lilinote.k12.hi.us/STATE/BOE/POL1.NSF/85255a0a0010ae82852555340060479d/da81bd16b557a9590a2566a30007780f?OpenDocument

State of Hawaii, Board of Education. (1995). *Policy 2110 Abstinence-based education.* Retrieved from http://lilinote.k12.hi.us/STATE/BOE/POL1.NSF/85255a0a0010ae82852555340060479d/1bb88fd5ec2ea5940a2566a3000110ef?OpenDocument

State of Hawaii, Board of Education. (2008). *Policy 4540 High school graduation requirements and commencement policy.* Retrieved from http://lilinote.k12.hi.us/STATE/BOE/POL1.NSF/85255a0a0010ae82852555340060479d91ae48edb6f3e0140a2566a3006f0dec?OpenDocument

State of Hawaii, Department of Health. (2007). *HIV/AIDS surveillance semi-annual report: Cases to June 30, 2007.* Retrieved from hawaii.gov/health/healthy-lifestyles/std-aids/aboutus/prg-aids/aids_rep/2h2007.pdf

State of Hawaii Department of Health. (2011). *HIV/AIDS surveillance annual report: Cases to December 31, 2010.* Retrieved from http://hawaii.gov/health/healthy-lifestyles/std-aids/aboutus/prg-aids/aids_rep/2h2007.pdf

State of Hawaii, Department of Health, Offices of Health Status Monitoring. (2012). *Live births in Hawaii, by mothers DOH race-ethnicity and mothers age for the year(s)-2000, 2001, 2002, 2003, 2004, 2005, 2006, 2007, 2008, 2009, 2010.*

Retrieved from http://www.hhdw.org/cms/uploads/Data%20Source_%20Vitals/Vital%20Statistics_Live%20Births%20in%20Hawaii_IND_00006.pdf

State of Hawaii, The Senate, Twenty-Sixth Legislature. (2011). Senate Bill 922: Comprehensive Sex Education. Retrieved from http://www.capitol.hawaii.gov/measure_indiv.aspx?billtype=SB&billnumber=922

Telljohann, S., Symons, C., & Pateman, B. (2009). *Health education: Elementary and middle school application* (6th ed.). New York, NY: McGraw Hill.

Tiongson, A. (1997). Throwing the baby out with the bathwater: Situating young Filipino mothers and fathers beyond the dominant discourse on adolescent pregnancy. In M. P. Root (Ed.), *Filipino Americans: Transformation and identity* (pp. 257–271). Thousand Oaks, CA: Sage.

Weitz, T., Harper, C., Shen, E., Acebo, R., Mojllajee, A., & Milliken, N. (2001). *Teen pregnancy among Asian and Pacific Islanders in California: Final report.* San Francisco, CA: UCSF Center for Reproductive Health Research & Policy.

U.S. Department of Health and Human Services, Office of the Surgeon General. (2001). *The surgeon general's call to action to promote sexual health and responsible sexual behavior.* Retrieved from www.surgeongeneral.gov/library/sexualhealth/call.htm

Yin, R. (2003). *Applications of case study research.* Thousand Oaks, CA: Sage.

Yin, R. (2009). *Case study research: Design and methods.* Thousand Oaks, CA: Sage.

Yoon, E., & Chien, F. (1996) Asian American and Pacific Islander health: A paradigm for minority health. *Journal of American Medical Association, 225*(9), 736–737.

CHAPTER 16

EXPLORING THE FILIPINO AMERICAN FACULTY PIPELINE

Implications for Higher Education and Filipino American College Students

Dina C. Maramba
State University of New York at Binghamton

Kevin L. Nadal
City University of New York

A diverse faculty population has been known to play an important role in the retention and persistence of students, specifically students of color. In fact, faculty of color often go above and beyond their roles as professors and researchers by serving as role models and providing a support system for students of color in their institutions (Castellanos & Jones, 2003; Trower, 2009). Furthermore, research has demonstrated the critical nature of diversifying faculty in institutions of higher education (Smith, Turner, Osei-Kofi,

The "Other" Students, pages 297–307

& Richards, 2004; Smith, Wolf, & Busenberg, 1996; Turner, 2002; Turner & Myers, 2000; Weinberg, 2008). With the rapidly increasing numbers and diverse demography of Asian American and Pacific Islander (AAPI) students attending college, it is fitting that attention also be given to studying AAPI faculty. Although there exists informative research studies about faculty of color (e.g., Allen, Epps, Guillory, Shuh, & Bonous-Hammarth, 2000; Turner & Myers, 2000) particularly African Americans, Latinos, and Native Americans, less attention has been given to examining AAPI faculty (e.g., Cho, 2002; Hune, 2006) and more specifically Filipino American faculty. There are a number of possible reasons for this discrepancy for AAPIs. First, because of the Model Minority Myth, which inaccurately portrays all AAPIs as successful and academically inclined, many may stereotype AAPIs as being model citizens who are well adjusted to the educational environment (Nadal, 2011). These assumptions about AAPI students can easily apply to AAPI faculty, who also become overlooked and misunderstood with regard to their experiences in higher education. Second, because AAPIs appear to be statistically well represented in various colleges and universities, it may be assumed that they are not a population that needs further examination or support. As seen within the context of the university environment, it is common for the AAPI population to be disregarded. For example, AAPI students tend to be ignored for outreach and support services (e.g., Suzuki, 2002), and the experiences of university AAPI administrators and faculty are often marginalized or go unnoticed (e.g., Hune, 2011; Maramba, 2011).

Moreover, examining specific statistics on AAPI faculty can be misleading. One research study indicated that AAPI faculty increased from 25,000 positions in 1993 to more than 41,000 positions in 2003 (a 62.85% gain), the largest number among faculty of color (Cook & Cordova, 2006). These numbers can be perceived as impressive and interpreted as AAPIs' gains in education, furthering the stereotype that this "successful" group has reached parity. However, some researchers heed caution in the interpretation of such statistics. Cho (2002) argues that the parity explanation, mainly based on quantitative measures, misrepresents AAPIs in a number of ways. First, the "overparity" representation most often leads to the supposition that AAPIs are now free from discrimination. Second, such statistics reinforce the model minority stereotype, pitting them against other populations of color who are "underparity." Furthermore, Nadal (2011) cites that with most data focusing on AAPIs as an umbrella group, there is a need to further examine the meaning behind the statistics or whether the trend is true for all AAPI ethnic groups. Similarly, another study found that in general, within the context of higher education faculty, AAPIs have the largest gender gap of any racial/ethnic group. In 2003, women in general made up only 39% of full-time faculty in higher education institutions, while professors of color tend to be men (59%) versus women (41%) (Cook & Cordova, 2006).

However, upon closer examination of these 2003 statistics, the gender gap for Asian American faculty is even more disparate, in that 67% of AAPI faculty are men and 32% are women. Although the number of Asian American women faculty more than doubled, there remains a faculty difference of more than 14,000 between Asian American men and women in full-time positions (Cook & Cordova, 2006). Although AAPI female faculty accounted for 30% of the total AAPI faculty in 1999–2000, with 36% assistant professors, 24% associate professors, and 14% full professors, they are concentrated at the junior faculty level and much less likely than AAPI males to be at the tenure rank of associate professor and above (Hune, 2006). While these numbers may be alarming, it may be necessary to disaggregate the data to see if these trends are true for all AAPI ethnic groups. For example, one report from the census found that Filipina American women are more likely to enter the labor force than Asian American women and the general American female population (Reeves & Bennett, 2004). Given this gender difference for the workplace in general, perhaps it is possible that Filipina American faculty members may have different experiences than other Asian American female faculty members as well.

Because the AAPI population consists of 48 ethnic groups (National Commission, 2010), with a great diversity in socioeconomic statuses, family histories in higher education, languages spoken, and immigration statuses, it is necessary to examine the experiences of specific Asian American ethnic groups. Attempting to give an accurate representation of the entire AAPI category would be nearly impossible (S. J. Lee, 2006). For example, while there may be some statistics that cite that Asian Americans are overrepresented in the academy, there are many other reports that reveal that many AAPI ethnic groups (e.g., Southeast Asians, Pacific Islanders, Filipino Americans) are actually statistically underrepresented in college (Nadal, 2011; Nadal, Pituc, Johnston, & Esparrago, 2010; Okamura, 1998). Also, by upholding the Model Minority Myth, the experiences of specific subgroups of the AAPI umbrella continue to remain unknown.

Although there have been a few important studies on Asian American faculty in general (Cho, 2002; Escueta & O'Brien, 1995; Hune, 2006; Johnsrud & Sadao, 2002; S. M. Lee, 2002), research that looks at faculty experiences of specific ethnic groups within the AAPI umbrella is close to nonexistent. Thus, the purpose of this study is to examine one ethnic group of the AAPI umbrella and to explore general statistics about Filipino American faculty. Filipino Americans are an important population to study for a number of reasons. First, a few empirical studies conducted on the college experiences of Filipino/a American undergraduate and graduate students reveal that having Filipino/a American faculty on campus is important to Filipino/a college students' well-being on campus (Maramba 2008a, 2008b; Nadal et al., 2010). These studies have also reported that the number of Filipino/a American faculty is lacking compared to the number of Filipino/a American college students. To date, there is no existing database on the numbers of Filipino/a American faculty. As with most national data, Filipino/a American numbers are aggregated within the Asian American category. Additionally, second to the Latino population, Filipino Americans are the second-largest and fastest growing immigrant population in the country (Rumbaut & Portes, 2001). Although Filipino Americans are the second-largest Asian American group in the United States and are projected to become the largest Asian American population in coming years, there is a dearth of literature focusing on this ethnic group in education, social sciences, and humanities (Nadal, 2011). Third, because Filipino Americans often experience educational and sociocultural disparities that differ from other Asian American groups, it is necessary to disaggregate the Asian American umbrella and understand the experiences of individual ethnic groups. It is also important to mention that within a historical and current context, the Philippines continues a very complex, postcolonial relationship with the United States. Since the beginning of the 1960s, the brain drain in the Philippines has meant consistently recruiting large numbers of nurses, other medical professionals, and to some extent, teachers to the United States (Nadal, 2011).

Given the lack of existing literature and information on Filipino American faculty, our study is an exploratory investigation of the current state of Filipino/a American faculty. We aim to survey the number of Filipino American tenured and tenure-track professors in the United States to provide a picture of the Filipino American faculty pipeline. We will focus on Filipino/a American faculty, specifically in the disciplines of humanities/arts/social sciences, in which most Filipino/a Americans tend to be underrepresented. Our research questions include the following: (a) How many Filipino American tenured and tenure-track faculty members are in the United States? (b) To which fields or disciplines do these Filipino American faculty members belong? (c) In what institutions or geographic locations do these Filipino American faculty members reside?

METHOD

Recruitment

A snowball sampling method was used to collect a comprehensive database of Filipino American faculty members. A recruitment e-mail was sent to various Filipino American, Asian American, and ethnic minority listervs and organizations that may have members with access or contact with Filipino American professors on a national level. Some of these organizations included the Filipino American National Historical Society (FANHS), the Association of Asian American Studies (AAAS), the National Association of Filipino American Associations (NAFAA), the Asian American Psychological Association (AAPA), and the people of color listserves through American College Personnel Association (ACPA), and American Educational Research Association (AERA). Announcements were also posted on various Filipino American and Asian American group pages on Facebook, and participants were encouraged to repost the announcements on their own personal Facebook pages. The recruitment e-mails and postings included a link to an online survey on SurveyMonkey, where participants were informed that the purpose of the survey was to collect the names of all of the Filipino American professors in the United States. The survey then asked for the following: (a) name of professor, (b) current university affiliation, (c) concentration or department, (d) doctoral institution (if known), (e) degree and concentration (if known), (f) tenure status and ranking, (g) gender, and (h) generational status (if known). To reach as many networks as possible, the survey was made available for 10 months, from July 2010 to May 2011. Participants could submit their own information or information about others from their campuses, communities, or social networks. Participants were informed that they could submit as many names as appropriate; they were then encouraged to forward the recruitment e-mail to their social networks in order to collect as many names as possible.

Analysis

The data was analyzed by a team of three researchers, which consisted of one Filipina American professor of higher education, one Filipino American professor of psychology, and one Filipina American undergraduate student of psychology. For the preliminary analysis, the team decided to include only the entries of professors from the social sciences, humanities, and related fields. The disciplines that were analyzed included, but were not limited to the following: anthropology, English, ethnic/cultural/American studies, education, psychology, economics, political science, fine arts, and public health. The main rationale for including only these fields was twofold: first, it has been documented that there is a large amount of Filipinos and Filipino Americans in the fields of medicine and nursing, and two, there is a lack of information regarding Filipino Americans in the social sciences. Professors of science, technology, engineering, mathematics, law, and business were also not included in the initial analysis, but they may be analyzed in future studies.

First, each of the entries was entered into a spreadsheet, which included all of the aforementioned categories. After duplicate entries were removed, entries of nontenured or nontenure-track faculty (i.e., adjunct instructors, lecturers, visiting faculty), individuals with doctorates but who are not in academia, and retired faculty members were also removed. Next, the researchers then searched each college or university website to verify that each entry was accurate and up-to-date, while also aiming to fill in missing data. When a website was not available, a phone call was made to the department or university to verify the information. Finally, entries were alphabetized and divided into three categories: assistant professor, associate professor, and professor.

Credibility and Trustworthiness

To ensure credibility of the study (Merriam, 1998), the final list was reviewed by two external auditors—one Filipino American professor in ethnic studies and one Filipino American community leader. Both individuals are well versed in the topic of Filipino American communities and are active in Filipino American national social networks. These debriefers provided valuable feedback for potential additions or errors in our inquiry.

Limitations of the Study

There were a few limitations for this study. First, our findings were bounded by a time frame of 10 months. Nevertheless, this is the first national investigation of Filipino American faculty to be conducted and provides for readers a glimpse of this population's status in the academic environment. Second, the study did not distinguish between American-born Filipinos and Philippine-born Filipinos nor did we differentiate between first generation or second generation. Although the authors recognize limitations in the current study, we also see these limitations as opportunities for future examination of this topic.

RESULTS

The survey yielded a total of 114 professors, which included 52 assistant professors, 46 associate professors, and 16 full professors. There were 61 women and 53 men. There were an array of disciplines or concentrations represented, including 16 professors of Asian American studies, 13 professors of psychology, 13 professors of education, 9 professors of English (or related fields), 9 professors of ethnic studies, 9 professors of sociology, 8 professors of American studies (or related fields), 7 professors of history, 4 professors of communications (or related fields), 4 professors of social work, 4 professors of the arts, 3 professors of Asian studies (or related fields), and 3 professors of public health (or related fields). There were two professors each of architecture/urban planning, economics, women's studies, and interdisciplinary sciences, and one professor each of anthropology, international education, Philippine literature, and political science. Almost half of the entries (N = 45) were from faculty members who resided in California. There were eight faculty members from Illinois; seven each from Hawai'i, New York, and Washington; five from Michigan; and six from Colorado. There were three professors from Minnesota and Maryland; two professors each from Alaska, Massachusetts, New Jersey, Oregon, Pennsylvania, and Rhode Island; and one professor each from Arizona, Missouri, North Carolina, North Dakota, South Dakota, Wyoming, Ohio, Mississippi, Texas, and Virginia. The majority of the entries (N = 102) received their doctorates in the United States; one person received a doctorate degree in the Philippines, and eleven were unknown. Due to missing data, there was not enough data to determine the percentage of participants that were U.S. or foreign born.

The researchers further analyzed the data of the tenured faculty (i.e., both associate and full professors). There were close to an equal number of women (N = 30) and men (N = 31), with nine women and seven men holding the rank of full professor. While data was missing for birthplace for the majority of the participants, it was reported that 9 out of the 16 full professors were born in the Philippines and that 2 were born in the United States (the birthplaces of six full professors were unknown). Furthermore, in looking at the full professors, the breakdown of fields and concentrations were also different from the total population: there were three each in history and psychology, two were in education, and one each in Asian studies (or related fields), American studies (or related fields), architecture, economics, ethnic studies, Philippine history, social work, and sociology. So although the total sample yielded a large number of faculty members from Asian American studies, ethnic studies, or American studies, the same percentage for each discipline was smaller for the full professor category.

DISCUSSION

The results of our study point to at least three conclusions. First, reliance on aggregated statistical data provides us with only a partial view of AAPI experiences in higher education. More specifically, there is a lack of information about specific AAPI ethnic groups, namely, Filipino Americans. Our impetus for this study was to explore the number of Filipino American tenure-track faculty in the social sciences. Based on our exploratory study, our findings indicated Filipino Americans are not well represented at the full-time tenure-track faculty level in the social science disciplines. If institutions and agencies had provided disaggregated data by AAPI groups and gender, we would have a more precise picture of the AAPI educational pipeline and in the case of this particular study, Filipino/a American faculty pipeline.

Second, our findings encourage a further examination of the Filipino American faculty pipeline. It is clear that in order to further diversify faculty of color in higher education, it is necessary to examine the recruitment and retention practices for Filipino American faculty. Higher education institutions must consider how they can provide a supportive environment for Filipino American faculty. The low number of tenure-track Filipino American faculty has grave implications for Filipino American college students. Therefore, of equal importance is to examine the numbers of Filipino American students entering the social science fields and pursuing an academic career. Given the increasing number of Filipino/a American college students, it is imperative that these students have role models and support systems that include Filipino/a American faculty. For example, as mentioned from previous studies (Maramba 2008a, 2008b; Nadal et al., 2009), mentoring and role modeling for Filipino American college and graduate students is lacking. Filipino American faculty can have a positive influence in encouraging Filipino American students to enter the academy. Therefore, future studies on this pipeline need to be further explored.

Third, we found that even within the social sciences, there is a heavier representation of Filipino American faculty in ethnic studies, Asian American studies, and American studies disciplines. Other less represented disciplines included education, psychology, economics, social work, and communication. There are two explanations to this compelling finding. First, it is possible that Filipino American students are more likely to enter ethnic, Asian American, and American studies disciplines when they pursue doctoral degrees. However, perhaps another explanation is that higher education hiring practices and recruitment are less likely to hire Filipino Americans in other social science fields. Although it is valuable to have Filipino American faculty in ethnic, Asian American, and American studies, we must also closely examine the reasons why there are lower numbers in other social science disciplines.

Finally, the geographic locations where Filipino American faculty members are found in U.S. institutions are another important finding. It may not be surprising that the majority, 54% (or 45 faculty), are located on the West Coast, with California having the largest number, as this matches the population breakdown of the Filipino American community in general. However, this also indicates that there is still much to be done in terms of addressing the hiring of Filipino American faculty across the country. While there are some states on the East Coast and in the Midwest with larger numbers of Filipino American faculty (e.g., Illinois, New York), most states have either one or no Filipino American faculty. With the exception of the University of Hawai'i Mānoa (N = 7) and San Francisco State University (N = 4), there are usually no more than two Filipino American faculty located in the same institution. For the most part, Filipino American faculty find themselves to be the only one at their institution, which may cause some to feel isolated and tokenized.

The lack of Filipino American faculty members may also have a detrimental impact on Filipino American students. The results from our study indicate that most colleges and universities do not have a Filipino American faculty member at their institution. Thus, it is possible that students may not have the role models that may encourage them to further their studies, perhaps perpetuating the cycle of the dearth of Filipino American faculty. Moreover, having a lack of role models may have a negative impact on Filipino Americans' sense of belonging in the college environment (Maramba, 2008a; Maramba, 2008b; Maramba & Museus, 2011, in press; Museus & Maramba, 2011). In addition, when an institution has only one Filipino American faculty member, there is a possibility for that individual to experience burnout, because of the potential responsibility of serving as a mentor for all of the Filipino American students.

To conclude, our exploratory study begins to raise very critical issues that higher education institutions must continue to address. The dearth of literature, empirical studies, and statistical data on Filipino American faculty is only scratching the surface of the issues that Filipino Americans face in higher education. Not having a stable faculty pipeline can lead to additional challenges for both Filipino American faculty and students. Retention and persistence of both populations becomes an issue as both lack role models and a support system within the higher education environment. Institutions must provide supportive work and education environments for Filipino Americans as it also benefits and contributes to inclusiveness and diversity for colleges and universities as a whole.

REFERENCES

Allen, W. R., Epps, E. G., Guillory, E. A., Suh, S. A., & Bonous-Hammarth, M. (2000). The Black academic: Faculty status among African Americans in U.S. higher education. *The Journal of Negro Education, 69*(1/2), 112–127.

Castellanos, J., & Jones, L. (2003). *The majority in the minority: Expanding the representation of Latina/o faculty, administrators and students in higher education.* Sterling, VA: Stylus.

Cho, K. K. (2002). Confronting the myths: Asian Pacific American faculty in higher education. In C. S. Turner, A. L. Antonio, M. Garcia, B. V. Laden, A. Nora, & C. L. Presley (Eds.), *Racial and ethnic diversity in higher education* (pp. 169–184). Boston, MA: Pearson Custom.

Cook, B. J., & Cordova, D. I. (2006). *Minorities in higher education: Twenty-second annual status report.* Washington, DC: American Council on Education.

Escueta, E., & O'Brien, E. (1995). Asian Americans in higher education: Trends and issues. In D. T. Nakanishi & T. Y. Nishida (Eds.), *The Asian American educational experience* (pp. 259–272). New York, NY: Routledge.

Hune, S. (2006). Asian Pacific American women and men in higher education: The contested spaces of their participation, persistence, and challenge as students, faculty, and administrators. In G. Li & G. H. Beckett (Eds.), *"Strangers" of the academy* (pp. 15–36). Sterling, VA: Stylus.

Hune, S. (2011). Asian American women faculty and the contested space of the classroom: Navigating student resistance and (re)claiming authority and their rightful place. In G. Jean-Marie, B. Lloyd-Jones, & L. Bass. (Eds.), *Women of color in higher education: Turbulent past, promising future.* Bingley, UK: Emerald Group.

Johnsrud, L. K., & Sadao, K. C. (2002). The common experiences of "otherness:" Ethnic and racial minority faculty. In C. S. Turner, A. L. Antonio, M. Garcia, B. V. Laden, A. Nora, & C. L. Presley (Eds.), *Racial and ethnic diversity in higher education* (pp. 185–201). Boston, MA: Pearson Custom.

Lee, S. J. (2006). Additional complexities: Social, class, ethnicity, generation and gender in Asian American student experiences. *Race, Ethnicity and Education, 9*(1), 17–28.

Lee, S. M. (2002). Do Asian American faculty face a glass ceiling in higher education? *American Educational Research Journal, 39*(3), 695–724.

Maramba, D. C. (2008a). Immigrant families and the college experience: Perspectives of Filipina Americans. *Journal of College Student Development, 49*(4), 336–350.

Maramba, D. C. (2008b). Understanding campus climate through voices of Filipino/a American college students. *College Student Journal, 42*(4), 1045–1060.

Maramba, D. C. (2011). Few and far between: Exploring the experiences of Asian American and Pacific Islander women in student affairs administration. In G. Jean-Marie, B. Lloyd-Jones, & L. Bass. (Eds.), *Women of color in higher education: Turbulent past, promising future.* Bingley, UK: Emerald.

Maramba, D. C., & Museus, S. D. (2011). Exploring college experience through the intersectionality of ethnicity and gender: The case of Filipino Americans. In S. D. Museus & K. A. Griffin (Eds.), *Using mixed methods to study intersectionality in higher education. New Directions for Institutional Research* (pp. 93–101). San Francisco, CA: Jossey-Bass.

Maramba, D. C., & Museus, S. D. (in press). Examining the effects of campus climate, ethnic group cohesion and cross-cultural interaction on Filipino American students' sense of belonging in college. *Journal of College Student Retention, 15*(1).

Merriam, S. B. (1998). *Qualitative design and case study applications in education.* San Francisco, CA: Jossey-Bass.

Museus, S. D., & Maramba, D. C. (2011). The impact of culture on Filipino American students' sense of belonging. *Review of Higher Education, 34*(2), 231–258.

Nadal, K. L. (2011). *Filipino American psychology: A handbook of theory, research, and clinical practice.* New York, NY: John Wiley & Sons.

Nadal, K. L., Pituc, S. T., Johnston, M. P., & Esparrago, T. (2010). Overcoming the Model Minority Myth: Experiences of Filipino American graduate students. *Journal of College Student Development, 51*(6), 1–13

National Commission on Asian American and Pacific Islander Research in Education. (2010). *Federal higher education policy priorities and the Asian American and Pacific Islander community.* New York, NY: USA Funds.

Okamura, J. Y. (1998). *Imagining the Filipino American diaspora: Transnational relations, identities, and communities.* New York, NY: Garland.

Reeves, T. M., & Bennett, C. E. (2004, December). We the people: Asians in the United States. Census 2000 Special Reports. *U.S. Census Bureau.* Retrieved from http://www.census.gov/prod/2004pubs/censr-17.pdf

Rumbaut, R. G., & Portes, A. (Eds.). (2001). *Ethnicities: Children of immigrants in America.* Berkeley: University of California Press.

Smith, D. G., Turner, C., Osei-Kofi, N., & Richards, S. (2004). Interrupting the usual: Successful strategies for hiring diverse faculty. *The Journal of Higher Education, 75*(2), 133–160.

Smith, D. G., Wolf, L. E., & Busenberg, B. E. (1996). Achieving faculty diversity: Debunking the myths. Washington, DC: Association of American Colleges and Universities.

Suzuki, B. (2002). Revisiting the model minority stereotype: Implications for student affairs practice in higher education. In M. K. McEwen, C. M. Kodama, A. N. Alvarez, S. Lee, & C. T. H. Liang (Eds.), *Working with Asian American college students* (pp. 21–32). San Francisco, CA: Jossey-Bass.

Trower, C. A. (2009). Toward a greater understanding of the tenure track for minorities. *Change, 41*(5), 38–45.

Turner, C. S. V. (2002). Women of color in academe. *The Journal of Higher Education, 73*(1), 74–93.

Turner, C. S. V., & Myers, S. L. (2000). *Faculty of color in academe: Bittersweet success.* Boston, MA: Allyn & Bacon.

Weinberg, S. L. (2008). Monitoring faculty diversity: The need for a more granular approach. *Journal of Higher Education, 79*(4), 365–387.

ABOUT THE EDITORS AND CONTRIBUTORS

EDITORS

Rick Bonus, PhD, is primarily associate professor of American ethnic studies and adjunct associate professor of communication at the University of Washington, but he also has strong interests in the conjunctions among ethnic studies, American studies, Pacific Islander studies, and Southeast Asian studies, particularly as they deal with the historical and contemporary phenomena of migration, transnationalism, interdisciplinary work, and multicultural pedagogy. His first book, *Locating Filipino Americans: Ethnicity and the Cultural Politics of Space* (Temple, 2000), is a study of transnational Filipino experiences in the United States within the contexts of U.S. imperial histories, labor recruitment, and ethnic community formations. He coedited the anthology, *Intersections and Divergences: Contemporary Asian American Communities* (Temple, 2002), a collection of essays that grapple with the heterogeneities, complexities, and contradictions of racialized group formations. He has written essays on the cultural politics of difference, media representations, and multicultural education. He earned his PhD in communication at the University of California, San Diego.

Dina C. Maramba, PhD, is associate professor of student affairs administration and affiliate faculty in the Department of Asian and Asian American Studies at the State University of New York (SUNY) at Binghamton. Her work focuses on equity and diversity issues within the context of higher education. Her research interests include the influence of educational institutions and climates on college access and success among underrepresented

The "Other" Students, pages 309–314

students of color and first-generation college students. She is also interested in the interplay between college students and their immigrant parents. Having presented her research nationally and internationally, her work has been published in student affairs and higher education journals including the *Journal of College Student Development*, *Journal of College Student Retention*, *Journal of Negro Education*, and the *Review of Higher Education*. Dr. Maramba is co-author of *Racial and Ethnic Minority Students' Success in STEM Education* (Jossey-Bass, 2011) and co-editor of *Fostering Success of Ethnic and Racial Minorities in STEM: The Role of Minority Serving Institutions* (Routledge, 2012). She was also involved in creating a documentary adopted by the Center for Asian American Media entitled *Silent Sacrifices: Voices of the Filipino American Family* (2001), which involved challenges faced by Filipino immigrant parents and their college-aged children. She earned her PhD in higher education at the Claremont Graduate University.

CONTRIBUTORS

Third Andresen, MEd, has been in the field of education and community organizing in Seattle's Filipino American community for 15 years. Third is a doctoral candidate in the College of Education, focusing on multicultural education at the University of Washington. He developed numerous courses in the Comparative History of Ideas (CHID) program and is teaching on topics of Civic Engagement and Hiphop, (Re)Thinking Diversity and Study Abroad Philippines. Third was the President of the University of Washington Filipino American Students' Association and was also a part of *Isang Mahal* (One Love), a Filipino American Arts Collective.

Tracy Lachica Buenavista, PhD, is an associate professor in the Department of Asian American Studies and a core faculty member in the doctoral program in educational leadership at California State University, Northridge. She teaches courses on immigration, race and racism, and the educational experiences of Pilipinos and other people of color in the United States. Her current research focuses on the college access, retention, and student-initiated activism of U.S. Pilipina/o students, as well as the relationship between race, gender, and (neo)colonialism in shaping Pilipina/o experiences. She received a PhD in education at University of California, Los Angeles and an MA in Asian American studies at San Francisco State University.

Roland Sintos Coloma, PhD, is associate professor and graduate coordinator in the Department of Humanities, Social Sciences, and Social Justice Education at the Ontario Institute for Studies in Education of the University of Toronto in Canada. His research and teaching focus on transnationalism, history, and social theory. The editor of *Postcolonial Challenges in Educa-*

tion (Peter Lang, 2009), his journal articles appear in *Paedagogica Historica, History of Education Quarterly, Curriculum Inquiry, Race Ethnicity and Education,* and *Qualitative Studies in Education.* He completed his PhD in cultural studies in education from The Ohio State University.

Patricia Espiritu Halagao, PhD, is associate professor of multicultural education and social studies in the College of Education at the University of Hawai'i, Mānoa. Her scholarship focuses on culturally responsive curriculum and pedagogy, particularly the education of Filipino Americans. She is co-founder of Pinoy Teach; Smithsonian Institution centennial online Filipino American curriculum; iJeepney.com; and project director of a federal grant, the Filipino American Education Institute (www.filameducation.com), which engages professors, teachers, and community to meet the needs of Filipino American students. She earned her PhD in education at the University of Washington.

Funie Hsu is a doctoral candidate at the Graduate School of Education, University of California, Berkeley. She is an American Educational Research Association Minority Dissertation Fellow. Her work is broadly informed by her experience as an elementary school teacher in the Los Angeles Unified School District.

Korina Jocson, PhD, is assistant professor of education in arts & sciences at Washington University in St. Louis. Her research and teaching interests include literacy, youth, and cultural studies in education. She has published in several scholarly journals and is the author of *Youth Poets: Empowering Literacies In and Out of Schools* (Peter Lang, 2008) and editor of *Cultural Transformations: Youth and Pedagogies of Possibility* (Harvard Education Press, forthcoming). She received her PhD in education in the area of language, literacy, and culture at the University of California, Berkeley, and completed her postdoctoral work at Stanford University School of Education.

Zeus Leonardo, PhD, is associate professor of education and affiliated faculty of the Critical Theory Designated Emphasis at the University of California, Berkeley. Before coming to Berkeley, Professor Leonardo was associate professor at Long Beach State University, a visiting professor at the University of Washington-Seattle, and acting director of the University of Washington's Center for Multicultural Education in the place of Professor James Banks. He graduated from the University of California, Los Angeles with a BA in English and PhD in education. He teaches courses and publishes in the areas of critical race theory, Whiteness studies, and social theories in education. His recent book is *Race, Whiteness, and Education* (Routledge, 2009).

Cheryl E. Matias, PhD, is assistant professor in the Urban Community Teacher Education Program at the University of Colorado, Denver. She received her PhD from the University of California, Los Angeles' Graduate School of Education with an emphasis on race and ethnic studies in education. Her master of arts in social and multicultural education is from Long Beach State University. She received her bachelor's and teaching credential from the University of California, San Diego and San Diego State University (respectively). Her research focus is on critical whiteness studies, critical race theory, and critical pedagogy. She also devotes much time to mother scholarship. She is a former teacher in both Los Angeles Unified School District and New York City Department of Education. She is a mother of twins and enjoys 1990s hip hop.

Reynaldo I. Monzon, PhD, is director of Student Testing, Assessment and Research at San Diego State University. As an educational researcher for the past 20 years, he has conducted various studies investigating cross-cultural and institutional factors affecting student performance and success. In particular, his passion has been to focus on issues affecting Filipino American students and their families. He received his PhD at the Claremont Graduate University/San Diego State University.

Kevin L. Nadal, PhD, is associate professor of psychology and the deputy director of the Forensic Mental Health Counseling program at John Jay College of Criminal Justice-City University of New York. He is the author of *Filipino American Psychology: A Handbook of Theory, Research, and Clinical Practice* (John Wiley & Sons, 2011), as well as over 40 publications focusing on Filipino American mental health; lesbian, gay, bisexual, and transgender (LGBT) experiences; and racial, gender, and sexual orientation microaggressions. He is a trustee with the Filipino American National Historical Society (FANHS), the president of the FANHS Metro New York Chapter, a fellow with the Robert Wood Johnson Foundation, and the recipient of the Early Career Contributions to Excellence Award by the Asian American Psychological Association. He earned his PhD in counseling psychology from Columbia University.

Jonathan Y. Okamura, PhD, is professor in the Department of Ethnic Studies at the University of Hawai'i, Mānoa. He is the author of three books: *Imagining the Filipino American Diaspora: Transnational Relations, Identities, and Communities* (Garland, 1998); *The Japanese American Historical Experience in Hawai'i* (Kendall/Hunt, 2001); and *Ethnicity and Identity in Hawai'i* (Temple, 2008). His primary research interests include race and ethnicity, racialization of Asian Americans, ethnic inequality in Hawai'i, minority access to higher education, and the global Filipino diaspora. He earned his PhD in anthropology at the University of London.

Allyson Tintiangco-Cubales, PhD, is associate professor of Asian American studies at San Francisco State University's College of Ethnic Studies. She is the founder and director of Pin@y Educational Partnerships (PEP), a service and teaching pipeline focused on the marriage of critical Filipina/o American Studies and critical pedagogy. Her research focuses on Filipina/o American youth; community studies; critical performance pedagogy; and Pinayism, a concept that she coined in 1995. She is currently a senior research associate with the Wangari Maathai Center, a fellow with Research Infrastructure in Minority Institutions (RIMI), and an Urban Fellow at the Institute on Civic and Community Engagement (ICCE). She serves as a consultant with the San Francisco Unified School District on the development of ethnic studies curriculum for high school students. She earned her PhD in education from the University of California, Los Angeles.

Antonio T. Tiongson, Jr., PhD is assistant professor of American studies at the University of New Mexico. He is co-editor of the anthology, *Positively No Filipinos Allowed: Building Communities and Discourse* (Temple, 2006). His research interests include youth cultural politics, comparative racializations, and empire. He is in the process of completing his manuscript, entitled *Claiming Hip Hop: Authenticity Debates, Filipino DJs, and Contemporary U.S. Racial and Global Diasporic Formations*, to be published by the University of Minnesota Press. His next two projects are a critical engagement with the comparative turn in both the social sciences and the humanities and mapping the contours of contemporary youth activism.

Charlene Bumanglag Tomas, PhD, a second-generation Filipina American, earned her PhD in cultural perspectives and comparative education at the University of California, Santa Barbara, with a specialization in sexual health and school health education; her emphasis is in cultural perspectives and comparative education. In the past year, she served as a Sexual Health Scholar at Morehouse School of Medicine under the leadership of Dr. David Satcher (16th U.S. Surgeon General). Her research interests are in health education, disenfranchised communities, and health policy. She continues to conduct work with diverse underserved communities nationwide.

Belinda Butler Vea, PhD, is a policy and program analyst for the University of California Office of the President, Student Affairs. Her primary areas of focus are on campus life issues, including student mental health, student wellness, alcohol and drug abuse and prevention, sexual assault and harassment, and campus violence. She oversees the administration of the University of California's Undergraduate Experience Survey, a census survey of all undergraduates enrolled at UC. Dr. Vea received her doctorate degree in 2008 in higher education and public policy from Claremont Graduate University, School of Educational Studies. She has consulted on issues related to higher education policies and programs that assist diverse populations as well as student access, retention, and success through higher education.

Benito M. Vergara, Jr., PhD, was born and raised in the Philippines, and he is the author of *Displaying Filipinos: Photography and Colonialism in Early 20th-Century Philippines* (University of the Philippines Press, 1995) and *Pinoy Capital: The Filipino Nation in Daly City* (Temple, 2009). He received his PhD in anthropology from Cornell University and has taught Asian American studies and anthropology at different universities in the San Francisco Bay Area. He also writes about movies at http://filmeyeballsbrain.com and blogs at thewilyfilipino.com.

INDEX

The "Other" Students, pages 315–330

B

C

F

G

H

I

J

K

L

M

Q

R

S

T

U

V

W

Y

Z

CPSIA information can be obtained at www.ICGtesting.com
Printed in the USA
BVOW08s1139150415

396247BV00004B/75/P